OXFORD WORLD'S

COMPLETE LE

PLINY THE YOUNGER (AD 61/2–c.112) was born into an equestrian family at Comum in northern Italy. After the death of his father, his uncle the Elder Pliny and the eminent consular Verginius Rufus became his guardians. After early schooling at Comum, he studied rhetoric under Quintilian at Rome. Following minor offices and brief military service, he became quaestor, plebeian tribune, and praetor under Domitian. After that emperor's assassination, he became a high civil servant as prefect of the treasury. Under Trajan in AD 100 he advanced to the suffect consulship, and in 103 was appointed curator of the Tiber. His crowning appointment came in 109–10 as governor of Bithynia-Pontus, where he probably died about two years later. The letters, part autobiography and part social history, cast a vivid light on Pliny's wide-ranging roles as advocate in the courts, as politician in the Senate, as cultivated littérateur, as man of property on his extensive estates, as provincial governor, and as devoted husband. They are also revealing on many aspects of social life in the early Empire, for example on education, on the treatment of slaves, on religion and the rise of Christianity, and on the eruption of Vesuvius.

P. G. WALSH was Emeritus Professor of Humanity in the University of Glasgow until his death in 2013. This is the sixth of his translations of Latin authors in Oxford World's Classics, following Apuleius, *The Golden Ass*, Petronius, *Satyricon*, Cicero, *The Nature of the Gods* and *On Obligations*, and Boethius, *The Consolation of Philosophy*. He also published extensively on Livy, on the Roman novel, and on patristic and medieval Latin.

OXFORD WORLD'S CLASSICS

*For over 100 years Oxford World's Classics have brought
readers closer to the world's great literature. Now with over 700
titles—from the 4,000-year-old myths of Mesopotamia to the
twentieth century's greatest novels—the series makes available
lesser-known as well as celebrated writing.*

*The pocket-sized hardbacks of the early years contained
introductions by Virginia Woolf, T. S. Eliot, Graham Greene,
and other literary figures which enriched the experience of reading.
Today the series is recognized for its fine scholarship and
reliability in texts that span world literature, drama and poetry,
religion, philosophy and politics. Each edition includes perceptive
commentary and essential background information to meet the
changing needs of readers.*

OXFORD WORLD'

PLINY THE YOUNGER

Complete Letters

Translated with an Introduction and Notes by
P. G. WALSH

OXFORD
UNIVERSITY PRESS

OXFORD

UNIVERSITY PRESS

Great Clarendon Street, Oxford OX2 6DP

Oxford University Press is a department of the University of Oxford.
It furthers the University's objective of excellence in research, scholarship,
and education by publishing worldwide in

Oxford New York

Auckland Cape Town Dar es Salaam Hong Kong Karachi
Kuala Lumpur Madrid Melbourne Mexico City Nairobi
New Delhi Shanghai Taipei Toronto

With offices in

Argentina Austria Brazil Chile Czech Republic France Greece
Guatemala Hungary Italy Japan South Korea Poland Portugal
Singapore Switzerland Thailand Turkey Ukraine Vietnam

Oxford is a registered trade mark of Oxford University Press
in the UK and in certain other countries

Published in the United States
by Oxford University Press Inc., New York

British Library Cataloguing in Publication Data

Data available

Library of Congress Cataloging in Publication Data

Pliny, the Younger
[Correspondence. English]
Complete letters / Pliny the younger ; translated with an introduction and
notes by P. G. Walsh.
p. cm.
Includes bibliographical references and indexes.
1. Pliny, the Younger—Correspondence. I. Walsh, P. G. (Patrick
Gerard) II. Title
PA6639.F5W3513 2006 876'.01—dc22 2006011797

ISBN 978–0–19–953894–2

18

Typeset in Ehrhardt
by RefineCatch Limited, Bungay, Suffolk
Printed and bound in Great Britain by Clays Ltd, Elcograf S.p.A.

ACKNOWLEDGEMENTS

THIS volume makes no claim to scholarly originality. I acknowledge my debt in particular to three predecessors. The first is to Betty Radice's revised Loeb edition, and in particular to the carefully compiled Index. When I reviewed this edition many years ago, I failed to pay adequate tribute to its solid merits. Secondly, in coping with the problems of Book X, I have profited greatly from the excellent contribution of Wynne Williams in the Aris and Phillips series; his edition of Pliny's correspondence with Trajan is a model volume for student use. But my greatest debt is to the masterly work of scholarship of A. N. Sherwin-White, to which I have constantly turned for enlightenment.

The solid contributions of nineteenth-century continental scholarship are not acknowledged here. But the image of John of Salisbury, 'We are dwarfs, standing on the shoulders of giants', should always be in the forefront of our minds as we attempt to transmit that accumulated knowledge to the next generation of readers and students.

I owe a great debt of gratitude to Judith Luna, for her encouragement at the early stages, and for her efficiency and courtesy in improving the typescript and guiding it through the press. Thanks, too, to Elizabeth Stratford for meticulously checking, correcting, and improving the typescript.

CONTENTS

ABBREVIATIONS

AJP	*American Journal of Philology*
ANRW	*Aufstieg und Niedergang der römischen Welt*
CIL	*Corpus Inscriptionum Latinarum*
CJ	*Classical Journal*
CP	*Classical Philology*
CW	*Classical Weekly*
GR	*Greece and Rome*
HSCP	*Harvard Studies in Classical Philology*
ILS	*Inscriptiones Latinae Selectae*
JRS	*Journal of Roman Studies*
Mnem.	*Mnemosyne*
OCD[3]	*Oxford Classical Dictionary*, 3rd edition
PBSR	*Papers of the British School at Rome*
REL	*Revue des Études Latines*
SCI	*Scripta Classica Israelica*
SIFC	*Studi Italiani di Filologia Classica*
TAPA	*Transactions and Proceedings of the American Philological Association*

INTRODUCTION

The Political Background of the Letters

THE extant letters of Pliny were all composed in the years between 97 and 112, during the principates of Nerva and of Trajan. But they contain references to events which date back half a century; moreover, Pliny's political stance can be fully understood only by consideration of the evolution of the principate from the days of Augustus.

When Augustus assumed direct control of a Rome which was exhausted by civil discord, he sought to mitigate the resentment of nostalgic Republicans by encouraging the myth of dyarchy, joint rule between the *princeps*, as he styled himself, and the Senate. Subsequent history exposed the hollowness of the claim. Pliny makes no direct criticisms of the reigns of Tiberius and of Gaius, but he waxes bitter about the servitude of the Senate under Claudius. Though that emperor showed deference to the Senate, his manipulation of the reins of power was demonstrated by his increasing control of the civilian treasury, by the appointments of governors of the senatorial provinces, and above all by the establishment of a court bureaucracy under the control of four imperial freedmen. The most prominent of these was Pallas, secretary of finance. In two letters Pliny draws attention to the obsequious behaviour of the Senate towards this 'slave' (as he inaccurately calls him, VIII 6.4). He cites the inscription on Pallas' tomb, which recorded that on his retirement the Senate decreed to him the insignia of a praetor, together with 15 million sesterces, distinctions 'wasted on such slime and filth' (VII 29.3). Pliny is so infuriated by this inscription that he looks out the decree in the Roman archives, and devotes a long and satirical letter to the voluntary degradation of the Senate in making this award (VIII 6).

The increasing despotism of Claudius' successor Nero was reflected in the savage persecution which followed his murder of his interfering mother Agrippina, and the death of his discreet adviser Burrus in 62. Following the condemnation and murder of Christians after the Great Fire of 64, and the conspiracy of Piso in 65, Nero ordered the execution or the enforced suicides (Seneca included) of about twenty senators, and the exile of another thirteen. Pliny waxes bitter not only about the systematic persecution of worthy men, but also about the informers who laid evidence of treason against fellow senators (see e.g. I 5.1). In more enlightened days Trajan cited Nero as exemplar of how an emperor should not behave. When he conducted an inquiry into allegations against his freedman Eurhythmus, Pliny cites with approval his remark: 'That freedman is not Polyclitus' (he was the notorious freedman of Nero), 'and I am not Nero' (VI 31.9).

Pliny was too young to witness the turbulent 'Year of the Four Emperors' which ensued when Nero failed to establish a successor, but his family doubtless welcomed the restoration of discipline with the accession of Vespasian in 69. The fiction of dyarchy was now totally dispelled; henceforward the Senate had to bow before the imperial bureaucracy. Vespasian held the consulship every year until his death except 73 and 78, and his son Titus, in addition to holding seven consulships with his father, was awarded the two powers which guaranteed his succession, the *proconsulare imperium* and the *tribunicia potestas*. Recalcitrant senators who refused to cooperate, like Helvidius Priscus, were banished; Priscus indeed was eventually executed. Philosophers who fomented opposition were exiled. Vespasian had no difficulty in ensuring the smooth succession of his son Titus in 79.

In spite of the authoritarian attitude of the emperor towards the Senate, Pliny's letters offer no criticism of Vespasian. It is doubtless significant that his uncle, the Elder Pliny, was a close confidant. He was a member of the emperor's council, and was appointed by him to various offices, including the command of the western fleet at Misenum, as our Pliny notes (III 5.7 and note; VI 16.4). It is less surprising that there is no criticism of Titus, in view of the brevity of his reign and his popular policies of banishing informers and discouraging charges of treason. He was popular, not only with the Senate, but also with Romans in general; he was 'the dear one and darling of the human race' (Suetonius, *Titus* 1). The Elder Pliny's friendship with the father extended to the son: he dedicated his monumental *Natural History* to him. The sudden death of the young emperor in 81 made thoughtful observers wonder whether this popularity could have been maintained had he lived longer; the repressive regime of Domitian which followed lent Titus' two-year reign a nostalgic glow, especially in view of the alleged coolness between the two brothers (see IV 9.2).

The shadow of Domitian's reign darkens the pages of Pliny's letters, which reinforce the jaundiced views of Tacitus in the *Agricola* and of Juvenal in his Fourth Satire. The combination of these three powerful voices, representative of the great majority of the Senate which condemned Domitian's memory after his death in September 96, has to be set against the more balanced estimate of Suetonius' biography and the flattering attentions of the poets Martial and Statius. A strong case can be made for the emperor's conscientious administration of the provinces, for his financial stringency, and for his attempt to maintain high standards of public morality. But Pliny's letters ignore these virtues. When he writes on the banishment of Valerius Licinianus, accused of sexual depravity with the Vestal Virgin Cornelia, he presents a lengthy indictment of the emperor for the barbaric cruelty of entombment of the allegedly innocent woman, supplemented with an accusation of Domitian's own sexual immorality with his niece, which led to her death after an abortion (IV 11.6). But the bulk of the vendetta against the emperor rightly details the executions and exiles of worthy opponents of the regime, together with condemnation of the despicable informers who laid charges of treason against the victims. Pliny is particularly severe on his *bête noire* Regulus for his harrying of the innocent (I 5), and there are also scathing condemnations of Messalinus (IV 22) and of Publicius Certus (IX 13). Pliny goes so far as to claim that he himself might have become a victim had Domitian lived longer, for an accusation laid by Mettius Carus was found on the emperor's desk after his death (VII 27.14). Pliny repeatedly and strenuously defends his own intrepid conduct during these troubled years, though his incipient career indicated no hindrance to its progress.

The peaceful succession to Nerva was ensured by the conspirators who had murdered Domitian. He was not their first choice, but he was acceptable to the body of senators as a moderate who had held the consulship twice. During the insecurity of the early months of his tenure (see IX 13), he revoked the oppressive measures of Domitian, recalling exiles and restoring confiscated properties, so that his sixteen-month reign was lauded as the restoration of liberty (IX 13.4; cf. Tacitus, *Agricola* 3). The ever-present danger from restive army-units was dispelled by Nerva's adoption in October 97 of the distinguished soldier Trajan as co-regent. At this time Trajan was governor of Upper Germany; he succeeded to the throne on the death of the elderly and ailing Nerva in January 98. For Pliny, the reign of Nerva marked the beginning of his standing as a senior political figure.

The principate of Trajan (98–117) was regarded throughout antiquity as a golden age. Adored by the common folk and worshipped by the soldiery, the new emperor won the unstinting devotion of the Senate, which he treated with such grave respect that there was general acknowledgement that the principate and liberty were at last reconciled. In 100, Pliny delivered his speech of thanks (for the award of his consulship) to Trajan in the Senate. This speech, the *Panegyricus*, has survived. In it, he depicts Trajan as the ideal prince, tracing his career from the governorship of Upper Germany in 96, with praise of his love of peace, his political moderation, and his generosity.

The cordial relations between the emperor and Pliny are reflected at many points in the letters. During the trial of Marius Priscus in January 100, Trajan showed concern for Pliny's lungs after he had spoken for almost five hours (so Pliny reports at II 11.15, without a hint of self-irony). He obtains the 'right of three children' not only for himself, but also for his friends Voconius Romanus and Suetonius (X 2, II 13.8, X 94–5). He is readily granted leave from his post at the treasury to dedicate a temple at Tifernum, and to attend to the affairs of his estate near by (X 8–9). He asks for and is granted a priesthood (X 13, IV 8). Above all, the reward of the governorship of Bithynia-Pontus, the friendly interest which Trajan shows about the progress of the arduous voyage, and the patient replies to Pliny's queries and requests from Bithynia as recorded in Book X, indicate the emperor's careful concern. The final extant letters (X 120–1), in which Pliny requests and receives permission for his wife Calpurnia to use the imperial transport system in order to return home more speedily, show that this cordial relationship continued throughout Pliny's tenure of his post.

Pliny's Career

Pliny was born in AD 61 or 62, the son of Lucius Caecilius, a wealthy landowner of Comum.[1] After primary and secondary schooling at Comum, he moved to Rome, where his tertiary education at the school of rhetoric was supervised by the renowned Quintilian and the Greek rhetorician Nicetes Sacerdos. His father had died earlier, and he was brought up under the care of the eminent Verginius Rufus and of his uncle, the Elder Pliny.

As explained in the note to I 14.7, the Republican ladder of offices (*cursus honorum*) had been revised by the emperor Augustus. A man seeking advancement to the Senate had first to hold one of the twenty minor offices (technically called the Vigintivirate) allocated by the emperor. Ten of the twenty were appointed to the Board of Ten for Judging Lawsuits (*decemuiri stlitibus iudicandis*); these took turns in presiding over the Centumviral court, which dealt with civil cases. The youthful Pliny was presumably selected for this role because he had already pleaded and won his first case there (I 18.3). Following this year's service, an aspirant was expected (though it was not mandatory) to gain experience of army service for a few months as a military tribune. A man of equestrian family might command an infantry or cavalry cohort, but Pliny's service in Syria was virtually in a civilian role, in which he supervised the accounts of the auxiliary forces. This was during the first years of Domitian's principate.

On his return to Rome, he became well known through frequent appearances as advocate in the Centumviral court, which assisted his rise to political eminence. Candidates for the twenty quaestorships were elected by the Senate, but as Pliny makes clear at II 9.1 f., a recommendation by the *princeps* was at once accepted, and it seems certain that Pliny made his way without the formality of election, for he later reveals that he was appointed with Calestrius Tiro as Domitian's assistant (*quaestor Caesaris*, VII 16.2), a role in which he was required to convey to the Senate communications from

---

[1] Evidence for the career of Pliny derives from two sources: from these letters on the one hand, and from inscriptions on the other. Especially valuable is the inscription on stone from Comum (*ILS* 20927), as well as the inscription from the neighbouring village of Fecchio (*CIL* v. 5667). For this and other inscriptional evidence, see A. N. Sherwin-White, *The Letters of Pliny* (Oxford, 1966), 732 f. The chief inscriptions are conveniently presented with translations by Betty Radice in the Loeb Pliny (*Letters and Panegyricus*, 1969), vol. ii, appendix A.

the emperor. His appointment as quaestor also gave him entry to the Senate.

On the revised ladder of offices, a non-patrician quaestor was next required to take up one of sixteen posts as aedile or as tribune of the plebs (*tribunus plebis*). Pliny reveals that he became a tribune, and that whereas the magistracy was widely regarded as a sinecure and an empty show, he had demanded due deference, and was ready to respond to citizens' appeals in the time-honoured way (*ius auxilii*; see I 23). The office seems to have provided over-zealous individuals with the opportunity to bring people to order (cf. VI 8.3), but in what circumstances is not clear.

The next step was election to the praetorship, which Pliny gained probably in 93. Of the twelve vacancies each year (Nerva later raised the number to eighteen), four were nominated by the emperor. It is uncertain whether Pliny was so preferred by Domitian, who did however permit him to hold the office a year early (see VII 16.2). The traditional function of praetors as guardians of the law was maintained; one presided over the Centumviral court, and others supervised criminal trials, and occasionally convened the Senate. Incumbents of the praetorship gained a high profile in organizing and financing public games; see VII 11.4, where Pliny mentions that he appointed a substitute to preside in his absence.

On laying down their office, ex-praetors were offered administrative posts at Rome or in the provinces. Pliny was appointed as prefect of the military treasury (*praefectus aerarii militaris*), where his duties were to pay out pensions to discharged troops from the 5 per cent tax imposed on inheritances, and the 1 per cent tax levied from auction sales. This was his final appointment under Domitian. At the close of the *Panegyricus*, he suggests that his career had prospered until the emperor 'proclaimed his hatred for good men' (doubtless with reference to the purge of 93–4, and the execution of the emperor's cousin Clemens in 95). Pliny's progress was 'halted', which suggests that he resigned or was replaced.

Following the assassination of Domitian in September 96, Pliny's career was revived. From January 98 to August 100, he was prefect of the treasury of Saturn (*praefectus aerarii Saturni*, so called because it was located in the temple of Saturn below the Capitol), jointly with Cornutus Tertullus. The *aerarium* was the civil treasury administered by the Senate, as distinct from the *fiscus*, the imperial treasury, which had control over taxation in the provinces. In August 100 he was raised to the suffect consulship for the months September to December.

In 103 his eminence was further signalled when Trajan acceded to his request for a priesthood. There was a vacancy to be filled in the augurate, and Pliny's pleasure at being nominated for this honour was redoubled by the knowledge that his idol Cicero had held the same priesthood—and at a later age (see X 13; IV 8). In the following year he was designated as curator of the Tiber, its banks and the city-sewers (*curator aluei Tiberis et riparum et cloacarum*). This was a highly responsible post, since flooding was a perennial hazard at Rome, as VIII 17 attests. During these years of the early second century Pliny continued to shoulder other responsibilities, as advocate and assessor in the Centumviral court, the Senate, and the emperor's council.

Pliny's crowning appointment came in 109 or 110 (the date is disputed). He was appointed by Trajan to govern the province of Bithynia-Pontus as 'propraetorian legate with consular power' (*legatus pro praetore consulari potestate*). Hitherto the province had been administered by the Senate, which had appointed proconsuls as governors, but recent scandals which implicated the leading officials Julius Bassus and Varenus Rufus prompted Trajan to assume direct control. Pliny had been involved in the extortion trials of these governors (see IV 9, V 20), so that he already had some acquaintance with the problems of the province. The sixty-one letters in Book X which he wrote to the bureaucracy at Rome reveal a fascinating glimpse of the range of problems which confronted him, as he sought to establish probity in the finances and administration of the cities. The letters cease abruptly before the third year of the tenure of his office; it seems certain that sudden death overtook him in the province, probably shortly after his wife had left for Italy on hearing of the death of her grandfather.

The Range of Topics in the Letters

In each of Books I–IX, Pliny systematically assembles letters which reflect the wide range of his activities and interests, public and private.[2] In this sense the letters are a form of autobiography. Though

---

[2] See the headings in Index I below.

political leaders like Sulla and Julius Caesar wrote 'diaries' (*commentarii*), the fully fledged autobiography in the modern sense does not appear in Latin until the *Confessions* of Augustine in the late fourth century. Thus the letters allow Pliny (like Cicero before him) to project his personality and his achievements in the various fields of his endeavours. By the same token, the letters cast a flood of light on numerous aspects of the world of AD 100. They can (and should) be read as a social history of the early empire.

(i) Pliny as Advocate and Assessor; the Centumviral Court, Senate, and Emperor's Council

Pliny made his name initially as a lawyer pleading in the civil court of the centumvirs, which by this date had expanded from a Board of 105 to one of 180. The court, over which a praetor presided, was divided into four panels (*consilia*) each headed by one of the Board of Ten for Judging Lawsuits, for the speedier handling of cases. Normally, therefore, each action was contested before a panel of forty-five judges, but in cases deemed to be of exceptional importance the four panels sat together (see IV 24.1). The entire range of disputes under the jurisdiction of the court is unknown, but it will have covered litigation about property, notably legacy-claims. Letter VI 33 provides a juicy example, in which an octogenarian father brings home a new wife and disinherits his daughter, the wife of an ex-praetor. Pliny modestly reports that friends have compared his speech on this occasion with the best of the orations of Demosthenes. This letter vividly describes the scene in the Basilica Iulia (the regular venue of the court, on the south side of the Forum) with hordes of spectators thronging the floor and the gallery. But another letter (II 14) laments the decline in oratorical standards in the court. Pliny describes most of the cases as 'slight and trivial', the pleaders are rude and raw youths fresh from the schools of rhetoric, and audiences consist of bevies of paid claqueurs, hired at three denarii to swell the audience and to voice ignorant support. When Pliny was not pleading, he was often called in to act as judge or assessor.

The Senate sat as a court of law when one of its members was indicted on a criminal charge. Prominent among these cases were accusations levelled against ex-governors of provinces for extortion. Pliny provides details of four such trials, with mention of a fifth.

These cases are reviewed *en masse* in VI 29, where Pliny instructs a young protégé on the improvements in legal procedures which have been introduced as a result of his efforts. The four detailed accounts of the trials present a clear picture of the conduct of such cases. First, the Senate nominates two of its members to act as advocates of the province concerned; in the trial of Marius Priscus (II 11), Tacitus serves with Pliny as counsel for the province of Africa. Priscus pleaded guilty, and the question to be decided was whether he should be compelled merely to make financial restitution or be exiled. Those who had bribed the governor to convict innocent men were then subpoenaed as witnesses. Pliny, as chief prosecutor, speaks for almost five hours (measured by water-clocks; see note to II 11.14). On the third day of the trial, senators then vote in order of seniority. When Caecilius Classicus is indicted by the province of Baetica in Spain (III 4 and 9) the same procedure is described. Pliny and Lucceius Albinus are named to appear for the province against the henchmen of Classicus, who has died in the meantime. In the other two cases, Pliny acts as defending counsel for Julius Bassus (IV 9) and Varenus Rufus (V 20, VI 13, VII 6) against indictments by the province of Bithynia. Again, there are two advocates on each side.

On three occasions Pliny proudly reports that Trajan invited him to join his council to act as assessor in investigations which bear on public policy (IV 22) or on which the emperor has been personally consulted (VI 22 and 31). He also served occasionally as assessor at the court of the city prefect (VI 11), which dealt with criminal charges against members of the lower classes.

(ii) Pliny as Politician: The Senate and the Emperor

Pliny's letters, in so far as they are devoted to the political scene, largely reflect and complement the exultant theme of the *Panegyricus*, that liberty has been restored. Pliny repeatedly harks back to the oppressive days of Domitian. So, for example, in VIII 14. 8 ff. he recalls a Senate of those days as 'fearful and speechless . . . wholly idle or wholly wicked . . . now a laughing-stock and now ripe for grief'. In this letter he is asking for advice on senatorial procedures, which he claims had fallen into abeyance in that era of tyranny. At IX 13 he celebrates the new spirit of freedom with an attack on Publicius Certus for his disgraceful record in that period, and he succeeds in having him rejected for the consulship.

None the less Pliny acknowledges that even in this enlightened age senators continue to refer to the emperor decisions which that body might have been expected to take themselves. Thus at VI 19, when he discusses abuses in electioneering in which candidates attract votes by offers of dinners, presents, and loans, the emperor is asked to remedy the evil. Again, at VI 5 in the trial of Varenus when controversy arises as to whether the defendant should be permitted to introduce witnesses, some senators urge that the emperor be asked to decide. Likewise, at V 13.7 the plebeian tribune Nigrinus proposes that the emperor should take action about advocates' fees, 'because the laws and senatorial decrees were being flouted'. It is doubtful that Trajan welcomed such deference, but old habits died hard.

(iii) Pliny and Roman Social Life

Since Pliny was frequently writing to friends remote from the capital, the social life in the city is a frequent topic. In I 9 he laments days wasted on the social round: 'If you were to pose to anyone the question, "What did you do today?", the answer would be: "I attended an investiture of the adult toga, or I was present at a betrothal or a wedding; one person asked me to witness his will . . ." ' Unlike Tacitus, Pliny does not waste his time at the races, at which thousands are 'so childishly keen . . . to see horses galloping and drivers hunched over their chariots' (IX 6.2; for Tacitus' presence, see IX 23.2). In spite of such high-mindedness, Pliny does visit the low theatre (VII 24.6), and this in spite of his enthusiastic approval of Trajan's earlier attempt to ban such shows (*Panegyricus* 46.4 ff.).

Pliny is more at home in the literary salon, where recitations of original works were now in vogue. He contrasts the enthusiasm of would-be poets (I 13: 'Throughout . . . April there has scarcely been a day on which someone was not offering a recitation') with the reluctance of invited audiences to attend (they 'either fail to turn up, or, if they do come, complain that they have wasted their day just because they have failed to waste it'). Another letter (VI 17) criticizes the chilly reception which some sophisticated listeners manifest. In reference to his own recitations, he reports criticisms of his readings of his speeches as distinct from other genres, which suggests that this had been an uncommon practice, and he offers an apologia for it (VII 17). He claims that his reading of the *Panegyricus* has enticed his audience to return for a third day (III 18.4). Similarly, when he offers a reading of his short poems, his audience dutifully turns up for a second day, and this despite his admission that he is said to read poetry more limply than speeches, so that he wonders whether to train one of his freedmen for the task (IX 34).

In his accounts of dinner-parties, Pliny contrasts the refinement of the food and entertainments at his own table with the vulgarity shown by other hosts. Thus at I 15, a letter rebuking Septicius Clarus for failing to keep his appointment for dinner, he specifies the modest but refined vegetarian fare which he provides by contrast with 'oysters, sow's tripe, sea urchins' at a more pretentious establishment. Similarly the entertainments are contrasted: he offers performers of comedy, a reader, and a lyre-player, and not 'performing-girls from Cadiz' as in the other establishment. In response to a complaint from his youthful friend Julius Genitor, he chides him for his criticism of the vulgar entertainment he experienced elsewhere ('wits and catamites and clowns roamed round the tables'), and suggests that other guests might regard the refined entertainment laid on by themselves with similar horror (IX 17). In another letter which describes a boorish dinner-party, he castigates the host for serving the best dishes to the privileged few, and for placing inferior food and wine before the rest of the company. Inevitably, he contrasts his own practice, which is more civilized: 'I invite [guests] for dinner, not for disgrace . . . my freedmen do not drink what I drink; no, I drink what they drink' (II 6.3f.).

Many letters record the deaths of friends (there is at least one obituary in each of the first nine books, communicating Pliny's conviction that man's hope for immortality lies in the achievements and writings he leaves behind). This sense of deprivation, one of Pliny's most civilized characteristics, is evident also in descriptions of friends driven by illness to thoughts of suicide, for example Corellius Rufus (I 12), and Titius Aristo, who awaits the physicians' reports before making a decision ('to ponder and weigh the motives for [death], and then to adopt or abandon the decision to live or die . . . is the mark of a noble mind', I 22.10). Pliny pays tribute also to old men like Spurinna, who ward off death's approach by the regular round of physical and mental exercise ('A well-ordered human existence gives me the same pleasure as the fixed course of the stars' III 1.2). In his comments on contemporaries, Pliny is invariably charitable, except when reporting on ex-informers like Regulus, whose discomfiture in the new era of liberty he savours (I 5), whose legacy-hunting he abominates (II 20), and whose extravagant mourning for his son he repeatedly mocks (IV 2 and 7). Even so, he finds words of praise for him when reporting his death, as a man who knew the value of oratory (VI 2).

(iv) Pliny and his Extended Family: Slaves and Freedmen

Pliny was married three times. We are told nothing about his first wife. His second died in 97 (IX 13.4); she was the daughter of Pompeia Celerina, with whom Pliny continued to have a close relationship, for she readily offered him hospitality and loans of money when he requested it (III 19.8, VI 10.1). Some years later, probably in 104, he married his third wife Calpurnia. Pliny describes his relationship with her as idyllic; he appreciated her concern for him when he was speaking in court or giving a recitation ('She sits close by, concealed by a curtain, and listens most avidly to the praises heaped on me. She also sings my verses and adapts them to the lyre . . . It is not my time of life or my body which she loves . . . but my fame', IV 19.3 f.). To modern eyes this reads more like a father–daughter relationship, but the letters he writes to her later, in 107, when she is away convalescing, reveal a close conjugal affinity, almost worthy of inclusion in attestations of courtly love (VI 4 and 7; VII 5). Further letters report her miscarriage (VIII 10 and 11), which like-wise reflect tender affection. At this time Pliny was optimistic that they would be able to start a family, but the hope was never fulfilled.

Towards his slaves and freedmen Pliny adopted the humanitarian approach increasingly evident in the Rome of his day, as reflected, for example, in Seneca, *Letters* 47. The most conspicuous evidence of this attitude in Pliny is in VIII 16. He laments the illnesses and deaths of servants, but states that he has two consolations: 'The first is my readiness to grant them their freedom . . . and the second is my permitting those who remain slaves to make a sort of will . . . They . . . bequeath their possessions, with the proviso that they are con-fined to the household, for the household is for slaves a sort of republic and citizen-state.' In another letter, composed about the same time, he writes of 'the life-threatening maladies of my servants, and indeed the deaths of some of them' (VIII 19.1), for which his only solace is to retire to his studies. He mentions in particular his reader Encolpius, 'mainstay of my serious studies and joy of my relaxation', who has coughed up blood (VIII 1.2), and his freedman Zosimus, 'reciter of comedies . . . a seasoned lyre-player', who also 'reads speeches, histories, and poetry . . . expertly'. Zosimus has earlier been so dear and valuable to Pliny that he had been sent to Egypt to regain his strength after repeatedly spitting blood (V 19). This concern for the health of his servants surfaces again when he praises the health-giving atmosphere of his estate near Tifernum: 'My servants too nowhere live a healthier life than here . . . I have never lost a single one' (V 6.46).

Pliny regularly refers to his staff as *mei* ('my servants') without specifying whether they are freedmen or slaves. We may reasonably assume that the more cultivated among them had been manumitted, and that they sat at table with him (so II 6.4). On the other hand, the more menial servants who rowdily celebrate the feast of the Saturnalia at Laurentum (II 17.24) will have remained slaves. Pliny makes an interesting observation in discussion of the servants of Calpurnia's grandfather Fabatus: he states that some of them who had already been informally manumitted were to have their status made official by the visit of a passing magistrate. Their admittance into the ranks of the citizens, he remarks, will benefit the local community: 'I am keen that our native area should be advanced . . . especially in the number of its citizens' (VII 32). Such manumission would not, however, be extended to uneducated slaves such as those who work on Pliny's estates (III 19).

(v) Pliny's Views on Education

The Roman system of education was a continuation of the tripartite division in the Hellenistic world. Girls as well as boys (see V 16.3; Martial 9.68.2) attended the primary school under the *litterator* about the age of 7, and secondary school under the *grammaticus* about the age of 11. When they received the toga of manhood at 13 or 14, they proceeded to the school of rhetoric, often until the age of 20. Not all children went out to primary or secondary school, for many were privately instructed at home by an educated member of the household. In a letter to Corellia Hispulla, Pliny remarks of her son: 'Until now consideration of his boyhood has kept him closely bound to you. He has had teachers at home, where there is little or even no opportunity of going astray' (III 3.3).

Pliny's chief interest was in tertiary education, both in his native town of Comum and in Rome. A letter to Tacitus recounts an encounter with a young man who is a student at Milan, since there were no teachers at Comum. Pliny suggests to local parents that if they club together to contribute the equivalent of the cost of travel, lodgings, and food at Milan plus a little more, he will be willing to undertake a third of the salaries of teachers whom they appoint. He adds that he would have pledged the entire sum, but this might lead to abuses, 'for I see this happening in many places where teachers are hired at public expense' (IV 13.6). The abuses refer to canvassing for the posts; the parents will ensure that they get the best appointments only if they have to pay for them. Pliny's generosity is motivated not only by local patriotism, but also by concern for the moral welfare of students when away from parental supervision.

This concern to safeguard young students from sexual abuse is also evident in Pliny's activity at Rome. Two letters report that he is investigating a possible teacher for the young charges of friends. In one, Pliny stresses to Corellia Hispulla that her son has 'outstanding physical beauty, and at this hazardous stage of life, one who is not merely a teacher but also a protector and guide must be sought out' (III 3.4). He recommends Julius Genitor, from whom 'he is to learn first upright behaviour, and then eloquence. One cannot properly learn the second without the first' (III 3.7). In another Pliny conscientiously undertakes the rounds of all the teachers. With characteristic modesty he relates how on one visit to a lecture-room, the badinage of the band of students was reduced to silence on his august entry. There was clearly a wide choice of teachers available, for he remarks that 'in this business of choosing a teacher, some can feel resentful . . . I must bear not only resentment, but also enmity . . .' (II 18.5).

(vi) Pliny, Roman Religion, and Christianity

For many Romans, including Pliny and his idol Cicero, the state religion was inextricably bound up with Rome's history and her mission to dominate the world. Pliny was especially gratified when Trajan at his request awarded him a priesthood, the more so since it was the augurate, which Cicero before him had also held (IV 8). In this spirit of traditional Roman piety, he dedicated a temple at Tifernum, the township which acknowledged him as patron (III 4). He installed statues both there and in his native Comum, 'for particular preference in a temple of Jupiter' (III 6.4). At the behest of soothsayers he enlarged a shrine of Ceres on his estate near Tifernum to accommodate the crowds of locals who attended her feast (IX 39). He recounts at length the entombment alive of the errant Vestal Virgin Cornelia (IV 11; this had in fact occurred several years earlier in the dark days of Domitian, whom he was at pains to disparage). When he became governor of Bithynia-Pontus, he sought to impose Roman forms of consecration of temples there until Trajan vetoed this plan (X 49–50).

As an apologist for the traditional religion, Pliny reacted with dismay to the remarkable rise of Christianity in the province of Bithynia. He wrote a long and celebrated letter to ask the advice of the emperor on how to treat the new sect, and elicited a brief but equally celebrated reply (X 96 and 97). His conscientious investigation of the growth and practice of the new religion reveals that it had already existed in the province as early as AD 90. He states that there are numerous Christians 'of all ages, every rank, and both sexes'. They assembled 'at dawn on a fixed day [of the week], to sing a hymn antiphonally to Christ as God, and to bind themselves by an oath . . . to avoid acts of theft, brigandage, and adultery, not to break their word, and not to withhold money deposited with them when asked for it'. Following the ceremony they departed, but again assembled to take food; this was probably the *agape*, the love-feast first described in Paul's First Epistle to the Corinthians (11: 17 ff.). Pliny finds these Christians guiltless of any crimes. To establish their innocence, he even interrogates under torture two maidservants, 'who were called deaconesses'. None the less, he ordered the execution of those who refused to renounce their adhesion to the sect, because of their 'wilful obstinacy' (*contumacia*, disobedience to a judicial command). He asks the emperor's advice on how to proceed with the investigation.

Trajan in reply commends his governor's actions. Though 'Christians are not to be sought out', once indicted they are to be punished if they refuse to deny their religion and to worship the Roman gods. Thus the emperor makes it clear that adhesion to Christianity constitutes a crime, even if no criminal activity is involved. Trajan adds, however, that anonymous denunciations are to be disregarded as contrary to the spirit of the age. The emperor clearly by this statement distances himself from the practice of informers in the reign of Domitian.[3]

(vii) Pliny and Natural History: The Eruption of Vesuvius

Pliny's close relationship with his uncle, who had become his adoptive father, led him to share the Elder Pliny's interest in natural philosophy. At VIII 8 he describes how the Clitumnus in Umbria emerges from its course with such force as to defy the laws of gravity. In another letter (VIII 20) he discourses at length on the floating islands of lake Vadimon. As governor of Bithynia-Pontus, he surveys the ground near Sinope to assess whether it will support an aqueduct (X 90), and investigates the possibility of diverting the waters of lake Sophon from their natural course into the Black Sea so as to connect it by a canal to the river which flows westward into the Propontis (X 41 and 61). He is fascinated by the behaviour of the dolphin which loves to sport with the boy whom it selects as its favourite (IX 33).

The most celebrated of the letters concerned with natural phenomena are those describing the eruption of Vesuvius in August 79, which Pliny penned at the request of his friend Tacitus, who used them as a source in a lost section of his *Histories*. After a premonitory earthquake in 63, the volcano buried Pompeii in sand, stones, and mud, Herculaneum in liquid tufa, and Stabiae (modern Castellamare) in ashes. The first of the two letters (VI 16) describes the eruption as the backcloth to the heroic death of the Elder Pliny. As commander of the fleet at Misenum, he had (with the enthusiasm of the scientist) ordered a galley to allow him to investigate the appearance of a remarkable cloud ('The pine tree . . . best describes its appearance and shape, for it rose high up into the sky on . . . a very long trunk, and it then spread out . . .'). But then 'the journey begun in a spirit of research he now undertook with the greatest urgency', for he received an urgent appeal for rescue, and he launched other ships. At Stabiae, where his friends were in a state of panic, he calmly dined and retired to sleep, but had to be roused as the danger loomed nearer. Escape over the mountainous sea now proved impossible.

[3] For more detailed discussion of these celebrated letters, see Sherwin-White, *Letters of Pliny*, 691–712 and 772–87, and W. Williams, *Correspondence with Trajan from Bithynia* (Warminster, 1990), 138–44.

The party emerged on to the beach with pillows covering their heads as protection against falling pumice-stones. There Pliny's uncle died from asphyxiation.

As the central theme of this first letter was the heroism of his adoptive father at Stabiae, so the second letter (VI 20) depicts the heroism of the 17-year-old at Misenum. We smile indulgently as Pliny in tranquillity reflects on the events of a quarter of a century earlier, and places himself at the centre of the dramatic events of August 24–5. As the buildings shake around his mother and himself, he coolly guides her out of the town, followed by a stream of panic-stricken townsfolk looking to him for salvation. When the black cloud from the volcano descends to ground level, engulfing them in blinding darkness, he takes his mother aside to avoid the hazard of being trodden underfoot by the crowds pressing from behind them. When daylight returns, they behold a countryside covered in ash 'as though by snow'. They trudge back into Misenum, calmly awaiting news of the fate of Pliny senior, while blood-curdling prophecies ring out from hysterical neighbours.

The two letters combined form a memorable description of the eruption and its devastating progress over the countryside. Pliny does not, however, detail its calamitous effects upon Pompeii, Herculaneum, and Stabiae.

(viii) Pliny as Littérateur

Though Pliny enjoyed his prominent role as senator and advocate at Rome, he frequently claims in the first nine books that he is never so happy as when he is closeted with his books in retirement at Laurentum and Tifernum. He divided his time there between his own compositions and his assessments, invariably flattering, of the works of his friends. The letters record three speeches of individuals of his literary circle, the historical writings of Tacitus, Suetonius, and two others, and above all the poetic compositions of seven versifiers. If Pliny is any guide, the loss of the writings of Pompeius Saturninus, contributor to all three genres (I 16), is particularly regrettable. In sum, this group of literary men attests the vigour of the intellectual life of Trajan's day.

Pliny regarded himself pre-eminently as an orator, and most of his time in retirement is devoted to revision of his numerous speeches. No fewer than fifteen letters discuss these, including two (III 13 and

18) which refer to his *Panegyricus*. He devotes long discussions to his
theories of oratory, being especially concerned with the traditional
controversy of the merits of Atticism, the compressed and factual
presentation, over Asianism, the richer and more flowery mode. Like
Cicero and Quintilian, his former teacher, Pliny claims to espouse a
mixture of styles, employed according to the context. Atticism,
he suggests, is more appropriate for discussion of practical issues
in the courts, whereas a more florid style is more suitable in speeches
such as the *Panegyricus* (so III 18.8 ff.). But in general he inclines to
the more ebullient style, and in a long defence of it (IX 26), he
equates it with greater richness of vocabulary and freer use of figures
of speech.

The tedium involved in revision of speeches, together with the
example of friends, may have encouraged Pliny to try his hand at
verses, and specifically at hendecasyllabics, but he himself claims
that an epigram of Cicero was the direct inspiration (VII 4.3 ff.). He
sends the first batch of poems to his friend Paternus at Comum,
explaining that he beguiles his leisure-time with them 'when in my
carriage; or in the bath, or during dinner'. He forewarns his friend
that some topics are risqué and the language is coarse, but he
emphasizes that like Catullus he does not wish his readers to assume
that his verses are reflections of his lifestyle (IV 14). This proviso
proved all too necessary for another friend, who reported that when
the poems had been discussed in his circle, their vulgarity had
elicited criticism. Pliny was roused to make a spirited response, citing a long list of eminent forebears who likewise indulged in sportive
and indecent versification (V 3).

At a more elevated level, in a letter of advice to a youthful associate
on how to develop his literary powers, he suggests among other
recommendations that his friend should compose poems which are
'pungent and brief'. He underlines the message by breaking into
elegiac couplets, and points out that the finest orators trained themselves in this way, for such poems (specifically hendecasyllabics) contain 'accounts of love, hatred, anger, mercy, and elegance, in short,
all features of life' (VII 9.11–13), such as the orator evokes. Pliny
doubtless preaches to himself here.

Pliny claims that 'there is virtually no lover of literature who does
not regard me likewise with affection' (I 13.5). The letters indicate
that he is on friendly terms with all the literary giants of the day,

Juvenal excepted. He is especially pround of his close connection with Tacitus, to whom eleven of his letters are addressed. The sequence of them reflects the development of their friendship. After serving together as prosecutors in the trial of Marius Priscus (II 11.2), they are on sufficiently affable terms for Pliny to ask Tacitus to recommend suitable candidates as teachers of rhetoric at Comum (IV 13), and for Tacitus to request a detailed account of the eruption of Vesuvius (VI 16 and 20). Thereafter Pliny acknowledges his pleasure that their names are increasingly paired in literary contexts (VII 20), and he is bold enough to send Tacitus details of his role in the extortion case of Baebius Massa in the hope that Tacitus will incorporate this in his *Histories* (VII 33). The climax to Pliny's enthusiasm at their joint celebrity is reached when he records that Tacitus at a dinner-party describes himself to a new acquaintance as a writer, and is asked: 'Are you Tacitus or Pliny?' (IX 23.3).

Whereas Pliny's relations with Tacitus were as devoted pupil to master (VIII 7), his connection with another notable historian, Suetonius, was of solicitous patron to a protégé. In the year 97 he dispels his friend's fears that an unpropitious dream may cause him a bad day in the courts, and he proposes to cover for him in his role as advocate (I 18). At I 24 he is helping him to buy a property at an economical price. A little later he reveals that he has obtained for his young friend a post as military tribune and was graciously arranging to have the post transferred to a relative (III 8). But by V 10 Suetonius' talents are becoming known, perhaps after recitations of his *De uiris illustribus* (his *Lives of the Caesars* were published later, under Hadrian); Pliny castigates his slowness in publication. A later letter confirms this change in the relationship, for Suetonius is begged to advise a remedy for Pliny's frailty at reading verses (IX 34). It seems likely that Pliny invited his friend to serve on his staff in Bithynia, for when he asks Trajan by letter to award the historian the 'right of three children', he states: 'I have begun to love him all the more, the more I have now come to know him from close at hand' (X 94.1). For the probable role of Suetonius in gathering and publishing Pliny's letters, see below (pp. xxxiv f.).

The poet Martial was another contemporary with whom Pliny reveals his acquaintance. The obituary (III 21) which he composed on hearing of Martial's death informs us that he paid the poet's travelling-expenses, when he retired to his native Spain, 'as a gesture of friendship and an acknowledgement of the verses he composed about me'. With characteristic modesty Pliny cites the lines before adding: 'You will respond that his writings will not be immortal. Perhaps they will not be.' A similarly just judgement is expressed of the epic composed by Silius Italicus on the Hannibalic war. Of this extant poem, the *Punica*, Pliny writes, in an obituary devoted largely to Silius' chequered career, 'He composed poetry with greater diligence than genius' (III 7.5).

In this roll-call of notable literary figures, the Elder Pliny naturally holds a prominent place. In response to a friend's request, a complete bibliography of his uncle's works is provided, with brief commentary on each (III 5). After listing his one hundred and two books, his nephew adds: 'Are you surprised that such a busy man completed so many volumes . . .? Your surprise will be greater if you know that for a period he pleaded in the courts, that he died in his fifty-sixth year, and that his middle years were preoccupied and hindered by duties of the greatest importance' (III 5.7). He describes the Elder Pliny's daily routine both at Rome and in retirement, when not a minute was lost from his books: 'Only the time for the bath deflected him from his books. (When I say "the bath", I mean when he was in the water, for when he was being scraped and towelled, he was either listening to or dictating something.) . . . For he believed that any time not devoted to study was wasted' (III 5.15 f.). It has already been noted how his zest for enquiry led to his death in the eruption of Vesuvius (VI 16).

(ix) Pliny as Man of Property

Though Pliny retired to his estates primarily to seek the solitude conducive to his literary activities, part of his leisure was devoted to supervision of his properties at Laurentum, Tifernum, and Comum; not least because he was in part financially dependent on the returns from their produce. He frequently complains of the meagre returns which they bring him, as at II 4.3: 'Because of the poor state of my modest farms, the returns are rather small or uncertain.'

Of his three properties, that at Laurentum was the least pretentious (see plan of the house, p. 308). The house itself, described in detail in II 17, was ample, 'large enough for my needs', but 'not expensive to maintain', but the property was not extensive: 'I have nothing there but the house and garden, and the beach immediately beyond . . . there I . . . cultivate not my non-existent land but myself with my studies' (IV 6.2). At Comum, Pliny had inherited his mother's property (II 15). He speaks of doing the rounds of his 'modest holdings, lending an ear to the many complaints of the country folk, skimming through the accounts unwillingly' (V 14.8). By 107 he has acquired further estates by a legacy, a part of which he generously sells to a close friend of his mother for substantially less than its market value (VII 11 and 14).

Pliny's most extensive property is that near Tifernum in Umbria. He devotes a lengthy letter (V 6) to a description of the capacious mansion with its woodland, extensive vineyards, and open fields (earlier, at III 19, he debates whether to purchase a neighbouring estate identically described, so that it seems probable that he had incorporated it with his own). He states that he prefers this estate to 'any in Tusculum or Tibur or Praeneste' (V 6.45), in other words, to the properties of the wealthy in the vicinity of Rome. As when visiting Comum, he is assailed with the complaints of tenants (VII 30.3, IX 36.6), together with the problem of neglected accounts (IX 15).

In two letters he complains of the difficulty of leasing his farms, 'an exceedingly troublesome task, for suitable tenants are a rare commodity' (VII 30.3). In 107 he reports that 'in spite of large-scale lowering of rents, the arrears of debts have increased . . . several tenants have lost all interest in reducing their debts.' One remedy which he investigates is to lease the farms 'not for money but for part of the produce' (IX 37.2–3). A letter of particular interest (VIII 2) describes how eager buyers had purchased his vine-crop in advance, in anticipation of a bumper harvest, but when it proved disappointing, Pliny awarded them a generous rebate. 'Other people', he remarks at the head of this letter, 'visit their estates to return richer, but I myself go to return poorer.'

(x) Pliny as Provincial Governor

The letters of Book X, collected posthumously (probably by an official in Pliny's entourage), describe his activities as governor of Bithynia-Pontus.[4] When Trajan appointed him to this position in

---

[4] See Williams, *Correspondence*, 5 ff.; A. H. M. Jones, *Cities of the Eastern Roman Provinces* (Oxford, 1971), 148 ff.; B. J. Harris, 'Bithynia', *ANRW* 7.2 (1980), 883 ff.

109/110, the province had been part of the Roman Empire for more than 170 years. The Greek monarch Nicomedes IV had at his death bequeathed the kingdom of Bithynia to the Roman people in 74 BC, but Mithradates of Pontus then invaded it, and only after he was subjugated was Pompey able to establish Bithynia-Pontus as a Roman province in 63 BC. He divided the territory of Bithynia among eleven self-governing cities, the local officials of which were required to collect the taxes for Rome, provide supplies for Roman armies, and organize transport and lodgings for visiting Roman officials. The traditional tripartite structure of government, assembly, council, and magistrates, was retained in each city, but henceforth the assembly merely approved decisions of the council. Each city appointed delegates to the two provincial councils of Bithynia and Pontus, but these over-arching bodies exercised little power, and are never mentioned by Pliny.

Under the late Republic and earlier emperors, the governor was a magistrate of praetorian rank formally appointed by the Senate as proconsul, but by Trajan's day the province was notorious for maladministration. Under emperors from Augustus onwards, more governors were indicted for extortion from this province than from any other. Trajan accordingly appointed Pliny as his direct representative, with the title *legatus Augusti pro praetore consulari potestate*. The title makes clear that he was Trajan's deputy with praetorian power (earlier governors had been ex-praetors). The addition to his title, *consulari potestate*, was a mere sop to the ex-consul, allowing him to be attended by six lictors instead of the five allotted to other legates.

Since the administration of the province was almost wholly the charge of the cities, Pliny's role in the maintenance of public order, in scrutinizing finances, and in authorizing large-scale projects was conducted with the officials of the cities. Seven of the cities in Bithynia, and five in Pontus, are cited in the letters. In Bithynia, Nicomedia, the erstwhile capital of the Greek kingdom, presented him with a range of problems: he proposes to establish a fire-brigade to counter fires (letter 33), to build an aqueduct (37), to divert the waters of a lake for more efficient transportation (41), to rebuild a temple (49), and to deal with problems of slaves (31 and 74). Nicaea, rival of Nicomedia for pre-eminence in the province, confronts him with the indictment of a prominent citizen from Prusa (81), with property-disputes (83), and with the proposal to build a theatre (39).

At Prusa, the finances and provision of public works demand his attention (17B), together with a proposal for a new bathhouse (23 and 70). Apamea, as a Roman colony established by Julius Caesar or Mark Antony, claims exemption from taxation and also financial self-government (47). Claudiopolis, like Prusa, wishes to build a new bathhouse, for which Pliny requests an architect from Rome (39.5 ff.). Finally, Byzantium, strictly in the province of Thrace, but now administered from Bithynia, has been awarded a military contingent to support the city-magistrates, and Pliny pleads for similar provision at Juliopolis (77).

It will be clear from this survey that cities normally required permission from Rome to initiate projects such as aqueducts, theatres, and baths. This was to ensure that money was prudently spent and to prevent corrupt contracts. Throughout the tenure of his governorship Pliny was particularly vigilant in ensuring financial probity in the cities. He had served less than two years in the province when the letters suddenly cease. As the normal tenure of a governorship was three years, it seems virtually certain that he died in the province.

Epistolography at Rome

Whereas published epistles in Greek were common, and especially from the third century onwards, the arrival of epistolography as a prose genre at Rome came much later.[5] Though there is evidence of publication of letters composed by the elder Cato and by Cornelia, mother of the Gracchi, in the second century BC, the earliest surviving collection is that of Cicero a century later. This massive anthology comprises 914 letters in all, largely from Cicero's pen but some also from his correspondents. For Pliny, Cicero as letter-writer is the essential model (we are here concerned neither with the poetic epistle represented in Horace and Ovid, Martial and Statius, nor the philosophical type, represented by Seneca as the chief Latin counterpart to Plato and Epicurus). Cicero's letters perform two main functions for the benefit of today's readers as for his correspondents:

---

[5] See now M. Trapp (ed.), *Greek and Latin Letters: An Anthology with Introduction* (Cambridge 2003), and Catharine Edwards, 'Epistolography', in S. Harrison (ed.), *A Companion to Latin Literature* (Oxford 2005), ch. 19.

first, they offer a view from the inside of many facets of the political, social, and domestic concerns of the day, and secondly, they depict Cicero's own leading role in them. Autobiography was still in its infancy as a genre at Rome, being represented almost entirely by military and political memoirs, and for Cicero the letters serve as a substitute for self-projection.

Pliny, likewise, is not slow to proclaim his own virtues and his many-sided accomplishments, but in the very different political and social atmosphere of the day, especially as they impinge on the men and women of the *haute bourgeoisie*. The collection, numbering 246 letters in Books I–IX, all from Pliny himself, and 121 in Book X shared between Pliny and the emperor Trajan on the problems of provincial administration, can thus be exploited as a primer of Roman social history, as the classification of topics in Index I indicates.

Literary Style, Publication, and Dating of the Letters

Pliny regarded epistolography as a third genre of creative literature additional to his orations and his verses. What style, then, was to be adopted in the presentation of the letters? When he offers advice to his youthful friend Fuscus Salinator on the literary exercises he should practise to further an orator's career, amongst other suggestions he writes: 'I am keen . . . that you should devote some care to letter-writing . . . we look to epistles for language which is compressed and unadorned' (VII 9.8). In another letter, in which he praises Pompeius Saturninus, he states: 'Recently he read out to me some letters, which he said his wife wrote. I thought that what was being read to me was Plautus or Terence freed of the metre' (I 16.6). Taken together, these passages indicate that the prose epistle should be composed in a plain but educated style, and this is why, for young students of today, their Latin is more suitable as being more comprehensible than the speeches of Cicero or the history of Livy.

While 'plain but educated' serves as a general assessment of Pliny's epistolary style, the dramatic content of some letters tempts him to embark on more flowery discourse. One obvious example is the ghost story recounted to Licinius Sura (VII 27), where Pliny imaginatively creates a dramatic and atmospheric narrative. Other similarly dramatic accounts include the dream of Fannius (V 5), the poetic description of the floating islands on lake Vadimon (VIII 20), the anecdote of the sportive dolphin (IX 33), and of course the account of the eruption of Vesuvius and the heroism of the Elder Pliny (VI 16).

When Pliny dispatched letters to selected correspondents, he had copies made and filed with the intention of later publication.[6] The dedication to Septicius Clarus which precedes Book I indicates that he intended to publish groups of selected letters at staggered dates. Some scholars have suggested that Books I–IX were issued tidily in three triads (I–III, IV–VI, VII–IX), others that each book was published separately, and others still that Books I–IX were published simultaneously.

Study of the chronology of the early letters suggests the further possibility that Books I–II formed the first volume. All the letters of Book I can be dated to the reign of Nerva and the first months of Trajan's principate. Book II contains further letters from this period 97–8, but others must be assigned to the year 100. Pliny may have gathered and published Books I and II before undertaking the duties of the consulship in September of that year. The wide range of letters in Book I has no single dominant topic; by contrast, Book II has as its centre the lengthy account, covering two letters (II 11–12), of the extortion trial of Marius Priscus and Pliny's prominent role in it. Artistically set against these is a second letter devoted to Pliny's life away from city-business, the description of his estate at Laurentum (II 17). The final letter of Book II offers a light-hearted close to the volume with three anecdotes portraying Regulus as legacy-hunter.

The continuity of themes pervading Books III–VI suggests that they are closely harmonized, but both the large number and the careful balance of the numbers of letters (21 and 30 in Books III and IV, and 21 and 34 in V and VI) encourage the speculation that Pliny published them in two separate volumes. As in Book II, there is a dominant letter in Book III portraying an extortion trial, that of Caecilius Classicus (III 9) and round it are assembled artistically the diverse themes of his uncle's writings, panegyrics of the deceased poets Martial and Silius Italicus, obituaries and testimonials, and notable events in the social life of the capital, including recitations, a dinner-party, and the consternation caused by the murder of a cruel

---

[6] This discussion of how the letters were published is inevitably speculative; see Sherwin-White, *Letters of Pliny*, 20–41.

grandee by his slaves. Book IV likewise centres on an extortion trial, that of Julius Bassus (IV 9). The letters round it again offer a mélange of public business in the Senate and the Centumviral court, and of Pliny's private affairs. The letters devoted to literary matters now include references to his burgeoning role as versifier. Virtually all the letters in Books III and IV can be dated to between 100 and 105, encouraging the speculation that the two books were published together in that latter year.

As in these earlier books, in Books V and VI Pliny groups shorter letters with pleasing variation of topics around a more extended topic. In Book V this is the description of his estate near Tifernum (V 6), and in Book VI the two letters requested by Tacitus on the eruption of Vesuvius (VI 16 and 20). The accumulation of a series of short letters towards the close of Book VI suggests that Pliny was seeking a balance between the length of the two books. The letters in both can be dated predominantly to the years 105 to 107, and were probably published in 107.

The letters of Books VII–IX may likewise have been subdivided into two volumes. Most of those in Books VII–VIII can be dated to 107–8, though a few may have been incorporated from earlier years. By contrast, Book IX gives the impression that Pliny has filled it out with several epistles from earlier years. Moreover, the large number of letters in the book, and the brevity of many of them, reinforce the impression of a shortage of more substantial correspondence. It is striking that there is little discussion of political affairs in this book. We may conclude that these three books were published in two volumes, VII–VIII in the first, and IX in the other, late in 108 or early in 109.

The correspondence with Trajan, which occupies the whole of Book X, comprises the earlier exchange of private letters (1–14), and those sent and received when Pliny was governor of Bithynia-Pontus. Of the first small group, letters 1–11 date from 98–9, shortly after Trajan's accession, 12 is to be assigned to 101–2, 13 to 104, and 14 to either 102 or 106. These letters will have been gathered and published together with 15–121, not by Pliny himself nor in his lifetime, but by a person with access to the imperial archives. It is feasible that the work was carried out under the supervision of Suetonius, for as a close associate of Pliny he probably served on his staff in Bithynia (see X 94.1), and, more important, he became a prominent figure in the imperial bureaucracy in the later days of Hadrian. Indeed, he became the imperial secretary for correspondence until Hadrian dismissed him from this post (*Historia Augusta, Hadrian* 2.3), so that he had unrestricted access to the Roman archives. He could then have arranged for the publication of Book X in the 120s or 130s.

In the course of editing, the bald headings on the letters replaced the more courtly versions of the originals. Evidence from papyri and inscriptions also shows that letters to and from the imperial court included the date and place of origin. These too will have been struck out in the course of editing.

A note on writing materials. At I 6.1 Pliny, when out hunting, sits by the nets, 'armed not with hunting-spear or lance, but with pen and tablets'. At III 5.15 his uncle when travelling has his secretary by him 'with a book and writing-tablets'. From the days of Catullus and Cicero, these were wax-coated wooden tablets, hinged together by straps, and small enough to be held in the hand. They were incised with a stylus for preliminary drafting, which could later be deleted to allow repeated use of the tablets. By Pliny's day there is evidence of the introduction of parchment 'tablets' (Martial 14.7 and 184), but it is not certain that Pliny used them. The versions of the letters finally sent were inscribed on papyrus with a split reed dipped in ink made from soot and gum, or from the juice of the cuttlefish. Such writing in ink could be erased by a sponge, and the paper reused.

NOTE ON THE TEXT AND TRANSLATION

THIS translation is based on the text of the letters edited by R. A. B. Mynors (Oxford, 1963), which is faithfully reproduced in the Loeb edition (ed. B. Radice, 1969). It rests on three separate manuscript traditions, which Mynors labels α, β, γ, and which are popularly known as the Nine-book, Ten-book, and Eight-book versions.

The Nine-book tradition is represented by two ninth-century manuscripts M and V, and V does not survive after V 6, leaving M as the sole representative of this tradition for V 7 to IX. The Ten-book tradition (β) provides the sole evidence for Book X; no manuscript survives after V 6, so that we are dependent on printed editions for the rest. The Eight-book version (so called because it does not contain Book VIII) has no complete surviving manuscript, and provides the least reliable readings of the three. Mynors helpfully prefaces his edition with a book-by-book survey of the available evidence from the three traditions. The section numbers of Mynors' text are given in the margins.

The existence of the letters as we have them is attributable to the heroic endeavours of the Italian and French humanists. They assembled them from widely dispersed texts of the three traditions. There is an enlightening brief account by Reynolds in L. D. Reynolds (ed.), *Texts and Transmission* (Oxford, 1983), 316–22.

In translating the letters I have sought to bear in mind two categories of readers. A carefully selected anthology is the ideal text for young students grappling with the Latin, because the language is simpler and more straightforward than that of Cicero's speeches or Livy's history. For these students I have provided a more literal and careful version than the admirably fluent rendering of Betty Radice in the Loeb edition. But the second (and much larger) group of readers will approach the letters independently of the Latin. For them I have attempted, as far as possible, to provide an idiomatic English version without straying from the essential sense of the original.

The letters are virtually all addressed to learned friends who are equally at home in Greek and in Latin. Pliny on occasion, with some affectation, employs a Greek expression to convey his meaning. I have resorted to French to convey a similar effect. But where he quotes from Homer or other Greek writers in a more extensive way, I have translated literally into English.

SELECT BIBLIOGRAPHY

Editions and Commentaries

Durry, M., *Lettres X et Panégyrique* (Paris, 1959).

Guillemin, A.-M., *Lettres I–IX* (Paris, 1927–8).

Mynors, R. A. B., *Letters I–X* (Oxford, 1963).

Radice, B., *Letters and Panegyricus*, 2 vols. (Loeb, 1969).

Schuster, M., and Hanslik, R., *Letters and Panegyricus* (Leipzig, 1958).

Sherwin-White, A. N., *The Letters of Pliny* (Oxford, 1966). See also the extended reviews by C. P. Jones, *Phoenix*, 22 (1968), 111–44, and by F. Millar, *JRS* 58 (1968), 218–24.

Stout, S. E., *Letters I–X* (Bloomington, Ind., 1962).

Williams, W., *Correspondence with Trajan from Bithynia* (Warminster, 1990).

General

Ash, R., ' "Aliud est enim epistolam, aliud historian scribere" (*Ep.* 6.16.22)', *Arethusa*, 36 (2003), 211–25.

Augustakis, A., ' "Nequaquam historia digna": Plinian Style in Ep. 6.20', *CJ* 100 (2005), 265–73.

Balsdon, J. P. V. D., *Life and Leisure in Ancient Rome* (London, 1969).

Barnes, T. D., 'Legislation against the Christians', *JRS* 58 (1968), 32–50.

Bennett, J., *Trajan, Optimus Princeps* (London, 1997).

Bradley, K., 'Writing the History of the Roman Family', *CP* 88 (1999), 237–50.

Bütler, H. P., *Die geistige Welt des jüngeren Plinius* (Heidelberg, 1970).

Crook, J., *Consilium Principis* (Cambridge, 1955).

Delia, D., *Alexandrian Citizenship* (Atlanta, 1991).

De Neeve, P., 'A Roman Landowner and his Estates: Pliny the Younger', *SIFC* 10 (1992), 335–44.

Duncan-Jones, R. P., 'The Finances of the Younger Pliny', *PBSR* 20 (1965), 177–88.

Du Prey, P., *The Villas of Pliny from Antiquity to Posterity* (Chicago, 1996).

Edwards, C., 'Epistolography', in S. Harrison (ed.), *A Companion to Latin Literature* (Oxford, 2004), ch. 19.

Felton, D., *Haunted Greece and Rome: Ghost Stories from Classical Antiquity* (Austin, Tx., 1999).

Gonzalès, A., *Pline le Jeune: Esclaves et affranchis à Rome* (Besançon, 2003).

Grainger, J. D., *Nerva and the Roman Accession Crisis of AD 96–99* (London, 2000).

Griffin, M., 'Pliny and Tacitus', *SCI* 18 (1959), 139–58.

Grimal, P., *Les Jardins romains*[2] (Paris, 1969).

Guillemin, A.-M., *Pline et la vie littéraire de son temps* (Paris, 1929).

Hammond, M., 'Pliny the Younger's Views on Government', *HSCP* 49 (1938), 115 ff.

Harris, B. F., 'Bithynia', *ANRW* 7.2 (1980), esp. pp. 883–94.

Henderson, J., *Pliny's Statue: The Letters, Self-portraiture, and Classical Art* (Exeter, 2002).

—— 'Knowing Someone through their Books: Pliny on Uncle Pliny, Ep. 3.5', *CP* 97 (2002), 256–84.

Higham, T. F., 'Dolphin Riders', *GR* 7.1 (1960), 82 ff.

Hoffer, S. E., *The Anxieties of Pliny the Younger* (Atlanta, 1999).

Hutchinson, G. O., *Latin Literature from Seneca to Juvenal* (Oxford, 1993).

—— *Cicero's Correspondence: A Literary Study* (Oxford, 1998).

Jackson, R., *Doctors and Disease in the Roman Empire* (London, 1988).

Jones, A. H. M., *Cities of the Eastern Roman Provinces* (Oxford, 1971).

Jones, B. W., *The Emperor Domitian* (London, 1992).

Jones, C. P., *Plutarch and Rome* (Oxford, 1971).

Jones, N. F., 'Pliny the Younger's "Vesuvius" Letters', *CW* 95 (2002), 31–48.

Kraemer, C. J., 'Pliny and the Early Church Service', *CP* 29 (1934), 293–300.

MacDougall, E. (ed.), *Ancient Roman Villa Gardens* (London, 1987).

Magie, D., *Roman Rule in Asia Minor* (Princeton, 1950).

Malherbe, A. J., *Ancient Epistolary Theorists* (Atlanta, 1988).

Meiggs, R., *Roman Ostia*[2] (Oxford, 1973).

Murgia, C. E., 'Pliny's Letter and the Dialogus', *HSCP* 89 (1985), 171–206.

Myers, K. S., 'Docta Otia: Garden Ownership and Configuration of Leisure in Statius and Pliny the Younger', *Arethusa*, 38 (2005), 103–29.

Oberrauch, L., 'Et statim concidit: Bemerkungen zum Tod Plinius des Alteren', *Mnem.* (2000), 721–5.

Pitcher, R. A., 'The Hole in the Hypothesis: Pliny and Martial Reconsidered', *Mnem.* (1999), 554–61.

Riggsby, A. M., 'Pliny on Cicero and Oratory', *AJP* 116 (1995), 123–35.

—— 'Self and Community in the Younger Pliny', *Arethusa*, 31 (1998), 75–98.

Roller, M., 'Pliny's Catullus: The Politics of Literary Appropriation', *TAPA* 128 (1998), 265–304.

Rudd, N., 'Stratagems of Vanity', in T. Woodman and J. Powell (eds.), *Author and Audience in Latin Literature* (Cambridge, 1992), ch. 2.

Rutledge, S. H., *Imperial Inquisitions: Prosecutors and Informants from Tiberius to Domitian* (London, 2001).

Sherwin-White, A. N., 'The Date of Pliny's Praetorship', *JRS* 47 (1957); repr. as Appendix IV in *The Letters*.

—— 'Trajan's Replies to Pliny: Authorship and Necessity', *JRS* 52 (1962), 114–125.

Slater, W. J., 'Hand-outs at Dinner', *Phoenix*, 60 (2000), 107–22.

Smallwood, E. M., *Documents of Nerva, Trajan, and Hadrian* (Cambridge, 1966).

Sordi, M., *The Christians and the Roman Empire* (London, 1986).

Southern, P., *Domitian: Tragic Tyrant* (London, 1997).

Stout, S. E., *Scribe and Critic at Work in Pliny's Letters* (Bloomington, Ind., 1954).

—— 'The Coalescence of the Two Plinies', *TAPA* 86 (1955), 250 ff.

Syme, R., *Tacitus*, 2 vols. (Oxford, 1958).

—— 'Pliny's Less Successful Friends', *Historia*, 9 (1960), 362–79.

—— 'People in Pliny', *JRS* 58 (1968), 135–51.

Tanzer, H. H., *The Villas of Pliny the Younger* (New York, 1924).

Testard, M., 'Carmenque Christo quasi deo dicere', *REL* 72 (1994), 138–58.

Townend, G. B., 'The Hippo Inscription and the Career of Suetonius', *Historia*, 10 (1961), 99–109.

Trapp, M. (ed.), *Greek and Latin Letters: An Anthology with Introduction* (Cambridge, 2003).

Traub, H. W., 'Pliny's Treatment of History in Epistolary Form', *TAPA* 86 (1955), 213–32.

Van Buren, A. W., 'Pliny's Laurentine Villa', *JRS* 38 (1948), 35 ff.

Vidman, L. *Étude sur la correspondance de Pline le Jeune avec Trajan* (Prague, 1960).

Wolff E., *Pline le Jeune ou le refus de pessimisme* (Rennes, 2003).

Further Reading in Oxford World's Classics

Juvenal, *The Satires*, trans. Niall Rudd, ed. William Barr.

Suetonius, *Lives of the Caesars*, trans. Catharine Edwards.

Tacitus, *Agricola and Germany*, trans. Anthony Birley.

—— *The Histories*, trans. W. H. Fyfe, revised by D. S. Levene.

A CHRONOLOGY OF PLINY THE YOUNGER

All dates are AD

61/2	Birth of Pliny.	54–68	Nero emperor
		68–9	Year of the Four Emperors
c.69–c.75	Schooling at Comum. Death of father; adoption by uncle.	69–79	Vespasian emperor
76	Tertiary education begins under Quintilian at Rome.		
79	Present at eruption of Vesuvius.	79–81	Titus emperor
c.80	Vigintivirate; presides over Centumviral court.		
c.82	Military tribune in Syria.	81–96	Domitian emperor
c.90	Quaestor; chosen as *quaestor Caesaris*.		
c.92	Serves as *tribunus plebis*.		
c.93	Elected praetor.		
c.94–6	Prefect of the military treasury.		
Jan. 98–Aug. 100	Prefect of the treasury of Saturn	96–Jan. 98	Nerva emperor
Sept.–Dec. 100	Suffect consul.	Jan. 98–117	Trajan emperor
c.104–7	Curator of the Tiber.		
c.109–11	Governor of Bithynia-Pontus.		
c.112	Presumed dead.		

COMPLETE LETTERS

BOOK ONE

1 Gaius Pliny sends greetings to his friend Septicius Clarus[1]

On numerous occasions you have urged me to assemble and to pub- 1
lish such letters as I had composed with some care. I have now
assembled them without maintaining chronological sequence, for I
was not compiling a history, but as each happened to come to hand.*

What remains is that you should not repent of your advice, nor I 2
of obeying you. On that assumption I shall seek out those still lying
neglected, and I shall not expunge any which I intend to add to the
collection in future. Farewell.

2 To his friend Arrianus Maturus   c.97–8

I foresee that your arrival is to be somewhat delayed, so I am present- 1
ing for your inspection the book which I promised you in earlier
letters. I beg you to read and correct it as you usually do, more
especially because I do not seem to have written anything before with
as much *élan*. This is because I have tried to imitate Demosthenes, 2
your invariable model, and Calvus,* who has lately become mine,
though only so far as figures of speech go, for the impact of these
great men can be attained solely by 'the favoured few'.* The subject 3
matter* itself did not militate against such rivalry with them (I fear I
speak without shame), for it was presented almost entirely in impassioned speech, and it roused me as I slumbered in lengthy idleness, if
a person like me can be so roused. But I did not entirely eschew the 4
grandiloquence of our Cicero, whenever I was prompted to stray a
little from my path in not inappropriate passages that charm, for the
effect which I sought was to stimulate, and not to depress.

You are not to think that I am craving your indulgence for this 5
stylistic departure. Indeed, in order to provoke your criticism the
more, I shall confess that both my friends and I are not averse to
publishing the work, provided that you vote in favour of what may be

---

[1] Hereafter the salutations have been abbreviated. See Explanatory Notes for short
descriptions of Pliny's correspondents, and Index II: Pliny's Correspondents, for all
letters to the same recipient.

6 a mistake on my part. Clearly I must publish something, and I pray that what I have ready may be most suitable; you hear my aspiration to idleness! Several reasons prompt my need to publish, above all the fact that the works which I have already issued* are said to be in men's hands, though they have lost the glamour of being new. But perhaps the booksellers* are tickling my ears. If so, let them keep at it, so long as this deception of theirs gives me a good impression of my writings. Farewell.

3 *To his friend Caninius Rufus*

1 How goes it at Comum, your favourite spot and mine? And that delightful house of yours close to the town, with that colonnade in which it is always spring, that grove of plane trees with their abundant shade, that watercourse sparkling like emeralds, the lake lying below* at your service, the walk so soft yet firm underfoot, the bath-house which gets its fill of the sun as it courses round, the dining rooms, some catering for a number and others for the few, the bedrooms for rest at night and during the day? Do they claim and

2 share you with each other? Or are you called away, as often in the past, on frequent trips to review your domestic affairs? If they are claiming you, what a lucky and blessed soul you are! If not, you are 'one of a crowd'.*

3 Why not assign those shallow and shoddy concerns to others, for it's time you did, and apply yourself to your books in this time of boundless and slothful retirement? Make this your business and leisure, your work and relaxation. Devote your waking hours to this,

4 and your sleeping hours too. Create something and shape it, so that it becomes yours for ever. Whereas all else will pass to a succession of owners, this will never cease to be your own from the moment it begins to exist. I know well the mind and talent which I stir to action. Strive only to be as outstanding in your own eyes as you will appear to others, if you do. Farewell.

4 *To Pompeia Celerina, his mother-in-law*   *c.*97

1 What amenities you have in your houses at Ocriculum, Narnia, Carsulae, and Perusia!* At Narnia there is even a bathhouse! My letters make these available, so there is no need for you to write

now, as the brief note which you wrote earlier is enough. I swear that 2
my own properties are not so much mine as are yours. The difference between yours and ours is that your domestics welcome me
with more attention and concern than do my own.

Perhaps you will get the same treatment should you at some time
break your journey at ours. I should like you to do this, first so that 3
you may enjoy our hospitality as we enjoy yours, and secondly so
that my servants may finally rouse themselves, for they await my
coming without concern, almost offhandedly. The fact is that when 4
masters are tolerant, the fear felt by their slaves is dispelled through
their growing used to us, whereas they rouse themselves when there
are new arrivals, and they strive to win the favour of their masters by
attention to others rather than to ourselves. Farewell.

5 *To his friend Voconius Romanus* early 97

Did you ever see anyone more fearful and abject than Marcus 1
Regulus, following Domitian's death?* The crimes which he perpetrated under Domitian were no less than those in Nero's day, but
he hid them more successfully. He began to be apprehensive that I
was angry with him, and he was not mistaken, for I *was* angry.

He had lent his support to the trial of Arulenus Rusticus,* and 2
had rejoiced at his death to the point of publicly reciting and publishing a written version, in which he launched an attack on Rusticus,
even calling him 'the ape of the Stoics', and adding 'branded with
Vitellius' scar'* (you recognize his eloquence!). His lambasting of 3
Herennius Senecio* was so immoderate that Mettius Carus asked
him: 'What concern of yours are my dead victims? Did I harass
Crassus or Camerinus?'* (Regulus had laid accusations against them
in Nero's day.)

Regulus believed that I was angry at his behaviour, and so he had 4
not even invited me to his public reading. He also recalled with what
hostility he had assailed me in the Centumviral court. I was appear- 5
ing on behalf of Arrionilla, the wife of Timon, at the request of
Arulenus Rusticus,* and Regulus was on the opposing side. Part of
our plea rested on the view of Mettius Modestus, that excellent man
who was then in exile, for Domitian had excluded him. Regulus,
look you, comes forward and says: 'I want to know your view of
Modestus.' You appreciate my danger if in replying I had expressed

approval, and the disgrace if I had expressed disapproval. I can only say that the gods were with me at that moment. 'I shall answer', I said, 'if the Centumviral court is to pass judgement on him.' He

6 repeated: 'I want to know your view of Modestus.' I in turn said: 'It used to be the case that witnesses were questioned about the accused, and not about the convicted.' He made a third attempt: 'I am not asking now for your view of Modestus, but for your view of

7 his patriotism.'* 'You ask me for my view,' I said, 'but I regard it as improper even to ask questions about one already sentenced.' He was silenced, and I was praised and congratulated for avoiding on the one hand damage to my reputation by giving a reply perhaps opportune but certainly dishonest, and on the other the trap set by so insidious a question.

8 So, being now terrified by his feelings of guilt, he laid hold of Caecilius Celer and then of Fabius Justus, begging them to forge a reconciliation between us. This was not enough for him; he approached Spurinna,* and addressed him in grovelling entreaty, as is his most downcast manner when he is afraid: 'Please visit Pliny at home early in the morning; be sure to make it early in the morning, for I cannot bear the strain any longer. Ensure by any way you can that he feels no anger towards me.' I had just woken up when a messenger came from Spurinna: 'I am coming to see you.' 'You certainly aren't,' I replied. 'I will come to you.'

9 We ran into each other in the colonnade of Livia,* as we were making for each other. He retailed Regulus' instructions and added a plea of his own, but brusquely, as befitted the best of men speaking on behalf of one wholly unlike him. I said to him: 'You must decide

10 for yourself what reply you think should be made to Regulus. I must not deceive you; I am waiting for Mauricus'* (he had not yet returned from exile), 'so I cannot give you a reply either way, for I intend to do whatever he decides. It is right that he should take the lead, and that I should go along with him.'

11 A day or two later Regulus himself encountered me as we were paying our formal visit* to the praetor. He came up behind me, and asked to have a private word. He said that he feared that what he had said some time ago during a process in the Centumviral court was lodged deep in my mind. That occasion was when he was replying to Satrius Rufus* and myself—'Satrius Rufus, who is no rival of

12 Cicero, and is satisfied with the style of utterance of our day.' I

answered that I now realized that he had said that maliciously, because he was himself admitting it, but that the remark could have been interpreted as respectful. 'I myself do vie with Cicero,' I said, 'and I am not content with the eloquence of our age, for I regard it 13 as utterly stupid not to posit for imitation all that is best. But now that you remember this lawsuit, why have you forgotten the one in which you asked me for my view of the patriotism of Mettius Modestus?'

He grew markedly pale (though in fact he is always pale), and in faltering tones he said: 'My question was designed to damage not you but Modestus.' (Note the viciousness of the man, for he did not conceal his desire to damage an exile.) He offered 14 in addition a remarkable reason. 'In a letter which was read out before Domitian,' he said, 'Modestus wrote: "Regulus, the most depraved of all two-legged creatures." ' Modestus had been wholly truthful in penning this.

This was virtually the end of our conversation, for I had no wish 15 to take the matter further. I wanted to keep all my options open until Mauricus came. I am well aware that Regulus is *dur à réprimer*,* for he is wealthy, leader of a faction, well regarded by many, and feared by more, fear being an emotion stronger than affection. It is possible, 16 however, that those supports may be shaken, and collapse, for the popularity of evil men is as fickle as the men themselves.

However, to keep repeating what I have already said, I await Mauricus, a serious man of practical wisdom whose many experiences have schooled him, the sort of man who can visualize the future from past events. My own decision on whether to take action or to remain quiet* will rest on his advice.

I have written this account to you because it is right that in view of 17 our shared affection you should know not only all that I have done and said, but also what I plan to do. Farewell.

6 *To his friend Cornelius Tacitus* before 98

You will laugh at this, and your laughter is in order. This acquaint- 1 ance of yours has captured three boars,* and most handsome ones at that. 'What, you yourself?' you ask. 'Yes, but without totally abandoning my idle and restful life. I would sit by the nets, armed not with hunting-spear or lance, but with pen and tablets. I would contemplate some subject and jot it down, so that if I returned empty-handed, my tablets would be full.'

2   You are not to despise this manner of study, for it is remarkable how the mind is roused by exercise and movement of the body. To start with, the woodland all around, the solitude, and the silence

3 imposed by the hunt are great incentives to thought. So when you go hunting you can adopt my advice, and carry your tablets as well as your food-basket and flask, for you will find that Minerva roams the mountains no less than Diana.* Farewell.

7 *To his friend Octavius Rufus*   September 97

1 Observe the lofty eminence on which you have set me when you ascribe to me the same power and the same dominion as Homer allots to Jupiter Greatest and Best:

> Part of his prayer the Father granted, part denied,*

2 for I can likewise part grant and part refuse your prayer. It is certainly right for me, especially as you demand it, to demur at representing the Baetici against a single individual,* but it does not square with my good faith and integrity, which win your affection, to confront in court the province to which I have been closely attached

3 through my many services and toils and even dangers. So I shall cling to this compromise: of the alternatives which you seek, I shall choose the course which does justice not merely to your inclination but also to your good judgement. I am in fact to take seriously not so much your momentary whim, excellent man though you are, as what will win your lasting approval.

4   I expect to be in Rome about 15 October, and to maintain this position in person to Gallus,* with my expressions of loyalty and yours. For now, you can assure him of my benevolence. 'He nodded

5 with his dark brows',* for why should I not chat with you in Homeric lines, seeing that you do not allow me to converse with you in your own? I am fired with such enthusiasm* for them that I think this reward alone could induce me to be bribed to oppose the Baetici in court.

6   I almost omitted to mention what ought to be the last thing to leave unmentioned. Your excellent dates have joined me here, and they must now engage with my figs and mushrooms. Farewell.

8 *To his friend Pompeius Saturninus* 96–7

Appropriately enough, the arrival of your letter, in which you 1
demanded that I send you one of my compositions, coincided with
my own decision to do so. Thus you have spurred on this horse
already eager, simultaneously depriving yourself of any excuse to
avoid the toil of reading it, and me of the embarrassment of demanding that you do; for it is hardly right for me to show reluctance 2
towards your offer, or for you to be oppressed by your own request.
But you are not to anticipate any new work from this idle fellow, for
I intend to ask you to read again at leisure the speech which I
delivered before my fellow townsmen* prior to dedicating their
library. I recall that you have already made some general observa- 3
tions on it, so now I am begging you not merely to peruse it in the
round, but also to examine the detail with your usual critical faculty.
I shall then also after correction have the option of publishing or of
withholding it. Indeed, this process of correction will perhaps guide 4
my hesitant steps on whether to publish it or not. Quite frequent
reconsideration will either establish its unworthiness for publication,
or will make it worthy in the course of scrutiny.

Yet the reasons for this hesitation of mine lie not so much in the 5
writing as in the nature of the subject matter, for it is rather too
boastful and elevated. It will weigh heavily on my modesty (though
the style itself is restrained and subdued) because I am compelled to
dwell upon the generosity of my parents and myself. The topic is 6
two-edged and ticklish, even though the need justifies it. For if
praise even from other people often sounds unwelcome to people's
ears, how hard it is to ensure that a speech dwelling on oneself and
one's kin does not sound oppressive! For we tend to loathe true
worth, and still more the fame and repute which attend it. It is only
when such honourable deeds lie buried in obscurity and silence that
we subject them to less disparagement and criticism. For this reason 7
I have often asked myself whether I should have composed this
speech, such as it is, for others as well as myself. That it was written
for my own benefit I was reminded by the fact that many things
which are essential in the performance of an action lose both their
usefulness and their esteem once they are concluded. To look no 8
further for instances of this, what was more useful than to commit to
paper the reason for my generosity? This was the means by which I

succeeded, first of all in dwelling on honourable reflections, secondly in visualizing their nobility in more extended thought, and finally in guarding against the regret which accompanies impulsive generosity.*

9 These considerations gave birth to what we may call the practice of despising money, for though nature has constrained all of us to keep it under lock and key, my fondness for munificence, on which I have reflected long and hard, has freed me from the chains of greed by which the generality of people is bound, and my generosity seemed more likely to win praise because I was drawn to it not by a sort of impulse, but by a considered plan.

10 In addition to these motives there was the fact that I was pledging money not for shows or gladiators,* but for year-by-year expenses towards the rearing of freeborn children.* Moreover, pleasures which delight the eye and the ear, so far from demanding approval, ought not to be encouraged but rather played down in public addresses.

11 Indeed, to induce a person gladly to undertake the wearying toil of bringing up children, we must successfully deploy not merely

12 rewards but also refined exhortations. If physicians use more wheedling words in prescribing a healthy but not pleasurable diet, how much more fitting was it in the public interest to recommend by genial words a service which is highly useful but not equally popular! This was particularly important, since I had to endeavour to explain that what was being conferred on parents should be approved by the childless also, so that the privilege granted to the few would be

13 patiently awaited and deserved by the rest. But just as at that time I was intent on the general welfare rather than on my own self-projection, when I wanted the purpose and outcome of my gift to be understood, so now in considering publication I fear that I may perhaps appear to have ministered to my own praise rather than to the advantages of others.

14 Moreover, I keep in mind the fact that the greater magnanimity attributes the rewards of worthy behaviour to our moral awareness rather than to our good repute. Esteem ought to be the outcome rather than the motive, and, if by some chance it does not accrue, it is

15 no less noble in having deserved that esteem. Indeed, people who dignify their good deeds by recounting them are thought not to announce them because they have performed them, but to have performed them in order to announce them. In this way, what would have been a fine action when recounted by another fades from view

when the one who performed it himself recounts it. For when people cannot nullify the deed, they attack the boasting which accompanies it. Thus if you have done something which should go unmentioned, the action itself incurs blame; but if you do not keep quiet about something praiseworthy, you yourself get the blame.

In my case a personal obstacle presents itself, for I delivered this 16 very speech, not before the citizens but before the city council, in the Senate House and not in the open. My fear is therefore that having 17 avoided popular approval and applause when delivering the speech, it is rather inappropriate to seek it now by publishing it. So having distanced myself from the very people whose interests were being consulted by interposing the door and the walls of the Senate House, so as not to give the impression of canvassing them, I fear that, by now publicizing myself before them, I may be seeking out the very persons to whom my generosity is irrelevant, apart from the example it sets before them.

You have heard the reasons for my hesitation, but I shall defer to 18 your advice, for the authority it wields will afford me a sufficient reason to proceed. Farewell.

9 *To his friend Minicius Fundanus* 97

It is remarkable how we account, or seem to account, for each indi- 1 vidual day in Rome,* but not for a number of days combined. If you 2 were to pose to anyone the question, 'What did you do today?', the answer would be: 'I attended an investiture of the adult toga,* or I was present at a betrothal or a wedding;* one person asked me to witness his will,* a second to plead for him in court, a third to act as assessor on the Bench.'* These duties seem necessary on the day you 3 perform them, but once you reflect that you have spent every day doing the same things, they seem pointless, and much more so when you retire from Rome, for it is then that you recollect: 'How many days I have wasted, on what tedious pursuits!'

This is my own reaction once I am in my residence at Laurentum,* 4 reading or writing or just indulging in the physical relaxation on which the mind depends for its support. I hear or say nothing which 5 I regret having heard or spoken; no one in my presence criticizes another with unkind insinuations, and I have no harsh words for anyone—except myself, when my writing falls below standard. No hope, no fear agitates me; no gossip disturbs my mind. Conversation is confined to myself and my books.

6   What straightforward, unblemished living this is! What delightful and what honourable leisure, nobler than virtually any active occupation! The sea and shore, my true and private *maison des Muses*, how many thoughts do you inspire, and how many do you dictate!

7   This is why you too must at the first opportunity abandon this city din, this pointless bustle, these quite foolish toils, devoting yourself

8   to your studies or to leisure, for as our friend Atilius* most learnedly and also most wittily remarked, it is better to seek relaxation than to do nothing. Farewell.

10 *To his friend Attius Clemens*   98

1   Liberal studies in this city of ours are flourishing as splendidly as
2   ever before. There are many outstanding examples of this, but it would be enough to cite one, the philosopher Euphrates.* When I was serving in the army in Syria* as a mere youth, I became closely acquainted with him—indeed, in his home. I worked hard to win his affection, though the effort was superfluous, for he is accessible and
3   straightforward, and entirely practises the civility which he preaches. I only wish that I myself had fulfilled the hope which he then entertained of me, as much as he greatly enhanced his own virtues—or perhaps it is that I admire them the more because I now appreciate them better.

4   Yet even now I do not sufficiently understand them. Just as it takes an artist to pass judgement on a painter or sculptor or modeller, so
5   only a philosopher can appreciate a philosopher. However, to such insights as are granted to me the many qualities in Euphrates are so outstanding and crystal-clear that even moderately learned men are attracted and struck by them. In argument, he is precise, earnest, and elegant, and often he even achieves the grandeur and sweep of a Plato. In discussion he is fluent, wide-ranging, and particularly charming, the sort of person who can lead on and impress even those
6   who confront him. In addition, he is tall and handsome, with flowing hair and a long white beard. These features may be regarded as
7   accidental and of no consequence, but they induce the greatest respect. There is nothing repellent or depressing in his deportment, but rather a profound seriousness. Your reaction on meeting him

would be one of respect rather than apprehension. His manner of life is wholly blameless, and this is matched by his friendliness. He rebukes not people but faults; he corrects men rather than censures them. You could listen closely and adhere to his advice, and long to have him continuing to persuade you, after he has done so.

A further point: he has three children, two of them boys, whom he 8 has reared most carefully. His father-in-law, Pompeius Julianus,* has attained distinction and fame both in his life generally and notably in this alone: though he himself has been a leading figure in the province, and though there were possible matches with the highest families, he chose for his son-in-law one outstanding in philosophy rather than in social eminence.

Yet why do I go on about a man whose company I cannot enjoy? Is 9 it to vex myself the more, because it is impossible? For I am torn away by my official duties, which though most important are also most troublesome. I take my seat on the Bench, sign petitions, present accounts, write countless letters of a most unliterary kind. When 10 the occasion offers, I tend sometimes to recite my grumbles about these to Euphrates, who consoles me, and also maintains that it is not merely a part but in fact the most noble part of philosophy* to conduct public affairs, to investigate and to pass judgements, to promote and to wield justice, and to put into practice what the philosophers preach. However, he does not persuade me of this one thing: that it is 11 better to conduct these public affairs rather than to spend whole days with him in listening and learning.

So this is what I urge you all the more to do, since you are fancy-free. When you come to Rome in the near future (and for this purpose you must come the sooner), allow him to polish and to perfect you. Unlike many, I do not begrudge others a blessing which I 12 myself forgo. On the contrary, I get a feeling of pleasure if I see that things denied to me are available to my friends. Farewell.

11 *To his friend Fabius Justus*

You have sent no letters to me for quite a while. Your excuse is that 1 you have nothing to write. Well, then, just write that you have nothing to write, or nothing beyond the introductory greeting which our forebears used to use: 'If you are well, that's fine; I am well.'* I'm 2 satisfied with that, for it's the main thing. Do you think I'm joking?

My request is deadly serious. Do let me know how you are doing, for I cannot remain ignorant without being deeply concerned. Farewell.

12 *To his friend Calestrius Tiro* 97–8

1 I have sustained a very heavy loss, if the deprivation of so great a man can be called a loss. Corellius Rufus has died*—in fact it was suicide, which aggravates my pain, as it is the most grievous form of

2 death when it is seen to occur neither naturally nor inevitably. For whatever the circumstances of death by disease, the very fact of necessity is a great consolation, whereas in the case of those taken from us by suicide, our grief is irreparable, because we believe that they could have had a long life.

3 In fact, Corellius was constrained by supreme reasoning,* which for philosophers is the equivalent of necessity, and by conscious decision, yet he had numerous reasons for living—the highest rectitude, the highest repute, the greatest authority, and in addition to these, a daughter, a wife, a grandson, and sisters, and among all

4 these cherished ones some true friends. But he was tormented by such a lengthy and harsh illness that these rewards for living were outweighed by reasons for dying.

I heard him state that at the age of thirty-two he was afflicted with gout.* This was a hereditary condition, for clearly diseases, like other

5 things, are transmitted by a sort of succession. During his green years he fought and overcame the disease by dieting and by virtuous living. More recently, as the disease worsened with the onset of old age, he endured it with strength of mind, despite suffering agonies

6 beyond belief and the most degrading tortures, for by that stage the pain was not, as earlier, confined to his feet, but roamed at large through all his limbs.

In Domitian's time I visited him when he was bedridden in his

7 house close to the city. His slaves retired from his chamber (this was a practice he maintained whenever one of his more trustworthy friends came in, and even his wife, who was wholly privy to every

8 confidence, used to leave). He swivelled his eyes round,* and said: 'Why do you think I endure this dreadful pain for so long? I want to survive that brigand,* if only for a single day.' Had you endowed him with a physique to match such spirit, he would have achieved what he wished.*

God, however, attended his prayer, and once he had obtained it,
he now felt untroubled and free to die, sundering many attachments
to life since they were of less account. His illness had worsened, 9
though he sought to control it by self-restraint. But as it maintained
its hold, with strength of mind he fled from it. A second and a third
and a fourth day came while he declined to eat. His wife Hispulla
dispatched Gaius Geminius, a mutual friend, to me with the most
melancholy news that Corellius was intent on death, and was
unmoved by the entreaties of their daughter and herself. I was the
last resort, she said, as one who could recall him to life. I hastened 10
there, and had almost reached him when Julius Atticus* brought a
message, again from Hispulla, that even I would make no impression, for his decision to die had hardened more and more inflexibly.

In fact, he had said to the physician who was placing food before
him: '*Je me suis décidé*',* a phrase which affected my mind with a
sense of loss as much as of admiration. I contemplate the sort of
friend, the sort of man I am now without. He completed his sixty- 11
seventh year, a reasonable age for the sturdiest of us; I acknowledge
that. He escaped from an interminable illness; I acknowledge that.
He died with his dear ones surviving him, and at a time of prosperity
for the state, which was dearer to him than all else; that too I acknowledge. Yet I lament his death as though he were young and in glowing 12
health. I lament it—you can consider me a weakling in this—on my
own account, for I have lost the witness, guardian, and teacher of
my life. In short, I shall say what I said to my boon-companion
Calvisius* while my grief was fresh: 'I fear that for me life will be of
less account.'

So you must send me some words of consolation, but do not say, 13
'He was an old and sick man', for I am aware of that. Make it
something original and impressive, such as I have never heard or
read before, for the consolations such as I have heard and read come
to me unbidden, but are unequal to this great grief. Farewell.

13 *To his friend Senecio*   97

This year has unearthed a healthy crop of poets,* for throughout the 1
whole month of April* there has scarcely been a day on which someone was not offering a recitation. I am delighted that the literary
life is flourishing, that people's talents are sprouting and showing

2 themselves, though audiences are sluggish in attending. Most people
   sit around in resting places,* and while away in gossip the time for
   listening. From time to time they ask to be told whether the reader
   has come to the podium, whether he has finished his introduction, or
   whether he is a good way through his material. It is only at that point
   that they make their way in, and even then slowly and reluctantly;
   and they do not see the performance through, but make off before
   the end, some discreetly and stealthily, others openly and brazenly.

3   By contrast, within our parents' recollection, so the story goes,
   Claudius Caesar was strolling on the Palatine.* On hearing the sound
   of voices, he asked what it was about, and when he was told that
   Nonianus* was giving a reading, he made a sudden and unexpected
4 entry during the performance. But nowadays individuals with nothing whatever to do, though invited long before and repeatedly
   reminded, either fail to turn up, or, if they do come, complain that
   they have wasted their day just because they have failed to waste it.

5   This makes all the more praiseworthy and impressive the attitude
   of those who are not put off from their enthusiasm for composition
   and recitation by these lazy or superior airs of audiences. I myself
   have failed hardly anyone. True, most of the performers have been
   my friends, for there is virtually no lover of literature who does not
   regard me likewise with affection.

6   For these reasons I have stayed on in Rome longer than I had
   planned, and now I can head back to my place of retirement, and
   write something not for recitation.* This is to ensure that I may not
   appear to have been a lender rather than a listener to those whose
   recitations I have attended, for as in other matters so in the obligation of attending readings, the favour is nullified if we demand it in
   return. Farewell.

14 *To his friend Junius Mauricus*   97

1 You beg me to keep an eye open for a husband for your brother's
   daughter.* It is right that you should impose this task on me in particular, for you know how much I have looked up to him and loved
   him as the most outstanding of men. You know too the repeated
   encouragement with which he fostered my youthful years, together
   with the praises which ensured that I emerged deserving of them.
2 There is no more important or welcome task which you can allot to

me, and none which can be more honourable for me to undertake, than to choose the young man who can fittingly father grandchildren for Arulenus Rusticus.

This task would in fact have involved a lengthy search, were it not 3 that Minicius Acilianus* is available, and as it were, readily available. The most intimate regard he has for me is that of one young man for another (he is only a very few years younger), and the respect he shows is that towards one of advanced years; for he is eager to 4 be moulded and educated by me in the way I used to be by the two of you.

He is a native of Brixia, from that Italian region of ours* which still keeps and preserves a great deal of the modesty, sobriety, and indeed the provincialism of old. His father, Minicius Macrinus,* is a leading 5 equestrian; he had no wish for further advancement, for though the deified Vespasian designated him as a praetorian,* he was most insistent in preferring honourable retirement to our—shall I say ambition, or high status? The young man's maternal grandmother, Serrana 6 Procula, is from the township of Patavium.* You know the manner of their behaviour there, yet Serrana is a model of sobriety even to Patavians. He also has an uncle, Publius Acilius,* who is a man of seriousness, practical wisdom, and almost unique reliability. In short, there can be nothing in his entire household which is not as acceptable to you as anything in your own.

As for Acilianus himself, he is intensely energetic and hard- 7 working, though he is totally unassuming. He has held successively the quaestorship, tribunate, and praetorship* without the least reproach. He has thus already released you from the need to canvass on his behalf. He has the looks of a real gentleman, with a rosy 8 countenance and high colour. He is genuinely handsome in physique, with the fitting air of a senator. Such factors are in my view certainly not to be disregarded, for they are, so to say, as the reward bestowed on girls for their chastity.

I should perhaps add that his father is financially well endowed. 9 When I see in my mind's eye the pair of you for whom I seek a son-in-law, I think I should say nothing about wealth, but when I consider attitudes at large, and beyond these the legal requirements* of the state, which ordain that men's finances should be regarded even as paramount, it seems that this too should not be ignored. Certainly, when one thinks of the greater number of descendants to come, money too must be taken into account in choosing a marriage alliance.

10   You may perhaps think that I have given free rein to my affection, and that I have exaggerated these qualities more than the facts allow. But I give you my word and pledge that you will find all these recommendations far more impressive than my account of them. It is true that I have the most glowing affection for this young man, as he well deserves, but it is the nature of such affection not to overload him with praises. Farewell.

15 *To his friend Septicius Clarus*

1 Shame on you! You promised to come to dinner, and you never came!
2 I'll take you to court,* and you will pay to the last penny for my losses, and quite a sum! Ready for each of us were a lettuce, three snails, and two eggs, barley water* with honeyed wine cooled with snow (you must add the cost of the snow as well, in fact the snow in particular, as it melts in the dish). There were olives, beetroot, gourds, onions, and countless other delicacies no less elegant.* You would have heard performers of comedy, or a reader, or a lyre-player,* or even all three, such is my generosity!
3   But you preferred to dine at some nobody's house, enjoying oysters, sow's tripe, sea urchins, and performing-girls from Cadiz.* You'll be punished for this, I won't say how. What boorishness was this! You begrudged perhaps yourself, and certainly me—but yes, yourself as well. What joking and laughter and learning we
4 would have enjoyed! You can dine in many houses on more elaborate fare, but nowhere more genially, innocently, and unguardedly. In short, you must try it out, and in future, unless you make your excuses to others instead, you must always make them to me. Farewell.

16 *To his friend Erucius*   97

1 Earlier I was fond of Pompeius Saturninus* (I speak of a friend of mine*), and I would praise the variety, adaptability, and wide range of his talent* before I knew him. But nowadays he captivates me
2 wholly and has me firmly in his grasp. I have heard him handling cases in court with vigour and passion, yet equally with polish and

adornment, whether his speeches were prepared or unrehearsed. He has at his fingertips appropriate aphorisms in abundance; his word-arrangement is sonorous and seemly; his vocabulary is high-sounding and traditional. All these aspects are remarkably attractive when borne along in passionate flow, but they also please when reconsidered.

You will share my view when you take up his speeches, which 3 you will readily compare with any of the orators of old whom he seeks to rival. But he will impress you even more with his historical 4 writing by reason of its succinctness or lucidity or charm, and the brilliance and grandeur of the narrative. As for the orations, they have the same impact as his own speeches, except that they are more condensed, concise, and contracted.

Then again, he composes verses on the lines of those of Catullus 5 or Calvus,* and indeed they are as good as those of Catullus or Calvus. What elegance and sweetness they contain, and the bitterness of love!* True, he includes some rather harsher pieces among the smooth and light compositions, but this is purposeful, done in imitation of Catullus or Calvus.

Recently he read out to me some letters, which he said his wife 6 wrote. I thought that what was being read to me was Plautus or Terence freed of the metre. Whether they were composed by his wife, as he maintains, or by his own hand, as he denies, he deserves equal credit; for he either penned them himself, or he has moulded the girl he married* into so learned and elegant a wife.

So he is with me* throughout the day. I read him before I write, and 7 again once I have written. I read him too when at leisure, though he does not seem to be the same man. So I urge and advise you likewise 8 to do the same. The fact that he is a living author ought not to prejudice his works. If he had flourished among men on whom we have never set eyes, we would be searching out not only his books but also his portraits. So are his distinction and popularity to wane because he is still with us and because we have had more than our fill of such writing?

But it is wicked and spiteful to refrain from admiring a man 9 wholly worthy of admiration, merely because it is our fortune to see and address and hear and embrace him, and bestow on him not only our praise but also our affection. Farewell.

17 *To his friend Cornelius Titianus*   97–8

1 Loyalty and a sense of obligation are still observed among men, for
there are some who maintain their friendship even with the dead.
Titinius Capito* has obtained permission from our emperor* to be
2 allowed to erect a statute of Lucius Silanus in the Forum. It is a
noble intention, and one worthy of high praise, to exploit one's
friendship with the emperor for such a purpose, and to assess the
3 degree of one's influence by conferring distinctions on others. It is
Capito's obsessive practice to show observance to famous men. The
scrupulousness and enthusiasm with which he tends the portraits
of men like Brutus, Cassius, and Cato* in his home whenever possible
is remarkable. He also glorifies the lives of all most celebrated men in
4 outstanding verses. We can realize from such affection for the virtues
of others that he himself is plentifully endowed with them. The
distinction due to Silanus has been bestowed on him, and by looking
to immortality for him Capito has gained it for himself. For it is as
noble and striking a gesture to erect a statue in the Forum of the
Roman people as to be commemorated by one. Farewell.

18 *To his friend Suetonius Tranquillus*   97

1 You write that you have had a bad fright from a dream,* and that
you fear that you may sustain a reverse in the court case, so you
ask me to seek an adjournment* for a day or two, or at any rate for the
day closest at hand. It is difficult, but I will try, 'for a dream comes
2 from Zeus'.* But what matters is whether you usually dream what
will actually take place, or the opposite. When I think back to the
following dream of my own, your fear seems to augur a happy
outcome.

3   I had agreed to represent Junius Pastor, and I dreamt that my
mother-in-law approached me on bended knees, and begged me not
to take on the case. I was still a mere stripling, and was about to plead
in the Four Courts* against very powerful politicians who were also
friends of Caesar. Each one of these circumstances could have caused
4 me mental paralysis following such a melancholy dream. But I
reasoned that 'to fight for one's native land was the best and sole
omen',* for my promise to appear seemed to me to be my native land,
and indeed something dearer than my native land. Things turned

out well, and the speech I made opened men's ears to me, and also opened the door to my successful career.

So you must consider whether you too can follow this example, 5 and turn that dream of yours to good account. Or if you think as safer the rule of thumb adopted by all who are circumspect, 'If in doubt, don't do it', do write back to say so. I shall devise some 6 expedient and plead your case so that you can take it over when you wish. There is no doubt that your situation differs from mine.* A case in the Centumviral court can under no circumstances be adjourned, but for you a solution though difficult is possible. Farewell.

19 *To his friend Romatius Firmus*   *c.*97

You are a fellow townsman of mine; we were students and comrades 1 together from an early age. Your father was a friend of my mother and my uncle, and of myself as well in so far as the difference between our ages allowed. So there are substantial and important reasons why I should take in hand and further your social status. The 2 fact that you are a town-councillor is a sufficient indication that you are worth 100,000 sesterces.* Accordingly I am offering you 300,000 more to advance your resources to the requirement for an *eques.* In that way your status not merely as a councillor but also as an equestrian will be a source of pleasure to me.

Our long-standing friendship guarantees that you will keep this 3 gift ever in mind. I refrain from offering even that advice which it would be incumbent on me to offer, if I was not aware that of your own accord you will conduct yourself in the most temperate way in the rank which I have bestowed on you. For one's social status is to 4 be treated with the greater discretion when we are also to keep in mind the generosity of a friend. Farewell.

20 *To his friend Cornelius Tacitus*

I often argue with a certain man of learning and experience,* who in 1 forensic speeches approves of nothing so much as brevity.* I grant 2 that we must observe it, if the case allows; otherwise to pass over essential points is a betrayal of one's trust, as also is hasty and brief mention of issues which should be rammed home, implanted, and repeated. The topics for the most part gain additional impact 3 and weight with fuller discussion. A speech is to the mind what a sword is to the body; its effect is achieved as much by holding back as by thrusting.

4   At this point my friend deploys authorities against me, pointing out to me from among the Greeks the speeches of Lysias,* and those of the Gracchi and of Cato* from our Latin tradition; and it is true that very many of these are pruned and concise. I counter with Demosthenes, Aeschines, Hyperides,* and many others against Lysias, and with Pollio, Caesar, Caelius, and above all Cicero* against the Gracchi and Cato. Cicero's longest speech* is said to be the best. In fact, like other good things, the longer a good book is, the better it

5   is. You observe how in the case of statues, emblems, pictures, and finally dimensions of human figures, many animals, and also trees, it is the size more than anything which gains favour, so long as these are well executed. The same holds good for speeches; length in fact lends a sort of authority and beauty to the volumes themselves.

6   These arguments, and many others which I often present to express the same viewpoint, my friend sidesteps, for he is hard to pin down and is slippery in argument. So he goes on to claim that the very advocates on whose speeches I rely delivered speeches

7   shorter than the published versions. I take the opposite view,* which is supported by the witness of many speeches by many spokesmen, including the *Pro Murena* and the *Pro Vareno* of Cicero, in which the accusations, brief and unadorned, are depicted solely by the headings of the various charges. These make it clear that Cicero made numerous statements that he left out when the speeches were

8   published. Cicero also says that in defence of Cluentius he followed the old procedure,* and conducted the entire case alone; and further, that in defence of Gaius Cornelius his speech lasted four days. This removes all possible doubt that the speeches which he delivered more extensively, as was essential, over several days, he later cut back and pruned, and thus abridged them in one admittedly large but none the less single volume.

9   It may be claimed that a well-delivered speech is one thing, and the published version another. I know that quite a few hold this view, but my belief (I could be wrong) is that while a speech well delivered may not be good when published, a good published version must have been good when delivered, for the published version is the copy

10 and as it were *l'archétype** of the verbal version. For this reason we

find in all the best speeches countless spontaneous figures of speech, even in those which were merely published without having been delivered. For example, in the speech against Verres:* 'The sculptor, who was he? Who was that chap? Oh yes, you do well to remind me. They said it was Polyclitus.' So what this shows is that the delivered version is that which is fully developed and is as close as possible to the written version, so long as the speaker is accorded the appropriate and due time; if this is refused him, the fault is in no way his, but a serious lapse on the part of the judge.

The laws support this belief of mine,* for they provide abundant 11 time, and they counsel speakers to be expansive, in other words to be conscientious, rather than brief, for brevity cannot be conscientious except in the most limited cases. My further observation is what 12 experience, that outstanding teacher, has taught me. I have often pleaded, have often been a judge, and often an assessor. Different approaches influence different people, and often minor considerations lead to momentous outcomes. Men's judgements differ, and so do their inclinations, so that people listening to the same case at the same time often react differently, and sometimes identically but from different impulses. Moreover, every individual inclines to his 13 own insight, and accepts as the strongest argument the statement of another which tallied with his own prior view. So all must be fed some observation which they can grasp and acknowledge.

Regulus* on one occasion remarked to me, when we were pleading 14 in court together: 'You think that you must follow through every issue in a case; I set my sights at once on the jugular, and press home my attack there.' True, he presses home the issue which he has selected, but his choice is often awry. My retort was that his 15 idea of where the jugular was could be the knee or the heel! 'Since I cannot identify the jugular,' I said, 'I investigate and try every approach; in fact *je n'y laisse rien*.' It is like working on the land. 16 I tend and cultivate not just the vines, but also the fruit-bushes, and not just the bushes, but also the fields. In those fields I sow not only grain and wheat, but also barley, beans, and other vegetables. So too in composing a speech I scatter arguments like seeds over a wider area, so that I can gather up the issues which emerge. This is because the thoughts of judges are no less hard to fathom, 17 and just as uncertain and deceptive as the hazards of wild weather and the soil.

I always keep in mind the praise lavished on that outstanding orator Pericles by the comic poet Eupolis:*

> Besides the rapid movement of his thought,
> Persuasion of a kind sat on his lips.
> Thus he beguiled. Yet of all orators
> Alone he left his sting upon men's ears.

18 But neither that persuasion nor that beguiling could have been attained by the great Pericles himself by brevity or rapidity or both (for they are different qualities) without his supreme ability. Pleasing and persuading people demand fluency of speech and leisurely timing; leaving a sting in the minds of listeners can be achieved only by 19 one who implants it rather than bestows a pinprick. Append to this what a second comic poet* said, also about Pericles:

> His lightning and his thunder shattered Greece.

His is no pruned or lopped-off utterance, but one which is broad, high-sounding, and sublime, with thunder and lightning which in short confounds the entire world.

20 'Yet the mean is best.' Who denies it? But the man who falls short fails to keep the mean as much as he who overshoots, the spokesman 21 who is too terse as much as he who is too diffuse. So you often hear the comment 'meagre and lacking body' as much as 'undisciplined and repetitive'. The second is said to have gone beyond the subject matter, the first not to have covered it. Both are equally guilty, the one through feebleness and the other through virility. The second fault admittedly has the greater lack of polish, but the greater talent. 22 In saying this, I am not approving the character whom Homer describes as *prolixe*, but rather the one who uttered

> Words which fall like snowflakes in the wintertime.

Not that I fail to regard with the greatest approval the one who speaks

> few words, but with the utmost clarity.*

But if given the choice, I opt for an utterance like the winter snows, that which is copious and continuous but also abundant, in short what is godlike and heavenly.

23 'But many prefer a short speech.' True, but they are sluggards, and it is nonsense to regard their indolent fripperies as informed

judgement. Indeed, if one were to take their advice, it would be better not just to speak briefly, but not to speak at all.

This is my opinion as yet, but I shall change it if you disagree, 24 though I beg you to explain clearly why you do. For though I ought to yield to your authority, I think it better on this important topic to be prevailed upon by reason rather than by authority. Accordingly, if 25 I seem to be on the right track, write to tell me so in as brief a missive as you like, but do write, for you will be bolstering my judgement. If I am mistaken, compose a letter of the greatest length. It is surely not bribery on my part to have required the need for a short letter from you if you agree with me, but for an extended one if you disagree? Farewell.

21 *To his friend Plinius Paternus*

My boundless respect for your intellectual judgement extends equally 1 to your scrutinizing eyes; not that this says much (I would not have you complacent), but since you are as smart as I am—that too does say a lot for you! But all joking apart, I think that the slaves I bought 2 on your recommendation are suitable. Their honesty is still in question, for so far as slaves go, our judgement rests on hearsay rather than our eyes. Farewell.

22 *To his friend Catilius Severus* 97

For some time now I have been held fast in Rome, and moreover in a 1 state of acute anxiety. What is troubling me is the lengthy and stubborn illness of Titius Aristo,* a man whom I both admire and love uniquely. In dignity, integrity, and learning he is unsurpassed, so that in my eyes this is not an individual who seems to be on the brink of the utmost danger, but literature itself, together with all worthy accomplishments.

What great experience he has in both private and public law! 2 What a grasp of affairs and precedents and former times he possesses! There is nothing you would wish to learn which he cannot teach you. At any rate, whenever I seek some abstruse information,* he is a treasure-house of knowledge. His conversation is so reliable 3 and so authoritative, the pauses in his speech so deliberate and attractive! Is there anything which he cannot call to mind at once?

Yet he often pauses in doubt, pondering the various arguments which with his keen and impressive judgement he draws forth from their source and from first principles, and then distinguishes them and weighs them.

4 Then too how thrifty are his eating habits, and how modest his grooming! I often envisage his bedchamber and the bed itself as a
5 kind of reflection of old-time simplicity. What adorns them is his magnanimity with its indifference to mere show, and its total commitment to integrity of mind; he seeks his reward for upright behaviour not from the good opinion of the people, but from his
6 actions themselves. In short, you will not readily find a single one of those who parade their enthusiasm for philosophy in bodily adornment to compare with this man. Indeed, he does not attend the gymnasia or the colonnades;* he does not divert the leisure hours of others and his own with lengthy discussions, but dons his toga and involves himself in public affairs, aiding many as advocate in the
7 courts, and still more with counsel. He yields to none of these philosophers his pre-eminence in chaste life, devotion, justice, and courage.

If you were present, you would be astounded at the patience with which he endures this illness, how he confronts the pain, postpones quenching his thirst, and bears the unbelievable heat of fevers with-
8 out flinching or throwing off his covers. He recently summoned me and a few besides myself of whom he was particularly fond. He asked us to consult the physicians about the outcome of his illness, intending if it was incurable to depart deliberately from life,* but, if it was
9 merely difficult and lengthy, to withstand it, and to remain alive; for, he said, he owed it to his wife's entreaties, to his daughter's tears, and also to us his friends not to betray our hopes by suicide, so long as those hopes were not idle.

10 My view is that this decision is particularly difficult, and deserving of outstanding praise. It is a tendency shared with many to hasten one's death under some impulse and emotional urge, but to ponder and weigh the motives for it, and then to adopt or abandon the decision to live or die as reason dictates, is the mark of a noble mind.

11 In fact, the physicians promise me a happy outcome, and all that remains is for God to consent* to their promises, and finally deliver me from this worry. Once freed from it I shall get back to my house at Laurentum,* to my books, that is, and my writing-tablets and

leisure for study, whereas at present I have no time to read or write anything as I sit by him, and in my anxiety no desire either. So now 12 you know my fears, my hopes, my future intentions. You in turn must write and tell me of your activities, past and present, and your future aspirations, but on a happier note than this. It will be an immense reassurance to me in my troubled state of mind if you have no complaints to report. Farewell.

23 *To his friend Pompeius Falco* 97

You ask my view on whether I think you should plead in the courts 1 when you are a tribune.* What matters most is your idea of the nature of the tribunate, whether it is an empty shadow and undistinguished title, or an inviolable office which is not to be reduced in importance 2 by anyone, not even by the incumbent. I was perhaps in error when tribune* in believing that I had some status, but I refrained from pleading in the courts as though I had. My first reason was because I thought it degrading that the official in whose presence all should stand, and to whom all should give precedence, should stand while all remained seated; that one who could order each and every person to be silent should be reduced to silence by the hourglass; and that though it was sacrilegious to interrupt him, he should be subjected even to insults, appearing to be a sluggard if he endured them without reprisals, or arrogant if he imposed them.

I envisaged also the perplexity if my client or opponent formally 3 appealed to me: was I to intervene with the veto* and lend him help, or to stay mute and say nothing, converting myself into a private citizen as if I had resigned the magistracy?

For these reasons I chose to appear before all as tribune rather 4 than before the few as advocate. But once again I shall say that what 5 matters most is your view of the nature of the tribunate, and the role which you impose upon yourself. The wise man must assume that role in such a way as to sustain it throughout. Farewell.

24 *To his friend Baebius Hispanus*

My close friend Suetonius Tranquillus* wishes to buy the small estate 1 which a friend of yours is said to be putting up for sale. I am writing 2 to you to ensure that he buys it at a fair price, for in that way the purchase will please him. After all, a poor bargain is always unwelcome, above all because it seems to charge the new owner with stupidity.

3   The small estate has many features which excite my friend Tranquillus' appetite, so long as the price is congenial. It is close to Rome, and easily accessible; the house is a modest size, and the grounds are just big enough to entice him rather than to overstretch him there.

4   The fact is that owners who, like my friend, are scholars regard as plenty just enough land to enable them to clear their heads, restore their eyes, saunter along its boundaries, tread its solitary path, come to know each modest vine, and count the fruit-bushes.

I point this out to you to enable you to appreciate better the great debt he will owe me and I will owe you, if he buys this modest estate, which these amenities recommend, at such a favourable price as to leave no possibility of regret. Farewell.

BOOK TWO

1 *To his friend Romanus*

The public funeral of Verginius Rufus,* that citizen of the highest 1
eminence, greatest celebrity, and an equally blessed life, has after
several years presented to the eyes of the Roman people a striking
and also memorable display. He lived on for thirty years following his 2
hour of glory. He read poems and historical works* composed about
him, and lived to witness his later reputation. Three times he held
the office of consul, thus achieving the highest status of a private
person, for he declined to become emperor.

He escaped the clutches of Caesars who suspected and even hated 3
him for his merits, and at death he left safely installed one who was
an excellent person and a close friend. It was as if he had been held
back for this very distinction of a public funeral. He lived beyond 4
his eighty-third year, enjoying supreme peace of mind and revered
status in equal measure.

He enjoyed stable health, except that his hands used to tremble,
but without causing him pain. It was only his approach to death
which was rather grim and protracted; even so, his attitude towards
it was praiseworthy. When at his consulship he was rehearsing his 5
speech of thanks to the emperor, and chanced to lift up a rather
heavy book, its weight caused it to slip from his hands owing to his
age and standing posture. When he bent down after it and was pick-
ing it up, he missed his footing on the smooth and slippery flooring,
and he fell and fractured his hip. It was incompetently set, and with
the handicap of his age, it failed to join properly.

The funeral obsequies bestowed great distinction on the emperor, 6
on our times, and on the Forum and Rostra. The panegyric was
delivered by Cornelius Tacitus as consul,* adding the final touch to
Verginius' happy lot, for Tacitus is the most eloquent of spokesmen.
So Rufus died with his fill of years and his fill of distinctions, includ- 7
ing those which he rejected, leaving us to look vainly for him and
to miss him as the symbol of an earlier age. My personal loss is
especially severe, because I loved him as much as I admired him, and
not merely as a statesman; for to begin with, we came from the same 8

district,* from neighbouring towns, and our estates and properties lay cheek by jowl. Secondly, he was bequeathed to me as my guardian,* and showed me the fondness of a father. So when I stood for office, he honoured me with his vote, and, likewise, he hastened from his areas of retirement to inaugurate all my magistracies, though he had for long given up obligations of that kind. Likewise on the day when the priests usually name those whom they consider most worthy of a priesthood, he always put forward my name.*

9   Then again, during this most recent illness, he feared that he might be appointed as one of the quinquevirs* whom the Senate had decided to set up to reduce public expenditure. Although numerous friends, former consuls ripe in age, were still alive, he chose me at my early age to present his excuses. His actual words were: 'Even if I had a son, I would still have commissioned you.'

10   These are the reasons why I must seek your intimacy to grieve for his death as though it were before its time—if it is the right thing, that is, to lament or even to label it as his death at all, when it is the bodily close rather than the life of so great a man which has reached

11 its term. For he remains alive, and will always remain alive, and his presence will continue to be felt even more widely in men's recollections and conversations now that he has vanished from our sight.

12   I should like to write to you on many other matters, but my mind is focused wholly on this one consideration. It is Verginius who is on my mind, Verginius who is before my eyes, Verginius whom I see and address and embrace. His apparitions though illusory are fresh. Perhaps we shall have and already have fellow citizens equal in their merits, but not one equal in fair fame. Farewell.

2 *To his friend Paulinus*

1 I am angry. Whether I should be I am not sure, but I am angry. You know how love-feelings are sometimes unjust, often intemperate, and always *susceptibles*.* But what provokes them is weighty and perhaps just. Anyway, it is as if my anger is as justified as it is fierce. I am con-

2 siderably angry because I have not heard from you for so long. There is only one way you can prevail on me, which is to send me, now at long last, streams of the lengthiest letters, for in my eyes this is the only genuine means of excusing yourself. All other excuses will not

ring true. I won't hear of 'I was not in Rome', or 'I was too busy'. As for 'I was somewhat out of sorts', even the gods would not buy that!

I am on my estate,* enjoying the two fruits born of leisure, books and idleness. Farewell.

3 *To his friend Nepos*

Though Isaeus' great reputation* had preceded him, we found him 1 still greater in the flesh. His command of words is fluent, abundant, and rich. He invariably speaks off the cuff, but as though he has spent ages composing his remarks. He converses in Greek, or rather in Attic. His preliminaries are polished, unadorned, mellifluous, but from time to time weighty and challenging. He asks his audience to 2 suggest a number of subjects for disputation, and allows them to make the choice from them, and often also the side he is to take.* He rises, wraps his cloak around him, and begins. He has every aspect immediately and in almost equal measure at his fingertips. Abstruse notions come to his mind. His expressions—and what expressions! —are studied and polished. A great deal of reading, and a great deal of writing, shine out of his spontaneity. His introductions are 3 appropriate, his narratives clear, his polemics sharp, his summaries powerful, his embellishments elevated. In short, he instructs, charms, and moves* his audience, and you would find it hard to select the most impressive aspect of the three. His *enthymemata* are numerous, and so are his syllogisms,* the first abridged and the second fully formed; it is quite an achievement to construct these even with the pen. His powers of recall are astonishing; remarks made off the cuff are reintroduced with more profound consideration, and without the loss of a word. He has attained this 4 great *habileté* by study and constant practice, for night and day he acts and hears and speaks nothing else.

He is over sixty, and still a practitioner of rhetoric and nothing 5 else. No class of men is sounder, more straightforward and more honourable than this. Those of us who slog away at real-life disputes in the public sphere become acquainted with much depravity, however reluctantly, but fictitious cases conducted in school and lecture-hall 6 are unarmed combat, inflicting no damage, though no less rewarding, especially for the old—for what in old age is more rewarding than the most pleasurable activities of one's youth?

7   For this reason I regard Isaeus as not merely supremely eloquent,
but also supremely blessed. If you are not eager to make his
8 acquaintance, you are a man of stone or iron. So you must come at
least to hear him, if not on other business or to see me. Did you never
read of a man from Gades* who was so roused by the name and fame
of Titus Livy that he came from the end of the earth to set eyes on
him, and as soon as he had seen him he departed? To fail to regard
as worthwhile an acquaintance which is as pleasant, charming, and
civilized as can be, is an attitude which is *malappris*, uneducated,
sluggish, and virtually degrading.

9   You will respond: 'But I have with me authors no less eloquent to
read.' True enough, but reading is always on the cards, whereas
listening is not. Then, too, the spoken word is much more moving
according to the general view, for though a written version may be
more incisive, the impact of delivery, facial expression, bearing, and
10 gestures of a speaker lie deeper in the mind. But perhaps we regard
as apocryphal that anecdote of Aeschines,* who after reading out a
speech of Demosthenes to the admiring public of the Rhodians, is
said to have added: 'But what if you had heard it from the beast
himself?' Yet if we believe Demosthenes, Aeschines' delivery was
bien distinct. But Aeschines confessed that the composer of the
speech had declaimed it far better.

11   All this points to your need to come to hear Isaeus or to ensure
that you have heard him. Farewell.

4 *To his dear Calvina*

1 If your father had owed money to several people, or to any individual
other than me, perhaps you would have wondered whether to take on
an inheritance which would have been oppressive even for a man.
2 But I have been guided by my obligation as a relative, and have paid
off all those who were being somewhat—perhaps troublesome is the
wrong word, but attentive. So I have emerged as his sole creditor.
While he was still alive, and when your marriage was being arranged,
I contributed 100,000 sesterces towards your dowry, in addition to
the amount that your father promised you, which came virtually
from me (for he could pay it only by drawing on my finances). So
you have a striking assurance of my generosity, relying on which you
must protect your father's good name and honour.

To encourage you with deeds rather than words to do this, I shall give instructions that the entire sum owed me by your father will be credited to your account.* You need not fear that this gift will be a ₃ burden on me. True, my resources are quite modest,* and my high station is expensive; and because of the poor state of my modest farms, the returns are rather small or uncertain, I am not sure which. But these diminishing returns are made up by my modest living, the source from which my generosity flows free. For I must restrain its ₄ course so that I do not disgorge too much and it runs dry. But that restraint I am to exercise in other projects; in your case its accounts will readily square, even if they rise beyond due limits. Farewell.

5 *To his friend Lupercus*

I am sending you the speech which you have often requested* and ₁ which I have often promised, but as yet not all of it, for a section of it is still being polished. In the meantime it is not unreasonable to ₂ submit to your judgement the parts which I think have gained the final touch. I beg you to lend them the close scrutiny of a written report, for up to this time I have never had any work on hand which demanded the application of greater care. Whereas in my other ₃ speeches my diligence and honesty alone were subject to the assessment of the world at large, in this case my patriotism will be before them as well. For this reason the written version has expanded, in my pleasure at enhancing and extolling my native soil, and no less in ministering to its protection and fame. But you must prune these ₄ passages in so far as reason demands, for whenever I contemplate what readers dislike and what they favour, I realize that I must win their approval by applying restraint to the text as well.

But at the same time as I demand this stringency from you, I am ₅ forced to beg a different favour; namely, that you relax your severity in a number of places, for I must offer some concessions to the ears of young people, especially if the subject matter does not militate against it. So, for example, it is right that descriptions of places. which will appear quite often in this written version, should be treated in the manner not only of the historian, but also of the poet.* But if some person surfaces who thinks that I have treated the theme ₆ more exuberantly than the seriousness of a speech demands, his gloom, so to speak, must be lifted by the other sections of the speech.

7 I have at any rate tried to sustain the interest of classes of readers, however different, through applying several types of utterance;* and in spite of my fear that one section or another may meet with the disapproval of some by virtue of their individual temperaments, it still seems possible for me to have confidence that the varied nature
8 of the speech may recommend itself as a whole to everyone. Take the example of banquets. Though as individuals we refrain from trying some dishes, we one and all usually heap praise on the whole dinner. Those foods which our appetite rejects do not banish the attraction of those which take our fancy.
9 I would like what I send to be regarded as expressing, not my belief that I have been successful, but rather that I have toiled hard to be successful, and perhaps not in vain, if only in the meantime you run your careful eye over these sections, and later over those that
10 follow. You will claim that you cannot achieve this with sufficient care unless you first acquaint yourself with the whole speech. That I grant. However, for the moment these parts will become more familiar to you, and some of them will be such as can be improved
11 section by section. Take, for example, the head or some limb which has been broken off a statue. You could not infer from it the symmetry and uniformity of the whole, but you could assess whether the
12 fragment itself was sufficiently artistic. Some books likewise contain initial passages* and are circulated for no reason other than that some section is considered perfect even apart from the rest.
13 The pleasurable experience of conversing with you has carried me along too far. But I will finish now, so as to avoid going beyond the limit which I think should be imposed on a speech as well. Farewell.

6 *To his friend Avitus* 97–8

1 It would take too long to delve deeper—and it is of no importance— into how it happened that I, who am far from being a close friend, dined at the house of an individual who thought himself refined and
2 attentive, but was in my eyes mean and extravagant; for he served himself and a few of us* with choice fare, but the rest with cheap food and tiny portions. He had further separated out small flasks of wine into three categories, not to offer the possibility of choice, but to forestall the right to refuse. The first category was for himself and

for us, the second for his friends of lesser account (for he ranks his friends at different levels), and the third for his freedmen and ours.

The man reclining next to me noticed this, and asked if I 3 approved. I said no. 'What is your practice?' he asked. 'I put the same food before all,' I replied, 'for I invite them for dinner, not for disgrace.* Those whom I have made equal at table and on the couches, I make equal in all respects.' 'Even the freedmen?' he asked. 4 'Yes, the freedmen too, for then I regard them as fellow guests, not freedmen.' He rejoined: 'That costs you a packet!' 'Far from it,' I replied. 'How come?' he asked. 'Because, I suppose, my freedmen do not drink what I drink; no, I drink what they drink.'

Indeed, if you are abstemious it is not a heavy expense to share 5 with a number what you yourself enjoy. What must be suppressed and 'reduced to the ranks'* is economizing on expenses, for you will attend to this more honourably by your own modest appetite than by insulting others.

Why do I recount this? To ensure that the extravagance at table of 6 certain men, by masquerading as frugality, does not deceive you, a young man of noble disposition. It befits my affection for you, whenever such an incident occurs, to exploit it as an example to warn you what you should avoid. So bear in mind that there is nothing you 7 should avoid more than the novel alliance of extravagance and meanness, traits most demeaning when distinct and separate from each other, but still more so when they are merged. Farewell.

7 *To his friend Macrinus* 97–8

Yesterday a triumphal statue was decreed by the Senate to Vestricius 1 Spurinna* on the proposal of the emperor. It was not an award like those given to many who have never stood in the battle-line, have never seen a military camp, and in short have heard the din of the trumpet only in stage-shows. No, it was like that given to those who achieved this distinction by sweat, blood, and deeds, for Spurinna 2 established the king of the Bructeri* upon his throne by force of arms, and by the threat of war he subdued that fiercest of nations by terrifying them—the most noble species of victory.

So this was the reward gained for valour; and as consolation in 3 grief the distinction of a statue has been bestowed on his son Cottius,* whom he lost while he was away.* The tribute was unusual in the case

of a young man, but this too was merited by his father, for this heaviest of wounds which he sustained needed to be healed by a
4 sizeable application. But in addition Cottius himself had exhibited so glowing an indication of character that his short and constrained life needed to be extended by this kind of immortality, for his integrity, high seriousness, and authority were such that he could challenge in merit those elders with whom he has now been ranked in distinction.
5 As I see it, this distinction was not merely directed towards the memory of the dead man and to assuage the grief of his father, but also to be an inspiration to others. The establishment of such august rewards for our young men, as long as they are worthy of them, will incite our youth to practise the virtues. Our political leaders will likewise be encouraged to rear children,* both by the joys they experience from those who survive, and by such glorious consolations from those which have been lost to them.
6 These are the reasons, private no less than public, which prompt my joy at the erection of the statue of Cottius. I loved the young man in his perfection with the same intensity with which I now find his loss unbearable. It will be pleasant for me from time to time to gaze on this statue, from time to time to look back towards it, to halt
7 below it, and to stroll past it. For if the statues of the dead positioned in our houses alleviate our grief, how much more do those that are set in crowded locations, which remind us, not only of the outward forms and features of those men, but also of their distinction and glory. Farewell.

8 *To his friend Caninius* 98–100

1 Are you at your books, or fishing, or hunting, or at all three at once? They can all engage you together at that lake Comum of ours, for the lake contains fish, the woods surrounding the lake are the haunt of beasts, and that deepest of retreats offers abundant prospects of
2 study. But whether you are busy with all of them, or with just one, I cannot say 'I begrudge you'; I am merely irked that I too cannot participate, for I yearn for these activities as sick men yearn for wine and baths and spring-waters. Will I never sever these close-confining
3 bonds,* if I am refused permission to loose them? I do not think that I ever can, for fresh duties are superimposed on long-standing ones before those earlier ones are discharged. With all these chains and

fetters a greater column* of activities extends further every day. Farewell.

9 *To his friend Apollinaris* 97

The candidature of my friend Sextus Erucius* finds me on edge and 1 worried. I am greatly concerned, feeling for my second self the anxiety which I did not experience on my own behalf; and in general my self-respect and reputation and status are being called into question. I obtained for Sextus the broad stripe* and the quaestorship 2 from our Caesar, and on my recommendation he obtained the right to apply for the tribunate. If he does not attain this office on the approval of the Senate, I fear that I may seem to have misled Caesar. For this reason I must make every effort to ensure that the senators 3 all regard him in the same light as the emperor did on my assurance.

Even if this motive did not fire my eager support, I would still be keen to lend aid to this wholly worthy, most serious, and most learned young man, who in short is entirely deserving of all praise, as is his whole household. For his father is Erucius Clarus, a man of integrity, 4 old-fashioned manners, eloquence, and long practice in handling cases in the courts, which he defends with the utmost probity and a similar tenacity, yet with equal moderation. His uncle is Gaius Septicius,* the most genuine, straightforward, frank, and reliable person I know. All the family vies in that affection for me which they 5 equally share, and now I can show my thanks to all of them through this one member. So I am contacting all my friends, pleading with them and canvassing them. I do the rounds of private houses and public places, and with all the authority and influence I can muster I try my hand at entreaties. I do beg you to consider it as equally urgent to shoulder some part of my burden. If you ask me to return 6 the favour, I will reciprocate—and even if you do not ask me. People are fond of you, they cultivate you, and attend on you. Only reveal your wish, and there will be no shortage of men eager to comply with it. Farewell.

10 *To his friend Octavius* late 97

What an easy-going fellow you are, or rather a hard-hearted, virtu- 1 ally cruel one, since you cling to your outstanding works for so long!

2 For how long will you bear a grudge against yourself and against me? You begrudge yourself the meed of greatest praise, and me the pleasure it imparts. You must allow your works to be borne on all men's lips and to roam as widely as the language of Rome itself. Our anticipation has been great and lengthy; you ought not to go on disappointing us
3 and putting us off. Some of your verses have become known, and in spite of your reluctance have broken out from their prison. Unless you claw these back into your collection, like runaway slaves they will
4 at some point find someone who claims them as his own.* You must keep before your eyes our mortal lot, from which you can liberate yourself by this one memorial,* for all else is frail and fleeting. Death and non-existence descends on everything as on us men ourselves.

5 In your usual way you will say: 'My friends must see to it.' My pious hope is that you have friends so faithful, so learned, and so industrious that they both can and will undertake such concentrated care and attention. But you must beware of inadequate foresight, in expecting from others a task which you fail to impose on yourself.

6 So far as publication goes, follow meantime your own inclination, but at any rate arrange a recitation, so that you may then become amenable to publication* and finally experience the pleasure which
7 long ago I anticipated without rashness for you. I see in my mind's eye the crowds, the enthusiasm, the applause—and also the silence which lies in store for you. When I speak or recite, it is the silence which pleases me as much as the applause, so long as it is alert and
8 thoughtful, and eager to hear more. So cease to deprive your works by this interminable delay of the great reward which lies in store for them, for when that delay goes beyond bounds, one fears that it may be labelled sluggishness, idleness, or even cravenness. Farewell.

11 *To his friend Arrianus* early 100

1 You are usually delighted at any event in the Senate worthy of that order, for though in your preference for a peaceful life you have retired from Rome, concern for the dignity of the state is lodged in your mind. So let me tell you of the event of recent days, which the celebrity of the central figure made notorious, which the stern precedent it set made salutary, and which the importance of the case made of perennial significance.

2 Marius Priscus* was indicted by the Africans whom he governed

as proconsul. He pleaded guilty, and asked for assessors* to be appointed. Cornelius Tacitus and I, who had been bidden to represent the provincials,* believed that it was in keeping with the trust reposed in us to inform the Senate that Priscus by his monstrous savagery had overstepped any charges for which assessors could be appointed, for he had received money for the condemnation and even the execution of innocent persons.

Catius Fronto* in reply pleaded that no investigation should be 3 made beyond the law covering extortion. He is a man with the greatest expertise at extracting tears, and he filled all the sails of his speech with the breeze, as it were, of compassion. There was considerable 4 dispute, with considerable shouting on both sides, some maintaining that the Senate's judicial inquiry was limited by legal principle, and others claiming that its discretion was free and unfettered, and that the punishment should be measured by the guilt of the defendant. In the end Julius Ferox,* the consul-designate, who is a man of 5 uprightness and probity, proposed that in the meantime assessors should indeed be appointed for Marius, but that the persons to whom he was alleged to have sold the punishment of innocent men should be summoned. This proposal was not merely carried, but 6 after those major disagreements it was absolutely the only one which won support. Such outcomes demonstrate that benevolence and pity exercise an initial impact which is penetrating and considerable, but that gradually mature thought and reason stifle them and cause them to subside. The result is that a position maintained by many in 7 mingled shouting finds no one willing to defend it when the rest are silent, the reason being that assessment of factors cloaked by turmoil becomes clear once you detach it from that turmoil.

The men who had been summoned to attend, Vitellius Honoratus 8 and Flavius Marcianus,* then arrived. One of them, Honoratus, was accused of having procured the exile of a Roman knight and the execution of seven of his friends for 300,000 sesterces, and the other, Marcianus, of having purchased for 700,000 sesterces the multiple punishments of one Roman knight, for the victim had been beaten with clubs, condemned to the mines, and strangled in prison.* Honoratus, however, was withdrawn from the Senate's judgement 9 by a timely death. Marcianus was led into the Senate, while Priscus stayed away. This was why the ex-consul Tuccius Cerealis* used his right as a senator to demand that Priscus be informed.* The reason was that he thought that if Priscus appeared in person, he would attract greater pity or greater odium, or alternatively (this is my preferred opinion) it was because it was the fairest procedure that the joint accusation should be defended by both, and that if they could not be acquitted both should be punished.

10 The case was adjourned until the Senate next met. It was a most majestic scene. The emperor as consul* presided, and in addition the month of January brings to Rome both the public and the senators in great numbers. Moreover, the importance of the case, the anticipation and gossip which had swelled with its postponement, and the inherent interest of people in acquainting themselves with important and unusual events, had aroused the whole population from all

11 quarters. Picture my anxiety and apprehension at having to speak in that gathering on such an important issue, and in the presence of the emperor. True, I had performed a number of times in the Senate, and indeed there is nowhere I am usually listened to with greater favour. But on that occasion the entire scene seemed unprecedented, and

12 affected me with unprecedented apprehension. Apart from the factors I have mentioned, the difficulty of the case confronted me; in the dock was one who only recently had been a consular and only

13 recently a septemvir* in charge of feasts, but now was neither. So it was a considerable burden to accuse a man already condemned, a man who though under the weight of a monstrous accusation was fortified by the pity felt for a condemnation already decided.

14 Somehow or other I composed my mind, gathered my thoughts, and began to speak. My anxiety was counterbalanced by the approval of my listeners. I spoke for almost five hours, for four further water-clocks* were added to the twelve of the largest size already allotted to me. Thus the very factors which had seemed forbidding and hostile

15 before I spoke turned out to be to my advantage once I began. Caesar in fact showed me such great support,* and also such great concern (it would be an exaggeration to call it anxiety) that he more than once counselled my freedman, who stood behind me, that I should not strain my voice and lungs, for he thought that I was extending myself more vigorously than my slender physique could stand.

 Claudius Marcellinus* spoke in response to me on behalf of

16 Marcianus. The Senate was then dismissed and ordered to reconvene the next day, for by that time a speech could not be begun without its being cut short by the arrival of darkness.

Next day Salvius Liberalis* spoke on behalf of Marius. He is a 17
clever, well-organized, sharp, and eloquent speaker, and in this case
he brought forth all his skills. Cornelius Tacitus spoke most elo-
quently in reply, with that *majesté* which is the outstanding feature of
his eloquence. Catius Fronto delivered a second speech on behalf of 18
Marius. It was a notable performance, and, as the occasion now
demanded, he devoted more time to pleas for clemency than to a
defence. The evening closed in on his speech, but without forcing
him to cut it short.

Accordingly the summings-up* extended to a third day. This
was the fine old practice, by which the Senate was adjourned
at nightfall, summoned on three days, and confined to three days.
Cornutus Tertullus,* the consul-designate and an outstanding man 19
who stands four-square for the truth, proposed that the 700,000
sesterces which Marius had received should be deposited in the
treasury,* that Marius should be debarred from Rome and Italy,* and
Marcianus from these and from Africa as well. At the close of his
proposal, he added that because Tacitus and I had performed our
function as advocates with care and courage, the Senate believed
that we had acted in a manner worthy of the roles allotted to us.
The consuls–designate and all the consulars as far as Pompeius 20
Collega expressed agreement.* Pompeius proposed that the 700,000
sesterces should be paid into the treasury, that Marcianus should
suffer relegation for five years, and that the sentence on Marius
should be confined to the punishment for extortion which he had
already suffered.

Both proposals attracted many supporters, with perhaps more 21
favouring this less restrictive or milder one; for even some of those
who seemed to have agreed with Cornutus attached themselves to
Pompeius, who had made his proposal following their decision. But 22
when the division took place, those who had taken their stand by the
consuls' chairs* began to support Cornutus' proposal. Then those
who were allowing themselves to be counted with Collega crossed to
the other side, and Collega was left with few supporters. He subsequently complained at length about those who had urged him on,
and notably Regulus, who had left him high and dry maintaining the
proposal which Regulus himself had formulated. Regulus' thinking
is in general so inconsistent that he is both extremely forward and
extremely circumspect.

23   Such was the end of a most august trial. But *un procès** of some
importance is left hanging. Hostilius Firminus,* a staff-officer of
Marius Priscus, has been involved in this case, and was heavily and
severely embarrassed, for it was proved, both from the account-
books of Marcianus* and from a speech which Firminus himself
made in the council at Lepcis, that he had lent his assistance to
Priscus in a most despicable commission, that he had by bargaining
extracted from Marcianus 50,000 denarii, and had moreover received
10,000 sesterces* in the most disgusting role of 'perfumer', a role not
incompatible with the lifestyle of a man who is always spruce and
24   close-shaven. On the proposal of Cornutus it was agreed that his
case would be raised at the next meeting of the Senate, for chance or
guilt had on this occasion kept him away.
      You have the news from the city; now write back with your news
25   from the country. How are your fruit-trees, your vines, your crops,
and those very frisky sheep of yours? In short, if you do not reply at
equal length, from now on you must expect only the briefest note.
Farewell.

12 *To his friend Arrianus*   early 100

1   The *procès* which, as I recently wrote, was the unfinished business
from the trial of Marius Priscus, has now been rounded off and
cleaned up, though perhaps not satisfactorily.*
2   When Firminus was brought into the Senate, and answered
the charge which you know, different proposals followed from the
consuls–designate.* Cornutus Tertullus proposed that Firminus be
expelled from the senatorial order, and Acutius Nerva that he should
not be considered when lots were drawn* for the provinces. This
second proposal, apparently milder, prevailed, but in general it is
3   harsher and more unkind. What can be more wretched than to be
stripped and deprived of the distinctions owed to a senator, yet not
freed from the toils and troubles? What is more oppressive for one so
profoundly disgraced than not to skulk in isolation, but to present
oneself for sightseeing as a showpiece in that exposed eminence?
4   Again, what in public life is less appropriate and seemly than to
sit in the Senate under senatorial censure, to be ranked with the
very men by whom one has been censured? And though debarred
from a governorship because of loathsome behaviour as a deputy, to

pass judgement on governors, and though condemned for gross misconduct to condemn or acquit others?

Yet such was the decision of the majority. Votes are counted, 5 but not weighed carefully. Public decisions can be reached in no other way, yet nothing is so inequitable as equality itself,* for though practical wisdom is not equally shared, the right to vote is shared by all.

I have fulfilled my promise, and discharged the pledge made in my 6 earlier letter, which I presume you have now received because of the time which has elapsed—for I entrusted it to a fast-moving and conscientious courier,* unless he has met with some obstacle en route. Your role is now to repay me for the first and the second with letters 7 such as can return with abundance of news. Farewell.

13 *To his friend Priscus*

You for your part have most eagerly seized opportunities to oblige 1 me, and I for mine feel indebted to none more gladly than to you, so 2 I have decided to seek your help in particular, and it is my most fervent wish that it will be granted for two reasons. You are in command of a really massive army,* a position which gives you abundant scope for bestowing favours. Secondly, you have held this office for a long time, during which you have been able to advance your own friends.

Now turn your attention to mine—not many of them, though you 3 may have preferred them to be many, but just one or two; and one in particular, Voconius Romanus,* is enough to satisfy my moderation. 4 His father was an eminent member of the equestrian order, and even more eminent was his stepfather, who was more a second father, deserving of this title because of his devotion to the son. His mother* too was from the top drawer. Only recently he was a priest in Nearer Spain* (you are aware of the discernment and high seriousness of that province). When we were pupils together, I regarded him with close 5 and friendly affection. He has been my boon-companion both in Rome and in retirement. We have shared both earnest and light-hearted pursuits. Could there be anyone more faithful as a friend, or 6 more pleasant as a companion? His conversation, his voice, and his features are wonderfully attractive. Then too as an advocate in the 7 courts he has a talent that is lofty, refined, attractive, fluent, and

learned. The letters he writes would make you believe that the
8 Muses speak Latin. My boundless affection for him is no greater
than his for me. Indeed, ever since we were both young men, I have
with the greatest eagerness bestowed on him all the favours that my
years permitted. I recently obtained for him from our most noble
emperor the 'right of three children'.* Though this privilege has been
granted only sparingly and with discrimination, the emperor gave
9 his assent to me as if it were his own choice. There is no way in
which I can maintain these kindnesses of mine other than by
enhancing them, especially as Voconius' attitude towards them is so
grateful that while receiving earlier kindnesses he becomes deserving
of those to follow.

10   You are now apprised of the sort of man he is, and how estimable
and dear he is to me. I am asking you to ennoble him in a way
befitting your character and your status. In particular, you must feel
affection for him, for though you can accord him the most honourable rank, you can grant him nothing more honourable than your
friendship. I have briefly outlined for you his pursuits and his character, and thus in short his entire mode of life, to enable you to
become more aware of his fitness for your friendship which will
attain the closest intimacy.

11   I would have pressed my pleas further, but you for your part
would not have wished to be solicited at length, and I for mine would
have solicited you throughout, for the person who makes the most
persuasive request is he who proffers the reasons for it. Farewell.

14 *To his friend Maximus*   97

1 You are right. I am preoccupied by Centumviral cases,* which cause
me more hard work than pleasure. The majority of them are slight
and trivial; only occasionally does one crop up which is notable for
2 the fame of individuals or the importance of the business. And
besides, there are few individuals with whom it is a pleasure to plead.
The rest are presumptuous, largely unknown youths who have
crossed over from schools to the courts to practise declamations.
They are so lacking in respect and so heedless that my friend Atilius*
seems to have hit the nail on the head when he said that boys in
public life begin with Centumviral cases as they do with Homer in
the schools;* for in the courts as in the schools what is most important

has begun to be the first to be handled. But goodness, before my time ₃
(this is how our elders like to put it) there was no opportunity for
young men (even the most high-born) unless they were brought in
by an advocate* of consular rank, for this was the respect with which
this noblest of professions was venerated.

But now the barriers of modesty and respect are breached, and all ₄
avenues are open to all; they are not ushered in, but they burst in.
Listeners attend them who are like the performers; they are hired
claques, purchased with money. They meet with the contractor. The
dole is handed out as openly in the middle of the basilica* as in the
dining room. They proceed from one case to the next at the same
rate of pay. This is why with some wit they are called 'Sophocleses'; ₅
the Latin name attached to them is 'Tommy Tuckers'.* But the dis- ₆
gusting practice blacklisted in both languages is growing every day.
Yesterday two of my announcers* (they are of the same age as those
who have recently put on the man's toga) were drawn in to swell the
applause for three denarii each. That is how much it costs to become
really eloquent. This rate of pay ensures that the benches, however
numerous, are filled, that a huge circle is assembled, and that unend-
ing shouts are raised when the MC gives the signal. The signal is ₇
necessary because the audience does not understand or even listen—
for most of them do not listen, but they applaud as loudly as any. If ₈
at any time you pass through the basilica, and you are keen to know
how each advocate is performing, there is no need to mount
the rostrum or even to lend an ear. You can easily guess; just grasp
that the one who wins the loudest applause is the least competent
speaker.

Larcius Licinus* was the first to inaugurate this practice of audi- ₉
ence-participation, but only so far as inviting people to listen. At any
rate this is what I recall my teacher Quintilian* telling us. He used to
tell this tale: 'I was the pupil of Domitius Afer.* He was pleading in ₁₀
the Centumviral court in his sonorous and stately way (that was the
manner of his speaking) when he heard from close by* some monstrous and strange shouting. He was astonished, and fell silent.
When the noise subsided, he resumed where he had broken off.
There was further cheering, and again he fell silent. When silence ₁₁
ensued, he began again. The same thing happened a third time.
Finally he asked who was speaking. The reply came "Licinus". He
then abandoned the case. "Centumvirs," he said, "this profession is

12 doomed." ' What in general was beginning to die when it seemed to Afer to have already died, is now almost totally dead and laid to rest. I am ashamed to recount the speeches and the affected accents in which they are delivered, together with the effeminate cries with
13 which they are greeted. The only thing missing from their chanting is the clapping, or rather nothing but cymbals and tambourines. As for the howling (for no other word can express the applause, unfit-
14 ting even in the theatre), it is wholly overdone. As for myself, service to my friends and consideration of my time of life still delay and keep me here, for I fear that perhaps I may appear to have fled, not from these unworthy scenes but from the toil involved. But I attend less often than was my custom, and this is the beginning of gradual retirement.* Farewell.

15 *To his friend Valerianus*

1 How are your ancient Marsian lands* treating you? And your new purchase? Are you pleased with the property now that you have bought it? That doesn't often happen, for nothing is as pleasing once
2 you have acquired it as when you were keen to get it. My mother's estate* isn't treating me well. I'm pleased that it's my mother's, and in general my lengthy coping with it has given me a thick skin. This is the end of my non-stop grumbling, because I'm ashamed to be grumbling. Farewell.

16 *To his friend Annius* 100–1

1 In keeping with your attentiveness in other respects, you remind me that the additional clauses left by Acilianus,* who made me his partial heir, are to be regarded as invalid because not attested in his will.
2 This is a provision of which even I am not unaware, for even those otherwise completely ignorant know of it. But I have established my own law,* so to say, to protect the intentions of deceased persons as executed, even if they should be inadequate in law. Clearly these
3 codicils were written in his own hand, so though they are not attested in the will, I will regard them as attested, especially as there
4 is no opening for an informer.* If it were to be feared that the state would seize any donation made by me, I would perhaps have to be more hesitant and circumspect. But since an heir can give away

anything buried in an inheritance, there is nothing to impede my law, for the laws of the state do not conflict with it. Farewell.

17 *To his friend Gallus*

You express surprise that my Laurentine, or Laurentian if you pre- 1 fer, estate* gives me so much pleasure, but you will no longer be surprised when you get to know the charm of the house, the convenience of the location, and the expanse of the shore. It is tucked 2 away seventeen miles from the city, so that once the necessary tasks of the day are completed, one can stay there,* leaving the business of the day unimpaired and well ordered. There is more than one route to it, for the roads both to Laurentum and to Ostia* head in the same direction, but you must leave the Laurentine road at the fourteenth milestone, and the Ostian road at the eleventh. The road which takes you on from both is partly sandy, making it rather too heavy and long for a coach and pair, but short and soft on horseback.

The view is varied at different points, for at one moment wood- 3 land confronts you and the road narrows, and at the next it widens and extends through the broadest meadows. There are many flocks of sheep and many herds of horses and cattle there. When winter drives them down from the mountains, they grow sleek on the grass and the warmth of spring.

The house, though large enough for my needs, is not expensive to maintain. At the front of it there is an entrance hall which is modest 4 without being dingy. Beyond it are colonnades shaped like the letter D, which wind round and enclose a small but cheerful courtyard. The colonnades afford the best possible refuge against stormy weather, for they are protected by glass frames, and much more by the overhanging roof. Facing the centre of these is a cheerful inner hall, 5 and next to it is a quite handsome dining room, which runs out onto the shore. Whenever the sea is buffeted by the south-west wind, the room is lightly lapped by the last foray of the spent waves. It has folding doors, or windows as big as the doors, all round, and so from both sides and the front it looks out onto the equivalent of three seas. To the rear, it looks back towards the inner hall, one colonnade, the courtyard, the other colonnade, and then the entrance hall, woods, and distant mountains.

To the left of the dining room, a little further set back, there is a 6

large room, and then a second and smaller one, which by one window lets in the rising sun, and by the other holds it captive as it sets. From this window, too, the room looks out at the sea lying below
7 from a longer but safer distance. Interposed between this room and the dining room is enclosed a nook which holds and intensifies the heat of the wholly unclouded sun. This serves as both a winter retreat and a gymnasium for my staff, for all the winds subside there except those which bring in the rain-clouds, and dispel the day's
8 brightness before depriving this area of its use. Adjoining this nook is a room which bends round like the arc of a circle, and which from all its windows follows round the circuit of the sun. Into its wall is fitted a cupboard which acts as a sort of library, containing books that
9 are not to be merely read but repeatedly read. Next to this is a sleeping apartment with an intervening passage. The floor of the passage is raised on supports, and is fitted with pipes. When the steam-heat is produced, it distributes it on both sides and provides it with a beneficial temperature. The remaining part of this side of the house is reserved for the uses of the slaves and the freedmen, though most of the rooms are so elegant that they can lodge guests.
10 On the other side of the dining room there is a most elegant chamber, and adjacent to it one which can serve as a large private room or a small dining room, bright with abundance of sun and of glistening sea. Behind it lies another room with an antechamber; its height makes it suitable in summer, and its protective walls in winter, for it is sheltered from all the winds. A further room with antechamber is joined to this by a common wall.
11 Next to this is the cooling-room of the baths. It is large and spacious, and from facing walls project two baths curved in shape. They are big enough when you consider that the sea is at hand. The anointing-room, the hypocaust, the sweating-room come next, followed by two reclining-rooms, elegant rather than luxurious. Attached to them is our wonderful heated pool, from which swim-
12 mers have a view of the sea. Near by is the games court, which meets the full warmth of the sun when the day has now commenced its downward path.

Here a tower rises, with two sets of apartments on the ground floor, with two above. There is also a dining room which claims a view of the vast expanse of the sea, the huge extent of the shore, and
13 its most attractive houses. There is also a second tower, with a room

in it which is visited by both the rising and the setting sun. Behind it are a wide wine-cellar and a granary, and on the ground floor there is a dining room which experiences nothing from the sea when it is stormy except the noise of the breakers, and even that when it is wearied and exhausted. The tower looks out upon the garden and the drive which encircles it.

The drive is lined with a hedge of box, or by bushes of rosemary 14 where the box fails (for where it is shielded by the buildings, the box flourishes, but it wilts under the open sky when it is exposed to the wind and the sea-spray, however far away). Close to the drive on its inner circuit is a gentle, shady path* which is soft and yielding even 15 to bare feet.

The garden is clothed in large numbers of mulberries and figs, for the soil is especially fertile with regard to these trees, but more hostile to all others. The dining room on the other side from the sea enjoys an outlook just as fine as that over the sea. It is encircled in the rear by two suites of rooms, beneath the windows of which lie the approach to the house and another sleek kitchen garden.

At this point a covered passageway extends, almost like a public 16 building;* it has windows on both sides, more of them facing the sea, and fewer which alternate with them facing the garden. When the day is cloudless and still, all the windows lie open, but when there are troublesome winds on one side or the other, they are kept open harmlessly on the windless side. In front of the passageway is a 17 strolling area scented with violets; the passageway itself accentuates the warmth of the sun that beats upon it by reflecting it. It both retains the sun and restrains and keeps at bay the north wind, so that it is as cool behind as it is warm in front. It likewise acts as a brake on the south-west wind, and thus halts and breaks the force of these wholly divergent winds with one of its sides or the other. This is its charm in winter, but it is more charming still in summer, for with its 18 shade it cools the strolling area before midday, and after midday the nearest part of the drive and garden. As the day waxes and wanes, its 19 shadow becomes shorter and then longer on one side or the other. The passageway itself gets absolutely no sunshine when the sun at its fiercest beats down on its roof. In addition it lets in and circulates the western breezes through the open windows, so that it is never stuffy with fetid and unshifting air.

Over beyond the strolling area, the passageway, and the garden is 20 my favourite suite of rooms, truly my favourite, for I had it built myself. It contains a sun-room which looks out on the strolling area on one side, and on the sea on the other, and it gets the sun on both. The bedroom from its folding doors looks out on the passageway,

21 and from its window on the sea. Facing the wall which lies between these is an alcove quite elegantly set behind the bedroom, and, by closing or opening the glass doors and the curtains, it can reduce or extend the size of the bedroom. It takes a bed and two armchairs. The sea lies beneath it, houses lie in its rear, and woods over and beyond. It both separates and mingles all the vistas from as many windows.

22 Attached to it is a chamber for sleeping at night. There, nothing is heard of the voices of confidential slaves, or the gentle sound of the sea, or the lashings of storms; and nothing is seen of lightning flashes, or even of daylight unless the windows are open. The reason for this dense and buried seclusion lies in the intervening passage which separates the bedroom wall from that of the garden; thus the empty

23 space absorbs all the noise. A tiny hypocaust is set by the bedroom, and by means of a narrow window it expels the heat below or confines it, as the situation demands. Next to it is another bedroom with an antechamber extended to meet the sun; it catches it as soon as it rises, and though after midday the sun slants in, it is still retained.

24   When I retire to this suite, I regard myself as being away even from my house, and I take great pleasure in it, especially at the Saturnalia,* when through the rest of the house the roof resounds with the uninhibited behaviour and the festive shouts of the holidays; for then I do not impede the games of my household, and they do not interrupt my studies.

25   The only thing missing from these amenities and delights is running water, but the house does have wells, or rather springs, for they rise close to the surface; indeed, it is a remarkable feature of this shore that wherever you uncover the earth, a ready supply of water confronts you. It is pure, not even slightly affected by such close

26 proximity to the sea. Logs in abundance are provided by the nearest woodland, and the colony of Ostia provides the other resources. Then too there is a village* from which we are separated by a single dwelling, and this supplies all that a plain-living man needs. In the village there are three baths for hire, a considerable convenience if it happens that a sudden arrival or too short a stay makes us disinclined to heat our bath at home.

The shore is adorned with the roofs of houses, some in unbroken 27
line and others spaced out, offering most pleasing variation. They
present the appearance of as many cities, whether you view them
from the sea, or when walking on the shore itself. Sometimes a long
spell of balmy weather makes the seashore soft, but more often it is
hardened by the regular impact of the breakers. The sea, it is true, 28
does not contain lots of expensive fish, but it does produce soles and
excellent prawns. Our estate also provides supplies from inland,
especially milk, for, whenever the herds make for water and shade,
they come in from the pastures and gather there.

So now do you think I am justified in making this retreat my 29
home and habitation, and loving it? If you do not long for it, you
are too much the city-slicker. I pray that you will long for it, for then
all these splendid endowments of my modest house may gain in
addition the greatest recommendation from your company here.
Farewell.

18 *To his friend Mauricus* mid-97

What more pleasant task could you have imposed on me than to 1
seek out a teacher for the children of your brother? For through
your kindness I am going back to school,* reliving, so to say, the
most pleasant period of my life. I sit among the young as I used to,
and I also become aware of the considerable authority which my
researches have brought me in their eyes.

Quite recently they were exchanging loud pleasantries in a crowded 2
lecture-hall, though there were many present of senatorial rank.* But
when I entered, they were silent. I would not have mentioned this if
it did not redound to their credit rather than to mine. I also wanted
you to entertain the hope that your brother's sons can likewise show
good manners as students. It now remains for me, once I have 3
listened to all the performers, to report to you my views about them
individually, and so far as I can by letter,* make you feel that you have
heard each and all of them. I owe this commitment and concern to 4
you and to the memory of your brother particularly in this important
respect. For what is of greater importance to you both than that the
children (I would have said your own children, but these days you
love your nephews more!) should be found worthy of their father and
their uncle? I would have claimed this charge for myself even if you

5 had not imposed it on me. I am well aware that in this business
of choosing a teacher some can feel resentful, but on behalf of
your nephews I must bear not only resentment, but also enmity*
with the same equanimity as parents feel on behalf of their children.
Farewell.

19 *To his friend Cerialis* 100

1 You urge me to recite my speech* to a number of friends. Because you
2 urge me, I shall do so, though I am extremely hesitant, being well
aware that speeches when read out lose their entire impact and passion, and virtually their claim to be speeches. This is because what
usually recommends and ignites them is the assemblage of judges,
the gathering of advocates, the prospect of the outcome, the repute
of the several participants, and the divided support of the partial
audience.* Then too there are the speaker's gestures, his movements
as he moves forward and bustles this way and that, and the vitality of
his body which harmonizes with the shifting movements of his
mind.

3 This explains why people who perform sitting down, though still
possessing for the most part the same abilities as when they are
standing, are weakened and weighed down by the very fact that they
4 are seated. Indeed, when men read out their speeches, this hinders
their eyes and hands, the chief agents of effective delivery. Hence it
is less surprising that the concentration of listeners wanes, for there
are no outward gestures to beguile them by flattery or to rouse them
by stinging barbs.

5 Then too the speech under discussion is combative and, so to say,
argumentative. Nature has also conditioned us to believe that people
6 should take the same pains to listen as we have taken to compose; yet
how few right-minded listeners are there who do not get greater
pleasure from mellifluous and resounding utterance than from that
which is dry and compressed? True, this disharmony between styles*
is quite reprehensible, but it does exist, for it usually happens that
listeners and judges demand different things, though as a general
rule the listener ought to be influenced particularly by the factors
7 which would chiefly register with him if he were a judge. It is however possible that in spite of these difficulties the new approach may
lend charm to the written version. (New, that is, with us; for the

Greeks have something not at all dissimilar,* though from a different
viewpoint. It was their custom to refute laws which they maintained 8
were opposed to previous legislation by comparing them with other
laws, and in the same way I had to argue that my demands were in
keeping with the law of extortion by arguing from that law itself and
from others.) Though this approach is far from attractive to the ears
of inexperienced listeners, it ought to win favour commensurately
greater in the eyes of the learned as it wins less in the eyes of the
ignorant. If we decide to go ahead with the reading, I shall invite all 9
who are best instructed.

But at this point clearly you must ponder whether the recitation
should take place. Set out all the considerations which I have mooted
on each side, and make the choice where reason has prevailed. Such
a rational choice will be demanded of you, whereas my excuse will be
my compliance. Farewell.

20 *To his friend Calvisius*

Pay your penny and hear this princely story, or rather stories,* for this 1
latest one has reminded me of earlier ones, and it does not matter
which to begin with for preference.

Verania, wife of Piso* (I mean the Piso whom Galba adopted) lay 2
seriously ill. Regulus approached her.* To begin with, what cheek, his
coming to a sick woman when he had been bitterly hostile to her
husband, who had utterly hated the sight of him! Enough said, if he 3
had merely come. But he also sat close to her couch, and asked her
the day and hour of her birth. On hearing these he arranged his
features, concentrated his gaze, pursed his lips, juggled his fingers,
and made a calculation. Then nothing more. After keeping the poor
lady on tenterhooks for ages, he states: 'This is a critical time for you,
but you will survive. To ensure that you get a clearer picture, I shall 4
consult a soothsayer* whom I have often tried out.' He there and then 5
conducted a sacrifice and claimed that the entrails were in harmony
with the message of the stars. The lady was disposed to believe him
in her hour of danger. She asked for additions to be made to her will,
and appended a legacy for Regulus, Then her illness got worse. On
her deathbed she cried out that he was a wicked deceiver, worse than
a perjurer, for the oath that he had sworn was on the survival of
his own son.* This conduct of Regulus is as barbaric as it is frequent. 6

He calls down the gods' anger, which he himself daily beguiles, upon the head of an unfortunate boy.

7   Velleius Blaesus,* the rich ex-consul known to you, was struggling in his final illness. He wished to alter his will. Regulus, fondly hoping to obtain something from the new one (for he had recently begun to pay court to him) urged and begged the physicians to prolong the
8 man's life in any way they could. Once the will was witnessed, he became a different man, changed his tune, and said to the physicians: 'For how long are you going to torture the poor fellow? Why do you begrudge him an easy death, when you cannot prolong his life?' Blaesus died, and as though he had heard every word, he left Regulus not a penny.

9   Are these two stories enough, or do you demand a third in accord
10 with the scholars' law?* There is another at hand. Aurelia,* a well-endowed lady, had put on some very fine garments before signing her will. Regulus turned up to witness it, and said: 'Please bequeath
11 to me those garments.' Aurelia thought that he was joking, but he was serious in his insistence. To cut a long story short, he prevailed on the woman to open up the document, and to bequeath the garments she was wearing to him. He watched her as she appended it, and looked it over to see whether she had done so. In fact, Aurelia is still alive, but he put that pressure upon her as though she were on her deathbed. And this, mind you, is the man who accepts inheritances and legacies* as though he earns them!

12   *Mais pourquoi je me fâche?* In this community for a long time now wickedness and dishonesty have gained no less—and indeed
13 greater—rewards than have decency and virtue. Cast your eye on Regulus. Through his crimes he has risen from poor and humble circumstances to such great wealth that, as he himself told me, when he was working out how quickly he would reach sixty million sesterces, he had come across a twin set of entrails* which presaged
14 that he would attain a hundred and twenty million. He certainly will, if he continues as he has begun, and dictates the terms of wills not his own to the people to whom they belong. This is the most disreputable type of fraud in existence. Farewell.

BOOK THREE

1 *To his friend Calvisius Rufus*

I doubt whether I have spent any time more delightfully than   1
that during my recent stay with Spurinna,* so much so that when I
grow old (if old age is granted me) there is no other I would wish
to emulate, for there is no pattern of living more out of the ordinary
than his. A well-ordered human existence gives me the same pleasure   2
as the fixed course of the stars, especially so in the case of old men.
A cluttered and disorganized mode of life is not at that stage
inappropriate for the young, but for old people an entirely tranquil
and well-ordered existence is apposite. For them, sustained activity
is outdated, and ambition is degrading.

The regimen that Spurinna most steadily maintains reflects this.   3
With a sort of routine and fixed circuit he undertakes in order those
unimportant activities—unimportant, that is, except that they are
carried out daily.

In the early morning he keeps to his bed. At the second hour* of   4
daylight he asks for his shoes, and takes a three-mile walk, exercising
his mind no less than his body. If friends accompany him, the most
dignified conversation takes place; if not, a book is read, and sometimes too when friends are with him, so long as they are not bored.
He then sits down, and there is either more reading, or for prefer-   5
ence, conversation. After a short time, he climbs into his carriage,
taking either his wife, a model woman for all to imitate, or one of his
friends, most recently myself. How fine, how exquisite was that tête-   6
à-tête! How evocative of the old days! What events and what person-
alities one would hear of! In what rules of conduct would you be
steeped, though he has imposed the restraint which his moderation
demands, namely not to appear to lay down the law.

When he has covered seven miles, he goes on foot again for a mile.   7
He then returns to his chair or retires to his room and his pen, for he
writes highly learned lyrics, not merely in Latin but also in Greek.
They are marvellously sweet and smooth and gay, and their charm is
enhanced by the integrity of their author.*

When the hour for the bath is announced (in winter at the ninth   8 hour, and in summer at the eighth), he walks naked in the sun as long as there is no wind. He then throws a ball forcefully for some time, since with this type of exercise too he wars on old age. After his bath he lies down, and for a short time postpones the prospect of food; in the meantime he listens to the reading of a work of a more relaxing and pleasurable kind. During this entire period his friends are free to do the same, or something different, if they prefer.

9 The dinner set down is as elegant as it is simple, served on antique dishes of solid silver. Corinthian ware* is also employed, for he delights in it without being obsessed by it. The dinner is often punctuated with readings of comedy, so that even gastronomic pleasures are spiced with study. The meal extends for a time after dark even in summer, and no one finds the party overlong in such friendly company.

10 Hence, though he is in his seventy-eighth year, his hearing and his
11 sight are unimpaired. He is physically mobile, and his only concession to old age is discretion. This is the type of life which I anticipate in prayer and thought, and as soon as calculation of my age allows me to sound the retreat, I shall embark upon it with the greatest eagerness. Meanwhile I am exercised with a thousand tasks, but in
12 these too Spurinna offers me both consolation and example. For as long as it was honourable, he performed public duties, held magistracies, governed provinces,* and through the wide scope of his labours he has deserved the leisure he enjoys. So I set for myself the same course and the same goal, and I now witness it in your presence. Thus if you see me continuing to run for too long, you can summon me to observe the terms of this letter of mine, and bid me retire once I have escaped the charge of idleness. Farewell.

2 *To his friend Vibius Maximus*

1 The favour which I myself would have extended to your friends, if the same opportunity were available to me, I now appear justified
2 in begging from you for mine. Arrianus Maturus* is a leading citizen of Altinum.* When I call him a leading citizen, I refer not to his wealth, which he has in abundance, but to his integrity, justice,
3 serious demeanour, and practical wisdom. I turn to his advice on business matters, and to his judgement on my writings, because his loyalty, truthfulness, and intelligence are absolutely outstanding.

His affection for me equals yours, and I cannot describe it more 4
glowingly than that.

He is not ambitious, and he has accordingly confined himself to
his equestrian rank, though he could easily rise to the very top. None
the less, I must see to his ennoblement and further progress. So I 5
regard it as important to advance his distinction without his expectation or knowledge—perhaps indeed against his will. But that
advancement is to be one which brings glory, yet without being
burdensome. I beg you to bestow on him some distinction of this 6
kind at your first opportunity. Both he and I will be most gratefully
in your debt, for though he does not seek the favour, he will accept it
as thankfully as if he eagerly sought it. Farewell.

3 *To his friend Corellia Hispulla*

Your father* was a man of high seriousness and the greatest integrity, 1
and I am not sure whether my esteem or my love for him was the
greater. For this reason, and also because of my particular affection
for you (which I owe both to his memory and to my respect for you),
I must be eager and also assiduous as far as I can to ensure that your
son turns out like his grandfather. I express my preference for his
grandfather on his mother's side, though his paternal grandfather
was also famous and highly regarded, and his father and uncle too
have won prominence by their distinguished fame. He will be like 2
them all on reaching maturity only if he is endowed with honourable
principles, and the most important consideration is the person from
whom he is especially to imbibe them.

Until now, consideration of his boyhood has kept him closely 3
bound to you. He has had teachers at home,* where there is little or
even no opportunity of going astray. But now his studies are to be
advanced beyond your threshold, and we must now cast round for a
teacher of Latin rhetoric in whose school strictness, probity, and
above all propriety must be implanted. For this young man of ours 4
has, in addition to the other endowments of nature and of fortune,
outstanding physical beauty, and at this hazardous stage of life one
who is not merely a teacher but also a protector and guide must be
sought out.

For this reason I can, I think, recommend to you Julius Genitor.* 5
Though I am fond of him, my assessment is not hindered by my

affection, which is based on that assessment. He is a serious person with no faults, a man even a little too prickly and uncompromising

6 for the easygoing standards of our day. For his rhetorical ability you can trust the judgement of more than one, for fluency of speech is clear and obvious, and so immediately recognizable. But people's personal lives contain hidden depths and substantial hiding-places; so far as this goes, you must accept me as the guarantor on Genitor's behalf. Your son will hear nothing from this man which is not to his profit, and he will learn nothing which it would be better for him not to know. Genitor will remind him just as often as you or I of the ancestors who weigh upon him, and the importance of their names which he must bear.

7 So with the gods' support you must entrust him to the teacher from whom he is to learn first upright behaviour, and then eloquence.* One cannot properly learn the second without the first. Farewell.

4 *To his friend Caecilius Macrinus* 100

1 Though not only friends who were with me at the time but also people at large with their comments appear to have approved my

2 action, I attach great importance to your opinion. While I would have preferred to seek your advice in this matter before the decision was made, I am extraordinarily eager to have your judgement on it even though it is decided.

I had hurried off to Etruria to lay the foundations of a public building* at my own expense, for I had been granted leave from my prefecture of the treasury.* Then ambassadors from the province of Baetica, who intended to lay a complaint against the proconsul Caecilius Classicus,* requested the Senate that I should represent

3 them. My colleagues,* excellent men bound to me by close ties of affection, tried to excuse and extricate me with prefatory mention of the necessary duties which we share. The decree of the Senate was quite laudatory, to the effect that I should be assigned to the provin-

4 cials as their protector, provided that they obtained my consent. The ambassadors were again ushered in, and again sought me (by then I was present) as their advocate. They begged for my loyal support which they had enjoyed against Baebius Massa,* and they claimed my formal attachment to them as patron.* The agreement of the

Senate ensued in the clearest terms, and this usually heralds a formal decision. Then I stated: 'Conscript Fathers, I no longer believe that I have advanced just reasons for exemption.' Both my unassuming words and my argument won approval.

What impelled me to follow this plan was not merely the unanim- 5 ity of the Senate, though this was the weightiest reason, but also certain other aspects of lesser account, which were none the less relevant. I remembered that our predecessors had on their own initiative pursued with accusations injustices inflicted even on individual foreigners, and this induced me to believe that it would be all the more contemptible to disregard the rights of states who received us as their guests. Moreover, when I recalled the considerable 6 dangers* I had undergone in that earlier advocacy on behalf of the Baeticans, I thought it important to preserve the merit of that former service by undertaking this new one. For it is in the nature of things that you undermine your earlier kindnesses if you do not reinforce them with new ones, for however often you put people under an obligation, if you refuse them a kindness just once, they remember only that one rejection.

I was further motivated by the fact that Classicus had died,* and 7 thus what is often the most melancholy feature in cases of this kind, namely the hazardous plight of a senator, was not in question. I therefore realized that gratitude for my advocacy would be no less than if he were alive, whereas the odium would be non-existent. And 8 finally I reckoned that if I performed this duty for the third time,* I would have a readier excuse if some individual became involved whom it would be undesirable for me to indict. There is, after all, some limit to be set on all obligations; then too the best excuse for remaining free then is to bow to authority now.

You have heard the motives for my strategy. What remains is for 9 you to come down on one side or the other. I shall be just as delighted by your frank disapproval as by your weighty approbation. Farewell.

5 *To his friend Baebius Macer*

I am pleased that you are repeatedly reading the works of my uncle* 1 with such care that you wish to possess all of them, and you ask for all their titles. I shall perform the role of an index, and I shall also 2 inform you of the order in which the books were written, for this too is knowledge which scholars are pleased to have.

3   *One book on throwing the javelin from horseback.** He wrote this when serving as a prefect of cavalry, devoting to it ingenuity and care in equal measure.

*Two books on the life of Pomponius Secundus.** My uncle was held in unique affection by this man, so he wrote this work as a tribute owed to the memory of a friend.

4   *Twenty books on the wars in Germany.** In this he assembled all the wars which we have waged against the Germans. He embarked on this when he was soldiering in Germany. He was prompted by a dream, in which as he lay asleep there stood before him the ghost of Nero Drusus,* who after victories over a huge area of Germany died there. He entrusted his memory to my uncle, and pleaded with him to deliver him from the injustice of oblivion.

5   *Three books on education.** He divided this work into six rolls because of its length. In it he educates the orator from the cradle, and completes his training.

*Eight books on ambiguity.** He wrote this in Nero's last years, when slavery had made hazardous every sort of writing which inclined to some independence or nobility of thought.

6   *Thirty-one books continuing where Aufidius Bassus left off.**

*Thirty-seven books on natural history.** This is a work both extensive and learned, one no less varied than nature herself.

7   Are you surprised that such a busy man completed so many volumes, many of them so detailed? Your surprise will be greater if you know that for a period he pleaded in the courts, that he died in his fifty-sixth year,* and that his middle years were preoccupied and hindered by duties of the greatest importance,* and also by his

8   friendships with emperors.* But he had a keen intelligence, astonishing concentration, and little need for sleep. From the time of the Vulcanalia* he would begin work by lamplight, not to take the auspices, but to start studying at once while it was fully dark, in winter from the seventh or at latest the eighth hour, and often from the sixth. True, he fell asleep very readily; on occasion sleep would

9   overcome and leave him as he worked at his books. He would make his way before dawn to Vespasian (for that emperor likewise employed the hours of darkness), and after that to the posts allotted

10   to him. On returning home he would devote the rest of the day to

his studies. After a snack (like the men of old, during the day he would eat sparingly and informally) he would often in summer spend any leisure time lying in the sun; a book would be read, and he would make notes and take excerpts; for there was no book which he read without excerpting it. He used to say that there was no book so bad that it was not useful at some point.

After sunbathing he would often bathe in cold water, then after a 11 light lunch* he slept for a very few minutes. After that, as if a new day had dawned, he worked at his books till dinner-time. Over dinner a book was read, on which he took notes at great speed. I recall that 12 once when the reader mispronounced some words, one of my uncle's friends made him go back, and forced him to go over them again. My uncle said to him: 'But surely you understood?' When his friend agreed, my uncle said: 'So why did you order him back? We have lost ten lines and more* through your interruption.' Such economy he 13 exercised with regard to time. In the summer he would quit the dinner-table while it was still light, and in winter during the first hour of darkness. It was as though some law had laid it down.

This was the pattern of his life when in the midst of his labours 14 and the bustle of the city. In retirement only the time for the bath deflected him from his studies. (When I say 'the bath', I mean when he was in the water, for when he was being scraped and towelled,* he was either listening to or dictating something.) When on a journey, as 15 though freed from other preoccupations he devoted himself solely to study. His secretary sat by him with a book and writing-tablets; in winter his hands were shielded with gauntlets so that not even the harsh temperature should deprive him of any time for study. For this reason even when in Rome he was conveyed in a chair. I recall his 16 rebuke to me for walking: 'You could', he said, 'have avoided wasting those hours.' For he believed that any time not devoted to study was wasted. It was through such concentration that he completed those 17 numerous volumes, and also bequeathed to me one hundred and sixty notebooks of select excerpts written on both sides of the paper in the tiniest script, so that when you take this into account the number is multiplied. He himself used to say that when he was a procurator in Spain, he could have sold those notebooks to Larcius Licinus* for 400,000 sesterces, and at that time they were somewhat fewer.

When you recall the volume of his reading and writing, you would 18 surely imagine that he had never held any public offices, nor been a friend of the emperor; again, when you hear the amount of toil which he devoted to his studies, that he did not read or write enough. For what could those busy duties not have hindered, and what could such concentration not have achieved? This is why I often smile when people call me an earnest student, for by comparison with him I am the laziest creature alive. But is it just me—for I am distracted partly by official duties and partly with services to friends?* Which one of those who spend their whole lives on literature, when compared with my uncle, would not blush at appearing to devote themselves to sleep and idleness?

20   I have prolonged my letter, though I had planned to pen only what you were seeking, namely, what books he had left. But I am sure that this additional information will please you no less than the books themselves, for this can move you not merely to read the books, but also by the goad of imitation to work away at something similar. Farewell.

6 *To his friend Annius Severus*

1   From an inheritance that came my way I have purchased a Corinthian statue*—quite a small one, but a fine piece nicely finished, so far as I can tell. Mind you, my expertise, perhaps minimal in general, is certainly so in this area. But even I can appreciate this statue, for it is unclothed, and so it does not conceal possible defects, or fail to reveal its virtues. The figure is of an old man in a standing position. Bones, muscles, sinews, veins, and even wrinkles give it a lifelike appearance. His sparse hair is swept back; he has a broad forehead, frowning features, and a thin neck. His arms hang loose, his chest is flat, and his belly pulled in. The rear view, in so far as a rear view can, indicates a person of the same age. The bronze itself, so far as the true colour shows, is old, of early date. In short, every detail is such as can detain the eyes of a craftsman, and delight those of the novice. This is what impelled me to buy it, ignoramus though I am.

    My purpose in buying it was not to keep it at home (I do not in fact have any Corinthian ware as yet), but to have it set in some populous place in my native region, and for particular preference in a temple of Jupiter, for it seems to be a gift worthy of a temple and worthy of the god. So undertake this task, as you regularly undertake all the tasks which I impose on you. Commission a pedestal to be

made from any marble you choose, and have my name inscribed on it
with my titles,* if you think that these too should be appended. I shall 6
dispatch the statue itself to you as soon as I find someone who is not
inconvenienced by it, or I shall bring it myself, as you will prefer. For
my plan is to hurry off with it, if the situation of my office allows it.
You will be pleased at my promise to come, but you will frown when 7
I add 'just for a few days', for tasks which do not yet allow me to
leave do not permit me to be away for longer. Farewell.

7 *To his friend Caninius Rufus* c.103

It has recently been announced that Silius Italicus* has committed 1
suicide by starvation in his villa at Naples. His reason for dying was 2
his illness. He had developed an incurable tumour, and the weariness
it induced caused him to hasten his death with resolute determination. Until the day of his death his life was happy and successful,
except that he lost the younger of his two children. However, his
elder son, the better of the two, is doing well and has in fact attained
the consulship.*

Silius had besmirched his reputation under Nero, for it was 3
believed that he voluntarily turned informer, but after becoming a
friend of Vitellius* he had conducted himself in a prudent and genial
way. He had gained distinction as proconsul of Asia. He had erased
the stain of his former busy activity in praiseworthy leisure. He 4
became one of the most prominent figures in the state, but without
exercising power or incurring odium. People paid early morning
visits to him, and cultivated him. For much of the time he lay on his
couch, and invariably spent the days in his room attended by many
without thought of his wealth,* and when not occupied with writing
indulging in highly learned conversation.

He composed poetry with greater diligence than genius, and on 5
several occasions he held recitations to submit his writings to the
judgement of others. Most recently, at the prompting of his years, he 6
retired from Rome and settled in Campania. He did not budge from
there even on the accession of the new emperor.* This was much to 7
Caesar's credit, for allowing such licence, and to Silius' also for
presuming to exploit such freedom. He was *un connaisseur*,* to the
point of being criticized for his mania for buying. He owned a num- 8
ber of villas* in the same region; he would fall in love with his new

purchases, and neglect the former ones. In every place he had many books, many statues, and many busts. He not merely possessed but also revered them, especially those of Virgil, whose birthday he would celebrate with greater devotion than his own, and above all at
9 Naples, where he used to visit Virgil's tomb* as if it were a shrine. He enjoyed this peaceful existence beyond his seventy-fifth year, being frail rather than feeble in body. He was the last to be chosen as consul by Nero, and he was likewise the last to die of all those whom Nero
10 had made consuls. What is also noteworthy is that he was the last of Nero's consulars to die, and Nero died when he was consul.

As I recall this, I am struck with pity for the frailty of the human
11 condition. What is so confined and short as even the longest life of man? You must think that it is no time since Nero was still with us, yet meanwhile not one of those who held the consulship under him
12 has remained alive. Yet why do I find this surprising? Not long ago Lucius Piso, father of the Piso who was killed in Africa* by Valerius Festus by a despicable deed, used to say that in the Senate he did not see one of those whom as consul he had called upon for their opinions.

13 Within such narrow limits is the lifespan of such a huge number confined, that the celebrated tears of Xerxes* seem not merely pardonable but also praiseworthy. For we are told that when that king surveyed his mammoth army, he wept at the thought of the early
14 death overhanging so many thousands. But if it is not granted to us to expend our fragile and fleeting days on famous deeds (for the opportunity for this lies in another's hands*), let us all the more devote it at least to writing, and in so far as a long life is denied to us,
15 let us bequeath something to attest that we have lived. I know that you do not lack the spur, but none the less my regard for you summons me to urge on even a galloping horse, as you likewise often urge me. *La lutte, c'est bonne,** when friends spur on each other by mutual exhortation to embrace the love of immortality. Farewell.

8 *To his friend Suetonius Tranquillus*   101–3

1 It is in accordance with the general respect you show to me that you take such pains to beg me to have the tribunate (which I obtained for you from the most distinguished Neratius Marcellus)* transferred to
2 your kinsman Caesennius Silvanus. I myself would have found it

most gratifying to see you made a tribune, but it is no less pleasing to see another advanced through your agency. I do not regard it as appropriate, when one is eager to honour a man with distinctions, to begrudge him his claim to observance of his family, for this claim is more noble than any distinctions. I further realize that, while it is a 3 splendid thing to be as deserving of kindnesses as to bestow them, you will win praise on both counts, since you are assigning to another the distinction which you yourself have deserved.

In addition, I am aware that I too will gain some prestige, since as a result of your gesture it will not remain unknown that my friends are able not merely to wield the office of tribune, but also to bestow it. For this reason I am falling in with your most honourable wish, 4 for as yet your name has not been entered on the army-lists, and I am free to put Silvanus in your place.* I hope that your gift is as welcome to him as is mine to you. Farewell.

9 *To his friend Cornelius Minicianus* 100

I can now detail to you all the difficulties I have experienced in 1 the public indictment involving the province of Baetica; for it had 2 many ramifications, with quite frequent hearings and considerable variations. Why the variations, and why the series of hearings?

Caecilius Classicus, a disgusting, blatantly evil man, had in his capacity as proconsul in that province governed in a manner no less brutal than squalid. This was in the same year that Marius Priscus* governed Africa. Priscus was a native of Baetica, and Classicus was 3 from Africa. Hence the *bon mot* of the Baeticans which circulated (for grievances, too, often elicit witticisms): 'I dealt a nasty one, and got one back.' But whereas Marius was indicted publicly by a single 4 community* and by many individuals privately, Classicus was set upon by the whole province. Classicus forestalled the accusation by 5 dying, whether by chance or suicide, the cause of his death being uncertain though suspicious. It seemed credible that he had wished to end his life, since no defence could be offered, but on the other hand it was surprising that he had escaped the shame of condemnation by dying when he had shown no shame in performing acts worthy of condemnation.

In spite of this, the Baeticans persisted with the indictment, even 6 when he was dead. This was licit according to the laws, but the

practice had fallen into abeyance, and was now reintroduced after
a long interval. The plaintiffs further stated that they were bringing
charges against the allies and agents of Classicus,* and they demanded
7 that they be investigated, citing each by name. I represented the
Baeticans conjointly with Lucceius Albinus,* who is a fluent and
elegant speaker. We had for some time liked each other, but as a
result of this shared obligation I have begun to feel a more glowing
8 affection for him. The desire for prestige, particularly in matters
intellectual, *ne veut pas partager*, but between us there was no competition or rivalry, for in bearing the yoke equally we were striving in
the interests of the case and not of ourselves. Both its importance
and its usefulness seemed to demand that we should not shoulder
9 this great burden by each making a single speech. We feared that
time, our voices, and our lungs would give out on us if we wrapped
these numerous charges and all the defendants into one bundle. We
feared too that the concentration of the judges might be not merely
wearied, but also baffled by the plethora of names and charges; and
then again that favour for each of them, when combined and intermingled, might win for each individual the collective impact of
all of them. Finally, we feared that the most powerful among
them would offer the least important defendants as a sort of expi-
ation, and themselves slip through the net while others were pun-
10 ished. Good will and canvassing become dominant when concealed
11 under the cloak of stern sentencing. We also took into account that
exemplary tale of Sertorius,* who ordered the strongest and the
weakest individual among his soldiers to pull off the horse's tail—
you know how the story goes! For we too realized that such a large
number of defendants could be bested only if we picked them off
one by one.

12 We took the view that the first essential was to prove Classicus
guilty. This was the most appropriate way to pass on to his allies and
agents, for these allies and agents could not be found guilty unless he
was a wrongdoer. We at once attached to Classicus two of them,
Baebius Probus and Fabius Hispanus, both of them being very
13 influential, and Hispanus also very eloquent. So far as Classicus was
concerned, our efforts were swift and straightforward, for he had left
a written account in his own hand of the money he had received from
each transaction and each indictment. He had also sent arrogant and
boastful letters to some lady-friend at Rome. These are his actual

words:* 'All hail! I'm on my way to you, having gained my freedom, for I've sold a parcel of Baetica and made a cool four million.'

Hispanus and Probus cost us a lot of sweat. Before embarking on 14 the charges against them, I thought it vital to take pains to establish that their carrying out of orders was a crime.* Had I not done this, finding the agents guilty would have been futile, for the defence on 15 their behalf was not denial of the charges, but a plea for pardon on the grounds of necessity, for they claimed that being provincials they were forced through fear to carry out every command of governors. Claudius Restitutus,* who replied to me on behalf of the defence, and 16 is a practised, careful speaker, ready for any argument however unexpected, often remarks that he was never so befuddled and confused as when he saw that the arguments in which he placed all his trust had been forestalled and wrenched out of his speech for the defence.

The outcome of our strategy was that the Senate decreed that the 17 possessions which Classicus had before going to the province should be set apart from the rest, and bequeathed to his daughter, while the remainder was conferred on the persons he had plundered. A further clause decreed that the money which he had paid to his creditors should be returned. Hispanus and Probus were relegated for five years,* so serious was the charge against them, whereas at the outset it was uncertain whether it was a crime at all.

A few days later we indicted Claudius Fuscus, son-in-law of 18 Classicus, and Stilonius Priscus, who had been a tribune of a cohort under Classicus. The outcome differed for each of them, for Priscus was banished from Italy for two years, and Fuscus was acquitted.

At the third hearing we thought it most convenient to assemble 19 several defendants together, for we feared that, if the investigation was dragged out too far, those hearing the case would be glutted and rather bored with it, with the result that the justice and severity which they administer would be enfeebled. Then again, the remaining defendants were in general lesser figures, held back for the occasion. The one exception was Classicus' wife. Though her complicity was suspected, there did not appear to be sufficient proof to convict her. As for Classicus' daughter, likewise one of the accused, there 20 were not even any suspicions attached to her, so when I reached her name at the end of my speech—by the end of the case there was no need to fear, as there had been at the outset, that the reliability of the

entire indictment would be diminished in this way—I thought it the most honourable course not to bear heavily on her, since she did not
21 deserve it, and I made the point openly and in sundry ways. Not only did I question the ambassadors on whether they had informed me of any irregularity which they were sure could be factually proved. I then sought the advice of the Senate: did they think that I would launch such eloquence as I possessed like some weapon at the throat of an innocent woman? Finally I rounded off the whole topic with these closing words: 'Someone will ask: So are you a judge in this case? No, I am not, but I recall that I was assigned from the judges' bench* to undertake the prosecution.'

22 This was the end of a case which involved so very many defendants. Some were acquitted, but more were condemned and also
23 relegated, some for a period and others for life. The same senatorial decree registered in fullest testimony its approval of our diligence, honesty, and integrity, a worthy reward which alone was com-
24 mensurate with our great labours. You can visualize how exhausted we were by reason of our numerous speeches and verbal exchanges, and the interrogation, support, and refutation of so many witnesses.
25 Again, how taxing and troublesome it was to say no to the secret pleas of friends of so many defendants, and then to face their opposition openly! I shall cite one of these replies which I gave when some of the very judges were loudly protesting to me on behalf of a highly influential defendant. I remarked: 'He will be just as innocent as now if I recount all the facts.'*

26 You can gather from this the extent of the challenges, and also the abuse which we endured, admittedly for only a short time, for honesty momentarily gives offence to those who oppose it, but thereafter wins respect and praise from those same persons.

27 I could not have given you a clearer picture of the trial. You will say, 'It was not so important. Why have you saddled me with such a long letter?' Very well, don't keep asking what goes on in Rome. And bear in mind that the letter is not so long, in that it has taken in all those days, all those hearings, and finally all those defendants and
28 indictments. I think I have described them all with as much brevity as carefulness.

But I was rash to claim carefulness, for all too late something which I have passed over occurs to me. You will have it, though it will be out of place—this is a technique of Homer's,* and many writers follow his example. It is in general quite an elegant device, though that is not the reason why I shall employ it.

One of the witnesses, either because he was angry at being called 29 up against his will, or because he had been suborned by one of the defendants to weaken the indictment, prosecuted Norbanus Licinianus, one of the investigating ambassadors, on a charge of collusion in the case of Casta, wife of Classicus. The law has pro- 30 vided that the trial of a defendant should be completed before any investigation of a prevaricator,* the reason doubtless being that the honesty of an accuser is best assessed from the accusation itself. But 31 Norbanus obtained no protection from the order prescribed by law, nor from his status as ambassador, nor from his official role as investigator. Such was the flaming hatred in which he was engulfed; for he was in general a wicked person who had exploited the era of Domitian like many others. On this occasion he had been chosen by the province to conduct the investigation, not because he was a decent and honest man, but because he was an enemy of Classicus, who had previously banished him.

Norbanus demanded a postponement and a statement of the 32 charges, but he obtained neither and was compelled to reply to the charges there and then. When he did so, his wicked and debased character caused me to doubt whether it was a show of assurance or of integrity, for it was certainly carefully prepared. There were many 33 accusations more damaging than that of prevarication. Indeed, two ex-consuls,* Pomponius Rufus and Libo Frugi, adduced damning evidence that in Domitian's day he had appeared before a judge in support of the accusers of Salvius Liberalis.* He was condemned, and 34 relegated to an island.

So when I indicted Casta, my main attack was that her accuser had been brought down on a charge of prevarication, but my attack was vain, for the outcome went the other way and was unprecedented: that the defendant should be acquitted, though her accuser had been condemned for prevarication. You will ask what our reaction was to 35 all this. We pointed out to the Senate that it was from Norbanus that we had been informed of the indictment by the state, and that we must now learn it afresh, since he was found guilty of prevarication. So during his indictment we remained seated. Norbanus subsequently attended every day of the trial, persisting to the end with his attitude of steadfastness or shamelessness.

36   I am asking myself whether I have again left something out, and again I almost have. On the final day Salvius Liberalis issued a weighty rebuke against the remaining ambassadors, on the grounds that they had not prosecuted all the defendants as prescribed by the province. Since he is a forceful and eloquent spokesman, he put them in a difficult position. I defended them as excellent individuals, and they were most grateful. They publicly declare that they owe it to me that they survived that whirlwind.

37   This will be the end of the letter, really the end. I shall add not a single letter, even if I still think of something which I have left out. Farewell.

10 *To his friend Vestricius Spurinna and to Cottia*   100–1

1   When I was staying with you recently, I refrained from informing you that I had written an account of your son.* Why? First, I wrote it, not for your benefit, but to meet the demands of my affection and my grief. Secondly, you had heard that I had given a recitation (as, Spurinna, you yourself told me), and I assumed that you had heard

2   at the same time of the subject of my recitation, Then again, I feared that if I reminded you of your most harrowing grief, I might cause you distress during the festive days. Even now I am uncertain whether to send at your request merely the work which I recited, or

3   to add what I plan to hold back for a second volume; for it does not satisfy my feelings to furnish in a single volume my most affectionate and hallowed recollections, since his fame will be ensured more

4   widely if it is disseminated in serial form.* But in my uncertainty whether I should show you all that I have written or whether I should withhold certain parts at the present time, I decided that it was more consonant with honesty and friendship to send you all of it, especially as you guarantee that it will remain closeted with you until a decision is made whether to publish.

5   One further thing: I ask that you should with like honesty inform me of anything which you think should be added, amended, or omit-

6   ted. It is hard for you as yet to turn your mind to it in your grief. Yes, it is hard, but just as you would advise a sculptor or painter, when fashioning a representation of your son, what features he should emphasize or change, so you must mould and guide me in the same way, for I am trying to achieve a likeness not frail or fleeting, but one

that is in your opinion immortal. The more authentic and fine and finished it will be, the longer it will survive. Farewell.

11 *To his friend Julius Genitor*

Our friend Artemidorus* is so full of kindness by nature that he heaps 1 exaggerated praise on his friends for their services. So he is singing the praises of my deserving merit as well. What he says is true, but 2 more than I deserve. It is a fact that when the philosophers were banished* from Rome, I visited him in his residence outside the city, and my visit was all the more noteworthy, and therefore more hazardous, because I was a praetor.* Then, too, when he was in need of quite a substantial sum of money to pay a debt which he had incurred for the noblest of reasons, at a time when most of his high and mighty wealthy friends were humming and hawing, I borrowed the money and passed it to him without charging interest. Moreover, 3 I did this at a time when seven of my friends had been executed or banished. Senecio, Rusticus, and Helvidius* had been executed, and Mauricus, Gratilla, Arria, and Fannia* had been banished; scorched as I was with all these bolts of lightning hurled around me, certain sure signs made me prophesy that the same fate overhung me.

However, I do not think that I have deserved the outstanding 4 reputation such as Artemidorus proclaims; it is merely that I avoided disgrace. For in so far as my youth allowed, I loved and admired his 5 father-in-law Gaius Musonius,* and, when I was serving in the army as a tribune in Syria, I was already then joined in close friendship with Artemidorus himself. That was the first occasion when I gave evidence of some insight, for I appeared to realize that he was a sage, or one closely approximating to a sage. Indeed, of all those 6 today who call themselves philosophers, you will find scarcely one or two who manifest such integrity and truthfulness. I say nothing of the physical endurance with which he bears winters and summers alike. He yields before no hardships, makes no concessions to the pleasures of food and drink, and exercises firm control over his eyes and thoughts.* These are impressive traits in others; they are trivial in 7 Artemidorus compared with his other virtues, as a result of which he has deserved to be chosen by Gaius Musonius from all the suitors of every rank to be his son-in-law.

As I recall these facts, it is gratifying that he heaps such praise on 8 me in the presence both of others and of you, though I fear that he exaggerates. To return to the point I made at the beginning, his

9 kindness often leads him to overstep the mark. This is the one fault in which this man, who is in general supremely wise, seems to err—an honourable one, but none the less a fault, that he thinks his friends are of greater worth than they actually are! Farewell.

12 *To his friend Catilius Severus*

1 Yes, I will come to dinner, but here and now I state my terms: it must be informal and inexpensive, plentiful only in Socratic conversation,*

2 with a time limit set even on that. Your duties with early morning callers* will lie ahead. Not even Cato* was allowed to collide with

3 them, though Caesar's rebuke* to him was not without praise. He relates that when the persons whom Cato encountered uncovered his head, and discovered the identity of the drunkard, they blushed for shame. 'You would have thought, not that they had caught Cato red-handed, but that he had caught them.' Could Cato's high repute have been signalled more clearly than that, since when even drunk he was such a revered figure?

4   However, our dinner-party must have a limit imposed not only on preparations and expense, but also on time, for we are not the kind of people whom even our enemies cannot censure without also praising us. Farewell.

13 *To his friend Voconius Romanus*   100–1

1 At your request I am sending you the written version of the speech* in which as consul I recently expressed our thanks to the best of

2 emperors; I was about to send it even if you had not requested it. I should like you to give thought not only to the splendid content, but also to the difficulty inherent in it. Whereas in other speeches the unfamiliar content holds the attention of the reader, in this case all that was said is known and noised abroad. The result is that the reader has leisure and freedom to devote himself solely to the mode of expression,* and it is more difficult to give satisfaction in this when

3 it is assessed in isolation. I only hope that the reader directs his attention alike to the order of topics, the transitions from one to the next, and the figures of speech; for sometimes even uncivilized

people are outstandingly good at invention of topics and at impressive delivery, but clever arrangement and varied use of figures are denied to all except the initiated. We should not always aspire to lofty and elevated expression. Take the analogy of a painting; nothing 4 brings out light better than shadow.* In the same way the lowering of tone is as appropriate as the raising of it.

However, why do I explain this to a man of such great learning? 5 Instead, I must beg you to mark the passages which you think need correction, for I shall more readily believe that you approve the rest if I know the passages of which you disapprove. Farewell.

14 *To his friend Acilius*

Larcius Macedo,* a praetorian, has suffered at the hands of his slaves 1 a ghastly fate which merits notice more than in a mere letter. True, he was in general an arrogant and savage master, too forgetful, or rather, all too aware, that his father had been a slave. He was taking a 2 bath at his residence in Formiae* when suddenly slaves surrounded him. One took him by the throat, another battered his face, and a third pummelled his chest, belly, and (disgustingly) his private parts. When they thought that he was senseless, they threw him on the hot pavement to see if he was alive. Whether because unconscious or feigning unconsciousness, he lay stretched out and motionless, giving the impression of being quite dead.

Finally he was carried from the bath as though overcome by the 3 heat. His more trusty slaves took over, and his concubines came rushing round, moaning and shouting. In this way he was both roused by their voices and revived by the cool temperature indoors. By opening his eyes and moving his body he indicated (for now it was safe) that he was alive.

Those slaves made off in different directions. Many have been 4 caught, and the rest are being hunted. Macedo was revived with difficulty, but died within a few days. However he had the consolation of vengeance, for while still alive he was avenged as murdered individuals usually are.* You realize to what dangers and insults and 5 derision we are exposed. No man can remain untroubled because he is relaxed and gentle, for masters are murdered through wickedness rather than considered judgement.

So much for that. What other news is there? There is none, for 6

otherwise I would add it. There is still some paper vacant, and today's holiday* allows me to compose more. I shall make a further point with regard to the same Macedo which aptly occurs to me. When he was bathing in the public baths* at Rome, a surprising
7 event occurred which the outcome has shown was portentous. His slave laid his hand gently on a Roman knight as a request to allow them to pass. The knight turned, and with the flat of his hand struck not the slave who had touched him, but Macedo himself with
8 such force that he almost fell over. In this sense, the baths have for Macedo successively proved to be the scene first of abusive treatment, and then of his death. Farewell.

15 *To his friend Silius Proculus*

1 You ask me when I'm away from Rome to read and scrutinize your writings to see if they are worth publishing. In your recourse to pleas, you offer a parallel, for when you request that I devote to your writing any spare time I take from my own, you add that Cicero* showed remarkable kindness in nurturing the talent of poets.
2   But I need no request or exhortation, for on the one hand I have the most scrupulous respect for poetry,* and on the other I have boundless affection for you. So I will do what you desire both care-
3 fully and gladly. However, I think that I can say in reply here and now that your work is splendid, and should not lie unpublished, so far as I could judge from the pieces which you recited in my presence; that is, so long as your delivery did not beguile me, for you read
4 so very charmingly and skilfully. However, I am sure that my ears do not lead me on to cause the sharp edge of my judgement to be blunted by the charms of listening. Its acuteness may perhaps be dulled and deadened, but it cannot be forcibly removed or extracted.
5 So this is no rash pronouncement which I make about the work as a whole; I shall try it out part by part in reading it. Farewell.

16 *To his friend Nepos*

1 I think that I have noted that some deeds and words of men and
2 women are more celebrated, but that others are greater. My belief was strengthened by a conversation I had yesterday with Fannia.* She is the granddaughter of the famous Arria,* who was both a

consolation and an example to her husband at his death. She told me
many things about her grandmother which were no less impressive
than that, but are less well known, and I think you will find them as
remarkable as you read them as I did when I heard them.

Caecina Paetus,* her husband, was ill, and so was her son, and both 3
were at death's door. Her son died. He was remarkably handsome
and equally modest, and dear to his parents as much for other considerations as for being their son. She organized his funeral and 4
arranged the ceremonies so discreetly that her husband knew nothing of it. Indeed, whenever she entered her husband's room, she
pretended that their son was still alive, and was even improving. To
his frequent enquiry about the son's progress, she would reply: 'He
has slept well, and has happily taken some food.' When her tears, for 5
long restrained, overcame her and burst forth, she would leave and
then yield to her grief. After crying to her heart's content, she would
dry her eyes, compose her features, and go back to her husband as if
she had left her son's loss outside.

That celebrated action* of hers in unsheathing the dagger, piercing 6
her breast, extracting the dagger, passing it to her husband, and
crowning all with the immortal, almost godlike words 'Paetus, it does
not hurt', was certainly an outstanding deed. But as she did these
things and said these words, never-ending fame lay before her eyes;
all the greater was it, therefore, without the reward of perennial
fame, to conceal her tears, to bury her grief, and to play the role of a
mother when her son was lost to her.

When Scribonianus raised a rebellion* against Claudius in 7
Illyricum, Paetus had joined his faction, and when Scribonianus was
killed, Paetus was escorted to Rome. As he was embarking, Arria 8
pleaded with the soldiers that she too should be taken aboard.
'Doubtless,' she said, 'since he is a consular, you will provide him
with some slaves to feed and clothe him, and to put on his shoes.
I shall do all these things by myself.' When she was refused, she 9
hired a small fishing-boat, and followed the huge ship in her tiny
craft. When the wife of Scribonianus was laying information before
Claudius* about the rising, Arria said to her: 'Am I to listen to
you, when Scribonianus lay slain in your arms, and yet you go on
living?' This incident makes it clear that her decision to die a most
noble death was not unpremeditated. Indeed, when her son-in-law 10
Thrasea* begged her not to take the path to death, and among other

things remarked, 'So if I had to die, would you wish your daughter to die with me?', she replied: 'Yes, if she lives as long and as harmoni-
11 ously with you as I have lived with Paetus.' This reply had intensified the concern of her household, and they kept a more vigilant eye on her. She realized this, and said: 'You are wasting your time, for you can ensure for me a coward's death, but you cannot prevent my
12 dying.' Saying this, she jumped from her chair, and with great force struck her head on the wall opposite, and collapsed. When she came round, she said: 'I told you that I would find some harsh way to die if you refused me an easy one.'

13   These words must surely strike you as more impressive than that famous utterance, 'Paetus, it does not hurt', to which they led. While those final words have become hugely famous, these earlier ones are not current at all. So this exemplifies my initial remark, that some sayings are more celebrated, but others are greater. Farewell.

17 *To his friend Julius Servianus*   *c.*100–1

1 Is all well? Your letters have stopped coming for some time now. Is all perhaps well, but you are fully stretched? Or are you perhaps not
2 fully stretched,* but with few or no opportunities to write?* Do relieve my anxiety, for I cannot keep it under control. Do relieve it, even by dispatching a special courier. I will pay his travelling-expenses, and I will also reward him provided that he tells me what I long to know.

3   I am well, if being in suspense and on tenterhooks is being well, for at every hour, with the welfare of the dearest of friends in mind, I await with apprehensions at what can happen to a person. Farewell.

18 *To his friend Vibius Severus*   *c.*102

1 My position as consul* imposed upon me the task of offering thanks to the emperor in the name of the state. Once I had performed this duty in the Senate as tradition demanded, in accordance with the nature of the location and the occasion, I thought it most appropriate for me, as a loyal citizen, to embody the same material in a more
2 extended and luxuriantly written version.* My motive was first to applaud with sincere praises the emperor's virtues, and secondly to offer prior counsel to future incumbents on the best possible way to strive for the same renown—not laying down the law as a

schoolmaster, but by offering a precedent. For it is an excellent ₃
notion to prescribe what an emperor should be, but it is also oppressive and almost arrogant, whereas to praise this best of emperors,
and in this way to indicate to his successors as from some lofty
vantage-point the beacon which they are to follow, is just as useful
without being overbearing.

I had wanted to recite this written version among a company of ₄
friends, so I informed them, not by dispatching formal notices or
programmes, but with messages 'if convenient' or 'if absolutely free'
(at Rome, in fact, no one is ever 'absolutely free' or finds it 'convenient' to listen to someone reciting his work). What has given me no
little pleasure is that in spite of this, and really foul weather as well,
they assembled on two days running, and when in my modest way
I would have wished to put an end to the recital, they demanded that ₅
I continue for a third day. Should I believe that this was a tribute
paid to me, or to the literary exercise? I opt for the second, for these
literary recitals, which had almost died out, are being revived.*

But what was the subject matter in which they showed such sus- ₆
tained interest? Surely it was the stuff which after no more than a
moment used to oppress us even in the Senate, where we had to
endure it. But now we find some willing to recite, and others willing
to listen, for three days! This is not because the compositions are
more fluent than before, but because they are written in an atmosphere of greater freedom and therefore of more pleasure. So this too ₇
will redound to the praise of our emperor, that an exercise earlier as
loathed as it was hypocritical has now become as popular as it is
genuine.

But it was with some wonder that I registered approval of both the ₈
enthusiasm and the good judgement of my audience, for I observed
that what they appreciated above all were the unadorned passages. I ₉
bear in mind that I have read out only to the few what I have written
for the world at large, but the serious demeanour of my listeners
gives me the pleasant expectation that their opinion will be shared by
people generally. Just as in days gone by the theatres taught performers to sing badly, so now I am led to hope that these same theatres
may possibly teach them to sing well.

All who compose to give pleasure will write the kind of things ₁₀
which they have noted give pleasure. So far as I am concerned, I am
sure that for this type of content the argument for a more luxuriant

style prevails, since the more restrained and severe presentation*
seems more artificial and alien than what I have composed in a more
genial and buoyant mode. However, I pray all the more eagerly that
the day will sometime come (I only hope that it has come already)
when these charming and ingratiating modes of expression may
abandon their tenure of the scene, however justified, in favour of
what is disciplined and plain.

11   Here then are my efforts over the three days. On behalf of both
the exercise and myself, I wanted you to obtain as much pleasure in
reading them in your absence as you would have gained by being
present. Farewell.

19 *To his friend Calvisius Rufus* 100

1 I want to consult you on a matter of property. A neighbouring estate*
which actually forms a wedge into mine is up for sale. It has many
attractions which excite me, but just as many features which dis-
2 suade me. What chiefly attracts me is the splendid prospect of the
combined properties. Then there is the aspect, as useful as it is
pleasing, and the possibility of visiting both with the one outlay
of effort and of travelling-expenses. Then again, having the one
superintendent and virtually the same bailiffs, and maintaining and
equipping the one residence, and merely keeping an eye on the other.

3   The calculation involved includes the cost of furniture, domestic
staff, landscape gardeners, workmen, and hunting equipment, for it
makes a huge difference whether you concentrate these in one place,
4 or apportion them among several. Against acquisition is my fear that
it may be injudicious to subject so sizeable a property to the same
vagaries of weather and the same natural hazards. It seems safer to
confront the uncertainties of fortune with a varying range of properties. Also relevant is the great pleasure experienced in a change
of location and climate, as well as the journeying between one's
properties.

5   But the main factor which dominates my thinking is that the lands
are fruitful, rich, and well watered; they comprise open fields, vineyards, and woodland, which provides timber* and from it a modest
6 but steady return. But this fertility of the earth is being exhausted by
inadequate cultivators; for the previous owner quite often sold what
the farm-labourers had mortgaged, so that while for the moment he

reduced their liabilities, he drained their resources for the future,
and when these ran out, their debts mounted again. So we shall have 7
to equip them with slaves,* and they will be more expensive because
they will have to be reliable, for neither I myself nor anyone at all
there keeps chained slaves.

The final thing for you to know is the likely purchase price. It is
three million sesterces. Mind you, at one time it was five million,
but owing to the dearth of farm-labourers and the economic slump*
of these days, the returns from the land have been reduced, and with
them the value of the estate.

You ask whether I can readily raise the three million. My wealth is 8
almost entirely invested in land, but I lend some money at interest,
and it will not be difficult to borrow. I shall obtain some money from
my mother-in-law,* whose wealth I deploy just like my own. So this 9
problem must not weigh with you, as long as the other matters are no
obstacle. I would like you to ponder these as carefully as possible, for
both in matters generally and in the allocation of finance you have
abundance of both experience and practical wisdom. Farewell.

20 *To his friend Maesius Maximus* 103–4

Do you remember often reading of the great controversies arising 1
from the *lex tabellaria*,* and the great esteem or censure it conferred
on the proposer? Nowadays, however, the procedure is approved in 2
the Senate with no disagreement, as being the best. On the day of
the elections* everyone requested a wax tablet.

With open voting in public we had earlier been more intemperate 3
than in the free-for-all in those public assemblies. The time limit for
speeches was not maintained; no moderation was shown in establish-
ing silence; people did not even observe propriety in remaining
seated. Loud and confused shouting was heard from every side; all 4
were rushing forward with their candidates; there were long lines in
the centre of the hall with many circling round them—an undignified
mêlée. To such an extent had we abandoned the custom of our forebears, with whom everything was well ordered, under control, and
peaceful, upholding the dignity and decency of the Senate House.

There are old men still among us from whom I often hear that the 5
procedure at elections* was as follows. When the name of a candidate
was announced, there was total silence. He spoke on his own behalf.

He outlined his life, and adduced as witnesses and eulogists either
his former commanding officer or the governor he had served as
quaestor, or both if possible. He would then introduce in addition
some of the voters, who would each contribute a few dignified words.

6   This procedure was more effective than pleas. Sometimes a candidate would challenge a rival's origin, age, or even character.* The
Senate would listen with austere sobriety. As a result, candidates
7   who were worthy rather than influential gained the day. Nowadays
these proceedings have been marred by uncontrolled shouts of support, and recourse has been had to secret voting as a remedy. Meanwhile it has already served as that remedy, because it was a novel and
8   emergency measure, but I fear that as time goes on the remedy itself
may give rise to vices, the danger being that silent voting may be
quietly invaded by shamelessness; for how few evince the same con-
9   cern for what is honourable in secret as in public? Many show
respect for their reputation, but few for their conscience. But it is too
early to worry about the future. In the meantime, thanks to these
writing-tablets we shall have magistrates who have deserved election,
for just as in court cases* which assess financial compensation, so
in these elections when suddenly pressed into service we have
performed as honest judges.

10   My reasons for writing to you about this were first to report some
news to you, and secondly on occasion to raise with you political
issues. The opportunity for raising this topic comes less frequently
to us than it did to men of old, and for that reason we should be
11   more reluctant to forgo it. What point is there, for heaven's sake, in
those everyday greetings, 'How are things?' and 'Are you in good
form?' Our letters should also incorporate content which is not triv-
12   ial or mean or restricted to personal affairs. It is true that everything
is under the control of one man, who has alone undertaken the
concerns and toils of all for the common good. But from that outstanding source of kindness certain streams flow* down to us at a
health-giving temperature. We can draw on these for ourselves, and
also by our letters transmit them to our absent friends. Farewell.

21 *To his friend Cornelius Priscus*   101–4

1   I hear that Valerius Martial* has died, and I find it sad news. He was a
talented and intelligent man with a keen mind, the sort of poet with

abundant wit and gall, and an equal measure of openness. When 2
he was retiring from Rome,* I presented him with his travelling-
expenses as a gesture of friendship and acknowledgement of the
verses he composed about me. It was an ancient custom to honour 3
poets who had written eulogies* of individuals or of cities with distinctions or with money. But in our day this practice in particular,
like other splendid and notable customs, has lapsed. For now that we
have abandoned praiseworthy pursuits, we consider it pointless to
receive accolades.

Would you like to hear the verses for which I thanked him?* I 4
would refer you to the collection, if I did not remember some of
them. If you like these, you must look out the rest in his publications.
He is addressing his Muse, bidding her make for my house on the 5
Esquiline,* and to approach with deference.

> But be sure that you don't when drunk go knocking
> At that eloquent door when you're not welcome.
> He devotes all his days to stern Minerva,
> While for the ears of the court of Centumviri
> He works away at what men of later ages
> Can compare even with Arpinum's pages.*
> You will go more safely when late lamps burn;
> That is your hour, when Bacchus rages wildly,
> When the rose is queen, when men's hair is perfumed.
> Why, unbending Catos would then read me!

Surely it was right that he who penned these lines should then have 6
been waved off in the friendliest way, and should be mourned as a
close friend now he has died? For he gave me the greatest tribute that
he could, and he would have given more if that had been possible.
Yet what greater thing can a man bestow on a person than fame,
praise, and immortality? You will respond that his writings will
not be immortal.* Perhaps they will not be, but he composed them
believing that they would be. Farewell.

BOOK FOUR

1 *To Calpurnius Fabatus, his grandfather-in-law*

1 You are eager to see both your granddaughter* and myself after this considerable time. Your eagerness is appreciated by both of us, and is 2 certainly reciprocated; for we in turn are possessed by a longing to see you which is beyond belief, and we shall not postpone the visit any longer. So we are already packing our baggage, intending to hasten as quickly as the nature of the route allows.

3 There will be one delay, but a short one. We shall turn aside into Etruria, not to set eyes on our lands and property (this we can 4 postpone), but to perform an essential duty. There is a town close to our estate called Tifernum-on-Tiber.* The citizens adopted me as their patron while I was still virtually a boy. Their enthusiasm was in inverse proportion to their judgement! They make much of my 5 arrivals, regret my departures, and rejoice in my distinctions. So to return their favours (it is very uncivilized to be outdone in affection) I have had a shrine* built in the town at my own expense, and since the building is ready it would be impious to postpone its dedication 6 any longer. So we shall be there on the day of the dedication, which I have decided to celebrate with a banquet. We shall perhaps stay there on the following day as well, but this will induce us to hasten our journey to you all the more.

7 We only hope that we find your daughter* and yourself in good shape. We shall certainly find you in good spirits, if we reach you safe and sound! Farewell.

2 *To his friend Attius Clemens* *c*.104

1 Regulus has lost his son,* the sole misfortune which he did not deserve, though whether he thinks it a misfortune is uncertain. He was a boy with a keen but vacillating brain; yet he could have made 2 good if he had not been like his father. Regulus released him from paternal authority* to enable him to inherit his mother's estate, but once he was 'disposed of' (this was how the father's behaviour was characterized in common gossip), Regulus began to win him over

with a hypocritical show of kindness unusual in parents. It is hard to believe, but just think of Regulus!

But now that he has lost him,* he mourns him like a madman. 3
The boy had many ponies, some harnessed in pairs and others unfettered for riding; he also had dogs, larger and smaller, nightingales, parrots, and blackbirds. Regulus slaughtered all of them round his funeral-pyre. This was no grief, but a mere display of it. People are 4 thronging round him in astonishing numbers. They all loathe and hate him, but they rush up to him and mob him as if they approve and love him. To state my feelings in a nutshell, in fawning on Regulus they play the Regulus. He keeps himself in his gardens 5 across the Tiber, where he has covered a massive area with huge colonnades, and the river-bank with his statues,* for despite his monstrous greed he is extravagant, and in spite of his monstrous notoriety he plays the braggart.

So he is disturbing the city at this unhealthiest time of year, and 6 he regards this disturbance as a consolation. He says that he intends to marry, showing wrong-headedness in this as in other things. Soon 7 you will be hearing of the mourner's marriage, the old fellow's marriage, the first coming too early and the second too late. On what do I 8 base my prophecy? Not on any statement of Regulus—nothing is more untrue than that—but Regulus is sure to do what should not be done. Farewell.

3 *To his friend Arrius Antoninus* 104

Your tenure of two consulships in a manner reminiscent of leaders of 1 old, your proconsulship of Asia, matched by few others before or since (your modesty does not permit me to claim that there is not one), your pre-eminence, too, in the state in integrity, authority, and ripe years—these are august and splendid achievements. But for myself, I admire you even more for your activities in retirement. To 2 season that stern demeanour with matching amiability, to combine such friendliness with the height of seriousness, is as difficult as it is impressive. This you achieve in your conversation, agreeable beyond belief, and conspicuously in your writing; for when you speak, that 3 honey of Homer's fabled ancient* seems to issue forth, and as for your writings, the bees seem to fill and to entwine them with the sweetness of the blossoms.

Such at any rate was the effect on me in my recent reading of your
4 Greek epigrams and your iambic mimes. What culture, what charm
they embody, how agreeable and affecting they are! What clarity, what
propriety lie in them! I thought that I was handling Callimachus or
Herodas,* or such as is better than these—yet neither of these poets
5 wrote, or sought to write, poetry in both genres. To think that a
Roman can be so at home in Greek! I could swear that Athens herself
could not be so Attic!

Need I say more? I am envious of the Greeks, for you have
chosen to write in their language. There is no need to hazard what
you can express in your native tongue, since you have achieved
such outstanding productions in this alien and imported language.
Farewell.

4 *To his friend Sosius Senecio*

1 I have the greatest affection for Varisidius Nepos,* a diligent, upright,
and eloquent man; these qualities weigh most heavily with me. He is
a close relative of Gaius Calvisius,* my boon-companion and your
2 friend, for he is the son of his sister. I am requesting you to ennoble
him with a six-months' tribunate,* both for his own sake and for that
of his uncle. You will render a service to our friend Calvisius and to
Nepos himself, who is as worthy to be in your debt as you consider
3 myself to be. You have bestowed many kindnesses on many people; I
would presume to claim that you have awarded one to no one more
deserving, and to very few equally so. Farewell.

5 *To his friend Julius Sparsus*

1 The story goes* that, at the request of the Rhodians, Aeschines read a
speech of his own and then one by Demosthenes. Both were greeted
2 with tumultuous applause. I am not surprised that the written versions of these great men were greeted in this way, for recently men
of the greatest learning listened to a speech of mine* with the
same enthusiasm, approval, and also sustained concentration—for it
lasted two days—and this in spite of the fact that no comparison, no
competition, so to say, between this and some other speech stirred
3 the interest of the audience. The Rhodians were roused both by
the merits of the speeches themselves and by the challenge of the

comparison, whereas my speech won approval without the attraction of rivalry. Whether this reception was deserved, you will know once you read the written version, for its length does not permit me the preface of a longer letter. I must be brief at least where I can, so as to 4 win greater pardon for the expanded length of the speech itself, though its length does not outgrow the importance of the case itself. Farewell.

6 *To his friend Julius Naso*

Etruria has been battered by hail, and the report from across the Po* 1 is of a bumper harvest but with prices correspondingly dirt-cheap. My Laurentine estate* alone offers a return. In fact, I have nothing 2 there but the house and garden, and the beach immediately beyond. None the less, it is my only profitable property, for there I write a lot, and cultivate not my non-existent land but myself with my studies. Already I can show you a full cupboard of papers, the equivalent of a full granary elsewhere. So if you are keen on a reliable and rewarding 3 property, purchase something here! Farewell.

7 *To his friend Catius Lepidus*   *c.*104

I often tell you of the native energy possessed by Regulus.* It is 1 remarkable how he achieves whatever he embarks upon. He decided to mourn his son;* he mourns like no other. He decided to have the greatest possible number of statues and portraits of his son made; he sets to work on this in every studio, and has him fashioned in colours, wax, bronze, silver, gold, ivory, and marble. Recently he 2 gathered a huge audience, and declaimed a biography of his son. It was a mere boy's life, but he none the less declaimed it. He had a thousand copies transcribed and dispatched throughout Italy and the provinces. He wrote letters to the authorities, asking town council-lors to choose from among them their most articulate member to read each out before the citizens. This was done.

If he had directed this energy (or by whatever term you are to call 3 that determination to achieve whatever you want) towards better aims, how much good he could have achieved! But good men have less of that energy than evil ones, and just as 'ignorance breeds daring, while reflection breeds hesitation',* so a sense of restraint

4 weakens decent minds, while daring strengthens the corrupt. Regulus exemplifies this. He has weak lungs, clouded utterance, a hesitant tongue, the dullest imagination, and a non-existent memory*—in short, nothing but the brain of a madman—yet by his shamelessness and that very craziness he has attained a reputation as an orator.

5 So to describe him Herennius Senecio* turned Cato's definition* marvellously on its head: 'An orator is a wicked man unskilled at speaking.' I swear that Cato himself did not define the true orator as well as Senecio defined Regulus.

6 Is there some way you can do me an equal favour with a letter to match this? There is, if you write to tell me whether any of my friends in your township, or even you yourself, have had to read out, like some hawker in the Forum, this woeful book of Regulus. In Demosthenes' words,* 'raising your voice exultantly,and shouting

7 lustily'. For that book is so idiotic that it can rouse laughter rather than grief. You would think that it had been composed not about a boy, but by a boy! Farewell.

8 *To his friend Arrianus Maturus* 104

1 You congratulate me on my admission to the augurate.* You do well to congratulate me; first, because it is a splendid thing to merit the decision from our most dignified emperor, and secondly, since the priesthood itself is not only ancient and sacred, but is clearly hal-

2 lowed and celebrated because it is retained for life. Whereas other positions* are virtually equal in distinction, they are withdrawn as well as awarded. But for the augurate, fortune can play a part only in the possible award.

3 I regard the appointment as deserving of congratulation also because I have taken the place of Julius Frontinus,* an outstanding citizen, who nominated me for a priesthood every year without a break on the day for nominations. It was as if he was co-opting me in his place, and now the outcome has confirmed this in such a way that it has seemed not to have happened by chance.

4 You comment that you are especially pleased with my augurate because Cicero was an augur, and you are delighted that in honours I am following in the footsteps of him whom I am keen to emulate in

5 my writings. I pray that just as I have attained the same priesthood and the consulship at a much earlier age* than he did, so I may at least

in old age match his talent in some degree. Assuredly, however, 6 distinctions which are at the disposal of men may come to me as to many, but to match his talent is difficult and too much to expect, for it can be bestowed only by the gods. Farewell.

9 *To his friend Cornelius Ursus* 103

Julius Bassus,* a man struggling and celebrated in adversity, has in 1 recent days been standing trial. In Vespasian's time he was indicted by two private citizens; after being referred to the Senate, his case lay for a long time in abeyance, but he was finally acquitted and discharged. As a friend of Domitian, he felt endangered under Titus, 2 and was then relegated by Domitian. After being recalled by Nerva, he obtained the province of Bithynia, and was indicted on his return. The accusation against him was as vehement as his defence was conscientious. The voting was divided, but the majority inclined to mercy.

Pomponius Rufus was the prosecutor, a ready and forceful speaker 3 and Theophanes,* one of the Bithynian ambassadors, the firebrand and originator of the indictment, was his second string. I spoke for 4 the other side, for Bassus had imposed on me the task of laying the foundations of the entire defence. I was to speak of his positive qualities,* which were many, arising from the fame of his lineage and from the hazardous processes he had undergone. I was to speak of 5 the plotting of the informers,* which they were seeking to exploit for gain. I was to speak of the reasons why he had alienated all those most turbulent agitators such as Theophanes himself. Bassus had wanted me also to confront the most serious charge hanging over him, for though the other accusations* sounded more serious, he was on those counts deserving not merely of acquittal but also of praise.

What weighed heavily on this naive and unthinking person was 6 that he had received as a friend certain presents from provincials (for he had been quaestor* in that same province). His accusers labelled these thefts and plunder, while he called them gifts. But the law forbids the acceptance even of gifts. On this issue what was I to do? 7 What line should I take in his defence? Was I to deny the accusation? I feared that to admit it would be seen as acknowledging blatant theft. In addition, denial of a clear act would aggravate the charge rather than diminish it, especially as the defendant himself had not left his lawyers with *carte blanche*, for he had told many people, including the emperor himself, that the only small gifts he had received were on his birthday and at the Saturnalia,* when he had himself sent presents to several persons.

8   So was I to plead for pardon? I would have cut the defendant's throat if I had admitted that his guilt was so clear-cut that pardon alone could save him. Was I to defend his action as above board? That would have been no help to him, but would have exposed me as
9 bare-faced. Confronted with the problem, I decided to hold a middle course, and I think that I succeeded.

   My speech (as happens with battles too) was interrupted by night-fall. I had spoken for three and a half hours, with an hour and a half still available, for though the law* had permitted an accuser six hours and a defendant nine, the defendant had divided the time between myself and my seconder, so that I was to speak for five hours, and he
10 was to take up the rest. The success of my speech counselled me to opt for silence and to say no more, for it is rash not to be content with what has gone well. Moreover, I feared that my physical strength* would fail me if I again shouldered the burden, for it is more difficult
11 to resume a speech than to continue with one. There was the further danger that the rest of my speech when abandoned would induce a cold response, and when resumed would cause weariness. Take the parallel of a torch. It keeps its flame alive when continually shaken, but once put down it becomes very difficult to restore. In the same way the heat of a speaker and the concentration of a listener are maintained when unbroken, but weaken if there is an intermission
12 and relaxation. But Bassus implored me with repeated pleas, even almost to the point of tears, that I should take up my allotted time. So I complied, and put his interests before my own. It worked out well. I found the Senate's attention as lively and as fresh as if they had been roused rather than glutted by my previous speech.

13   Lucceius Albinus* took over from me so appropriately that our speeches are thought to have contained the variation of two orations
14 but the coherence of one. Herennius Pollio* made a forceful and dignified reply, and Theophanes again followed. He delivered this speech like the others with utter shamelessness, for though he was following after two speakers who were both ex-consuls and eloquent orators, he claimed his time somewhat too generously. He spoke until

darkness fell, and even as night drew on, for lamps were brought in. Next day Homullus and Fronto* spoke wonderfully well on behalf of 15 Bassus, and the evidence of witnesses took up a fourth day.

Baebius Macer, the consul-designate, proposed that Bassus should 16 be committed under the law of extortion, and Caepio Hispo* that assessors should be appointed without Bassus' loss of status. Both proposals were justified. 'How can that be,' you ask, 'when their 17 proposals were so different?' The answer is that Macer, following the law, regarded it as appropriate to condemn one who had illegally accepted gifts, while Caepio, since he believed that the Senate had the power (as in fact it has) both to soften and to intensify the rigour of the law, had some justification in proposing pardon of an action which was admittedly forbidden, but was not without precedent. Caepio's view prevailed; indeed, on rising to make his proposal he 18 was greeted with the applause usually accorded to speakers when they resume their seats. From this you can gather how wholehearted was the reception given to his words since there was such support when he seemed about to speak.

However, in the community at large as in the Senate, people's 19 views were divided. Those who favoured Caepio's proposal censured that of Macer as unbending and harsh, while those who agreed with Macer called the alternative proposal wishy-washy and also illogical, their argument being that it is unfitting for a man to remain a senator if assessors have been nominated to deal with him. There was also a 20 third proposal. Valerius Paulinus,* agreeing with Caepio, further recommended that, once Theophanes had reported on his embassy, he should be investigated, for it was claimed that in the course of the prosecution many of his actions made him liable under the very same law as that under which he had indicted Bassus. But the consuls did 21 not pursue this proposal,* in spite of the fact that it gained remarkable support from most of the Senate. However, Paulinus gained a 22 reputation for fair dealing and integrity.

When the Senate was discharged, Bassus was welcomed by a huge crowd of people making a great din and demonstrating great joy. The renewal of the long-standing saga of the dangers he had undergone had brought him popularity, as did his name, widely known for the hazards he had endured, and the unhappy and unsightly appearance of his aged and lofty frame.

This letter will be for you *un avant-coureur*, for you are to await 23 the full and substantial speech which follows. Your wait will be lengthy, for revision of such an important case cannot be undertaken lightly and speedily. Farewell.

10 *To his friend Statius Sabinus*

1 You inform me that Sabina,* who has left us as her heirs, has nowhere instructed us that her slave Modestus should be freed, but that she had left him a legacy with the appendage: 'To Modestus, whom I 2 have ordered to be freed.' You seek my opinion. I have conferred with legal experts, all of whom are agreed that he should not be freed, since his freedom has not been granted, and that a legacy is not his due since Sabina awarded it to him as her slave. But this seems clearly mistaken,* so I think that we should act as if Sabina had 3 written what she herself believed she had written. I am sure that you will fall in with my opinion, for you are always most scrupulous in observing dead persons' wishes, the understanding of which is for decent heirs as good as a law, and with us honourable conduct is no 4 less binding than is necessity with others. So let us allow Modestus to dwell in freedom and to enjoy his legacy as if Sabina had taken every careful precaution; in fact, she did take such precautions by her good choice of heirs. Farewell.

11 *To his friend Cornelius Minicianus*

1 Have you heard that Valerius Licinianus* is practising his profession in Sicily? I imagine that you have not yet heard this, for the news is fresh. Only recently this praetorian was regarded as one of the most eloquent pleaders, but now he has slumped to becoming an exile from being a senator, and a teacher of rhetoric from being an orator. 2 So in his prefatory remarks he stated sadly and heavily: 'What sport you have with us, Fortune, converting senators into teachers, and teachers into senators!'* There is so much anger, so much bitterness in this aphorism that he seems to me to have become a teacher in 3 order to say it. When he made his entry wearing a Greek cloak (for those who have been 'debarred from water and fire'* are not granted the right to wear a toga), he settled himself, surveyed his clothing, and said: 'I intend to deliver my speech in Latin.'

4   You will say that this was a melancholy and pitiable sight, but that

he deserved it for blackening those studies with the crime of sexual
impurity. He admitted this charge, but it is not clear that he did so 5
because it was true, or because he feared graver charges if he denied
it. For Domitian was raging and seething at being left high and dry
amid strong feelings of odium. He had wanted to bury Cornelia, 6
chief of the Vestals, alive* in his plan to add lustre to his era by
deterrents of this kind. So by his right as chief priest, or rather by his
monstrous behaviour as tyrant and by his free rein as despot, he
summoned the other priests, not to the Regia,* but to his Alban
residence. He then perpetrated a crime no less wicked than that
which he appeared to be avenging. He condemned Cornelia,* absent
and unheard, for sexual impurity, though he himself had not merely
defiled his brother's daughter* sexually, but had also killed her, for
that widow died as a result of an abortion. Priests were immediately 7
dispatched* to arrange the burial and the murder of Cornelia. She
stretched out her hands, now to Vesta, now to the other deities
with repeated cries, and most frequently with these words: 'Caesar
believes me guilty of sexual depravity, though through my conduct
of the ritual he has won victories and triumphs!'

It is not clear whether she uttered these words in flattery or in 8
derision of the emperor. She repeated them until she was led out to
her death. Whether innocent or not, she certainly behaved as though 9
innocent. Indeed, when she was escorted down into the underground
chamber, and her robe caught up on her way down, as she turned and
freed it, and the executioner offered her his hand, she turned away
and recoiled from him, rejecting his foul touch with a final gesture of
chastity, as if her person was demonstrably pure and spotless. With
successive movements of modesty, 'she took elaborate care to sink
down with due decorum'.* In addition, Celer,* a Roman knight, who 10
was charged with being a partner with Cornelia, as he was scourged
in public, repeatedly said: 'What have I done? I have done nothing.'

The outcome was that Domitian was livid, owing to the notoriety 11
incurred by his cruelty and injustice. He had Licinianus arrested,
because he had hidden a freedwoman* of Cornelia on his estate. He
was forewarned by responsible officials that if he wished to avoid
being scourged in public, he should have recourse to a confession as 12
a means of obtaining pardon. He complied. Herennius Senecio*
pleaded for him in his absence, adopting the 'Patroclus is dead'
technique:* 'I have become not an advocate but a messenger;

13 Licinianus has withdrawn.' Domitian welcomed this so enthusiastic-
ally that his joy betrayed him, and he said: 'Licinianus has acquitted
me!' He added that there was no need to harry him in his shame, and
indeed he allowed him to grab whatever he could of his possessions
before the confiscation of his goods, and he awarded him the mild
14 form of exile* as a sort of reward. However, through the clemency of
the deified Nerva, he was allowed to move from his place of exile to
Sicily, where he is now teaching, and in his forewords to his lectures
taking revenge on Fortune.

15   You observe how obediently I obey you, for I write to you not only
about affairs in Rome but also about those abroad with such diligence, harking back to earlier events. I believed in fact that because
you were away at the time, you had heard nothing about Licinianus
beyond the fact that he had been relegated for sexual depravity.

16 Common gossip reports the gist but not the sequence of events. I
deserve in turn to obtain from you an account of what is happening
in your town and neighbourhood (for noteworthy events often do
occur). In short, report whatever you like, as long as your letter is as
lengthy as mine. I shall count not only the pages, but also the lines
and the syllables! Farewell.

12 *To his friend Arrianus Maturus*   105

1 You are fond of Egnatius Marcellinus,* and you also often recommend him to me. You will love and recommend him all the more
2 once you learn of his recent action. After he had left for his province
as quaestor there, the scribe who had been assigned to him by lot
died before his salary was legally payable. He had been given the
money to hand over to the scribe. He understood and decided that it
3 should not remain in his charge. So on his return he consulted
Caesar,* and then on Caesar's authorization the Senate, on what they
wished him to do with the money.

The inquiry was minor, but was none the less an inquiry. The
scribe's heirs claimed it for themselves, while the prefects of the trea-
4 sury claimed it for the people. The case came to court. The lawyer
for the heirs spoke first, followed by the advocate for the state; both
spoke admirably. Caecilius Strabo proposed that the money be paid
into the treasury, and Baebius Macer* that it should go to the heirs.
Strabo gained the day.

You must applaud Marcellinus, as I did on the spot, for though the 5
approval he has gained from both emperor and Senate is more than
ample, he will be delighted to have your corroboration; for all who are 6
impelled by fame and repute evince surprising pleasure at applause
and praise emanating even from lesser men. In fact, Marcellinus
has such lofty respect for you that he holds your judgement in the
highest regard. And besides, if he becomes aware that news of his 7
action has travelled so far, he must inevitably be pleased that his
praises are sung so widely and swiftly as they journey abroad.* Somehow or other, men take more pleasure from widespread than from
resounding praise. Farewell.

13 *To his friend Cornelius Tacitus* *c.*104

I am delighted that you have reached the city safely. Your arrival has 1
come at a time when, if ever, I was most eagerly longing to see you. I
shall be staying for a very few further days on this Tusculan estate,*
to complete a little work which I have on hand, for I fear that if I 2
relax my concentration, now that it is almost finished, I may find it
hard to take it up again. But in the meantime, so that the matter may
lose none of its urgency, I am asking in this letter (which is, so to say,
hastening before me) for a favour which I intend to ask of you face to
face. But first you must hear the reasons for the request.

Recently I was in my native region* when the young son of a fellow 3
citizen of mine came to greet me. I asked him: 'Are you a student?'*
He replied: 'Yes.' 'Where?' I asked. 'At Milan,' he said. 'Why not
here?' I asked. Then his father, who was with him (he had in fact
brought him along), answered: 'Because we have no teachers here.'
'Why are there none? Surely it is very much in the interests of you 4
fathers here' (several of them were conveniently listening) 'that your
children should learn here rather than elsewhere. Where could they
reside more happily than on their native soil? Where could their
morals be better safeguarded than under their parents' eyes?* Where
could they live at less expense than at home? Surely it would be 5
inexpensive to hire teachers, if you put your money together,
and add towards their salaries what you now lay out on lodgings,
travelling-expenses, and purchases away from home (for you have to
buy everything when away from home)? As I do not as yet have any
children,* I am ready to contribute a third of what you raise together

6　as a gift to my native region as if it were a daughter or a parent. I
would pledge the entire sum if I did not fear that this gift of mine
might at some time be misused by canvassing for the posts, for I see
this happening in many places where teachers are hired at public
7　expense.* This failing can be confronted by one remedy only, namely,
if the right to hire is left to the parents alone, and the duty of making
the right choice is imposed on them by their need to contribute the
8　funds. People who are perhaps careless with other people's money
will at any rate be judicious with their own, and they will ensure that
only a deserving person obtains money from me if he is to obtain it
9　also from them. So make common agreement and work together.
Show greater initiative from my example, for I desire the sum I must
contribute to be as large as possible. You can grant nothing worthier
to your children, and nothing more welcome to your native region.
Let children who are born here be educated here. Let them from
their earliest childhood grow used to loving and thronging their
native region. I only hope that you bring in teachers so celebrated
that students from neighbouring towns come here for their learning;
and just as now your children flock to other areas, so in the near
future may students from other areas flock here!'

10　I thought that I should recount these details from earlier on and
from the start to allow you to realize what a favour it would be to me
if you undertook what I seek to impose on you. What I impose and
beg of you, in view of the importance of this matter, is that you cast
your eye around the horde of students who surround you* in admiration of your talent, and look for teachers whom we can inveigle
here, but on condition that I do not bind myself with pledges to
anyone. The reason for this is that I am leaving the choice entirely to
the parents. They must pass judgement and choose; I confine my
11　role to supervision of the project and my contribution. So if anyone
emerges who has confidence in his ability, he must go there on condition that he takes nothing from here except his own self-confidence.
Farewell.

14 *To his friend Paternus*

1　You are perhaps both demanding and anticipating a speech from me,
as you usually are, but I am bringing out for you from my outlandish
2　and frivolous stock some trifles of mine. With this letter you will

receive my hendecasyllables,* with which I beguile my leisure-time
when in my carriage, or in the bath, or during dinner. In these I ₃
incorporate my joking and my sport, my affection and my grief, my
complaints and my irritations. I treat a topic at one time with some
restraint, and at another in more elevated style,* and by this very
variety I try to ensure that different pieces attract different people,
and that some of them please everyone.

If several of these poems seem to you rather too coarse, your ₄
learning must cause you to reflect that those outstanding and highly
serious men who wrote verses like these avoided neither wanton
topics nor even explicit language. I have drawn back from such
treatment, not because I am too puritanical (why should I be?), but
because I am too cowardly. Yet in general I know that the most ₅
authentic rule of thumb for this lesser activity is that which Catullus
formulated:*

> True poets must themselves be chaste;
> Their verses need not be so clean.
> Such wit and charm they only have
> If they are pathic and obscene.

You can infer the value which I place on your judgement from the ₆
very fact that I have preferred you to assess them in their entirety,
rather than accord praise to selected pieces. Indeed, those pieces
which are most agreeable cease to appear so, once they begin to be
comparable with others. Moreover, the shrewd and subtle reader ₇
ought not to compare poems of different kinds, but judge them
individually, without regarding one that is perfect in its own category
as inferior to another.

But why should I say more? It is the height of foolishness to ₈
excuse or to recommend one's tomfooleries in an extended preamble.
The one foreword which seems necessary is that I intend to entitle
these trifles of mine 'hendecasyllables', a heading confined solely to
the discipline of the metre. So you can call them epigrams, or idylls, ₉
or eclogues, or short poems* as many do, or anything else you prefer;
I present them merely as 'hendecasyllables'. I ask you to be straightforward, and to tell me what your comments to a third party about
my book will be. My request is not difficult, for if this lesser work ₁₀
were my main or my sole literary achievement, it could perhaps seem
brutal to say: 'Look for something worth working on.' A gentle and

kindly formulation is: 'You have something worth working on.'
Farewell.

15 *To his friend Minicius Fundanus*

1 If there is one thing in the world which I count as my considered
view, it is my unique fondness for Asinius Rufus.* He is an outstanding person who has the greatest regard for decent men—for why
should I not reckon myself as one of them? He has moreover joined
to himself Cornelius Tacitus (you know the sort of man he is) in
2 close friendship. So, if you approve of both of us, you must take the
same view of Rufus, since similarity of character is certainly the most
tenacious bond in the establishment of friendships.

3 He has several children, for in this way, too, he has discharged the
obligation of the best of citizens. This is because he has sought to
exploit generously the fertility of his wife in an era in which the
rewards of childlessness make many regard even one child as a
burden.* He has despised their attitude, and has adopted the role
of grandfather in addition. For he is a grandfather; it is Saturius
Firmus* who has made him so, and you will feel affection for him as I
do, if like me you get to know him more closely.

4 All this is germane to your becoming aware of what a large and
numerous household you will oblige by a single act of kindness,
which I am led to seek initially in hope, but in addition by a kind of
5 good omen. I pray and prophesy that you will become consul next
year,* for both your merits and the emperor's appraisal tend to foretell
6 this. Coincidentally, in the same year the eldest of Rufus' sons,
Asinius Bassus, becomes quaestor.* He is a young man better even
than his father (I hesitate to claim this, but his father is anxious for
me to believe and state it, though the young man's modesty forbids
7 it). It is not easy for me to make you believe this of one you do not
know (though you habitually believe all I tell you), but he possesses
all the diligence and honesty, learning and talent, and finally application and memory, as you will find upon acquaintance with him.

8 I could wish that our era was so fertile in good qualities that you
would be obliged to prefer some other men to Bassus. I should in
that case be the first to encourage and advise you to cast your eye
9 round, and to ponder the best possible choice to make. As things
stand, however—but I am unwilling to speak too boastfully of my

friend. My only claim is that the young man is worthy of adoption by you as your son, after the fashion of our ancestors.* Men of wisdom like yourself should acknowledge as sons conferred by the state the sort to which we are wont to aspire as gifts of nature. It will be a 10 feather in your cap as consul to have as quaestor the son of a praetor, one whose relatives are consulars and who, in their judgement, though as yet a mere stripling, already in turn lends distinction to the family. So favour my prayers, fall in with my advice, and above all 11 pardon me if I seem to be over-hasty. The reason for this is because, to begin with, affection usually runs ahead of its desires, and secondly, in a state in which all business is conducted by those in possession, proposals which await their lawful time do not come to maturity, but arrive too late. And lastly, anticipation of what you long to achieve is itself a pleasure. Let Bassus at this time venerate you as consul; 12 become fond of him as your quaestor, and finally allow me, who have the utmost affection for both of you, to enjoy a twofold happiness. My affection for both you and Bassus is such that I intend to aid him 13 under any consul and your quaestor (whoever he may be), with all my resources, toil, and influence in his bid for high position. But it will give me considerable pleasure if consideration of both my friendship and your consulship bestows my support on that same young man—if, in short, you above all come to my aid in answer to my prayers, for the Senate most gladly defers to your decisions and puts the greatest trust in your testimony. Farewell.

16 *To his friend Valerius Paulinus*

Rejoice for me, for yourself, and for our state, because respect is still 1 paid to the intellectual life. The other day when I was due to speak in the Centumviral court, I could make my way through from the tribunal only by passing through the judges, for the rest of the court was swamped by a large crush of people. Moreover, a young man of 2 some distinction had his tunic torn, as often happens in a crowd, but he stayed on, clad only in his toga, for a full seven hours. For that 3 was the length of my speech,* delivered with much sweat and to much effect. So we must knuckle down, and not make other people's idleness an excuse for our own. Some come to listen, and some read;* all that we have to do is to beaver away at producing something worth hearing, and something worth the paper it is written on. Farewell.

17 *To his friend Clusinius Gallus* early 105

1 You remind and request me to undertake the case of Corellia* in her absence against the consul-designate, Gaius Caecilius.* Thank you for the reminder, but I resent your request, for while I need the reminder to be put in the picture, there is no need to ask me to do
2 something which it would be an utter disgrace not to do. Surely I cannot hesitate to defend a daughter of Corellius?* True, I am friendly with the man whom you urge me to oppose, though not a
3 close confidant. But in addition, there is his high status and the distinguished office* for which he is designated, towards which I must show respect all the greater because I have already discharged it. For it is a law of nature to desire that greater recognition be accorded to a
4 status which a person has himself attained. However, all these concerns seem flat and trivial to me when I reflect that it is the daughter of Corellius whom I am to support.

I see before my eyes the image of a man as dignified, venerable, and gifted as any which our age has produced. My admiration caused the growth of my affection for him, and contrary to one's usual experience, close acquaintance caused me to admire him still
5 more. For I did make that close acquaintance. He kept nothing hid-
6 den from me, sportive or serious, melancholy or joyful. I was a mere stripling, yet even then he showed me the regard and even, I shall presume to say, the respect accorded to an equal. When I was seeking offices, he became my sponsor and witness; when I embarked upon them, my escort and companion; when I wielded them, my counsellor and guide. In short, in every office I held, though he was then both enfeebled and elderly, he made himself as conspicuous as one
7 with youth and strength. How greatly he enhanced my reputation, both domestic and public; how greatly he furthered it even with the emperor.
8 For when there chanced to be some discussion in the presence of the emperor Nerva about young men of quality, and several people were praising me, for a moment or two Corellius maintained the silence which lent him additional authority in abundance. Then, in that dignified tone that you know well, he said: 'I must be more sparing in my praise of Secundus, because he does nothing without
9 taking my advice.' With these words he paid me a compliment to which it would have been excessive to aspire, for he implied that I

did nothing which was not conspicuously wise, for my every action followed the advice of the wisest of men. Then even when he was dying he told his daughter, as she often remarks: 'Through the benefit of a longer life I have gained many friends for you, but above all Secundus and Cornutus.'*

When I recall these words, I realize I must labour hard to ensure 10 that I do not appear to have betrayed in any respect the trust of that most far-seeing man. So I shall indeed represent Corellia with the 11 greatest enthusiasm, nor shall I refuse to incur resentment thereby. However, I think I shall elicit not only pardon, but also praise from the one who is, as you say, bringing a form of action which is perhaps novel because directed against a woman, if in this court case, whether to win justification or even commendation, I express these sentiments more broadly and more fully than the confines of a letter allow. Farewell.

18 *To his friend Arrius Antoninus*

How can I offer you clearer proof of my great admiration for your 1 Greek epigrams than by my attempt to imitate and render them in Latin? But they fall below your standard. The first reason for this is the feebleness of my talent, and secondly there is the dearth, or better, as Lucretius puts it,* the poverty of our native tongue. But if 2 these renderings of mine into Latin seem to you to possess some charm, how pleasing you must regard those which you published in Greek! Farewell.

19 *To his friend Calpurnia Hispulla*   *c.*105

You are a model of family devotion, and you loved your splendid 1 brother, matching his deep regard for you with equal affection. You love his daughter as if she were your own, and to her you re-enact the fondness not only of an aunt, but also that of the father she has lost.* For these reasons I have no doubt that you will be highly delighted to know that she is turning out worthy of her father, of you, and of her grandfather. She is highly intelligent, and exceedingly thrifty. Her 2 love for me is the index of her chastity. These qualities are enhanced by her enthusiasm for literature, which her love for me has fostered. She possesses and repeatedly reads and even memorizes my books.

3 What concern she shows when I am due to speak in court! And what delight, once the speech is finished! She posts individuals to report to her the assent and the applause which I have received, and the outcome which I have imposed on the judge.

Whenever I am giving a recitation, she sits close by, concealed by a

4 curtain, and listens most avidly to the praises heaped on me. She also sings my verses and adapts them to the lyre, with no schooling from a music-master, but with affection, which is the best possible teacher.

5 For these reasons I entertain the most sanguine hope that we will enjoy enduring harmony which will grow day by day. It is not my time of life or my body which she loves,* for these gradually decay

6 with age, but my fame. No other attitude befits one reared by your hands and trained by your instructions, for in her association with you she has set eyes only on what is pure and honourable, and finally she has grown to love me as the outcome of your recommendation.

7 For out of your respect for my mother,* whom you revered as a parent, you fashioned and encouraged me from my earliest boyhood, and you were wont to prophesy that I would become the sort of per-

8 son I appear to be in my wife's eyes. So we vie in giving you thanks— I because you have given her to me, and she because you have given me to her. It is as though you chose us for each other! Farewell.

20 *To his friend Novius Maximus*

1 I informed you of my reactions to each of your volumes* when I had perused them individually; now listen to my general judgement of

2 them in the round. The work is splendid, powerful, acute, and sublime. The language is varied, elegant, unsullied, rich in metaphor. It is also expansive, covering a broad canvas, which will bring you great applause. You have been borne along on your wide-ranging course by the sails of your talent and your resentment,* each of which lent

3 aid to the other. For talent has enhanced resentment with sublimity and grandeur, and resentment has added power and bitterness to your talent. Farewell.

21 *To his friend Velius Cerialis* c.105

1 What a sad and bitter misfortune has befallen the Helvidian sisters!*

2 Both have died in childbirth, each having given birth to a girl. I

grieve, but my grief is within bounds. It is a cause for lamentation that girls of the highest calibre have been cut off by their fertility in the first flower of youth. I mourn for the lot of the children, bereft of their mothers at the moment of birth; I mourn for their noble husbands, and I mourn on my own account, for with the greatest 3 constancy I have continued to love their father too since his death,* as my speech on his behalf and my books* attest.

Now only one of the three children survives, left alone as the stay and prop of a household which shortly before had the firm foundation of several supports. But my sorrow will find great solace and 4 repose if Fortune preserves him at least, strong and safe, as one equal to his famous father and famous grandfather. I am all the more concerned for his well-being and manners, because he has become the sole survivor. You know how soft-hearted and fearful I am in 5 my affections, which must make you less surprised that my fear is greatest for him in whom my hopes are highest. Farewell.

22 *To his friend Sempronius Rufus*   *c.*105

I have been present at a hearing held by our emperor, best of men, 1 for I was called in as assessor. Gymnastic games were held at Vienna* as a result of some person's bequest, and Trebonius Rufinus, an outstanding man who is a friend of mine, in his capacity as a city-magistrate* has caused them to be abandoned and abolished. It was claimed that he had no public authority to have done this. Rufinus 2 conducted his own case with a success which matched his eloquence. What won approval of his speech was his speaking on an issue of personal concern in a considered and dignified manner as a Roman and a good citizen.

When the judges were asked for their verdicts, Junius Mauricus,* a 3 man as steadfast and honest as can be, stated that the games should not be restored for the Viennese, and he added: 'I only wish that they could be abolished at Rome as well.' Firmly and bravely said, you 4 remark. Of course, but this is nothing new from Mauricus. He spoke no less courageously in the presence of the emperor Nerva, who was dining with a few people. Veiento* was next to him, and snuggled up against him—mention of the man says it all. Catullus Messalinus* 5 was mentioned in the course of conversation. He had lost the sight of his eyes, and the handicap of his blindness had intensified his savage

disposition. He showed no fear, shame, or pity, which was why Domitian would deploy him, like darts fired blindly and without
6 consideration, against each and every honourable man. All at table were discussing together Messalinus' wickedness and his blood-soaked views, when the emperor himself remarked: 'If he had gone on living, what do we think would have befallen him?' Mauricus said: 'He would be dining with us.'

7 I have diverged quite a way from my starting point, but deliberately so. It was decided to abolish the games, for they had corrupted the morals of the Viennese, just as our games here at Rome infect those of everyone. For while the vices of the Viennese are confined to their citizens, those of the Romans wander far and wide. As in the human body, so in the Empire at large the most serious disease is that which spreads down from the head. Farewell.

23 *To his friend Pomponius Bassus*

1 I was greatly pleased to discover from friends we share that in a manner worthy of your wisdom you are organizing your leisure and coping with it, living in a most beautiful region, exercising your body on both land and sea, participating in many discussions, listening a great deal, and reading and rereading a great deal, and though you
2 are a polymath, learning something new each day. This is the ideal old age* for a man who has held highly distinguished magistracies, commanded armies, and devoted himself wholly to the state for so
3 long as it was fitting. For we must devote our early and middle years to our native land, and our closing years to ourselves; this is what the laws prescribe* for us, for they restore a man when he is older in
4 years to a life of leisure. When will I be allowed to conform to this, when will I reach the age at which it will be honourable for me to imitate the example you set of living in most idyllic peace? When will my periods of relaxation away from Rome gain the title of peaceful repose rather than idleness? Farewell.

24 *To his friend Fabius Valens*   *c.*104

1 After I had spoken recently in a civil case before the four panels* of the Centumviral court, the thought occurred to me that as a young
2 man I had spoken similarly before the combined panels. As often

happens, my thoughts advanced further, and I began to recall with what associates I had shared the toil in this case and in that earlier one. I was the only one to have spoken in both. Such are the great changes introduced by the frailty of the human condition or the fickleness of Fortune. Some who had spoken earlier have died, and 3 others are in exile. Old age and illness have imposed silence on one, while another enjoys the great happiness of leisure. One man is commanding an army, while another has been diverted to duties of state through friendship with the emperor.*

In my own case, how numerous the changes have been! My 4 speech-making* has brought me advancement, then danger, and again advancement. My friendship with honourable men has benefited me, 5 thwarted me, and now again benefits me. If you calculate the years, you would regard it as a short period, but if you survey the changes of situation, it seems a lifetime. This can be a lesson to us not to lose 6 heart, nor again to repose trust in any situation, since we see such numerous changes in such an unstable round of events.

It is my regular practice to share with you all my thoughts, and to 7 advise you, following the same principles and examples with which I advise myself. This was the reason for this letter. Farewell.

25 *To his friend Maesius Maximus* 105

I earlier wrote to you that we must be chary in case the secret voting 1 might lead to some abuse. This has occurred. At the recent elections* several tablets were found to have many witticisms and disgusting comments inscribed on them. One of them contained the names of the campaigners* instead of the candidates! The Senate was furious, 2 and with loud cries implored the anger of the emperor against the man who had inscribed them. But the culprit cheated them and escaped detection; perhaps he was even one of the protesters!

What are we to think of that man's behaviour in private, seeing 3 that he deploys offensive wit at such a solemn moment and in such an important matter, one who, in short, in the Senate of all places is such a smart and elegant and fine fellow? In depraved minds such 4 permissive behaviour is reinforced by the self-assurance of 'For who will know?' That man asked for a tablet, obtained a pen, and bent his head. He has no fear of anyone, and no respect for himself. So we get 5 these mockeries worthy of the stage-shows. Where does one go from here? What remedies is one to seek? In whatever direction you go, the abuses are stronger than the remedies. 'But he who is over us will take care of that.'* His taxing vigilance day by day and his heavy labours are intensified by this sluggish yet lunatic scurrility of ours. Farewell.

26 *To his friend Maecilius Nepos*   105

1 You ask me to take in hand the rereading and correction of my volumes, which you have most carefully collected. I shall comply. For what task ought I more gladly to undertake, especially at your
2 demand? When a man like you, most serious, most learned, and most eloquent, one who in addition is most busy and is about to be governor of a massive province,* thinks it so worthwhile to carry my writings with him, I must make every effort to ensure that this item
3 of your baggage does not strike you as superfluous. So I shall try to ensure, first that these your companions are as agreeable as possible, and, secondly, that on your return you may find some which you wish to add to these. The fact that you are a reader is no slight incentive for me to embark on new writings. Farewell.

27 *To his friend Pompeius Falco*   104–5

1 For a third day I have been listening with the utmost pleasure and indeed with admiration to a recitation by Sentius Augurinus.* He calls them his short poems.* Many are composed with simplicity, many in lofty style; many are elegant, many are tender, many are
2 sweet-tempered, and many are cross. In my view no poetry of this type has been composed more competently for many years, unless perhaps I am beguiled either by my affection for him or by his
3 winning me over with his praises. For he has chosen as one theme the fact that I occasionally make sport with verses. I will go so far as to appoint you arbiter of my judgement, if I can recall the second line* of this very epigram, for I remember the rest and have now set the lines down:

4   My songs I sing in these shortened verses,
                   In which long ago my Catullus sang his,
                   As did Calvus and men of old. I don't care!
                   Pliny alone is for me all earlier poets.

> He leaves court behind, prefers to write short verses,
> Seeking a love affair. He believes he is loved.*
> Ho there, Pliny, worth a thousand Catos!
> All with love affairs, you must stop your loving.

You see how sharp and fitting and polished his writing is. I guarantee 5
that the whole book is redolent of this flavour, and I shall send it to
you as soon as he brings it out. Meanwhile show affection to the
young man, and be thankful to our times for such talent, which he
endows with honest manners. He spends time with Spurinna and
with Antoninus;* he is a kinsman of one, and a close friend of both.
From this you can gather how faultless the young man is, since he 6
wins such affection from most dignified elders. That famous saw* is
undoubtedly true, that 'One knows the sort of man he is from those
with whom he loves to associate'. Farewell.

28 *To his friend Vibius Severus*

Herennius Severus,* a man of the greatest learning, thinks it import- 1
ant to have in his library portraits of your fellow townsmen Cornelius
Nepos and Titus Catius.* He requests that if the originals are in your
town, as they are likely to be, that I arrange for them to be copied and
painted in colour. I am delegating this task to you particularly, first, 2
because you always carry out my wishes in a most friendly way;
secondly, because of your intense devotion for literature and your
intense regard for literary men; and finally, because you respect and
love your native soil and likewise all who have enhanced its fame. I 3
beg you to choose a most conscientious painter, for though it is
difficult to fashion a likeness from an actual person, it is supremely
difficult to imitate an imitation. I beg you not to allow the artist you
choose to stray from the original, even to improve it. Farewell.

29 *To his friend Romatius Firmus*　　　　　　　　early 105

Ho there, Romatius! The very next time there is a hearing, you must 1
somehow or other take your place on the judges' bench. There is no
chance of your relying on me to allow you to sleep untroubled. You
won't get away with your idling. Here comes the praetor, Licinius 2
Nepos!* What a keen and courageous praetor he is! He has levied a
fine even from a senator. The senator pleaded his case in the Senate,

pleaded in fact to be let off. The fine was remitted, but he got a
3 fright, had to beg, needed to be pardoned. Your reaction will be:
'Not all praetors are so harsh.' You are in error. True, only harsh
ones can establish or reintroduce such a precedent, but even the
most lenient can apply it, once it is established or reintroduced.
Farewell.

30 *To his friend Licinius Sura*

1 As a small gift from my native region, I have brought you a problem
2 wholly deserving of the boundless depths of your learning. There is
a spring* which rises in a mountain, runs down over rocks, and is
welcomed by a small dining-area which has been built up. There the
water is contained briefly, and then descends into lake Comum. The
remarkable feature of it is that three times each day the water level
3 rises and falls with regular increase and decrease. This is visible to
the naked eye, and affords the greatest pleasure to observe. As you
recline and dine by it, you also drink the water from the spring, for it
is ice-cold. Meanwhile, at fixed and regular intervals the water
4 drains away and fills up. If you place a ring or some other object in
the channel when it is dry, the water gradually laps over it and finally
covers it; then once again it is exposed and is gradually left high and
dry. If you keep watching it for some time, you can see the water
draining and returning once or twice more.

5 Is there some air-pressure which is less visible, and first opens up
and then closes the entrance and jaws of the spring, according as it
confronts the water when it is borne in, and subsides when it is
6 forced out? We see this occur in bottles and other similarly shaped
vessels, which have narrow necks and do not immediately offer
unimpeded passage; for they too, though inclined downwards, delay
the outflow with what we may call frequent hiccups, as the obstruct-
7 ing air causes certain delays. Or is the spring identical in nature with
the ocean, and just as the ocean is driven forward or sucked back, in
the same way is the modest volume of water alternately repressed
8 and forced out? Or just as rivers bearing their waters to the sea are
forced back by opposing winds or on confronting the tide, is there
9 some force that repels the outflow of the spring? Or is there a fixed
measure of water in the spring's hidden channels, and until it
gathers the amount which it has lost, is its flow smaller and more

sluggish, but once gathered, it pours forth in more lively fashion and in greater volume? Or is there some weight of water, lying hidden and unseen, which on being emptied, rouses and summons the spring, and once it is filled up, delays and constricts the water?

Please ponder the reasons behind this extraordinary phenomenon, for you are competent to do so. For my part, it is more than enough if I have sufficiently explained the outcome. Farewell.

BOOK FIVE

1 *To his friend Annius Severus*

1 A legacy has come my way which is modest but more welcome than the largest possible. Why more welcome than the largest? Pomponia Galla had disinherited her son, Asudius Curianus, and had left me as her heir; she had appointed as coheirs Sertorius Severus,* a praetor-

2 ian, and other distinguished Roman knights. Curianus petitioned me to present him with my share, and to aid him by a preliminary inquiry. He promised me that by tacit agreement my share would be

3 safeguarded. I replied that it did not accord with my standards of behaviour to adopt one position openly and another covertly; more-over, that it was not really the decent thing to present money to one who was both wealthy and childless; and finally, it would be of no service to him if I made a present of it, whereas it would be advanta-geous for me to renounce it, as I was ready to do, if it became clear to me that he had been unjustly disinherited.

4 At this, Curianus said: 'I am asking you to investigate.'* After a brief hesitation, I said: 'I will do so, for I do not see why I should consider myself less adequate for this task than I seem to you. But do remember at this stage that I shall have enough integrity to pro-nounce in favour of your mother, if that is what honesty prescribes.'

5 'As you wish,' he replied, 'for you will wish what is wholly fair.' I then appointed to advise me two of the most respected individuals in the state at that time, Corellius and Frontinus.* Flanked by them, I took my seat in my room.

6 Curianus put forward what he thought favoured his case. I made a brief response, for no one else was present to protect the integrity of the deceased lady. I then retired, and in accordance with the view of my advisers I said to him: 'Curianus, your mother had apparently just cause to be angry with you.'

Thereafter he posted an indictment in the Centumviral court
7 against the other heirs, but not against me. As the day of the suit approached, my coheirs were anxious to come to an agreement and to settle, not because they had lost confidence in their case, but through the fear induced by the times.* They were apprehensive at

what they saw had befallen many, in case they might find themselves
facing a capital charge as a result of the Centumviral judgement.
Some of them might have had their friendships with Gratilla and 8
Rusticus* charged against them. They asked me to discuss the matter 9
with Curianus.

We met in the temple of Concord,* where I said: 'If your mother
had enrolled you as heir for a fourth of her estate, what complaint
could you have made? Or again, if she had made you sole heir, but
had drained away your inheritance with legacies, so that no more
remained in your possession? So, after being disinherited by your
mother, you ought to be satisfied if you obtain a fourth part from her
heirs, though I shall add to it. You realize that you have not indicted 10
me, and that two years have now elapsed,* so that I have acquired it
all by uninterrupted possession. But to ensure that my coheirs find
you more willing to negotiate, and that your respect for me does
not deprive you of anything, I am for my part offering you the same
amount.'*

I have gained the reward, not merely of a good conscience, but
also of a fair reputation. So the said Curianus has both left me my 11
legacy and has signalled my gesture (which, unless I flatter myself,
showed old-world virtue) with conspicuous honour. I have penned 12
this account to you because it is my practice to discuss with you, no
less than with myself, whatever brings me pleasure or pain. Then
again I thought it unfriendly to deprive you of the joy which I was
feeling, for you have such great affection for me. And I am not such a 13
sage as to remain indifferent about whether actions which I believe I
have performed honourably have gained some recognition and a kind
of reward. Farewell.

2 *To his friend Calpurnius Flaccus*

I have received those very splendid thrushes, for which here in my 1
Laurentine villa I cannot make an equivalent return, either from
my city-store or from the storm-buffeted sea. So you will receive 2
instead a barren letter expressing simple gratitude, which does not
seek to vie even with Diomedes' crafty exchange* of gifts. But such
is your genial nature that you will be all the more forthcoming with
your pardon because my letter admits that it does not deserve it.
Farewell.

3 *To his friend Titius Aristo*

1 Your numerous services are both welcome and a pleasure to me, but none more so than your belief that you should not hide from me the fact that you have hosted much lengthy discussion about my slight verses, which was further protracted because of the varying range of judgements. You also report that there were some who, without censuring the works themselves, rebuked me in a friendly and open way 2 for writing and reciting them. To exacerbate my fault, my riposte to them is this: I grant that on occasion I write verses that are far from dignified; yes, I grant it; moreover, I also listen to recitations of comedies, I watch mimes, I read lyric poetry, and I appreciate Sotadics.* Then too there are occasions when I laugh, make jokes, sport, and—let me summarize all the forms of harmless relaxation— am human. As for those who are unaware that men of the greatest learning, high seriousness, and blameless manners have habitually 3 written such works, I do not resent their high opinion of my char- 4 acter, which causes them to express surprise at my writing them. But I am sure that those who are well aware of the great authors in whose steps I tread can be readily prevailed upon to allow me to stray from the straight path in the company of those writers, for it is praise- 5 worthy to emulate their jocular as well as their serious writings. I shall not mention any living author to avoid succumbing to any form of flattery, but am I to fear that what was fitting for Marcus Tullius Cicero, Gaius Calvus, Asinius Pollio, Marcus Messala, Quintus Hortensius, Marcus Brutus, Lucius Sulla, Quintus Catulus, Quintus Scaevola, Servius Sulpicius, Varro, Torquatus or rather the Torquati, Gaius Memmius, Lentulus Gaetulicus, Annaeus Seneca, and most recently Verginius Rufus,* is not fitting for me? And if these examples of private citizens are not enough, I can cite Julius, Augustus, and 6 Nerva, all deified, as well as Tiberius Caesar. I make no mention of Nero, though I am aware that such occasional activities do not become morally depraved because practised by wicked men; rather, they remain honourable because they are more frequently practised by good men. Among these we must number in particular Publius Virgil, Cornelius Nepos, and, earlier, Accius and Ennius.* Admittedly, they were not senators, but integrity of manners does not make social distinctions.

7 True, I give recitations, and I am not aware that they did, I

concede this, but they could rest happy with their own powers of judgement, whereas I am too unassuming in my resolve to believe that what I myself approve is sufficiently meritorious. So I propound 8 these causes for recitation: first, the performer concentrates more keenly on his writings out of respect for his listeners, and secondly, he takes decisions about any passages of which he has doubts by taking account of the opinions of what is a kind of advisory body. Further, he receives numerous suggestions from numerous people, 9 and even if he does not, he observes the reactions of individuals from their facial expressions, eyes, nods, applause, murmurs, and silences, for these offer sufficiently clear indications of the difference between their judgements and their humane sentiments. Accordingly, if by 10 chance any of those who attended take pains to read what has been recited, they will realize that I have changed or added certain passages, perhaps in keeping with their own judgements even if they have not intimated anything to me.

But I am now propounding my arguments as if I had invited the 11 public at large to a lecture-hall rather than friends to a private room. To have such friends in greater numbers is a source of pride to many, and a reproach to none. Farewell.

4 *To his friend Julius Valerianus* 105

This is a small matter, but the beginning of something big. A prae- 1 torian called Sollers* asked the Senate to allow him to hold a weekly market on his estate. Ambassadors from Vicetia* opposed it. Tuscilius Nominatus* was their advocate. The case was adjourned. At a second meeting of the Senate the ambassadors from Vicetia 2 arrived, without their advocate. They said that they had been misled, whether by some verbal misdirection or because they genuinely believed it. When Nepos the praetor* asked whom they had instructed, they replied that he was the same man as before. On being asked whether he had on that occasion represented them without payment, they replied that they had paid him 6,000 sesterces. When asked whether they had made a second payment, they said yes, 1,000 denarii.*

Nepos then commanded that Nominatus be brought to court. 3 Nothing further ensued that day, but my hunch is that the matter will go further, for many issues once touched upon and set generally in motion tend to creep on much further.

4   I have made you prick up your ears. How interminably and how fawningly you must now entreat me to ascertain what follows!* That is, unless you visit Rome first to get the news, and you prefer to witness it rather than read about it. Farewell.

5 *To his friend Novius Maximus*   c.105

1   I have been informed that Gaius Fannius* has died. This news has filled me with dismay and oppressive grief, first, because I loved this elegant and eloquent man, and secondly, because I used to exploit his judgement, for he was intelligent by nature, well tried by experience,
2   and most forthcoming with the truth. What saddens me as well is his personal misfortune, for he died without changing his will, and has left out some of whom he was especially fond, and has included some to whom he has become more hostile.

But this, such as it is, can be borne. What is more grievous is that
3   he has left his most noble work unfinished, for though distracted by his pleadings in court, he was writing an account of the deaths of men executed or banished by Nero. By now he had completed three volumes with nice judgement and careful research, composed in good Latin which bridges the conversational and the historical styles. The more often these books were being carefully read, the more eager he was to complete the rest.
4   For those at work on some immortal project, death seems to me to be always bitter and to come too early. For those who surrender to pleasure, and who live, so to say, for the day, each day forecloses their reasons for living. But for those who give thought to posterity, and prolong remembrance of themselves through their works, death at any time is too sudden, for it always cuts off some work which has been begun.
5   In fact, Gaius Fannius had a premonition long before of what actually occurred. He dreamt* in the silence of the night that he was lying on his couch dressed in his working-clothes, with his desk as usual in front of him. Then Nero seemed to him to enter, sat on the couch, took up the first volume which Fannius had published about the emperor's crimes, and read it through to the end. He did the same
6   thing with the second and third volumes, and then departed. Fannius was terrified. He interpreted this as indicating that this would be the end of his writing as it had been of Nero's reading, and indeed it was.

As I recall this, I feel pity for his having endured in vain all that 7
sleeplessness and all that labour. My mind is confronted by my own
mortality and my writings. I have no doubt that you too are most
fearful, for you will have the same thoughts for the works which you
have on hand. So as long as life lasts, let us strive to ensure that death 8
finds very little to destroy. Farewell.

6 *To his friend Domitius Apollinaris*

I was heartened by your concern and anxiety for me, for when you 1
heard that I intended to spend the summer on my Tuscan estate,* you
sought to dissuade me, believing that the region is unhealthy.* It is 2
true that the Tuscan shore extending along the coast is oppressive
and noxious, but my estate lies far back from the sea; indeed, it lies
below the Apennines, the most salubrious of mountains. So to help 3
you to dispense with all fear on my account, hear my recital of the
climate, the geography of the region, and the pleasant situation of
my villa. These details will be a pleasure both for you to hear, and for
me to recount.

The climate in winter is cold and frosty, so it repels and rejects 4
myrtles, olives, and other trees which delight in continual warmth.
However, it bears with laurels and yields most handsome ones,
though from time to time it kills them but not more often than
happens in the neighbourhood of Rome. In summer it is remarkably 5
temperate; the air is constantly stirred by currents, but more often
they are light breezes rather than winds. As a result many live to old 6
age. You can see grandfathers and great-grandfathers of men in
their prime, and you can hear old stories and talk of men of the
past, so that when you go there, you think that you were born in a
different era.

The appearance of the area is very beautiful. Think of some mas- 7
sive amphitheatre, one which nature alone can fashion. The broad
and expansive plain is ringed with mountains, on the topmost levels
of which are glades of tall and ancient trees, A good deal of varied 8
hunting* is available there, and woodland suitable for felling descends
with the mountain slopes. Between these areas of woodland are hills
whose soil is rich and fertile (no outcrop of rock readily meets the
eye anywhere, even if you are looking for it); they do not yield in
fertility to the broadest plains. The harvests that ripen there are

rich; true, they arrive rather late, but they are no smaller in size.

9 Below them, vineyards extend on every flank, presenting an identical appearance as they interweave far and wide. At the lowest level below

10 them plantations grow, and adjoining them are meadows and fields — fields which only strapping oxen and the strongest ploughs can break through, for when the ground is first ploughed, the soil cleaves fast, and comes out in such great clods that it is only finally subdued

11 when turned over nine times.* The meadows bloom with flowers like jewels; they nurture trefoil and other delicate plants which are always soft and fresh-looking, for they are all nourished by streams all the year round. Yet where much water gathers, there is no marshland because it lies on a slope, and any water which is attracted there and fails to be absorbed pours into the Tiber.

12 The river cuts through the middle of the fields. It can take boats, and it conveys all the produce down to Rome, though only in winter and spring, for in summer its level lowers, and with its dry bed it abandons its reputation as a massive river until the autumn, when it

13 claims it back. You will experience great pleasure by gazing out from the mountain over the countryside, for you will get the impression of looking not at the landscape but at some painting of a scene of extraordinary beauty. Wherever the eye settles, it will be refreshed by the variation and the pattern which is outlined.

14 The villa lies at the base of a hill, but the view seems to be from the top, for the hill rises so gently and gradually, and the slope is so deceptive, that you would think, not that you were mounting it, but that you had already done so. The Apennines lie in the rear, but at some distance. No matter how sunny and still the day is, the house welcomes breezes from them, but they are not piercing and excessive, but subdued, and they are played out because of the dis-

15 tance they travel. The house for the most part faces south, and in summer entices the sun from midday, and in winter from a little earlier, into a colonnade which is broad and correspondingly long. It contains several rooms, and also an entrance hall similar to those in days of old.

16 In front of the colonnade is a terrace divided into several sections of different shapes which are separated by hedges of box. From it a raised platform slopes downward, on which there are shapes of animals facing each other, fashioned from box. On the level below

17 there is acanthus, soft and virtually transparent. There is a walkway

round it enclosed by compact bushes cut into various shapes; close by there is a circular drive which encloses box in different shapes, and shrubs kept low by being cut back. The whole area is protected by a wall which is hidden from view by a tiered hedge of box.* Outside the wall there is a meadow; nature has made it as much worth seeing as 18 the garden just described, which was devised by human skill. Beyond it there are fields and many other meadows and plantations.

At the head of the colonnade a dining room juts out. Through its 19 folding doors it surveys the end of the terrace and immediately beyond it the meadow and the expanse of countryside. From the windows on one side it looks out onto the side of the terrace and onto a projecting part of the house, and on the other the grove and its foliage, which lie within the exercise-ground for horses close by. Virtually opposite the middle of the colonnade there is a suite of 20 rooms somewhat set back; it encircles a courtyard shaded by four plane trees. They surround a fountain in a marble basin, which gushes forth and refreshes the plane trees round it and the earth beneath them with its gentle spray. This suite of rooms contains a 21 bedroom which shuts out the daylight, shouting, and other sounds, and adjoining it is a dining room for everyday use by me and my friends. It looks out on the courtyard which I mentioned, on one wing of the colonnade, and on the general vista which the colonnade enjoys. There is also a second bedroom which the nearest plane tree 22 endows with greenery and shade. It is adorned with marble up to the dado, and has a mural depicting tree-branches with birds perched upon them, a scene no less charming than the marble. In this bed- 23 room there is a small fountain enclosed by a basin, the several jets around which combine to make a most pleasing whisper.

At the corner of the colonnade, the largest bedroom faces the dining room. From one set of windows it looks down on the terrace, from the other on the meadow, in front of which there is an orna- mental pool lying below the windows and enhancing the view from them, for it is pleasant both to the ear and to the eye, because the 24 water cascades down from a height and turns white when it enters the marble basin. This room is beautifully warm in winter, for it is constantly bathed in sunshine. Adjacent to it is the hot-air room, and if the day is cloudy the steam is injected and takes over the role of the 25 sun.

The spacious and cheerful room next to it, in which one disrobes

for bathing, is adjoined by the cooling-room, in which there is a good-sized swimming-pool shaded from the sun. If you want a bigger or warmer pool to swim in, there is one in the courtyard* with a well next to it, from which you can freshen up again if the warm
26 water is cloying. The cooling-room leads into a middle room, in which the sun provides a most genial service, though this is more in evidence in the hot room, for it projects outwards. This has three plunge-baths, two in the sun and the third at some distance from it,
27 though not from its light. Beyond the disrobing-room* a ball-court has been erected, big enough to cater for several kinds of exercise and for several circles of players.

Not far from the bath is a staircase which leads up to a covered gallery by way of three suites of rooms. The first of these suites overhangs the small courtyard with the four plane trees; the second is over the meadow, and the third over the vineyard with a view of
28 various sectors of the sky. At the end of the covered gallery there is a bedroom hollowed out of the gallery itself, which looks out on to the riding-circuit, the vineyard, and the mountains. Another room adjoining it meets the sun, especially in winter. Next comes a suite which connects the riding-circuit to the house. Such are the appearance and the perquisites of the front of the villa.

29 At the side there is a covered gallery* for summer use, which is set on an eminence, and which seems not so much to look out on the vineyard as to touch it. At its centre there is a dining room, particularly healthy since it welcomes a breeze from the Apennine valleys. It has very broad windows at the rear, from which the vineyard is visible; the folding doors also look out on the vineyard which is
30 visible through the gallery. On the side of the dining room which has no windows there is a staircase, which by means of a more private detour allows the access of things useful for dining. At the far end there is a bedroom which is afforded a view of the gallery no less pleasant than that of the vineyard. Beneath it there is the equivalent of a subterranean gallery, which in summer remains glacial with the enclosed cold; satisfied with its own air, it neither needs nor admits
31 breezes from outside. Behind these twin galleries, and beyond the dining room, a colonnade opens up which is cold up to midday but then heats up as evening draws near. This gives entry to two suites, in one of which there are four bedrooms, and in the other three; the sun's journey provides them successively with sunshine and shade.

Far, far more impressive than the arrangement and convenience 32
of the buildings is the riding-ground,* the centre of which lies open,
so that as soon as you enter, the whole complex is laid out before
your eyes. It is surrounded by plane trees which are clothed in ivy
and are green with their own foliage above and with that of other
plants below. The ivy travels round trunks and branches, and roams
across to link up with neighbouring plane trees. Between these
planes box-shrubs grow, and laurels circle outside the box-shrubs,
associating their shade with that of the plane trees. The straight 33
edge of the riding-circuit is broken at its end by a semicircular
curve, which changes its appearance. It is encircled and shaded by
cypresses, and becomes more overshadowed and darkened by the
thicker shade, but in the inner circuits, of which there are several, it
gets the most translucent daylight. In that area roses grow as well, 34
and the cool in the shadows is moderated by shafts of not unwelcome
sunlight.

At the far end of this curved sector, with its varied and manifold
twists and turns, a return is made to a straight lateral stretch, though
there is not just this one, but several separated by box-hedges lying
between them. At some points they are divided by lawns, and at 35
others by box-shrubs fashioned in a thousand shapes. Here and
there these form letters which spell out the names, now of the owner,
and now of the specialist gardener. Miniature obelisks* rise upward,
alternating with fruit-trees planted there. Amidst this creative work,
most characteristic of city-life, you suddenly confront the imitation
of an imported country-scene. The central open area is adorned at
both ends by plane trees of smaller height. Behind them on both 36
sides grow acanthuses with their slippery and pliant leaves, and next
come more shapes and names created from box.

At the far end of the circuit is a semicircular couch of white
marble, shaded by a vine which is supported by four slender pillars
of Carystian marble. From pipes within the couch jets of water
stream out as if ejected by the weight of those who sit there. The
water is caught by a hollowed stone and then held by a basin of
delicate marble, where it is controlled by some hidden means so that
it fills up without overflowing. The *hors d'œuvre* and the more sub- 37
stantial courses are placed on the circumference of the basin, while
the lighter ones float round on vessels shaped like tiny boats or birds.
A fountain opposite sends water shooting up and recovers it, for after

being ejected high in the air it falls back, and by the combination of fissures the water is both collected and expelled.

38 Close by the couch there is a facing bedroom which confers as much distinction on the couch as it obtains from it. Constructed in gleaming marble, it has folding doors which jut out into the greenery and lead out into it, and its upper and lower windows gaze up and down into further greenery. There is a hidden alcove, which is, as it were, part of the bedroom but also a second one. There is a bed in it, and though there are windows all round, the daylight is curtained by
39 the shade that overhangs it, for a most luxuriant vine struggles to mount to the roof of the whole building. You could recline there as if you were resting in a glade, except that you would not experience a
40 rain-shower as you would in the glade. Here too a fountain plays and at once retires. Marble chairs are arranged in a number of places, which please those wearied from walking as much as does the room itself. Tiny fountains play close by the chairs. The whole riding-circuit resounds with the noise of the streams which are channelled in, and which follow the controlling hand, watering now one area, now another, and from time to time all together.

41 Long before now I should have refrained from seeming to sing too loudly, if I had not decided to visit by letter every corner in your company. I did not fear that you would find it wearisome to read a description of what would not be wearisome to visit, especially as you could take a break should you so wish, lay down the letter, and take a seat. Moreover, I have been pandering to my affections, for I love the layout which I have for the most part arranged or which I
42 have developed from that put in train by others. To put it briefly (why should I not reveal to you my decided view or misconception?), I think the primary task of a writer is to scrutinize his title, to ask himself repeatedly what he has embarked upon, and to be aware that if he confines himself to his topic, his treatment cannot be long-winded. If on the other hand he summons and draws in extraneous
43 themes, it will be overlong. You know how many lines Homer takes to describe the arms of Achilles, and how many Virgil* expends on those of Aeneas, yet both treat their subject economically because they achieve what they set out to do. You observe how Aratus* follows up and gathers even the smallest stars, and yet he observes the due
44 limit, because this is no digression of his, but the subject itself. In the same way, 'to compare small things with great', I am attempting to

present the whole house before your eyes, and as long as I do not
introduce anything extraneous and irrelevant, it is the house being
described and not my letter describing it which extends itself.

But to ensure that I am not justly censured in terms of my own
law, if I linger longer in this digression, I shall revert to the topic
with which I began. You now know the reasons why I prefer my 45
Tuscan estate to any in Tusculum or Tibur or Praeneste.* Then, too,
in addition to the reasons I have given, I enjoy a leisure there more
profound and more rich, and therefore more carefree. I need not
wear a toga, no neighbour summons me, and all is peace and tranquillity; this very fact enhances the health-giving atmosphere of the
region, as if the sky were more cloudless, and the air clearer. When I 46
am there I am supremely healthy in mind and body, for my books
exercise my mind, and hunting my body. My servants too nowhere
live a healthier life than here; at any rate, up to now I have never lost
a single one* of those which I had brought to accompany me (forgive
my boasting). I only pray that in the days to come the gods may
preserve this joy for me, and this fair fame for the house. Farewell.

7 *To his friend Calvisius Rufus*

It is clear that a borough cannot be ratified as an heir, nor receive a 1
preliminary legacy, yet Saturninus,* who has deputed us as his heirs,
has bequeathed a fourth of his estate to our community, and later,
in place of that quarter, awarded it a preliminary legacy of 400,000
sesterces. According to the law, this is null and void, but according to
the wish of the dead man, it is ratified and definite. In my eyes (I 2
tremble to think how the legal experts will take what I am about
to say), the wish of the dead man is to be preferred to the law,*
especially as regards the bequest which he sought to bestow on
the native region which you and I share. Since I myself have made a 3
gift of 1,600,000 sesterces to the community, am I to refuse it the
400,000 from an external source which is only slightly more than the
one-third* due to me? I know that you will not dissent from my
judgement, since as the best of citizens you love the state as I do.
So what I should like you to do, when town-councillors are next 4
called to a meeting, is to state what the law is, but in a restrained
and unemphatic way, and then to add that in accordance with
Saturninus' instructions we are offering the community 400,000

sesterces. The gift and the generosity is his; our role is to be called merely compliance.

5 I have refrained from stating this in a letter to the council, first, because I remembered that the obligation of our friendship and the resources of your wisdom make it both desirable and possible for you to perform my role as well as yours. Secondly, I was afraid that in a letter I might not appear to have maintained the judiciousness

6 which it is easy for you to observe in conversation. For whereas one's voice itself controls language, facial expressions, and gestures, a letter bereft of all such graces is exposed to malicious interpretation. Farewell.

8 *To his friend Titinius Capito* 105–6

1 You urge me to compose a history, and you are not alone in urging this, for many have often suggested it to me. I am keen, not because I am sure that I would handle it appropriately (that would be a rash assumption without expertise), but because it seems to me an especially noble aim not to allow persons who are owed immortality to disappear, as also to prolong the glory of others together with one's

2 own. For me, no stimulus is so great as the love and longing for lasting fame, for this is the most worthy of human aspirations, especially if one has no awareness of personal guilt,* and accordingly no fear of the judgement of posterity.

3 So day and night I ponder if there is 'any path whereby I too can raise myself from earth', for that sufficiently meets my prayer, whereas 'to flit victorious on the lips of men'* is beyond my aspiration. 'Yet oh . . .'.* But history alone seems to guarantee that

4 sufficiency. Oratory and poetry win little favour without supreme eloquence, whereas history, however it is written, gives pleasure; for people are inquisitive by nature, and they are charmed by gaining knowledge of events however baldly presented, for even gossip and anecdote entice them.

The example of my family is a further stimulus which directs me

5 to the discipline. My uncle, who became also my father by adoption, wrote works of history* with scrupulous care, and the works of philosophers inform me that it is a most honourable thing to follow in the footsteps of one's forebears, so long as the path on which they paved the way was an honourable one.

So why do I hesitate? I have pleaded in important and serious 6
lawsuits, and even if my expectations arising from them are slight, I
intend to revise my speeches for fear that all that exacting toil may
perish with me, unless I put the finishing touches to them. For if you 7
take account of posterity, anything left unpolished is accounted as
not having been begun. You will say: 'But you can both rewrite your
speeches and write history.' I only wish I could, but both are such
mammoth tasks that to achieve one is quite enough. I began to plead 8
in court in my nineteenth year,* and now at last I see, though still
only dimly, the skills which an orator ought to manifest.

So what would be the outcome, if a new burden were added to 9
the old? True, oratory and history* have much in common, but there
are several differences in the characteristics they seem to share.
Both incorporate narrative, but in different ways. Oratory often has
fitting elements that are lowly and mean, deriving from common
life, whereas for history what is appropriate is all that is *recherché*,
noble, and lofty. Bare bones and modest muscles and sinews are 10
more often suited to oratory, whereas swelling thews and manes,
so to speak, befit history. Oratory wins supreme approval by its
passion, bitterness, and aggression, history by being drawn out,
equable, and even genial. In short, they differ in vocabulary, sound,
and structure. It makes the greatest difference whether it is, in 11
Thucydides' words,* a possession or a contest, the first of which is
history, and the second, oratory. For these reasons I am not disposed
to mingle and mix together the two dissimilar genres which differ
in their chief characteristics, in case I am confused by this great
jumble, and I handle the one as I ought to handle the other. So
meanwhile, to stick to the language of my profession, I beg leave for
an adjournment.

For the moment you must ponder what period in particular I 12
should tackle. Ancient history, already covered by others? The
research is available,* but the compilation burdensome. Or a recent
period not yet covered?* The animosity is oppressive, and the gratitude meagre. Apart from the fact that the monstrous vices of human- 13
ity entail more that is worthy of blame than praise, it will be said that
one's praise is too sparing and one's blame too censorious, even if
one's commendation is unbounded, and one's condemnation most
restrained. But these considerations do not hold me back, for I have 14
enough courage to be honest. I am asking you to prepare the ground

for the task you urge on me, and to choose the subject matter, so that once I am ready to start writing, no other just cause for hesitation and delay may emerge. Farewell.

9 *To his friend Sempronius Rufus* early 105

1 I had made my way down to the Basilica Iulia* in order to hear the speeches to which I was scheduled to reply after a two-day
2 adjournment. The judges were seated, the presiding decemvirs had arrived, the opposing lawyers were facing up to each other, and there was a protracted silence. At last a message arrived from the praetor. The centumvirs were discharged, and proceedings suspended. This was much to my delight, for I am never so well prepared as not to be
3 glad of a delay. The cause of the postponement was the praetor Nepos,* who was holding a judicial inquiry. He had published a brief edict, and he warned prosecutors and defendants that he would impose the provisions contained in the senatorial decree* appended
4 to the edict. By this decree all those pursuing business before the courts were ordered before speaking to swear that they had not given, promised, or guaranteed payment to anyone for legal advocacy. By these words and a thousand more it was forbidden to sell or to buy such legal assistance, but once the case was completed, it was per-
5 missible to make a gift of not more than 10,000 sesterces. This intervention by Nepos roused the praetor who was presiding over the Centumviral court. In order to give thought to whether he should follow Nepos' example, he bestowed on us some unexpected leisure.
6 Meanwhile Nepos' edict is arousing criticism or praise all over the city. Many are saying: 'We have found someone to straighten out bent practices! So were there no praetors before he came along? Who is this fellow who is seeking to correct the morals of the state?' But others are saying: 'He was absolutely right. Before entering on his magistracy he acquainted himself with the laws, read the senatorial decrees, comes down hard on the most disgraceful alliances, and refuses to allow the noblest of professions to be put up for
7 sale in the most demeaning way.' This is the sort of talk on all sides, and only the outcome will show which view will prevail. It is wholly unjust, but in practice accepted, that honourable or disreputable designs are approved or censured according as they turn out badly or successfully. So quite often the same actions win a reputation for

careful attention or empty-headedness, for independence or lunacy. Farewell.

10 *To his friend Suetonius Tranquillus*

I beg you to redeem the pledge made in my hendecasyllables, which 1 promised to the friends we share the publication of your writings.* Every day there are appeals and demands for them, and now the danger looms that the poems may be forced to accept a formal writ to show them. I myself am likewise hesitant about publishing, but 2 you have prevailed even over my delays and dilatory ways. So now you must break through the barrier of delay, or beware lest these works of yours, which my hendecasyllables cannot entice from you by flattery, are squeezed out of you by my abusive scazons. Your 3 writings are fully developed and perfected; the file does not give them a bright sheen, but impoverishes them. Allow me to see the title of your volume, allow me to hear that the works of my friend Tranquillus are being copied, read, and sold. It is right that in view of such a shared friendship I should experience the same pleasure from you as you enjoy from me. Farewell.

11 *To Calpurnius Fabatus, his grandfather-in-law*

I have received your letter informing me that you have dedicated a 1 most beautiful colonnade in the names of your son* and yourself, and that on the following day you promised money for the decoration of the gateways, so that the start of fresh generosity was the completion of that proposed earlier. I am delighted, first because of the fame it 2 brings you, some part of which reflects on me because of our kinship; secondly, because I realize that the memory of my father-in-law is prolonged by these most handsome works; and finally, because our native region wins renown,* as this is for me a delight no matter who adorns it, and the greatest delight since you have done so.

It remains for me only to pray that the gods continue to confer 3 that generous spirit upon you, and the longest period of years upon that spirit, for it is clear to me that once you have discharged this recent pledge, you will embark upon another. Once generosity has been roused to action, it cannot remain inactive, for the very exercise of it recommends its nobility. Farewell.

12 *To his friend Terentius Scaurus*

1 I decided to hold a recital of a modest speech which I am thinking of publishing, so I invited some people as a gesture of respect, and a few others to get from them an honest reaction. For I have two reasons for holding recitals: the first so that I am keyed up with anxiety, and the second so that I can receive advice, in case some error for which

2 I was responsible has escaped my notice. I obtained what I sought. I found people to give me generously of their advice, and I myself

3 noticed some things which I am to change. I have amended the written version which I have sent you. You will identify the subject matter* from the title, and the speech will explain the rest, for it must already be familiar enough to be understood without an introduction.

4 Please write and tell me your view of the speech as a whole, and of its parts, for I must be circumspect in withholding it, or more insistent on publishing it, if your authority inclines to one or to the other, Farewell.

13 *To his friend Julius Valerianus*   early 105

1 You ask me, and I promised if you did so to acquaint you with the outcome of the summons which Nepos issued in connection with Tuscilius Nominatus.

Nominatus was escorted in, and spoke on his own behalf, with no one indicting him, for the ambassadors from Vicetia not merely

2 refrained from charging him, but even lent him their support. The gist of his defence was that it was not his good faith as advocate which had been found wanting, but his resolve. He had come to court intending to plead, and he had even been seen in the Senate, but then he had become fearful in conversation with friends and had retired, for he had been warned not to offer such dogged opposition to the aspirations of a senator who was now battling not for the market, but for his influence, repute, and dignity, especially in the Senate. Otherwise, they said, Nominatus would incur greater odium* than he had

3 on the earlier occasion. As he left the chamber he was applauded, but only by a few. He reinforced his words with pleas and tears. Indeed, throughout his whole speech this practised performer made sure that he appeared to be begging to be let off rather than to be defending himself, for this approach was both more conciliatory and safer.

On the proposal of the consul-designate, Afranius Dexter,* he was 4
acquitted. The gist of Dexter's statement was that Nominatus would
have been better advised to have continued in support of the Vicetians' case with the same courage with which he had undertaken it.
However, since the type of guilt he had incurred had involved no
deceit, and it was established that he had committed no act deserving
of punishment, he should be acquitted on condition that he restored
to the Vicetians the money which he had received. The proposal 5
won universal agreement, with the exception of Fabius Aper. He
proposed that Nominatus be barred from advocacy for five years, and
though his show of authority attracted no one in support, he stood
resolutely by his proposal, and by citing the law* on senatorial procedure he compelled Dexter, who had made the initial proposal to
the contrary, to swear that his motion was in the interests of the
Senate. Though this demand was in harmony with the law, some 6
members railed against it, for he seemed to be censuring Dexter for a
proposal which was currying favour.

But before the votes could be declared, Nigrinus, a plebeian
tribune, read out an eloquent and important document,* in which he
complained that the provision of advocacy was for sale, as also was
collusion between prosecution and defence; that there was cooper-
ation over lawsuits; and that it was accounted fame to lay down large
and fixed financial returns from the spoils of citizens. He read out 7
sections of the laws, reminded senators of senatorial decrees, and
finally said that they should plead with the best of emperors to apply
a remedy himself to these great evils, because the laws and senatorial
decrees were being flouted.

A few days elapsed, and then a document came from the emperor 8
which was austere but couched temperately. You will be able to
read it, for it is in the public records.* How pleased I am that in the
matter of lawsuits I have always steered clear of not merely agree-
ments, gifts, and services, but also of honorific presents! True, one 9
should avoid dishonourable practices, not because they are illegal,
but because they are shameful, but it is none the less satisfying
to observe a public veto on what one has never allowed oneself to
do. Perhaps, or rather undoubtedly, I shall win less praise and less 10
public recognition for my own observance, once all will perform out
of necessity what I was accustomed to do voluntarily. Meanwhile I
enjoy the pleasant sensation as some keep labelling me a prophet,*

while others in sport and joking claim that an embargo has been placed on my plundering and my greed. Farewell.

14 *To his friend Pontinus Allifanus*

1 I had retired to my township when I was told that Cornutus Tertul-
2 lus* had accepted the post of curator of the Aemilian Way.* I cannot express how pleased I was, both for his sake and for mine; for his sake, because, though he may be a complete stranger to any ambition (as indeed he is), yet a distinction awarded to him unsought must be gratifying to him; and for me, because any position assigned to me is somewhat more pleasurable when I see one of equal prestige
3 bestowed on Cornutus. For it is just as welcome to be placed on a par with good men as to be advanced to high position; and is there anyone superior to Cornutus in virtue and in integrity, or, in every kind of praiseworthy activity, one more clearly moulded as a model of traditional behaviour?

My knowledge of him is not by reputation, though he enjoys in general the most signal and wholly deserved repute, but by personal experience over a long period and in important circumstances.
4 Together we cherish, and together we have cherished, almost every person of both sexes whom our age has produced worthy of imitation.
5 Our sharing of these friendships has bound us together in the closest bond of intimacy. There is in addition the bond of our relationship in public life, for as you know he was also, as if in answer to prayer, my colleague in the prefecture of the treasury, and again in the con- sulship. At that time I gained the deepest insight into the kind of man he was, and into the measure of his greatness, when I attended on him as my mentor, and reverenced him as a father,* a tribute which he deserved, not so much by his ripe years as by his experience of
6 life. For these reasons I congratulate myself as much as him in a public no less than a private capacity, for at last by their merits men are attaining distinctions, and not, as earlier, encountering hazards.*
7 I would draw out my letter indefinitely if I were giving free rein to my pleasure. I turn instead to my activities when this news reached
8 me. I was staying with my grandfather-in-law,* with my wife's aunt, and with friends whom I had long missed seeing. I was touring round my modest holdings, lending an ear to the many complaints of the country folk, skimming through the accounts unwillingly (for my

apprenticeship has been to documents and literature of a different kind). I had also begun to make my preparations for the journey back, for I am circumscribed by the brief period of my leave, and am 9 reminded of my duties especially by hearing of the office which Cornutus has obtained. I am keen that your Campania is simultaneously sending you back as well, so that on my return to Rome not a day of our close association may be lost. Farewell.

15 *To his friend Arrius Antoninus*

I discover how good your verses are especially when I imitate them. 1 Just as an artist rarely succeeds in painting a consummately beautiful face without demeaning it, so I stumble and fall short of the original. This is why I urge you all the more to publish as many poems as 2 possible, so that all can eagerly seek to imitate them, though none or very few can succeed. Farewell.

16 *To his friend Aefulanus Marcellinus*

I write these lines to you in great sadness, for the younger daughter 1 of our friend Fundanus* has died. I never saw anyone more sprightly and lovable than that girl, nor anyone worthier not just of a longer life, but of virtual immortality. She had not completed her fourteenth 2 year, yet she already had the practical wisdom of an elder and the serious demeanour of a matron, though she also possessed a girl's sweetness and a maiden's modesty. How she would cling to her 3 father's neck! How she would embrace those of us who were her father's friends, affectionately and modestly! What love she showed to her nurses, her attendants, and her teachers,* according to the duties of each! With what diligence and intelligence she applied herself to her studies! And how restrained and circumspect she was in her play! What self-control, endurance, and resolve, too, she showed in her final illness! She obeyed the doctors, encouraged her sister and her 4 father, and when her physical powers failed her, she kept herself going with her strength of mind, which endured in her to the end, 5 for neither her lengthy illness nor fear of death broke her spirit. This has left us with all the more affecting reasons to miss her and to lament her. What a truly sad and bitter death! 6

What a time to die, less fitting than her death itself! She was already betrothed to an outstanding young man; the wedding day* was

already chosen; we had already been invited. What joy transformed
7 into such grief! I cannot describe in words the ghastly wound which
pierced my heart when I heard Fundanus himself (for grief devises
many trials) giving instructions that the money which he had
intended to disburse on clothes, pearls, and jewels should be spent
8 instead on incense, ointments, and spices. True, he is a learned man,
and a philosopher,* for from his earliest years he has devoted himself
to higher systems of thought and to virtuous principles, but at
present he spurns all that he has often heard and declared, and
without regard for other virtues he is utterly committed to love of
9 family. You will pardon and even praise him if you ponder what he
has lost, for what he has lost is a daughter who mirrored his character no less than his face and features, and with remarkable likeness
wholly resembled her father.
10 So if you send him some lines about his wholly justified grief,
remember to address a consolation which is not censorious or over-
hearty, but one expressed with kindness* and gentleness. A lapse of
time will do much to help him accept his loss more readily; for just as
11 a wound still raw shrinks from the hands of healers, but then bears
with them and begs for them unasked, so mental grief while fresh
rejects and shrinks from any consolations, but then pines for them
and becomes resigned to them, if they are proffered with sympathy.
Farewell.

17 *To his friend Vestricius Spurinna*

1 I am aware of your enthusiasm for noble pursuits, and the pleasure
you feel when young men of the upper classes achieve something
worthy of their forebears, so with greater haste I am reporting to you
my attendance today in the audience assembled by Calpurnius Piso.*
2 He was presenting a recital of the learned and splendid content of
his *Translations to the Stars*,* which is composed in flowing, delicate,
and smooth elegiac couplets, which also attained grandeur when a
passage demanded it. For in apt and varied tones, at one point it rose
loftily and at another subsided; he mingled the high-sounding and
the subdued, the slight and the fully rounded, the serious and the
3 jocose, all with equal talent. He lent added attraction to his lines
with his most mellifluous voice, and his voice was enhanced by his
modesty of manner, for his features registered much blushing and

much anxiety, both of which are most attractive in a speaker. The fact is that in learned performances apprehension is somehow more appropriate in a person than self-confidence.

To refrain from further praise (though I should like to go further, 4 since these attainments are nobler in the young, and rarer in the nobility), once the recital was finished, I greeted the young man with long and enthusiastic embraces (a most incisive incentive in helpful advice). With my praises I roused him to proceed on the path on which he had begun, and to carry the torch on to his descendants as his ancestors had carried it to him. I also felicitated his mother, best 5 of women; and his brother, who emerged from the gathering with as much praise for his devotion to family as his brother had gained from his eloquence, for his initial anxiety and subsequent exhilaration on behalf of his brother during the recital were so impressively in evidence.

I pray that the gods may allow me to report such news more often. 6 My anxiety for this generation is that it should not be barren and unproductive, and my pressing concern is that our nobility should have in their houses something of beauty besides their ancestral portraits. At this moment such portraits seem to me to be silently praising and encouraging these young men, and to be acknowledging their presence, which is sufficiently great glory for both of them. Farewell.

18 *To his friend Calpurnius Macer*

All goes well with me, because all goes well with you. You have your 1 wife and your son with you, and you are enjoying the sea, the streams, the greenery, the fields, and your most delightful house. I have no doubt that it is most delightful, for in it retired a man who was more blessed until he became most blessed.* I am on my Tuscan estate, 2 combining my hunting with my literary activities. Sometimes I pursue them alternately, and sometimes simultaneously. At this moment I cannot declare whether it is more difficult to catch something or to write something. Farewell.

19 *To his friend Valerius Paulinus*

I note how humanely you treat your household, so I will openly 1 declare to you the tolerant way in which I treat mine. I always bear in 2 mind Homer's phrase,* 'He was gentle as a father', together with our expression, 'Father of the household'. But even if I were by nature harsher and more unsympathetic, my freedman Zosimus' illness would deeply distress me, and I must show him kindness all the greater now that he is in need of it.

3   He is an honest and dutiful man, and well educated. His specialization and selling-point, so to speak, is as a reciter of comedies, at which he is most adept, for his delivery is clear, correct, appropriate, and in good taste as well. He is a seasoned lyre-player, more than a reciter of comedies need be.* He also reads speeches, histories, and poetry so expertly that he gives the impression that this is the sole skill which he has learnt.

4   I have carefully explained all this to you to make you more aware of the numerous and pleasing roles he alone plays for me. Moreover, I have for long had an affection for him, and this has increased by
5   reason of those very dangers confronting him. It is a rule of nature that nothing rouses and ignites love so much as fear of loss, and I
6   have more than once entertained this fear, for a few years ago, when in the course of recitation he was straining himself to the utmost, he vomited blood. For this reason I sent him to Egypt, and after a lengthy sojourn abroad, he recently returned restored to health. But subsequently he put too much strain day after day on his vocal chords, and a cough gave him warning of his former weakness, and
7   he again vomited blood. For this reason I have decided to send him to your estate which you own at Forum Iulii,* for I have often heard you mention that the air there is healthy, and that the milk is most
8   suitable for treatment of this kind. I am therefore asking you to write to your household so that your villa may take him in as his home, and
9   also to provide him with expenses for whatever he needs. These requirements will be modest, for he is so thrifty and economical that he cuts back frugally not only on luxuries but also on things essential for his health. On his departure I shall give him enough money to cover his travelling-expenses to your estate. Farewell.

20 *To his friend Cornelius Ursus*   106–7

1   The Bithynians again! So soon after the case of Julius Bassus,* they have indicted the proconsul Varenus Rufus,* the very Varenus whom they had recently demanded and accepted as their advocate against

Bassus. When they were escorted into the Senate, they demanded an 2 investigation. Varenus asked that he too should be permitted to summon witnesses in his defence,* but the Bithynians objected, so the hearing was begun. I spoke in defence of Varenus, not without success; whether I spoke well or badly the written version of the 3 speech will show. For when speeches are delivered, Fortune is the controlling factor, for better or for worse. The memory, the voice, the gestures, the actual occasion, and finally, affection or loathing for the defendant, diminish or enhance greatly the approval a speech wins, whereas the written version is free from the resentment, free from the partiality, and is not affected by advantageous or adverse circumstances.

The speaker who opposed me was one of the Bithynians, Fonteius 4 Magnus,* who was very long on words but very short on facts. Most Greeks like him mistake verbiage for richness of content. Their convolutions of long and turgid period-sentences pour forth in a single breath like a torrent. As Julius Candidus* is quite wittily 5 wont to say, eloquence is one thing and loquacity is another. Eloquence is the gift of one or two at most (indeed, if we believe Marcus Antonius,* no one has it!), whereas what Candidus terms loquacity is the property of many, and particularly of all shameless individuals.

Next day Homullus made a clever, spirited, and cultivated defence 6 of Varenus, and Nigrinus'* speech indicting him was close-packed, dignified, and elegant. Acilius Rufus,* the consul-designate, proposed that the Bithynians be granted an investigation, and he passed over the application of Varenus without mention of it, which was a species of refusal. The consular, Cornelius Priscus,* was for granting 7 both accusers and defendant their applications, and his proposal prevailed with the majority. So we obtained our request, which, though not enshrined in the law and hardly customary, was fair. I will 8 not explain by letter why it was fair, so that you may hanker after the speech. If what Homer says* is true,

> For men pour louder praises on that song
> Which floats most recently about their ears,

I must be careful not to let the chattering of a letter despoil the charm and bloom of novelty which is the greatest recommendation of that little speech. Farewell.

21 *To his friend Pompeius Saturninus*   105–6

1 Your letter roused different emotions in me, for it contained news both happy and melancholy. Happy, because of its report that you are detained in Rome (you remark: 'Would that it were otherwise!', but I am content), and also because it promised that you would offer a recital as soon as I arrive. I am grateful that you are waiting for
2 me. The melancholy news is that Julius Valens is seriously ill. Yet this is not melancholy, since it is thought to be in his interest, for it is good for him to be delivered from his incurable illness with all possible speed.

3   But your further news is clearly not merely melancholy but also grievous, that Julius Avitus* has died when returning from his post as quaestor, and that he died on board ship, far from his most affection-
4 ate brother, and far also from his mother and sisters. This is of no concern to him now that he is dead, but it was so as he lay dying, as it is to those who survive him. The news is grievous also because this young man of such great talents has been snuffed out in his green years. He would have attained the highest eminence if his
5 qualities had reached full maturity. With what passion for intellectual studies he was fired! Think of all that he read, and all that he wrote! All this has departed with him, leaving no reward for poster-
6 ity. But why do I give free play to grief? There is no subject that is not all-consuming, if one gives it free rein. I will foreclose this letter so that I can foreclose also the tears which this letter has forced from me. Farewell.

BOOK SIX

1 *To his friend Tiro* 106–7

During the time I was in the Transpadane and you were in Picenum,* 1
I did not miss you so much, but now that I am in Rome and you are
still in Picenum, I miss you much more. One possible reason is that
the region in which we are often together puts me in mind of
you more keenly; or perhaps proximity more than anything else
intensifies the longing for absent friends, and the closer you get to
the hope of enjoying their company, the more impatiently you feel
their absence.

Whatever the reason is, you must rescue me from my distress, So 2
do come, or I shall head back to the place which I ill-advisedly left in
haste. My sole purpose in doing this would be to see whether you
might send me a letter like this one, once you find yourself in Rome
without me. Farewell.

2 *To his friend Arrianus* 106–7

During court-proceedings, I often keep looking out for Marcus 1
Regulus,* though I don't like to say I miss him. So why do I look out 2
for him? Well, he showed respect for oratory, he would look apprehensive, grow pale, write out his speeches (though he could not
memorize them). Then, too, he would paint round one or other of
his eyes (the right when about to speak for the plaintiff, the left for
the defendant); he would sport a white patch* over one eye, or transfer it to the other; he would always consult a soothsayer* on the
outcome of a case. All this arose from an excess of superstition, but
also from the great respect which he had for oratory. Then again, the 3
advocates speaking with him found two of his procedures quite
enjoyable: he would ask for unlimited time,* and he would muster an
audience to listen. What can be more enjoyable than to speak for as
long as you like while someone else gets the brickbats, and to be,
so to say, constrained to speak appropriately before an audience
gathered by another?

But whatever the merits of this, Regulus did well to die, and 4

would have done better to die earlier. Certainly nowadays he could have lived on without being a public menace,* under an emperor who
5 ensured he could do no harm. So it is quite in order to hanker after him at times, for since his death the custom of awarding and requesting two water-clocks or one,* or sometimes even a half, has become widespread and has taken root. For on the one hand speakers prefer to be done with speeches rather than to utter them, and on the other, those hearing cases would rather see the back of them than pass judgement. So prevalent is the indifference, the sloth, and in short the lack of respect for intellectual activities in the courts and judicial
6 hazards. Are we wiser than our forebears, or more devoted to justice than the very laws which assign so many hours* and days and adjournments? Our ancestors were dim and unconscionably slow, whereas we are clear in speech, swifter in understanding and more conscientious as judges because we rapidly dispose of cases with water-clocks fewer than the number of days in which the cases used
7 to be developed. Dear Regulus, despite your canvassing, you used to get from all the trust which very few vouchsafe today.

When I myself sit on the bench, a role which I perform more often
8 than that of speaker, I allow as many water-clocks as are demanded. I do this because I think it rash to guess how extensive a case as yet unheard will be, and to impose a time limit on an issue whose boundaries are as yet unknown, especially as a judge owes patience first and foremost to his own sense of obligation, for patience is an important element in administering justice. The objection may be made that some of what is said is irrelevant. True, but it is better that irrele-
9 vances be aired than that essentials be omitted. Moreover, you cannot identify irrelevances unless you have heard them out.

But we can discuss these things better face to face, together with other public shortcomings, for you too in your love for the common good often long to see improvements in things which are difficult to correct.
10 Now let us review our domestic concerns. Is all well with yours? There is nothing new in mine, but the blessings which continue are all the more welcome, and inconveniences become lighter because I have grown used to them. Farewell.

3 *To his friend Verus*

Thank you for undertaking the cultivation of the small farm which I 1
have bestowed on my nurse. When I gave it to her it was valued at
100,000 sesterces, but subsequently, with the decline in output, its
value has also depreciated. Now under your supervision it will
recover. Only bear in mind that I am entrusting to you not merely 2
the fruit-trees and the land (though these too are in your care), but
my modest gift, and it is important, for me the donor as for my nurse
the recipient, that it should be as productive as possible. Farewell.

4 *To his dear Calpurnia* 107

Never have my routine tasks* caused me to complain so much, since 1
they have not allowed me either to accompany you when you
departed for your convalescence to Campania,* nor to follow hot on
your heels once you had set out. At this time I long to be with you, to 2
witness with my own eyes what you are taking to build up your
physical strength, and to see whether your forgoing both the pleasures of relaxation away from Rome and the rich foods of the locality
leaves you unimpaired.

For myself, even if you were in rude health I would feel some 3
anxiety at being without you, for to have no news from time to time
of a person you love very dearly leaves you on tenterhooks and
deeply troubled. As things stand, because of both your absence and 4
your illness, various worries and uncertainty make me apprehensive.
I am subject to every fear, I have visions of every circumstance. In
the way of those obsessed by fears, my imagination dwells most of all
on what I loathe most of all. So with greater urgency I beg you to 5
relieve my apprehension with one or even two letters each day. I shall
be more free of anxiety as I read them, and fearful again once I have
read them. Farewell.

5 *To his friend Ursus* late 106

I reported earlier* that Varenus had succeeded in being allowed to 1
summon witnesses, and that this seemed fair to the majority, but
unfair to some, a view obstinately held in particular by Licinius
Nepos,* who at the next Senate in the course of discussion of other
matters spoke at length about that recent senatorial decree, and thus

2 raised afresh an issue which had been foreclosed. He further added
that the consuls should be asked to refer the question, under the
precedent of the law of bribery as affecting the law of extortion,
whether it should be agreed that for the future an additional clause
should be added, allowing defendants to have the same power as
3 prosecutors of investigation* and of summoning witnesses. Some
senators castigated his speech as too late, ill-timed, and unseason-
able, since it censured a decision already foreclosed which could have
been opposed at the time, when the opportunity to speak against it
4 had been neglected. Indeed, the praetor Juventius Celsus* fiercely
rebuked Nepos at some length for seeking to put the Senate to rights.
Nepos countered, and Celsus spoke again. Neither restrained his
insults.

5   I do not wish to recount their words, for I was affronted by them,
and for that reason I was all the more critical of certain senators who
in their eagerness to hear what was being said, kept darting now over
to Celsus, now to Nepos, according to which of them was speaking.
At one moment they seemed to be rousing and igniting them against
each other, at the next to reconcile them and to compose their differences. As though in some stage-show, they kept praying that the
emperor would look kindly on one or other for the most part, but
6 from time to time on both.* What I further found distasteful was that
each of them was aware of the other's proposals, for Celsus answered
Nepos in a speech already written out, and Nepos responded using
7 his tablets. Their friends had gossiped so much that before wrangling, the two of them knew each other's arguments as if by prior
agreement. Farewell.

6 *To his friend Fundanus*   late 106

1 Now if ever I should like your presence at Rome, and I beg you to be
there. I need a comrade to share my prayer and toil and anxiety.
Julius Naso* is standing for office. He is one of many candidates, and
good ones at that, so that to come out on top imparts distinction, but
2 is difficult. So I am on edge, stirred by hope yet apprehensive with
fear. I do not recognize myself as an ex-consul, for I see myself again
as a candidate for all the offices which I have exercised.

3   Naso deserves this attention because of his long-standing affection for me. Admittedly my friendship with him is not like that of a

father, for my youthful age could not make that possible, But when I was barely in my teens, his father* was signalled to me as an object of great praise; for he was a great enthusiast, not only for literary studies, but also for their practitioners. Almost every day he would attend, to listen to the teachers who were my mentors, Quintilian and Nicetes Sacerdos.* He was in general a man of distinction and high seriousness, and the recollection of him should be profitable to his son. But in the Senate today there are many who did not know 4 him, and though many others did know him, they have respect only for those who are still alive. This is why the son must strain and strive all the more without reference to his father's fame, which may confer great distinction, but waning influence.

In fact he has always industriously taken this stance, as if he 5 foresaw the time coming, so he has made friends and once made, has cultivated them. At any rate, as soon as he allowed himself to discriminate, he chose me as a person to love and to imitate. When I 6 speak in court, he stands attentively at my side; he sits in at my recitations. Moreover, he involves himself with my humble writings* especially at their first appearance, these days by himself, but earlier with his brother, whom he has recently lost, and whose role I must undertake and fulfil instead. For I mourn both for that brother so 7 undeservedly carried off by a premature death, and for Naso, now deprived of the aid of his excellent brother, and left only with friends to support him.

These are the reasons why I demand that you come and append 8 your vote to mine. It is greatly in my interest to show you off and to do the rounds in your company. Such is your authority that I believe that I will importune even my own friends more effectively if you are with me. Dispense with whatever holds you back. My pressing 9 situation, my reputation, and my high position demand it. I have adopted a candidate, and it is widely known that I have done so. I am the one who is canvassing, and I am the one risking the consequences. In short, if Naso is granted what he seeks, his will be the glory, but if he is rejected the failure will be mine. Farewell.

7 *To his dear Calpurnia*　　　　　　　　107

You write that my being absent from you causes you no little sadness, 1
and that your one consolation is to grasp my writings as a substitute

for my person, and that you often place them where I lie next to you.
2 I am happy that you are missing me, and that my books console you as you rest. I in turn keep reading your letters, repeatedly fingering
3 them as if they had newly arrived. But this fires my longing for you all the more, for when someone's letter contains such charm, what sweetness there is in conversing face to face! Be sure to write as often as you can, even though the delight your letters give me causes me such torture. Farewell.

8 *To his friend Priscus*

1 You both know and love Atilius Crescens.* Is there anyone of some slight distinction who does not know or love him? My affection for
2 him, unlike that of many, is of the closest kind. Our native towns are separated by a mere day's journey; we began to love each other when we were young boys, and that is the most passionate friendship there is. This intimacy continued later; with discernment it has strengthened rather than cooled, as those who have closer contact with either of us are well aware, for he broadcasts my friendship and boasts of it far and wide, while I for my part demonstrate my huge concern for his unassuming and retiring nature, and for his peace of mind.
3 Indeed, on one occasion when the rudeness of some candidate for the plebeian tribunate was causing him apprehension, and he mentioned it to me, I replied: '*Personne ne fera du tort, tant que je vivrai.*'*
    Why all this? It is so that you may know that Atilius cannot be
4 wronged while I stand idly by. You will repeat: Why all this? Valerius Varus owed him money. Varus' heir is our friend Maximus.* I am
5 fond of him, but you are more closely connected, so I am asking you, and indeed demanding by the rights of our friendship, that you ensure that my friend Atilius obtains not only his capital but also several years' interest. He is a man who keeps his hands wholly clear of other people's possessions, and is careful with his own. He draws no profits to sustain him, and his only takings come from his modest
6 income,* for he plies his literary studies, in which he shows great distinction, merely for pleasure and repute. Even the slightest loss weighs heavily on him, though getting back what one has lost weighs more heavily still.
7   Do relieve him of this headache, and relieve me likewise. Allow me to enjoy his charm and wit, for I cannot bear to see him melancholy

when his cheerfulness refuses to allow me to be depressed. In short, 8
since you know his ready wit, please ensure that injustice does not
transform it into gall and bitterness. You must judge from the
strength of his affection how strongly he feels when rebuffed. That
lofty and free-ranging spirit will not brook an insulting loss. Should 9
he have to bear it, I will regard it as a loss and insult to me—not with
such anger as I would feel if directed against me, but much more
intensely.

Yet why do I indulge in condemnations and virtual threats?
Rather, I ask and beg you, as I began, to ensure that he does not
believe that he has been neglected by me, and that I do not believe
that I have been neglected by you. You will ensure this if you have as
much concern for my feelings as I have for his. Farewell.

9 *To his friend Tacitus*   late 106

You recommend to me the candidacy of Julius Naso.* What, Naso's, 1
to me? You could be recommending my own to me. However, I shall
bear with it, and forgive you. I should have recommended him to
you, had I been away while you still lingered in Rome. Concern
tends to regard every step as necessary. I propose that you solicit 2
others; I shall be your agent, assistant, and participant as you make
your pleas. Farewell.

10 *To his friend Albinus*   107

After visiting the house of my mother-in-law at Alsium,* which for 1
some time belonged to Verginius Rufus,* the place itself renewed my
longing and sorrow for that best and greatest of men, for he had been
accustomed to spend his days there in retirement, and he used to call
it 'the wee nest of his old age'. Whenever I repaired there, my 2
thoughts and my eyes strove to seek him out. I was keen also to visit
his tomb there, and then regretted having visited it. For it is still 3
unfinished, not because of the difficulty of the work (it is modest,
and in fact small in size), but because of the sloth of the person to
whom the task has been deputed. I feel anger as well as pity that
nearly ten years after his death* his remains and ashes lie neglected
without an inscription, and without the name of one whose memory
and fame are widespread throughout the whole world. Yet he had 4

left instructions to ensure that his godlike and immortal achievement should be inscribed there in verses:

> Rufus lies here; of old by routing Vindex,
> He freed the imperial power for Rome, not for himself.

5 Loyalty in friendship is so rare, and forgetfulness of the dead so habitual, that we ought even to erect our own monuments, and
6 anticipate all the obligations of our heirs. Who is not to fear the fate that we see has overtaken Verginius? His fame makes the injustice done to him not only more undeserved, but also more notorious. Farewell.

11 *To his friend Maximus*

1 What a blessed day! When the city prefect called me in as assessor,* I listened to two young men of the greatest promise and the greatest ability, Fuscus Salinator and Ummidius Quadratus,* speaking on opposite sides. They are an outstanding pair, who will adorn not merely our times, but also our literature itself. Both showed remark-
2 able honesty and integrity unimpaired. They combined a handsome appearance, accents of pure Latin, manly tones, retentive memory, great originality, and judgement to match. One and all, these attributes delighted me. So did the fact that, in manifesting them, they regarded me as their guide and mentor. The audience listening got the impression that they were modelling themselves on me, and
3 treading in my footsteps. What a blessed day! I say again, a day to be marked on the calendar with the whitest of pebbles!* What can be more gratifying for the state than that young men from the noblest families should seek fame and high repute in oratory, and what aspiration could I entertain greater than to be proposed as a model for
4 men advancing on the right path? I beg the gods that I may experience this joy unceasingly. You will be my witness that I further pray to them that those who think it so important to model themselves on me may strive to outstrip me. Farewell.

12 *To Fabatus, his grandfather-in-law*

1 You must certainly not hesitate to recommend to me persons who you think need support, for on the one hand it is fitting that you

should lend assistance to many, and on the other that I should under- take whatever is relevant to your concerns. So I shall lend Bittius 2 Priscus* all the help I can, especially in my own field of the Centum- viral court. You bid me forget the letters which you wrote, as you put 3 it, 'with the heart's candour', but there are none which I recall with greater pleasure, for from them especially I realize the depth of your affection for me, since you have dealt with me as you used to do with your son. I do not hide that they were the more pleasing to me 4 because my conscience was clear, for I had discharged as energetic- ally as I could the tasks which you wished me to discharge. So 5 I repeatedly beg you always to rebuke me with the same frankness whenever I seem to be remiss (I say 'seem', for I shall never be remiss), because for my part I shall realize that you are motivated by the greatest affection, and you for your part will be pleased that I have not deserved such rebukes. Farewell.

13 *To his friend Ursus* 107

Did you ever see anyone in such toils and troubles as my friend 1 Varenus? He has had to defend, and virtually to seek again, the concession he had gained after a most contentious dispute. The 2 Bithynians brazenly attempted to erode and undermine the senator- ial decree in the presence of the consuls, and even to denounce the emperor in his absence.* He directed them back to the Senate, where they did not stop complaining. Claudius Capito* spoke disrespect- fully rather than with integrity, for he assailed the senatorial decree in the Senate. Catius Fronto* made a dignified and steadfast response. 3 The Senate itself behaved wonderfully, for even those who had refused Varenus his request voted that it should be granted, now that his application had been approved. They argued that it was right for 4 individuals to oppose the proposal while the matter was unresolved, but that all should stand by what the majority had decided. Acilius 5 Rufus* alone, together with seven or eight others—seven, in fact— persisted in his previous opinion. This small number included one or two whose momentary seriousness, or rather, affected seriousness, was laughed to scorn. But you must make your own assessment of 6 the great struggle in store for us when the battle proper is joined, since this preliminary and prelude has awakened these disputes. Farewell.

14 *To his friend Mauricus*

1 You invite me to your place at Formiae.* I shall come, provided that
you do not put yourself to any inconvenience. Such an agreement
allows me in turn to safeguard my own interests. For it is not the
sea and shore that I am after, but yourself, leisure, and freedom;
2 otherwise it would be better for me to stay in Rome. All things must
be ordered to suit someone else's convenience, or one's own. My
natural inclination is to go all out for nothing but the whole hog.
Farewell.

15 *To his friend Romanus*

1 You were not present at a marvellous episode, and nor was I, but the
story reached me the other day. Paulus,* a distinguished Roman
knight of exceptional learning, writes elegiacs. This is a family trait,
for he is a fellow townsman of Propertius, and indeed he numbers
2 him among his forebears. He was giving a recital, and he began
with the words: 'Priscus, you command me . . .'. At this, Javolenus
Priscus,* who was there as a close friend of Paulus, broke in: 'But I do
not command you.' Imagine the general laughter and the joking!
3 Priscus is indeed an odd fellow, yet he meets his obligations, is called
upon as adviser, and is also a community-adviser on the civil law.
This was what made the comment more comic and also more
4 remarkable. Meanwhile the eccentric behaviour of another brought
Paulus a lukewarm reception. So people intending to offer a recital
should carefully ensure not only that they themselves are sound in
mind, but also that the audience they invite are, too! Farewell.

16 *To his friend Tacitus*

1 You ask me to describe for you the death of my uncle, to enable you
to transmit a more truthful account* for the benefit of posterity. I am
grateful to you, because I realize that perennial glory is in store for
2 the manner of his death if it is extolled by you. It is true that he died
in a disaster which overtook the most beautiful of regions, and in a
calamity shared by communities and cities, so that his renown will
seemingly live for ever, and it is true also that he wrote numerous
works* which will also survive. But none the less, the undying quality

of your writings will greatly enhance his immortality. I myself 3
account as blessed those who by the gods' gift have been granted the
ability either to perform deeds worth chronicling or to compose
accounts which deserve to be read,* but I regard as most blessed those
who achieve both. My uncle will be numbered among these through
his books and through yours, and for this reason I more gladly
undertake and even demand the task you lay on me.

My uncle was at Misenum, where he held command of the fleet* in 4
person. Just after midday on 24 August my mother pointed out to
him the appearance of a cloud of unusual size and appearance. He 5
had relaxed in the sun, had then taken a cold dip, had lunched lying
down, and was at his books. He asked for his sandals, and mounted to
the place from which that remarkable phenomenon could best be
observed. A cloud was issuing up from some mountain which spectators from a distance could not identify; it was later established to
have been Vesuvius. The pine tree,* rather than any other, best
describes its appearance and shape, for it rose high up into the sky on 6
what one can describe as a very long trunk, and it then spread out
into what looked like branches. I believe that this was because the
cloud was borne upward while the pressure of wind was still fresh,
and then when this died down it was left unsupported, or was overcome by its own weight and so thinned out and became widespread.
Its appearance varied between white on the one hand, and grimy and
spotted on the other, according as it had thrust up earth or ashes.
My uncle, most learned man that he was, realized that this was 7
important, and should be investigated at closer quarters. He ordered
a fast-sailing ship to be made ready, and gave me the option of
accompanying him if I so wished. I replied that I preferred to work
at my books,* and it chanced that he had given me an exercise to
write.

As he was leaving the house, he received a letter from Rectina, 8
wife of Tascius.* She was panicking at the danger looming over her,
for her house lay below Vesuvius, and the only way of escape was by
ship. She begged him to rescue her from that great hazard. He 9
changed his plan, and the journey which had begun in a spirit of
research he now undertook with the greatest urgency. He launched
some quadriremes, and embarked in order to lend aid personally, not
merely to Rectina, but to many, for the attractiveness of the coast had
made it thickly populated. He headed swiftly into the area from 10

which others were fleeing, and maintained a straight course, steering straight towards the danger. He was so fearless that he dictated and had notes taken of all the movements and shapes of that evil phenomenon as he observed them.

11 By now ashes were falling on the ships, whiter and thicker the nearer they approached. Then pumice stones also descended, and stones which were black, charred, and split by the fires. Suddenly they were in shallow water and the shore-line barred their way with debris from the mountain. My uncle hesitated momentarily, wondering whether to turn back, but then, as the steersman advised that course, he said to him: 'Fortune favours the brave. Head for the villa

12 of Pomponianus.' This was at Stabiae, separated from the ships by the middle of the bay (for the shore gradually winds in a curve round the sea as it pours in). Though the danger had not yet drawn near, it was clearly visible, and would come very close as it spread. So Pomponianus had stowed his baggage into boats, having determined on flight if the opposing wind dropped. My uncle was then carried in by the wind, which was wholly in his favour. He embraced, consoled, and encouraged Pomponianus, who was panicking. Then in order to relieve his host's fear by a show of unconcern, he gave orders to be conveyed to the bath. After bathing, he reclined and dined in cheerful mood, or apparently cheerful, which was just as impressive.

13 Meanwhile from Mount Vesuvius widespread flames and fires rising high blazed forth in several places, their gleaming brightness accentuated by the darkness of the night. To calm people's apprehensions, my uncle kept saying that these were fires abandoned by peasants in their fear, and houses ablaze because they had been left untenanted. Then he retired to rest, and in fact he relaxed in sleep that was wholly genuine, for his snoring, somewhat deep and loud because of his broad physique, was audible to those patrolling

14 the threshold. But by this time the courtyard which gave access to his suite of rooms had become so full of ash intermingled with pumice stones that it was piled high. Thus if he had lingered longer in the bedroom the way out would have been barred. So he was wakened, and he emerged to join Pomponianus and the rest, who

15 had stayed awake. Together they debated whether to stay indoors or to roam in the open, for the buildings were shaking with frequent large-scale tremors; as though dislodged from their foundations, they seemed to shift now one way and now another, and then back

again. On the other hand, in the open they feared falling pumice 16
stones, however light and hollow. But comparison of the dangers
made them opt for the open. For my uncle, this was one rational
choice prevailing over the other, but for the rest, fear prevailing over
fear. They used strips of cloth to fasten pillows on their heads as a
protection against falling stones.

By now it was daylight elsewhere, but there it was night, blacker 17
and denser than any night, though many torches and lights of various kinds relieved it. They decided to go out onto the shore, and
to investigate from close at hand whether the sea now allowed any
departure, but it still remained mountainous and hostile. My uncle 18
lay down there on a discarded sail, and repeatedly drank cold water,
which he had requested. Then flames and the smell of sulphur her-
alding the flames impelled the rest to flight and roused him. Leaning 19
on two of his confidential slaves, he stood up and at once collapsed.* I
infer that his breathing was choked by the greater density of smoke,
and this blocked his gullet, which was often frail and narrow, and
often unsettled. When daylight was restored, two days after his eyes 20
had closed in death, his body was found intact and unharmed. It was
covered over, still in the clothes he had worn. It was more like
someone sleeping than a corpse.

Meanwhile my mother and I at Misenum*—but this is irrelevant to 21
a historical account, and you wanted to ascertain nothing other than
details of my uncle's death, so I shall end here, but with a single 22
addition. I have detailed everything at which I was present, and
which I had heard at the very time when the facts were most truth-
fully recorded. You must select what you particularly want, for it is
one thing to write a letter, and another to compose a history; one
thing to write for a friend, another to write for the world. Farewell.

17 *To his friend Restitutus*

I cannot refrain from pouring into your ear by letter, since I cannot 1
do it face to face, the slight irritation which I felt in the audience of a
certain friend of mine. A work was being recited which was exquis-
itely polished. Two or three of those present, eloquent men in their 2
own eyes and and in those of a few, listened as though they were deaf
and dumb. They did not part their lips, stir their hands, or even rise
to their feet because they were tired of sitting down. Why such high 3

seriousness, such superior wisdom, or rather such indolence, haut-
eur, ill-breeding, or rather mindlessness, to spend an entire day in
causing offence, leaving behind as an enemy one to whom you came
4 as a close friend? So are you yourself more eloquent? All the more
reason, then, not to be grudging, for he who is grudging is the
lesser man.

In short, whether your abilities are greater, or less, or identical,
offer praise to him who falls below you, or rises above you, or who is
your equal: to the one who is above you, because if he is not worthy
of praise, you yourself cannot obtain it; to the one who falls below
you, or is equal to you, because your own esteem depends on the
5 person whom you excel or equal being regarded as outstanding. For
my own part, I regularly go so far as to revere and admire all who
achieve something in the intellectual life, for it is a difficult, demanding, and exacting pursuit, which, when despised by people, despises
them in turn. But perhaps you think differently. Yet who is more
6 respectful and appreciative as a judge of literature than you? For this
reason I have revealed my annoyance to you particularly, for I could
associate you with me more than anyone in this matter. Farewell.

18 *To his friend Sabinus*

1 You ask me to undertake proceedings on behalf of the community of
Firmum.* Though I am overstretched, with numerous tasks on hand,
I shall try to do it, for I am keen to put under an obligation both that
distinguished colony by taking on the duties of advocate, and your-
2 self by undertaking this service so very pleasing to you. You often
proclaim to the world that you have gained my friendship for your
protection and prestige, so there is nothing which I should deny to
you, especially as you seek this on behalf of your native city; for what
pleas are more honourable than those which demonstrate patriotism,
3 or more effective than those of a dear friend? So you can pledge my
loyalty to your citizens of Firmum, whom I can now call mine
instead. That they deserve my hard work and eager support is
guaranteed both by their own distinction and above all by the likeli-
hood of their excellence, since your worthy self has emerged from
among them. Farewell.

19 *To his friend Nepos*　　　　　　　106–7

Are you aware that the price of land has risen, especially around 1
Rome? The reasons for this sudden increase have been the subject of
much discussion. At the last elections, the Senate issued the worthi-
est instructions that candidates should not host dinner-parties, dispense gifts, or deposit money.* The first two of these practices were 2
carried on both openly and without restraint, and the third though
covert was known to be taking place.

Our friend Homullus* then alertly exploited this unanimity of 3
the Senate as a proposal to demand that the Senate should inform
the emperor of this general desire, and should beg him with his
forethought to confront this abuse as he had confronted others. He 4
has done so, for he has invoked the law against bribery to restrict the
disgraceful and notorious expenses incurred by candidates. He has
ordered them to invest a third of their inherited wealth in real estate,
for he considered it a disgrace, as indeed it was, that candidates for
office were regarding Rome and Italy not as their fatherland but as
a lodging house and a stable, as if they were travellers from abroad.

So candidates are rushing around, trying to buy whatever they 5
hear is for sale, and ensuring that more properties are available for
purchase. If you are unhappy with your Italian estates, therefore, this 6
is the time, heaven knows, for selling them and buying in the provinces,* while those same candidates are selling there to buy here.
Farewell.

20 *To his friend Tacitus*

You say that your interest has been whetted by the letter which I 1
wrote to you at your request about the death of my uncle, and that
you are keen to know, when I was left behind at Misenum (I had
embarked on this topic but then broke off), not only what fears
but also what misfortunes I endured. So 'though aghast in mind at
recalling them, I shall begin'.*

Once my uncle had departed, I devoted the rest of my day to my 2
studies, for that was the reason why I stayed behind. I then took a
bath, had dinner, and then a disturbed and short-lived sleep. There 3
had been earth-tremors for many days previously, though they were
less terrifying because they were frequent in Campania.* But that

night they became so strong that everything around us seemed to be
4 not merely shifting but turning upside down. My mother broke into
my bedroom. I in my turn was already rising, intending to rouse her
if she was sleeping. We retired to the courtyard of the house, which
5 extended a short distance between the sea and the buildings. I am
uncertain whether I should call it resolve or foolishness (I was then
in my eighteenth year, you see), but I asked for a book of Titus Livy
and read it, and I also copied out passages (as I had begun earlier), as
though in relaxation. Suddenly a friend of my uncle appeared; he
had recently come from Spain* to join him. When he saw my mother
and myself sitting there, and me even reading a book, he rebuked
her for her forbearance, and me for my untroubled attitude. But I
concentrated on the book just as eagerly.

6 By now the first hour of daylight had arrived, but it was still
uncertain and listless. The buildings all round were shaking, and
though we were in the open, it was a confined space, and our fear of
7 falling buildings became great and definite. We then finally decided
to quit the town, followed by a stupefied mob. In what passes for
prudence at a time of panic, they preferred the decision of others to
their own, and in an extended column they pressed close to us and
8 drove us on as we departed. Once we were away from the buildings,
we halted. There we experienced many remarkable and many fearful
things, for the carriages which we had ordered to be brought out
were moved in opposite directions though on wholly level ground,
and did not remain stationary in the same tracks even though
9 wedged with stones. Moreover, we watched the sea being sucked
back and virtually repelled by an earth-tremor; at any rate the shore-
line had advanced, and left many sea-creatures stranded on the dry
sand. On the landward side there was a black and menacing cloud,
split by twisted and quivering flashes of fiery breath; it opened out
into extended shapes of flames, like lightning flashes, but greater.

10 Then that same friend from Spain spoke more urgently and pressingly: 'If your brother, if your uncle* is still alive, he desires your
safety. If he is dead, he wanted you to survive him. So why do you
postpone your escape?' Our answer was that we would not take
11 thought for our own safety while we were not sure of his. He did not
delay further, but burst out, and removed himself from the danger
with all speed.

Not long afterwards that cloud descended to ground level and covered the sea. It had encircled Capri and hidden it from sight, and made the promontory of Misenum invisible. My mother then 12 begged and encouraged and bade me flee in any way I could. She said that this was possible for a young person, but that she herself, being weighed down with years and a frail physique, would be happy to die if she were not responsible for my death. My riposte was that I would not seek safety without her. I then grasped her hand, and forced her to move faster. She reluctantly obeyed, reproaching herself for delaying me.

Ash was now descending, though slight in quantity. I looked back. 13 Dense blackness loomed over us, pursuing us as it spread over the earth like a flood. 'Let us turn aside,' I said, 'while we can see. Otherwise, if we stay on the road, we may be brought down and flattened in the darkness by the crowd accompanying us.' We had 14 scarcely sat down when darkness descended. It was not like a moonless or cloudy night, but like being in an enclosed place where the light has been doused. You could hear women moaning, children howling, and men shouting; they were crying out, some seeking parents, others children, and others wives, or recognizing them by the sound of their voices. Some were lamenting their own misfortune, others that of their families. A few in their fear of death were praying for death. Many were raising their hands to implore 15 the gods, but more took the view that no gods now existed anywhere, and that this was an eternal and final darkness hanging over the world. There were some who magnified the actual dangers with invented and lying fears. Some persons present reported that one part of Misenum was in ruins, and that another was on fire; it was untrue, but their listeners believed it.

A vestige of light returned, but to us it seemed to be not daylight 16 but an indication of advancing fire. In fact, the fire halted some distance away. But the darkness returned, and so did the ash, now abundant and heavy. We repeatedly stood up and shook it off, for otherwise we would have been buried and even crushed beneath its weight. I could boast that though encompassed by these great dan- 17 gers I uttered no groan or pusillanimous word, but what deters me is that I believed that I was perishing together with the whole world, and the whole world was perishing with me—a wretched consolation for my mortal lot, yet a powerful one.

At last the darkness thinned out and vanished into smoke or 18

cloud. True daylight came, and the sun also shone, but pallidly, as occurs at an eclipse. Our eyes, still trembling, were confronted with a scene of universal change, for everything was buried by deep ash
19 as though by snow. We returned to Misenum, tended our bodies as best we could, and in mingled hope and fear spent the night on tenterhooks and in uncertainty. The fear was stronger, for the earth-tremors continued, and many frenzied individuals made a mockery of their own misfortunes and those of others with terrifying proph-
20 ecies. Even then, however, we ourselves did not plan to leave, in spite of our experience and expectation of the dangers, until the message came about my uncle.

These details are in no way worthy of your history. You will read them with no intention of recording them. If they seem to you unworthy even of a letter, you will doubtless blame yourself for requesting them. Farewell.

21 *To his friend Caninius*

1 I am of the company of admirers of the ancients, but am not one to despise the talents of our own day, as some do. Nature is not so weary*
2 and exhausted that it produces nothing praiseworthy. Indeed, I recently listened to Vergilius Romanus* reading to a small group a work modelled on the Old Comedy. It was so good that it can at some time serve as a model for others.
3 I am not sure if you know him, but you ought to. He is the epitome of honest manners, refined talent, and literary versatility.
4 He has written graceful, sharp, and charming iambic mimes, and is supremely eloquent in this genre (for there is no category of writing which when perfected cannot be pronounced supremely eloquent). He has written comedies rivalling Menander and others of that age; you can regard these as on a par with those of Plautus and Terence.
5 Now for the first time he has made his appearance with Old Comedy, but he does not appear to be a beginner. He does not lack intensity, grandeur, subtlety, pungency, sweetness, or charm. He has paid hon-our to virtues, and attacked vices; he has deployed fictitious names
6 fittingly, and real names appropriately. Only with regard to myself has he exceeded the limit in generosity of judgement, but poets are permitted to transgress with regard to truth.
7 In short, I shall extract the book from him, and send it to you to

read or rather to memorize, for I have no doubt that you will not put
it down once you have taken it up. Farewell.

22 *To his friend Tiro*   106–7

A case of great importance has been conducted which concerns all 1
who are to be governors of provinces; it is important too for all who
naively entrust themselves to friends. Lustricius Bruttianus caught 2
his colleague Montanius Atticinus* red-handed in much criminal
activity, and reported it by letter to Caesar. Atticinus then added
insult to injury by laying an accusation against Bruttianus, whom he
had deceived. At the hearing which took place I was an assessor.*
Each of the two spoke on his own behalf, and both handled the issues
separately and *sommairement*, the kind of presentation which at once
divulges the truth. Bruttianus produced his will, written as he said 3
by the hand of Atticinus, for this was the means of demonstrating
both their intimate friendship and his need to complain about the
man for whom he had entertained such affection. He recounted clear 4
evidence of foul crimes.* Atticinus was unable to rebut them; he
retaliated in such a way that in his disgusting defence and his accusation he showed himself to be a scoundrel. For he had bribed a slave
of Bruttianus' scribe, had intercepted documents and tampered with
them, and, most sacrilegiously of all, he had exploited the charge
against himself by diverting it against his friend.

Caesar acted in the best possible way. He indicted,* not Bruttianus, 5
but Atticinus there and then. He was condemned, and banished to an
island.* Bruttianus was awarded a thoroughly deserved attestation
of honourable conduct, and indeed fame, since his resolution has
pursued him. For, having defended himself with the greatest dis- 6
patch, he launched a vigorous accusation, so that he has emerged as
incisive as he was virtuous and honest.

I have written to you about this to give you prior warning now that 7
you have obtained your province. You must rely on yourself totally,
and not trust anyone very much. Secondly, you must realize that if
any person does practise deception on you (I pray that this does not
happen), retaliation is at hand. But repeatedly ensure that there is no 8
need for this, for the pleasure of exacting reparation is not so great as
the humiliation of being deceived. Farewell.

23 *To his friend Triarius*

1 You insistently press me to take on a case in which you have a personal interest, and which in general is a noble cause, bringing good repute. Yes, I shall take it on, but not for nothing.* 'What?' you ask. 'Is it possible that you will refuse to do it for nothing?' It certainly is, for the fee I intend to demand is more honourable than

2 advocacy offered gratis. What I am asking as part of the bargain is that Cremutius Ruso* should be my fellow advocate. This is a regular practice with me, one which I have already repeatedly carried out with young men of high birth; for I have this zealous ambition to

3 parade fine young men in the courts, and to propel them to fame. I must bestow this attention on my friend Ruso if on anyone, whether because of his high birth or his exceptional affection for me. I regard it as very important for him to be seen and heard in the same cases

4 and also on the same side as myself. Do indulge me, indulge me before the time comes for him to speak, for once he has spoken you will thank me. I promise you that he will allay your anxiety, and satisfy my hopes and the importance of the case. He is a young man of outstanding qualities, who within a short time will introduce

5 others, if in the meantime we advance him. For no individual has such conspicuous talent from the start as not to need a subject, an opportunity, and also a sponsor and patron. Farewell.

24 *To his friend Macer*   106

1 In any action, what a great difference the identity of the person makes! The same deeds are either praised to the skies or relegated as the lowest of the low, depending on the fame or obscurity of the

2 person performing them. I was sailing on our lake Comum, when a friend of riper years pointed out to me a house and also a bedroom overhanging the lake. 'It was from that room', he said, 'that a woman

3 of our town some time ago threw herself down with her husband.' I asked him why. The husband, as a result of a long-standing illness, was festering with ulcers in his private parts. His wife demanded to take a look,* for, she said, no one would give him a more honest

4 opinion of whether he could be cured. Her examination removed all hope. She urged him to die, and herself became his companion in death—or rather she led him, was his inspiration, and compelled

him, for she roped herself to her husband, and threw herself into the
lake. Even I, a fellow townsman, had not heard of this until that 5
recent occasion, not because her action was less impressive than that
most celebrated deed of Arria,* but because she was socially humbler.
Farewell.

25 *To his friend Hispanus*

You write that Robustus, a distinguished Roman knight, journeyed 1
with my friend Atilius Scaurus* as far as Ocriculum, but has not been
seen anywhere since. You beg me to ask Scaurus to come, and to put
us, if he can, on any track in the investigation. He will come, but I 2
fear that it will be of no avail. For my suspicion is that something
untoward has befallen Robustus, as happened to my fellow townsman Metilius Crispus* some time ago. I had secured the rank of 3
centurion for him, and as he was leaving I also presented him with
40,000 sesterces with which to kit himself out and to smarten himself up. But thereafter I received no letters from him, nor any message that he had died. It is not clear whether he had been ambushed 4
by his slaves or together with them; what is sure is that neither he
nor any of his slaves has been seen again, and the slaves of Robustus
likewise. However, we must make the attempt, and summon Scaurus. 5
We must make the gesture in response to the praiseworthy pleas of
both yourself and that most honourable young man who with
impressive devotion and also impressive intelligence is searching for
his father. May the gods favour him in finding his father, as he has
already found the identity of his travelling-companion! Farewell.

26 *To his friend Servianus*   106–7

I am delighted, and I send my congratulations on your decision to 1
wed your daughter to Fuscus Salinator.* He comes from a patrician
family, his father is a most honourable man, and his mother merits
equal praise. The young man himself is devoted to his books and to
literature, and is also an eloquent speaker. He has a child's openness,
a young man's affability, and an elder's dignity. Nor does his affection for me deceive me. True, I have boundless affection for him, as 2
he has deserved for the services and the respect he has shown me,
but I am discerning, and the greater keenness of my judgement is

commensurate with my enhanced affection. As one who knows him
from experience, I promise you that you will have a son-in-law than
3 whom no better can be imagined. It remains for him with all speed
to make you a grandfather of children like himself. How blessed
that time will be, when I can take from your arms his children and
your grandchildren, as though they were my own children or grandchildren, and hold them as if my rights were equal to yours!
Farewell.

27 *To his friend Severus*   early 107

1 You ask me to think over what proposal as consul-designate you
should make to honour the emperor.* To formulate suggestions is
easy, but to choose between them is not, because his virtues offer
abundant material. However, I will offer a suggestion by letter, or for
preference face to face, if I can first reveal my doubts. I wonder
2 whether I should offer you the same advice as I gave to myself. When
I was consul-designate, I refrained from any semblance of flattery,
even if unintended. This was not because I was being independent
and true to myself, but from an understanding of our emperor, for
I realized that the greatest tribute I could pay him was to make no
3 proposal which I seemed forced to make. Then too I had in mind the
numerous distinctions bestowed on all the unworthiest recipients,*
from whom this excellent incumbent could be detached only by a
different kind of proposal. I did not gloss over this point by con-
cealment and silence, in case it might seem to be forgetfulness on my
part rather than personal choice.

4   This was what I did then, but the same tactic is not everyone's
choice, and indeed is not appropriate for all. Then again, the motive
for taking or avoiding some course of action varies with the circum-
5 stances of individual persons, situations, and occasions. So the recent
achievements* of this greatest of emperors offer the opportunity of
making some new, important, and heartfelt proposal. For this reason,
as I wrote earlier, I am uncertain whether to offer you the same
advice now as I offered myself then. But I have no doubt that I had to
lay before you my own procedure as part of my advice to you.
Farewell.

28 *To his friend Pontius*

I know what prevented you from being able to get to Campania* 1
before my arrival, but though you were away, you have moved here
lock, stock, and barrel; such an abundance of both urban and rustic
supplies have been offered to me in your name. I have accepted them 2
all in my unscrupulous way, for your servants begged me to do so,
and I feared that you would be cross with both me and them if I
refused. In future I shall impose limits on myself, unless you impose
them; and I have already threatened your staff that if they bring in
so many supplies again, they will have to take them all back. You will 3
say that I am to have the use of your possessions as if they are my
own. Very well, but I intend to be as sparing with them as with my
own. Farewell.

29 *To his friend Quadratus*   106–7

Avidius Quietus,* who showed not only particular affection towards 1
me but also his approval (which gives me equal pleasure), used often
to recount this observation of Thrasea* as well as many others: he
used to recommend undertaking three types of cases, those of
friends, those without an advocate, and those which established a
precedent. Those of friends require no explanation. Why those 2
without an advocate? Because in these above all both the resolve and
the humanity of the speaker were demonstrated. And why those
which established a precedent? Because it was of the greatest
importance whether a good or an evil principle was at stake. To these 3
types of case I shall—perhaps audaciously—add those which bring
fame and celebrity, for on occasion it is right to plead to gain glory
and repute, in other words to plead for oneself. So, since you have
consulted me, these are the boundaries I lay down for one of your
high position and sensitivity.

I am not forgetting that experience both is, and is held to be, the 4
best teacher of oratory, and I observe too that many with minuscule
talent and no education have achieved fluency in speaking by practising it. But I also find that the dictum which I have heard was Pollio's,* 5
or was ascribed to him, has the greatest truth: 'Adequate pleading
has brought me frequent pleading, but frequent pleading has
made me plead less adequately.' The reason for this is that through
excessive practice fluency rather than ability is acquired, and rashness

6 rather than dependability. It did not impede Isocrates* from being regarded as a supreme orator that he was hindered from public speaking by having a weak voice and a bashful attitude. So you must read and write and think a lot to be able to speak at will; you will speak when the desire to do so becomes imperative.

7 The balance I maintained was of this nature: sometimes I obeyed the law of necessity, which partakes of reason,* for I pleaded in some cases at the behest of the Senate. Among these are some that fall into the third of Thrasea's categories, namely those which establish a

8 precedent. I represented the Baeticans against Baebius Massa when the question was posed whether they should be allowed an investigation. It was granted. I again represented them in their complaint against Caecilius Classicus. The question was whether provincials should be punished for being the agents and lackeys of the pro-

9 consul. They paid the penalty. I indicted Marius Priscus, who when condemned under the law of extortion exploited the clemency of the law, though its rigour was insufficient to punish the monstrous

10 nature of his crimes. He was banished. I defended Julius Bassus on the grounds that his actions lacked circumspection and prudence, and were therefore in no sense criminal. His case was submitted

11 to the judges, and he remained a senator. Most recently I spoke on behalf of Varenus, who requested that he in turn be allowed to subpoena witnesses; the request was granted.* I pray that I may in the future be assigned to those cases particularly which it would be fitting for me to have undertaken voluntarily. Farewell.

30 *To Fabatus, his grandfather-in-law*

1 We must, I swear it, celebrate your birthday as gladly as our own, for our joy in ours is dependent on yours, since it is through your attentiveness and care that we are enjoying ourselves here with no worries about you there.

2 The villa Camilliana, your property in Campania, is admittedly ravaged by age, but the more valuable buildings remain undamaged

3 or are only very slightly affected. So we are ensuring that they are restored to the soundest possible condition.

Though I have many friends, I seem to have virtually none of the

4 kind you are looking for and which the situation demands, for they are all toga-clad city-dwellers, whereas supervision of country estates

requires some hardbitten country-dweller who does not regard physical toil as oppressive, nor the maintenance demeaning, nor the 5
lonely life depressing. Your thoughts on Rufus* are thoroughly commendable, for he was a close friend of your son. But I do not know
what he can do for us with regard to the estate, though I believe that
he is very well disposed. Farewell.

31 *To his friend Cornelianus* 107

I was summoned by our Caesar to join the panel of assessors at 1
Centum Cellae,* which is the name of the place. This has given me
great pleasure, for what could be more delightful than to observe the 2
emperor's justice, sobriety, and affability, and moreover in retirement from Rome, where these virtues are made most visible? There
were varying cases of such a kind as could test his judicial role by
reason of their differing types. Claudius Aristion,* chief citizen of 3
Ephesus, conducted his own defence. He is a generous soul who
courts popularity without causing offence. This had led to jealousy,
and a person was sent to inform against him by people of a wholly
different stamp. So he was cleared and acquitted.

Next day there was a hearing implicating Gallitta on a charge of 4
adultery.* She was married to a military tribune who was a candidate
for office. She had brought a stigma to her own reputation and to
that of her husband by a love affair with a centurion. Her husband
had reported this to the consular governor, who had written to the
emperor about it. Caesar reviewed the evidence of witnesses, dis- 5
honourably discharged the centurion, and also banished him. Since
the accusation had to be levelled at two persons, the issue of the
remaining punishment was still outstanding. But love for his wife
and a kind of self-blame for his own complaisance gave the husband
pause. Indeed, even after her adultery had been exposed, he had kept
her in his house, as if he was content to be rid of his rival. When he 6
was warned that he must go through with his accusation, he did so,
but unwillingly. However it was essential for her to be condemned,
even against the wishes of her accuser. So she was condemned,
and subjected to punishment according to the Julian law. Caesar
appended to the record of the sentence both the name of the centurion and a reminder about military discipline, to avoid appearing to
have all such cases referred to him.

7   On the third day a case was introduced which had raised much discussion and varying gossip. The will of Julius Tiro* was clearly
8 genuine in part, but was claimed to be partly forged. Sempronius Senecio, a Roman knight, and Eurhythmus, a freedman and procurator of Caesar, were made to answer the charge. While Caesar was in Dacia, the heirs had jointly composed a letter and begged him to
9 undertake a hearing. He had done so. When he returned, he had arranged a day. When some of the heirs, apparently out of respect for Eurhythmus, were for withdrawing the accusation, the emperor had made this splendid statement: 'That freedman is not Polyclitus, and I am not Nero.'* He had however granted the petitioners an adjournment, and after the expiry of the time limit he had taken his seat to
10 hear the case. Only two of the heirs put in an appearance. They demanded that all the heirs be compelled to plead, since all of them had laid the charge, or alternatively that they themselves too should
11 be allowed to abandon the case. Caesar spoke with the greatest seriousness and self-control. When the advocate of Senecio and Eurhythmus stated that the defendants were left under suspicion unless they were granted a hearing, the emperor remarked: 'Whether they are left under suspicion is not my concern; I am left under
12 suspicion.' He then turned to us and said: '*Comprenez bien** what we must do, since these defendants wish to complain at being allowed not to be charged.' Then, in keeping with the opinion of the councillors, he ordered all the heirs to be informed that they must either proceed with the indictment, or individually endorse the reasons for not proceeding. Otherwise he would go so far as to charge them with calumny.
13   You realize how diligently and seriously the days were spent, but each day the proceedings were followed by most enjoyable relaxation. We were invited to dinner each day, a modest meal, considering that the emperor was present. For some of the time we listened to entertainments, and for the rest, the night was prolonged with the
14 most agreeable conversation. On the final day as we departed we were sent guest-presents; such is the solicitous kindness shown by the emperor. For me the pleasure lay not merely in the serious hearings, the distinction of being an assessor, the charm and simplicity of
15 our shared meals, but also in the location itself. The very handsome house is ringed with bright green fields, and lies close to the shore. At this very time a harbour* is being created in the bay there, its left

arm protected by a most substantial mole, while work proceeds on
the right arm. An island projects in the harbour-mouth so that it 16
confronts and breaks the force of the sea borne in by the wind, and it
provides a safe passage on both sides for ships. The technique by
which it is being built up is worth seeing. An especially wide-decked
ship brings in huge rocks against it; these are thrown down on top of
each other, their very weight keeping them in place, so that gradually
they form a sort of rampart. A rocky spine already juts out and is 17
visible, ejecting and throwing up the waves, which dash against it up
to a monstrous height. There is a mighty din, and the sea all round
turns white with foam. Piers will later be superimposed on the rocks,
so that as time goes on they give the appearance of an island newly
formed. The harbour will bear—indeed, already bears—the name
of its founder,* and will form an especially safe haven, for this very
long stretch of shore which has no harbour will exploit its shelter.
Farewell.

32 *To his friend Quintilian*

You yourself are the last person to cut a figure, and you have brought 1
up your daughter in a manner befitting one who is your daughter and
the grandchild of Tutilius.* None the less, since she is to marry that
most honourable man Nonius Celer,* and since consideration of his
offices of state necessitates in him a certain measure of elegance, she
must show regard to the status of her husband by being clothed and
escorted in a manner which, without increasing her worth, lends her
some distinction and adornment. I am aware, too, how, while you rest 2
perfectly content, your resources are limited. So I am claiming to
shoulder a part of your expenses. As though I were a second father to
this daughter of ours, I am giving you 50,000 sesterces, and I would
give you more if I was not confident that your sense of propriety can
be prevailed to accept it and not reject it solely because this little gift
is so trifling. Farewell.

33 *To his friend Romanus*

'Put all away,' he said, 'discard the work begun.'* Whether you are 1
writing something, or reading, bid it be shifted and set aside; take up
like those famous arms this godlike speech (could I possibly be more

arrogant?). This is the really handsome one among my speeches, for
2 I am content to compete with myself. This one is on behalf of Attia Viriola,* and is notable for the distinction of her character, the unusual precedent set, and the importance of the judgement. For she is a woman of distinguished birth, married to a praetorian. She was disinherited by her octogenarian father within eleven days of his bringing home to his daughter a stepmother with whom he had become infatuated.

Attia was now seeking to recover her father's property in the
3 assembly of four panels.* The 180 judges (this is the sum of the four panels sitting together) took their seats. There were several advocates on the two sides, and the benches were jammed; and in addition a densely packed crowd of bystanders surrounded the very extensive
4 court-room in a circle which was thronged. Then, too, the bench of judges was crowded, and in the gallery of the basilica both men and women loomed over us in their eagerness to hear (which was difficult) and to see (which was easy). Fathers, daughters, even stepmothers all awaited with great anticipation.

5 The outcome was divided, for we prevailed in two of the four panels, and were defeated in two. Such a divergence was certainly
6 noteworthy and remarkable, given the same case, the same judges, the same advocates, and the same occasion. The chance outcome was one that did not seem to happen by chance; the stepmother, heiress to a sixth of the estate, lost her case. So did Suburanus,* who after being disinherited by his own father was with some shamelessness claiming the property of someone else's father, when he did not dare claim that of his own.

7 I have explained this to you, first, to acquaint you by this letter with what you could not infer from the speech, and secondly (I shall reveal my guile), so that you can read the speech more appreciatively if you seem not to be reading it, but to be present at the hearing. Though the speech is long, I am not without hope that it will gain
8 the favour of a very short one, for it retains its freshness by its abundant matter, its clear divisions, its several short anecdotes, and its varied eloquence. Many of the passages (I would not presume to claim this to anyone but you) are sublime; many are aggressive, and
9 many are delicate; for it was often necessary to interrupt those impassioned and noble passages to calculate and virtually to demand counters and a games-board so as to transform a speech appropriate

to the Centumviral court into the shape of a private hearing. I spread   10
my sails to express indignation and anger and grief, and I was borne
along by a succession of winds in this most noble case as on a bound-   11
less sea. To put it briefly, some of my close friends often reckon this
speech (I shall repeat myself) among the rest as my *On the Crown*.*
You will most readily decide whether that is true, for you have them
all off by heart, so that while you read this one, you can compare it
with the rest. Farewell.

34 *To his friend Maximus*

You did well to promise a gladiatorial show to our citizens of Verona,*   1
by whom you have for long been loved, respected, and honoured.
Moreover, this was a city from which you gained your wife, whom
you loved so dearly and esteemed so highly. To her memory some
public building, or some public show—and this most fittingly as a
funeral tribute*—was due. Then again, the request was made to you   2
with such unanimity that it would have seemed churlish rather than
resolute to have refused it. What was also impressive was your readiness and generosity in mounting it, for magnanimity too is displayed
in this way.

I do wish that the African beasts* which you had purchased in   3
great numbers had arrived by the appointed day. But though they
were detained by bad weather, and failed to arrive, you deserved to
gain the credit, because it was not your fault that you failed to
produce them. Farewell.

BOOK SEVEN

1 *To his friend Geminus*

1 This illness of yours which is so persistent frightens me, and, though I am aware of your supreme self-control, I fear that it may have an

2 impact on your behaviour. So I urge you to fight patiently against it, for this is both praiseworthy and efficacious. Human nature is in

3 keeping with my advice. At any rate, now that I am well, this is how I often broach the topic with my household: 'My hope is that if I chance to fall ill, I shall not long for anything which causes me shame or regret. But if the illness gets the upper hand, I am laying it down that you are not to give me anything without the doctors' permission. You are to know that if you do so, I shall punish you as others do when things are refused them.'

4 Indeed, once I did have a high temperature* from a raging fever. I finally cooled down and had a massage, and was taking a drink from the doctor. I stretched out my hand and told him to take my pulse.

5 The drink had by now been put to my lips, but I rejected it. Later, when on the twentieth day of my illness I was being got ready for a bath, and I suddenly noticed that the doctors were whispering to each other, I asked what the matter was. Their answer was that I could safely take a bath, but they were not altogether happy about it.

6 'So is it necessary?' I asked, and gently and serenely I abandoned hope of the bath, to which I was apparently now being carried, and instead ordered my mind and features to forgo it, just as the moment before I was looking forward to it.

7 I have written this to you, first so as not to counsel you without offering you a model, and secondly, to compel myself for the future to accept the same self-restraint, once I had bound myself by this letter as by a sort of pledge. Farewell.

2 *To his friend Justus*

1 What consistency is there in your simultaneously claiming that you are hindered by unremitting duties,* and your expressing a desire for my writings, which can scarcely obtain from people at leisure

any of the time which they proceed to waste? So I will allow the ₂ summer to pass, for it is always a busy and strenuous time for you, and finally in the winter, when it is likely that you can find some time at night at least, I shall look among my trifles for what I can best ₃ produce for you. Meanwhile it is more than enough if letters are not a hindrance—but I know they are, and so they will be shorter! Farewell.

3 *To his friend Praesens*

Why do you persist in spending so much time, now in Lucania, and ₁ now in Campania? 'The reason is', you reply, 'that I am a Lucanian, and my wife is a Campanian.' This is a reasonable excuse for a ₂ prolonged absence, but not for an indefinite one. So why don't you return to Rome some time, where your distinction and glory and friendships with both upper and lower classes reside? For how long will you play the monarch? For how long will you enjoy late nights as you wish, and lie in for as long as you like? For how long will your shoes never be worn, your toga remain on holiday, and your day be entirely free? It is time to revisit our problems, if for no other reason ₃ than to avoid letting those pleasures of yours flag through overindulgence. Come and greet us for a short time, to take greater pleasure in being greeted. Experience the crush of this Roman crowd, so as to take full delight in solitude.

But why do I foolishly dissuade one whom I am trying to entice? ₄ Perhaps these very exhortations may encourage you to bury yourself more and more in the leisure which I do not wish you to tear yourself away from, but merely to interrupt. If I were giving you dinner, I ₅ would mingle the sweet dishes with tangy and spicy ones, so that when your digestion was dulled and cloyed with the first, it could be sharpened by the second. Likewise I now urge you to season your most sweet manner of life from time to time with a few tart flavours. Farewell.

4 *To his friend Pontius*

You say that you have read my hendecasyllables.* Further, you ask how ₁ I came to write them, for I seem to you to be a serious person. I myself confess that I am not a trifler. I was never averse to poetry ₂

(I shall go back to my earlier days). In fact, at the age of fourteen I wrote a Greek tragedy. What was it like, you ask. I have no idea, but 3 it was called a tragedy. Then, when I was returning from military service, and was held up by winds on the island of Icaria,* I composed some elegiacs describing the sea there and the island itself. I also at one time tried my hand at heroic verses, and now for the first time at hendecasyllabics. Let me explain how and why they began.

In my Laurentine villa some books of Asinius Gallus* were being read to me. They were devoted to a comparison between his father* and Cicero. They contain an epigram of Cicero on his darling Tiro.* 4 Subsequently, when I had retired for a sleep at midday (it was high summer) and the sleep did not steal over me, I began to reflect that 5 the most eminent orators had practised this genre of writing,* both for recreation and to win esteem. I concentrated my mind, and, to my surprise because I was short of practice, I composed in quite a short period of time these verses on the theme which had stirred me to write.

6   When I was reading Gallus' book, in which he dared
       To award the palm to his father over Cicero,
       I chanced upon the wanton sport that Tully wrote,
       A work exceptional even from that genius.
       In it his serious concerns he lays aside;
       Therein he shows that minds of great men can rejoice
       In cultured wit and sundry varied pleasantries.
       For he complains that Tiro, with his gross deceit,
       Cheated his lover late at night, when he had dined;
       The meagre kisses owed to him Tiro withdrew.
       When I had read these lines, 'So why, then,' I enquired,
       'Am I concerned to hide so timidly my loves?
       Refusing to reveal, to acknowledge that I know
       The wiles of Tiro and his fleeting flattery,
       And thefts igniting further flames to fire me more?'*

7 I moved on to elegiacs, and with equal speed I rendered them as well, and seduced by such ease I appended more. Then when I returned to 8 Rome I read them to my friends, and they approved of them. Later I tried further metres at odd leisure times, especially when travelling.* Finally I decided to follow the example of many, and to complete a 9 separate volume of hendecasyllabics, and I am pleased with it. It is being read, copied, and even sung. Moreover, it is being set to music

on the harp and lyre* even by Greeks, for love of the book has taught them Latin.

But why should I be such a braggart? Yet poets are allowed to rave 10 like madmen. And I am citing not my own judgement, but that of others. This delights me, whether their judgement is sound or is mistaken. My only prayer is that later ages may likewise be mistaken or approve in the same way. Farewell.

5 *To his dear Calpurnia* 107

My obsession with longing for you is beyond belief. The reasons are 1 first, my love for you, and second, my being unaccustomed to living apart. Hence I spend a great part of the night awake, just picturing you, and likewise during the day, at the times when I used to visit you, my feet lead me (this is the absolute truth) to your suite, and eventually I leave it, feeling unwell and depressed, like a locked-out lover* on a deserted threshold. The one time when I am free of this torture is when I exhaust myself in court with friends' lawsuits. Just imagine, 2 then, the kind of life I am living, when my relaxation lies in hard work, and my consolation is in troubles and worries! Farewell.

6 *To his friend Macrinus* 106–7

An unusual and striking turn has occurred in the case of Varenus,* 1 though the outcome is still uncertain. It is said that the Bithynians have abandoned the accusation against him, regarding it as a rash endeavour. Do I say 'It is said'? The emissary of the province is in Rome, and he has brought a decree of the council to Caesar, with copies for many leading citizens, and also for us advocates of Varenus. Yet the notorious Magnus is still obdurate; indeed, he is most per- 2 sistently harassing the excellent man Nigrinus,* through whom he has approached the consuls, demanding that Varenus be compelled to furnish his accounts.

At this point I supported Varenus merely as a friend, having 3 decided to keep my mouth shut, for nothing would have been as prejudicial as that I, his advocate nominated by the Senate, should defend him as an accused person, when it was vital that he should not appear to be such. However, when Nigrinus had made that 4 request, and the consuls looked towards me, I remarked: 'You will be aware that I have good reason for my reticence once you grant a hearing to the ambassador from the province.' Nigrinus countered: 'To whom have the copies been sent?' I replied: 'To me among others.

5 I have the decree from the province with me.' 'So possibly the issue is clear to you?' he said. 'If you have a different perspective,' I

6 replied, 'I can have a better one.' Then Polyaenus the ambassador explained the reasons for their abandoning the indictment, and requested that no prior decision be taken before the emperor held a hearing.* Magnus then countered, and Polyaenus renewed his request.

7 My own interventions were few and brief, and for much of the time I kept my counsel, for my understanding is that on occasion the orator's task is to be silent rather than to speak.

Indeed, I recall that I have been of service to certain defendants on capital charges even more by silence than by the most punctilious

8 speech. A mother whose son had died (there is surely nothing to prevent me making a point about the orator's role, though my reason for writing this letter was different) had indicted his freedmen, who were her coheirs, on charges of forgery and poisoning.* This was before the emperor, and she had obtained Julius Servianus* as judge

9 for the case. There was a huge crowd before whom I appeared on behalf of the defendants, for the case was a most celebrated one, and men of the most eminent talents were pleading on both sides. The investigation put an end to the lawsuit in favour of the defendants.

10 Later the mother approached the emperor and claimed that she had unearthed fresh evidence. Suburanus was instructed to find time for a review of the case which had been finalized, if she could adduce anything new.

11 The mother's advocate was Julius Africanus, grandson of the celebrated orator* about whom Passienus Crispus remarked after hearing him: 'He's brilliant, heaven knows, quite brilliant, but to what purpose?' The grandson is a talented youngster, but somewhat clever-clever. He made a long speech, using up his permitted time. He then said: 'Suburanus, I beg you to allow me to add one word.'

12 Then everyone looked at me, expecting me to make a lengthy reply. I said: 'I would have countered if only Africanus had appended that one

13 word, for no doubt it would have contained all the new evidence.' I do not readily recall ever obtaining such vehement approbation by a speech as I obtained then by reticence.

On this present occasion my reticence up to now on behalf of

Varenus has gained similar approval and acceptance. The consuls, in 14
accordance with Polyaenus' request, held the entire issue in abeyance
for the emperor to decide. I await the hearing with some apprehension, for that day will either spell for me on behalf of Varenus freedom
from anxiety and time for relaxation, or it will impose on me with
renewal of anxiety the labours which have been interrupted. Farewell.

7 *To his friend Saturninus* 107

I thanked our Priscus* both very recently, and a second time at your 1
command; indeed, I was delighted to do so. It is gratifying for me
that you two excellent men, very dear friends of mine, have become
so close as to believe you are in each other's debt. For he too main- 2
tains that he derives particular pleasure from your friendship, and he
vies with you in your most honourable contest of affection towards
each other. Time itself will enhance this.

I find it frustrating that your activities at work distract you, for the
reason that you cannot devote yourself to your books. But if you can
settle one of your court cases by adjudication, and the other, as you
claim, by your own efforts, you will begin to enjoy your relaxation in
your own abode, and then when you have had your fill you can rejoin
me. Farewell.

8 *To his friend Priscus* 107

I must express the full measure of my delight because our friend 1
Saturninus* in letter after letter to me confesses the most profound
gratitude to you. Proceed as you have begun,* love this excellent man 2
with the greatest intimacy, for you will experience great pleasure
from his friendship, and not just for the moment. He is replete with 3
all the virtues, and above all with the supreme steadiness of his
affection. Farewell.

9 *To his friend Fuscus* 107

You enquire how I think you ought to study in the life of relaxation 1
which you have long been enjoying. What is especially useful, and 2
what many advise, is translation from Greek into Latin,* and from
Latin into Greek. This type of exercise engenders precision and

brilliance of vocabulary, abundant resources of figures of speech, force of exposition, and also, through imitation of the best writers, skill at devising similar concepts. At the same time things which might have eluded you when reading cannot escape the notice of the translator. All this promotes understanding and critical judgement.

3   When you have just read a passage, so as to memorize the content and the argument, there is nothing wrong in writing a sort of rival version, then comparing it with the one you have read, and carefully pondering what you and what the original have expressed more aptly. It is a matter for great self-satisfaction if your version is superior at some points, and for humiliation if the original is invariably better.

It will be in order from time to time to choose a very familiar
4 passage, and to compete with what you have chosen. This is a daring ploy, but not reprehensible, because the competition is private. Indeed, we observe that many who have engaged in competition of this kind have emerged with great praise, and in refusing to be disheartened have excelled those whom they were content to imitate.

5   You will also be able, after putting it out of your mind, to review what you have written, and to retain a great deal but to omit still
6 more, to insert new passages and to rewrite others. It is a laborious and hugely boring task, yet one whose very difficulty makes it fruitful, to rekindle afresh the enthusiasm and to recover the eagerness which has been dulled and has disappeared, and in short to graft fresh limbs, so to say, on an aged body, but without disturbing its earlier structure.

7   I am aware that at present your particular interest* is pleading in court, but I would not for this reason urge the invariable adoption of the aggressive, virtually warring style. Just as the earth is renewed by sowing different changes of seed, so our talents are refreshed by
8 different categories of reflection. I am keen that from time to time you should try your hand at a historical passage, and that you should devote some care to letter-writing, for often even a speech demands descriptions not merely appropriate to history, but also those virtually akin to poetry, and again we look to epistles for language which is
9 compressed and unadorned. It is also in order to relax by composing verses. I do not mean continuous poems of some length (for they can be completed only when at leisure) but those which are pungent and brief,* and which suitably punctuate activities and responsibilities,
10 no matter how extensive. They are termed 'pleasantries', but such

pleasantries sometimes attain celebrity no less than serious compositions. Indeed—for why should I not use verses to incite you to
verses?—

> Wax wins its praise, if soft and yielding it obeys 11
>   Skilled fingers, and when bidden becomes art,
> As now it fashions Mars, and chaste Minerva too,
>   And Venus now creates, and now her son;
> Likewise, as sacred springs not merely quench the flames,
>   But also foster flowers and green fields;
> So it befits men's talents to be shaped and formed,
>   Being instructed through wide-ranging skills.*

So it was that the finest orators, and the finest men too, used to train 12
and delight themselves, or rather, to delight and train themselves in
this way, since it is remarkable how the mind both concentrates and 13
relaxes by means of these. For they contain accounts of love, hatred,
anger, mercy, and elegance, in short, all features of life, and also of
political and legal affairs. Moreover, they embody the usefulness 14
common to other poems, for when we are freed from the requirements of the metre, we rejoice in the unfettered language of prose,
and with greater pleasure we write what comparison shows is the
readier medium.

Perhaps you have received more advice than you asked for, but I 15
have omitted one thing. I have not told you what I think you should
read, though I did advert to it when I stated what you should write.
You must remember to make a careful choice of authors of each genre.
As the saying goes, we are to read a lot, but not many authors. Those 16
to be read are so well known and approved that there is no need
to point them out; and in any case I have protracted this letter so
excessively that, in advising you what you should study, I have
deprived you of the time to do so. So why not return to your tablets,
and compose something as suggested here, or whatever you have
begun? Farewell.

10 *To his friend Macrinus* 106–7

When I have learnt the first part of a story, and the end has been 1
detached from it, I am keen to join it up, so I imagine that you are
similarly eager to learn the outcome of the case of Varenus and the

2 Bithynians.* Polyaenus spoke for the one side, and Magnus for the other. At the close of the speeches, Caesar said: 'Neither party will complain if there is a delay. I will undertake to investigate the will of
3 the province.'* Meanwhile Varenus' position is greatly strengthened, for it is doubtful whether the indictment is justified, since it is uncertain whether he is accused at all. For the rest, we pray that the province may not again take up what it is said to have condemned, and repent of its decision to repent. Farewell.

11 *To Fabatus, his grandfather-in-law* 106–7

1 You express surprise* that my freedman Hermes did not await an auction, but has sold to Corellia for 700,000 sesterces the lands which I had inherited and had ordered to be advertised for sale, representing my five-twelfths of the legacy. You add that they could have been sold for 900,000, which reinforces your query whether I
2 am to ratify his action. I do ratify it. Listen to my reasons for doing so, for I am keen that you approve, and that my coheirs excuse my dissociating myself from them because of an overriding obligation.
3 I regard Corellia with the greatest respect and affection. My first reason is that she is the sister of Corellius Rufus,* whose memory is
4 sacred to me. Secondly, she was an intimate friend of my mother. In addition, I have bonds of long standing with her husband Minicius Justus,* an excellent man; these bonds were particularly close with her son*—indeed, he presided over the games which I mounted
5 when I was praetor. When I recently visited you, Corellia informed me that she was eager to possess some land close to our lake Comum. I offered her any estate of mine which she wanted, and at the price she wanted, apart from those which belonged to my mother and
6 father, for I cannot relinquish them even to Corellia. So when the inheritance passed to me which included those properties, I wrote to her that they would be up for sale. Hermes carried the letter to her, and when she pressed him to sell her my share there and then, he assented.
So you realize that I must ratify my freedman's action which
7 accords with my disposition. It now remains for my coheirs to bear with my reason to sell separately the land which I need not have
8 sold at all. There is absolutely no obligation on them to follow my example, for they do not have the same bonds of friendship with

Corellia that I have. So they can look to their own interests; mine are subordinated to friendship. Farewell.

12 *To his friend Minicius*

I am sending you the written version of the speech which I have 1 composed at your request for your friend, or rather our friend (for what is there that we do not possess in common?), to use as occasion demands. I have sent it rather tardily so that you may have no time to improve it—in other words, to make a mess of it. You will have the 2 time, not perhaps to improve it, but to make a mess of it!* *Car vous autres puristes* delete all the best passages. Yet should you do so, I 3 shall regard it as all to the good, for later when any opportunity offers, I shall exploit your efforts as my own, and by virtue of your fastidiousness I shall get the praise—as though they are like the passages which you will find marked* and expressed otherwise in a note above them. For I suspected that you would regard the speech 4 as too puffed up, since it is rather high-sounding and sublime. So I thought it not out of the way to avoid paining you, and immediately to append something more compressed and meagre, or, to put it better, something meaner and inferior, though in your view more appropriate. For why should I not take every opportunity to attack 5 and criticize your spare style?

So far I have been trying to raise a smile from you at last during your busy round, but this point is in earnest. Be sure to repay me for 6 the travelling-expenses I have laid out in sending a courier for this specific purpose. I am sure that once you have read this you will castigate, not individual sections, but the whole of the speech. You will say that it is not worth a penny, when you are asked to pay for it! Farewell.

13 *To his friend Ferox*

The one letter indicates both that you are not and that you are at 1 your books. Do I speak in riddles? Indeed I do, until I declare my meaning. The letter states that you are not at your books, but it is so 2 polished that it could have been written only by one busy with his books. Alternatively, you are the most blessed man in the world, if you compose such addresses when idle and at leisure. Farewell.

14 *To his friend Corellia* 106–7

1 It is extremely decent of you both to ask and to demand that I should give instructions to accept from you as the price for the lands not 700,000 sesterces, the amount specified by my freedman, but
2 900,000, a twentieth part* of which you paid to the tax-collectors. I in my turn both ask and demand that you take into account what is fitting not only for you, but also for me, and that you allow me on this one issue to oppose you with the same spirit with which I often accede to your wishes in all things. Farewell.

15 *To his friend Saturninus*

1 You ask about my activities, but you know what they are. I am stretched by my public service, I lend aid to my friends,* and from time to time I work at my books. To involve myself in that third activity, not from time to time, but exclusively and always, I would not presume to call virtuous, but it would certainly be more blessed.
2 I should lament that all your activities are other than those you prefer,* if those which you perform were not so wholly admirable, for supervision of the affairs of one's country, and arbitration* between friends are both totally praiseworthy.
3 I knew that you would find friendship with my Priscus* congenial, I was aware of his openness and courtesy, and I am now apprised of his abundant gratitude, since you write that he recalls my services to him with such pleasure. Farewell.

16 *To Fabatus, his grandfather-in-law* 107

1 I enjoy the closest possible friendship with Calestrius Tiro,* who has been associated with me in both private and public connections.
2 We served in the army together, and we were quaestors of Caesar together. He preceded me in the office of tribune by virtue of the right of children; I caught him up in the praetorship when Caesar granted me a year's grace. I have often enjoyed relaxation at his residences, and he has often regained his health at my home.
3 He is now about to leave for his province of Baetica as proconsul,
4 by way of Ticinum.* I hope, indeed I am confident, that I shall readily persuade him to diverge from his route to visit you, if you wish formally to free the slaves* whom you recently manumitted in the

company of friends. You need not fear that this will be a nuisance for him, since he would not regard a journey round the world as over-long if made for my sake. So lay aside that excessive deference of 5 yours, and have regard for your own inclinations. He will be just as pleased to fall in with my request as I am to fall in with yours. Farewell.

17 *To his friend Celer*

Every person has his own reason for holding a recitation, and mine, 1 as I have often previously said, is to be prompted about anything which I have overlooked, as inevitably happens. This causes me all 2 the more astonishment at your writing that there were people who reproached me for reciting my speeches* at all—unless they think that speeches alone require no correction. I should be glad to enquire 3 of these people why they grant (if indeed they do) that there should be recitations of history, which is written not for empty show but for honest and truthful reporting; or again, tragedy, which needs a stage and actors, not a lecture-hall; or lyric poetry, which calls for a chorus and a lyre rather than a reader.

'But recitals in these genres are already accepted as customary.' So 4 should the person who introduced the practice incur blame? As for speeches, these too have often been recited, both by some Romans* and by Greeks. 'But recitation of a speech already delivered is redun- 5 dant.' This would be true if the speech were entirely unchanged, and made to all the same listeners precisely at that time. But if you intro-duce many new sections, or if you invite fresh listeners and others who have heard it but some time ago, why should recitation of your speech win less approval than publication of it? 'But it is hard for a 6 speech to be recited satisfactorily.' But this is a matter for the efforts of the one reciting it, not an argument against recitation.

I myself seek praise not while reciting, but when I am read, so 7 there is no form of correction which I disregard. Initially I scrutinize alone what I have written. Next I read it with two or three others. After that I pass it over to others to annotate, and if I am in doubt about them, I ponder their comments again with one or other of my friends. Finally I read out the speech to a number of people, and it is then, believe me, that I make the most incisive corrections, for I 8 concentrate all the more carefully for being more keyed up.

Respect for others, humility, and fear are the soundest critics, so
put it this way: 'Surely, if you are about to speak with some individual, however learned, and with him alone, you will be less on edge
9 than if you talk with many, even if they are ignorant? Surely, when
you rise to speak in court, it is then that you feel least confident, and
it is then that you long to change not most of your speech, but all of
it? This is especially so if you are performing on the larger stage,
with a bigger audience encircling you—for we show respect even to
10 dirty and shabby listeners. If you think that your exordium is being
criticized, do you not feel enfeebled, and lose heart? In my opinion,
this is because there is in numbers a sort of large-scale collective
discernment; whereas individuals show insufficient judgement, *en*
11 *masse* they show a great deal. So Pomponius Secundus,* the composer
of tragedies, used to say, if some more intimate friend happened to
think that a passage should be expunged when he believed it should
be retained: 'I appeal to the people.' So the silence or applause of
12 the audience led him to adopt his own or his friend's opinion. Such
was the great importance he attached to the views of the public. I am
not concerned whether he was right or wrong, for my practice is to
consult not the public, but particular chosen friends to whom I look
and whom I trust. In short, I take notice of them as individuals, and I
13 fear them when combined. I ascribe to fear what Cicero ascribes to
the pen;* apprehension is the most incisive corrective. It is fear which
inspires corrections, when we reflect that we are to offer a recitation,
fear when we enter the lecture-hall, fear when we are pallid and
aghast as our eyes circle round.
14 This is why I do not regret my regular practice, for I find it
most useful. So far from being put off by the idle gossip of your
acquaintances, I am asking you spontaneously to suggest something
15 in addition. I am never sufficiently conscientious. I reflect on the
great responsibility of entrusting a work to men's hands, and I cannot persuade myself that I am not to discuss often, and with many,
writings which one wishes will gain lasting and universal approval.
Farewell.

18 *To his friend Caninius*

1 You raise with me the question how the money which you have offered
to our fellow townsmen for an annual feast can be safeguarded after

you are gone. It is a worthy point to consider, but a proposal not
easy to solve. You could make over the capital to the town, but with
the fear that the money may dribble away. You could make a gift of
land, but being publicly owned it would be neglected. I find no 2
arrangement more suitable than the one which I myself made. I had
promised 500,000 sesterces to pay for the rearing of freeborn boys
and girls,* and to cover this I allotted land worth considerably more
from my estates to the city-agent; then I took the land back with the
imposition of a rental by which I was to pay 30,000 sesterces* a year.
By this means, the principal was secured for the state and the annual 3
return is fixed, and the land itself will always find an owner to work
it, because its produce greatly exceeds the rental. I am well aware 4
that I seem to have paid rather more than the sum I donated,* for the
need to pay the rental has reduced the value of the very handsome
property. But one must put the interests of the state before private 5
advantages, and lasting benefits before transient ones; and also look
to the interests of one's gift much more carefully than to one's own
resources. Farewell.

19 *To his friend Priscus*

I am upset by Fannia's* illness, which she caught when looking after 1
the Vestal Virgin Junia,* a task she initially discharged voluntarily (for
she is a relative) and later on the authority of the pontiffs, for when 2
the Vestals are forced to quit the hall of Vesta through severe illness
they are allotted to the care and guardianship of matrons. While
Fannia diligently discharged this duty, she contracted this dangerous
illness. Fevers oppress her, her cough worsens, and she is extremely 3
thin and extremely weak. The only strength left to her is in her mind
and spirit, which are fully worthy of her husband Helvidius and her
father Thrasea;* all else is slipping away, afflicting me not merely with
fear, but also with grief, for I grieve that this noblest of women is 4
being torn from our city's eyes, which will never perhaps see her like.
    What purity, what integrity, what dignity, what resolve! Twice she
followed her husband into exile, and because of him she was herself
banished a third time,* for when Senecio* was indicted for having 5
written volumes on the life of Helvidius, and when while defending
himself he had stated that he had been requested to write them by
Fannia, Mettius Carus asked her threateningly whether indeed she

had requested it, and she replied: 'Yes, I did.' And had she passed
on to Senecio her husband's diary, when he was commencing the
biography? 'Yes, I passed it on.' Was her mother* aware of this?
'No, she was not.' In short, no single word did she utter to escape
6 from the capital charge. Why, though the Senate had decreed their
destruction through the pressures and fear of the times, and her
possessions were confiscated, she preserved and retained those
volumes, and bore them into exile as the cause of that exile.

7   Yet how charming and genial she is, and how she inspires affection
as much as respect, a quality granted to few! Will there be any
woman after her whom we can establish as a model for our wives, and
to whom we men also can look for patterns of courage? Will there
be any whom we can likewise gaze upon and listen to in admiration,
8 like the heroines of history? Her very house seems to me to be
shaking and shattered* from its foundations, destined to fall upon her,
though as yet she has descendants. What great merits and what great
deeds will they manifest to ensure that she does not die as the last of
her line?

9   A further cause of my depression and pain is that again I appear
to be losing her mother, that renowned mother of this great woman
(for I can ascribe no greater glory to her). It is Fannia who brings her
back and restores her to us, and Fannia will take her with her. This
10 will afflict me with both a fresh wound and one reopened. I revered
and loved them both; which the more I do not know, and no preference did they seek between them. I discharged my services to them
in times of both prosperity and adversity. I consoled them when they
were banished, and I avenged them on their return.* Yet I have not
matched my services to them both, and for this reason I am all the
more eager that Fannia should survive, so that I may have continuing
time to pay my debts.

11   These are my anxieties as I write to you. If some god converts
them into joy, I shall not complain about my fear. Farewell.

20 *To his friend Tacitus*   ?106–7

1 I have read your book,* and, as carefully as I could, I have marked the
passages which I thought should be changed and those which should
be deleted. I for my part make it my practice to tell the truth, as you
for your part accept it gladly. None accepts criticism with greater

forbearance than those who deserve the greatest praise. I now await 2
the return of my own book* from you with your observations. What
a pleasant and splendid exchange this is! I take great delight in the
prospect (assuming that posterity pays some regard to us) that
reports will circulate everywhere of the harmony, frankness, and
loyalty we have shown each other in our lives. It will be an unusual 3
and notable fact that two men virtually identical in age and distinction,* and with some standing in the world of literature (I am forced
to speak of you rather unflatteringly, since I am describing myself as
well), have nurtured each other's writings.

I was still a mere youth when you were already flourishing in fame 4
and renown, and I was eager to follow your example, to be, and to be
thought to be, 'closest, but by a long distance'* to you. There were
many highly talented writers, but you seemed to me—our natural
likeness to each other inclined that way—the one whom I could and
should best imitate. So I rejoice all the more that in any conversation 5
about literature, our names are bracketed together, and when men
speak of you, my name at once crops up. There are some who are
esteemed above us both, but our ranking is of no account to me, as 6
we are linked together, for in my eyes he who is nearest to you ranks
as the highest. Why, you must have observed in wills that unless
someone has chanced to be a close friend of one or other of us, we
receive identical legacies, and indeed we are cited together. The 7
outcome of all this is that our affection for each other becomes still
more ardent, since our literary interests, characters, and reputations,
and above all the judgement of the public, bind us together with so
many bonds. Farewell.

21 *To his friend Cornutus*

I am following your instructions, dearest colleague,* and as you bid 1
me, I am taking precautions to cope with my eye-problem. I journeyed here in a covered carriage, enclosed on every side as if I were
in my bedroom. Here* I renounce not only my pen, but also my sight-
reading, and am confining myself to listening. I keep the rooms in 2
shadow by drawing the curtains but without totally excluding the
light. The covered passageway is kept half in shadow and half in
light by putting the shutters over the lower windows. In this way
I am gradually adapting my eyes to the daylight. I take a bath, 3

because that is beneficial, and wine, because it does no harm, but very sparingly. This has become my routine, and now my doctor is keeping an eye on me.

4   I was delighted to receive the guinea fowl, since it came from you. My eyes, though bleary, were sharp enough to see that it was a very plump bird. Farewell.

22 *To his friend Falco*

1 You will be less surprised at such a persistent request from me that you should bestow a military tribunate on a friend of mine, once you know his identity and his character. I can now both reveal to you his
2 name and describe him, now that you have given your promise. He is Cornelius Minicianus,* a notable figure in my native region, both in rank and in character. He is of distinguished family, and well endowed, keen on literature in the way of unproductive amateurs. He is also the most upright of judges, the most courageous of advo-
3 cates, and the most loyal of friends. You will believe that I have done you a good turn once you gain closer acquaintance with him, for he is equal to every distinction and every appointment. He is a most unassuming man, so I do not wish to praise him too highly. Farewell.

23 *To Fabatus, his grandfather-in-law*   107

1 I am glad that at present you feel strong enough to be able to meet Tiro at Mediolanum,* but, so as to maintain your strength, I beg you not to impose such heavy exertion on yourself, when your sum of years counsels against it. Indeed, I insist that you await him at home
2 and indoors—in fact, within the confines of your bedroom. True, I love him as a brother, but he must not demand from one whom I reverence as a father an obligation which he would not have imposed on his own father. Farewell.

24 *To his friend Geminus*   107

1 Ummidia Quadratilla* has died, shortly before her eightieth birthday. She retained her vigour until her final illness, and her body remained
2 compact and sturdy, more than is the norm for a married woman, She left the most edifying will at her death. She bequeathed two-thirds

of her estate to her grandson,* and a third for her granddaughter to inherit. I scarcely know the granddaughter, but I have the most intimate fondness for the grandson, an outstanding young man who inspires a sense of family affection among those beyond his blood-relatives. In his early days as a boy and a youth, in spite of his 3 handsome looks, he escaped all the tittle-tattle of malicious tongues. He married before the age of twenty-four, and would have become a father if the god had been kind. Though dwelling in the luxurious ambit of his grandmother, his way of life was extremely Spartan, though he was most deferential. She kept a troupe of pantomime 4 dancers, and indulged them more extravagantly than was fitting* for a woman in high society. Quadratus never watched them, either in the theatre or at home, nor did Quadratilla demand his presence. On one occasion she informed me, when she was entrusting me with 5 her grandson's studies, that it was her practice, as a woman enjoying the leisure of her sex, to relax with a game of draughts, or in watching her pantomime dancers; but before doing either of these things she always instructed her grandson to retire to his studies. It seemed to me that she did this more out of respect for him than out of affection.

You will be surprised at this, as I was. At the recent sacerdotal 6 games,* the pantomime performers were brought on as the commencement. As Quadratus and I were leaving the theatre together, he said to me: 'Do you know that today is the first time I have watched my grandmother's freedman dancing?' This was what her grandson 7 said, but good heavens, men with absolutely no connection with her were paying honour to her (I am ashamed to have said 'honour'). As they performed their service of flattery, they were rushing to the theatre, jumping up and down, clapping their hands, expressing admiration, and then reciprocating every gesture of their mistress as they sang. They will now receive the tiniest of bequests as a bonus for their activities in the theatre from an heir who failed to watch them.

I recount this because you for your part are not reluctant to hear of 8 any new event, and for me it is a pleasure to review by writing about it anything which has lent me delight. My delight springs from the dead woman's family feeling, and the honour bestowed on this best of young men. I am happy too that the house which at one time belonged to Gaius Cassius, head and founder of the Cassian school,*

9 will be under a master in no way inferior. For my friend Quadratus
will occupy and adorn it, and restore it to its ancient distinction,
fame, and glory, since he will emerge from it as great an orator as
Cassius was a jurist. Farewell.

25 *To his friend Rufus*   107

1 What a huge number of learned men lurk hidden and unknown
to fame through their unassuming nature or their inactive lives!
Yet when we are to make a speech or give a reading, we are apprehensive of those who publicize their literary skills, whereas those who
say nothing reveal their superiority all the more by greeting a
2 masterly work with reverential silence. What I now write describes
my experience of this.

   After Terentius Junior* had seen military service as an equestrian,
and had served with the greatest integrity as procurator in the province of Narbonensis,* he retired to his country estate, preferring the
life of most peaceful leisure to the public distinctions available to
3 him. When I was invited to stay with him, I regarded him as a decent
head of household and as a hard-working farmer, and I had in mind
to chat with him on issues in which I imagined him to be involved.
But once I had begun in this vein, he called me back to literature
4 with highly learned observations. How elegant was every word he
spoke in flawless Latin and Greek! His proficiency in both languages
is so striking that the one he uses at a particular moment seems to be
his speciality. The depth of his reading and his power of recall are
amazing; you would think that he lived in Athens, and not on a
country estate.
5   Need I say more? He kept me more on my toes, causing me to
respect these men, living like rustics in retirement, just as much as
6 the most learned people I know. I offer you the same advice; just as in
military camps, so in the field of letters there are a good number of
men of rustic appearance, whom you will find on close inspection to
be girt and armed and most eagerly talented. Farewell.

26 *To his friend Maximus*

1 The sickness of a certain friend* has recently brought to my notice
that we are most virtuous when we are ill, for who is gnawed by

greed or lust when he is out of sorts? He is not subject to love- 2
liaisons, does not aspire to high positions, is indifferent to riches, and
is satisfied with what little he has, as he is soon to leave it. It is then
that he is mindful of the gods, and remembers that he is a man. He
envies no one, admires no one, despises no one. He does not even pay
attention to or feed on malicious gossip. He pictures in his mind
baths and running streams, and these are the sum of his concerns 3
and prayers. For the future he aspires to a soft and easeful life, one of
harmless blessedness, if he should happen to survive.

So I can briefly prescribe for you and for myself what philosophers 4
try to teach in countless words and even in countless volumes: when
restored to health we are to persist in being what when ill we maintain
that we will be. Farewell.

27 *To his friend Sura*

Our leisure offers us the opportunity for me to play the pupil, and 1
you the master. So what I should very much like to know is whether
you believe ghosts exist* and have a form peculiar to them and some
supernatural power, or whether they are insubstantial and illusory,
acquiring shape merely from our fear. I am especially inclined to 2
believe in their existence from what I am told happened to Curtius
Rufus.*

While he was still a menial and little-known figure, he had become
a member of the staff of the governor of Africa. Late one afternoon
he was strolling in the colonnade when the figure of a woman, larger
and more beautiful than a human, appeared before him. He was
petrified. She told him that she was Africa, and had come to foretell
the future to him. She said he would repair to Rome, hold high
positions, and also return to that same province invested with the
supreme command; there he would die. The entire prophecy came 3
true. Moreover, as he neared Carthage and was disembarking, so
the story goes, the same figure met him on the shore. What is definite
is that when he fell ill he drew upon his past to foretell his future,
and on his happy days to presage his ill-fortune, for though none
of his entourage feared for him, he himself abandoned hope of
recovery.

Hear now this second story, which I shall recount as I heard 4
it; surely it is more terrifying and no less astonishing than the first.

5 At Athens* there was a sprawling, roomy house which was notorious and plague-ridden. In the silence of the night the clink of metal was heard. Then, to one of keener hearing, the distant rattle of chains was initially audible, and then resounded from close at hand. A spectre appeared, an old man bowed down with emaciation and filth, with a flowing beard and bristling hair. He wore fetters on his legs

6 and chains on his wrists which he kept rattling. As a result, the residents were kept awake in terror all through the grim and dread nights. Their lack of sleep induced illness and then, as their fear grew, death, for even during the day, though the ghost had retired, the recollection of it roamed before their eyes, and their fear survived longer than the causes of it. The house was then abandoned, and condemned to lie empty, left wholly to that spectre. But it was put up for sale, in case anyone unaware of that monstrous evil wished to buy or to rent it.

7 The philosopher Athenodorus* visited Athens. He read the advertisement, and on hearing the price he was suspicious because it was so cheap. So on making enquiries, he learnt the whole story, and in spite of it, or rather all the more because of it, he rented the house. When the day began to draw in, he ordered a couch to be laid for him in the front of the house. He asked for tablets, a pen, and a lamp, and consigned all his servants to the inner part of the house. He concentrated his brain and eyes and hand upon his writing, for fear that if his mind was unoccupied, he would imagine the presence of the apparitions which he had heard of, and arouse in himself empty fears.

8 At first the night was as silent there as elsewhere, but then there was the clank of metal and the movement of chains. The philosopher did not raise his eyes or abandon his pen, but he fortified his mind and stopped his ears. Then the noise intensified and drew nearer; now it was audible at the threshold, and now within the threshold. He looked back, and saw and recognized the spectre as it had been

9 described to him. It stood there, signalling with a finger as though summoning him. In response he gestured with his hand that it should wait a little, and again he bent over his tablets and his pen. The wraith rattled its chains over his head as he wrote. He again looked back at the ghost, which was signalling as before, and without

10 lingering he picked up his lamp and followed. The spectre proceeded with heavy steps, as though burdened with its chains. After diverging into the courtyard of the house, it suddenly glided away

and left him as he was accompanying it. Now left alone, he plucked some plants and leaves and marked the spot with them. Next day he 11 approached the magistrates, advising them to bid the place to be dug up. Bones were unearthed there, encircled and entwined with chains; the corpse had rotted with its time in the earth, and had left the bones uncovered and worn away with the chains. They were gathered and buried at public expense. Thereafter the house was free of the shades, which had been duly buried.

These details are attested by other persons, and I believe them; 12 but I can attest to others the truth of the story that follows. I have a freedman of some education. Sleeping in the same bed with him was a younger brother. My freedman seemed to observe a man sitting on the bed and applying scissors to his head, cutting off the hair from his crown. When daylight came, the crown of his head was shorn, and the hair was found lying there. A short period elapsed, and a 13 similar episode in turn lent credence to that earlier one. A young slave was sleeping among several others in the slaves' compound. As he tells the story, two figures in white tunics came through the window, cut his hair as he lay there, and retired the way they had come. The daylight showed that he too had been shorn, and his hair was scattered all around. Nothing untoward followed, except perhaps 14 that I was not indicted, though I would have been if Domitian, in whose reign these events occurred, had lived longer.* For found on his desk was a document laid against me by Carus. Since it is customary for persons indicted to let their hair grow long, this allows me to guess that the cutting of my servants' hair was an indication that the danger looming over me was averted.

So I ask you to apply your learning to this question, for it merits 15 your sustained and deep thinking. I am surely not unworthy to receive the benefit of your abundant knowledge? For though as usual 16 you may present the arguments on both sides, you must come down more strongly on one or the other, so as to leave me in no doubt and uncertainty, for my purpose in consulting you was to foreclose my vacillation. Farewell.

28 *To his friend Septicius*

You state that certain people have rebuked me in your presence for 1 exaggerated praise of my friends at every opportunity. I acknowledge 2

the charge and indeed embrace it, for what is more honourable than
the sin of generosity? But who are these acquaintances of yours who
know my friends better than I do? Granted that they know them,
however, why do they begrudge my making the most felicitous of
mistakes? My friends may not rise to the level of my praise, but it

3 makes me happy to believe so well of them. So let those people
direct their baleful attentions towards others, for there is no shortage
of those who call it discriminating to disparage their friends. They
will never succeed in persuading me that I am overfond of mine.
Farewell.

29 *To his friend Montanus*

1 You will laugh, you will then be angry, but then you will laugh,
2 should you read what you cannot credit unless you read it. On the
road to Tibur, less than a mile out, I recently noticed the tomb of
Pallas* with the inscription: 'For his loyalty and devotion to his patrons, the Senate decreed* to him the insignia of a praetor, together
with 15 million sesterces, but he was satisfied merely with the
distinction.'

3 I myself have never admired distinctions which originated from
fortune rather than good judgement. But this inscription reminded
me above all how ridiculous and pointless are those which from time
to time are wasted on such slime and filth. That scoundrel had the
audacity both to accept and to refuse distinctions, and even to present the proffered gifts before posterity as a model of modesty. But

4 why should I feel angry? It is better to laugh, in case such people
think they have obtained something important, when by such luck
they attain the status of laughing stock. Farewell.

30 *To his friend Genitor*   107

1 I am deeply pained by your loss of a pupil who, you write, showed
outstanding promise. Of course I realize that your studies have been
hindered by his illness and death, for you are most attentive to all
your obligations, and you show the most abundant affection towards
all those of whom you approve.

2 My Roman tasks follow me even here, for there are people seeking
3 to make me judge or arbitrator. Then too there are the complaints of

the peasants, who claim their right to trouble my ears following my lengthy absence. I am also oppressed by the need to let my farms, an exceedingly troublesome task, for suitable tenants* are a rare commodity. For these reasons I have precious little time to devote to 4 study, though I do work at it, for I am doing some writing and reading. But as I read, comparison makes me realize how badly I write, in spite of your cheering me up by comparing my speech which 5 vindicated Helvidius with Demosthenes' oration* against Meidias. In fact, I had that speech to hand when I was writing mine, not to challenge it (which would be shameless and almost lunatic), but to imitate it and follow in its footsteps, in so far as the gap between the strongest and the feeblest talent, and the difference between the cases, allowed. Farewell.

31 *To his friend Cornutus*

Claudius Pollio* desires your close friendship, and deserves it because 1 he desires it and also because of his affection for you. Scarcely anyone makes such a request unless he takes the initiative. He is in general upright, honourable, retiring, and excessively modest—if anyone can be too modest! When we served in the army together,* I formed a view 2 of him not restricted to that of the fellow soldier. He commanded a wing of a thousand cavalry; my orders from the consular legate were to audit the accounts of the cavalry and infantry units, and while I unearthed large-scale and disgusting greed with corresponding neg- lect, in Pollio's case I found the greatest honesty and scrupulous care. He was later advanced to most distinguished offices* as procur- 3 ator, and was never suborned by any opportunity to be diverted from his inherent attachment to incorruptibility. He never waxed overproud through his prosperity, and never in the wide range of his offices breached his unbroken reputation for kindness. With the same mental resolution he showed himself equal to hard work as now he copes with retirement. This leisure he interrupted and laid aside 4 briefly, and gained great praise thereby: he was taken on as assistant by our friend Corellius* in the purchase and allocation of lands,* a process resulting from the generosity of the emperor Nerva. He is indeed deserving of the highest repute to have gained the unquali- fied approval of that outstanding man, when there was available such a wide range of choice for the post.

5　　You can be assured of the degree of respect and loyalty which he shows to his friends from the attestations at death of many men, including one from that most dignified citizen Annius Bassus,* whose memory he preserves and prolongs with such grateful commendation that he has published a biography of him (for he accords to literature

6　the same respect he shows to other honourable pursuits). This was a noble gesture deserving of praise, since it is so unusual, for many invoke the memory of the dead only to grumble about them.

7　　This is the man, believe me, who is so very keen to cultivate you. So welcome and embrace him, in fact summon him and show him affection as if returning a favour. For in duties of friendship, the one who has taken the first step deserves to be rewarded rather than to be placed under an obligation. Farewell.

32　*To Fabatus, his grandfather-in-law*　　　107

1　I am delighted that the visit of my friend Tiro* has been a pleasure for you, and I am especially happy at your mentioning that you took the opportunity of the proconsul's presence to grant freedom* to a large number. For I am keen that our native area should be advanced in every material way, but especially in the number of its citizens, since this is the strongest accession to our cities.

2　　I am also pleased, though not for any ostentation, at your additional news that you and I have been celebrated both in a vote of thanks and in expressions of praise, for, as Xenophon remarks,* 'praise is the sweetest thing to hear', especially if you believe that you have deserved it. Farewell.

33　*To his friend Tacitus*　　　107

1　I prophesy (and my prophecy is not mistaken) that your histories* will be immortal, so I am all the more eager to be given a place in

2　them, as I freely admit. If we are usually careful to ensure that our features are portrayed by all the best artists, we must surely aspire to have our deeds penned by a writer and publicist like yourself.

3　　So I am describing to you an episode (in fact, it cannot have escaped your watchful eye, for it is in the public records,* but none the less I am describing it) so that you may be readier to believe that I shall be delighted if my role, which has won increased popularity because of the hazard it incurred, is enhanced by your genius and your testimony.

The Senate had allocated Herennius Senecio and myself as advo- 4 cates for the province of Baetica against Baebius Massa, and, after Massa was convicted, had passed a decree that his possessions should be lodged in state custody. Senecio ascertained that the consuls would be open to appeals against this decision, so he contacted me, and said: 'We have conducted in concert the indictment allotted to us, so let us also in concert approach the consuls, and request them not to allow the dispersal* of the property which they should keep in custody.' I replied: 'The Senate merely allocated us as advocates, so 5 consider whether our role is at an end, now that the Senate hearing has been completed.' He rejoined: 'You must impose whatever limit you like on your own account, for your relationship with the province* is confined to your services to them of recent date. But I was both born and held the quaestorship there.' Then I said: 'If that is 6 your firm and carefully pondered decision, I will support you so that any resultant odium from it may not fall on you alone.'

We approached the consuls, and Senecio explained the situation, 7 while I appended some comments. We had barely finished when Massa complained that Senecio had been motivated not by the good faith of an advocate, but by the hostility of a personal enemy, and he demanded that Senecio be indicted* for dereliction of duty. All 8 were aghast. Then I spoke: 'I fear, most distinguished consuls, that Massa may have exposed me to a charge of collusion with him by his silence, for he has not indicted me as well.' The statement was both welcomed there and then and achieved subsequent fame, being on many people's lips. Indeed, the deified Nerva* (for even when still 9 a private citizen he acknowledged actions directed to the public good) sent me a most dignified letter in which he felicitated not only myself but also our era for having shown an example (these are his very words) 'similar to those of days of old'.

Whatever the significance of this, you will make it better known,* 10 more celebrated, and of greater import, though I am not demanding that you exaggerate what really happened. History must not go beyond the truth, and for honourable deeds the truth is enough. Farewell.

BOOK EIGHT

1 To his friend Septicius   107

1 I have accomplished the journey* successfully, though with the one
2 snag that one of my servants fell ill in the most oppressive heat. In
fact, my reader Encolpius,* mainstay of my serious studies and joy of
my relaxation, coughed up blood when his throat was irritated by the
dust. How grim this will be for him, and what a harsh blow to me, if
this disqualifies him for intellectual work, when his entire charm lies
3 in it! Who will then read and savour my books as he does? To whom
will my ears be pinned* as they are to him? But the gods give promise
of a happier outcome. The discharge of blood has stopped, the pain
has diminished; then, too, he is a self-controlled patient, we are
exercised about him, and the doctors are attentive. Moreover, the
healthy climate, the retirement, and the relaxation give promise of a
cure as much as of leisure. Farewell.

2 To his friend Calvisius   107–8

1 Other people visit their estates to return richer, but I myself go to
return poorer. I had sold my vine-crop* to businessmen vying to buy
it. The price was enticing, both at the moment of sale and what
2 seemed in prospect, but their hopes were dashed. The quickest way
out was for me to offer them all an equal rebate, but that was not
quite just, and I hold the view that it is wholly admirable to practise
justice at home as well as abroad, in small things as well as in great,
and in our own affairs as well as in those of others. For if all sins are
3 equal, so are all merits. So I granted all of them an eighth of the price
which they had paid so that 'none should leave without a prize';* then
I made a separate arrangement for those who had expended the
largest amounts in their purchases, for they had both lent me greater
4 help and themselves sustained the greatest loss. So for those who had
laid out more than 10,000 sesterces, I added to the one-eighth, which
was conferred all round as a kind of general donation, a tenth of any
sum in excess of the 10,000.
5   I fear that I have not explained this too well, so I shall clarify it by

calculation of the figures. Any buyers who had chanced to lay out
15,000 sesterces received an eighth of that sum plus a tenth of 5,000.
In addition, when I recalled that some had paid over a fair amount of 6
what they owed, while others had put down a modest deposit, and
others still, nothing, I thought it wholly unfair that those who had not
been equally responsible in making payments should be made equal
recipients in the generosity of the rebates. So I granted a further 7
rebate of a tenth of the sum paid by those who had deposited the
money. This seemed the most appropriate way of both showing gratitude to each individual according to his past merits, and enticing all
of them not only to buy in future but also to put down the money.

This mode of calculation—or amenability—has cost me a great 8
deal, but it was worth it, for throughout the whole region the unprecedented rebate and the process have won praise. Moreover, the
purchasers, whom I treated, not by the same measuring-rod, as the
saying goes, but separately and in ascending order, have departed
under an obligation to me commensurate with their greater honesty
and decency. They have discovered that in my eyes it is not the case
that 'wicked and honourable men are equally respected'.* Farewell.

3 *To his friend Sparsus*

You indicate that you have found the book which I most recently sent 1
you to be by far the most congenial of all my writings. A certain very
learned person* holds the same view. This inclines me all the more to 2
believe that neither of you is mistaken, for it is hardly likely that you
are both wrong—but perhaps I flatter myself!* My own aspiration is
that each most recent work should appear impeccably finished, so
now, as against the speech which is in your possession, I am promoting the one which I have recently published, and which I intend to
share with you as soon as I find a reliable courier. I have whetted your 3
expectation, and I fear that the speech may fall below it when you
take it up. In the meantime, however, you must await it with the
assumption that it will please you, as perhaps it will. Farewell.

4 *To his friend Caninius*   107

Your plan to write on the Dacian war* is an excellent one, for what 1
subject is so recent, so wide, so sublime, and finally so poetic, and

2 though centred on most truthful events, so legendary? You will describe new rivers unleashed over lands, new bridges erected over rivers,* precipitous mountains overhanging the camps; a king, refusing to despair* as he was harried from his palace, and then from his life. Then, in addition to these topics, the celebration of two triumphs, the first over an unconquered nation, and the second that of most recent days.

3 But there is one most crippling difficulty: to find language to match the subject is an uphill and massive task even for a talent like yours,* however much it rises to the greatest heights and gains momentum from most splendid compositions. Additional toil lies in the fact that the barbaric and uncivilized names, notably that of the

4 king himself, do not run easily into Greek verses. But there is no impediment which cannot be alleviated by skill and care even if it cannot be wholly overcome. Moreover, if Homer is allowed to shorten, lengthen, and adapt malleable Greek words to lighten his verse,* why should you not be permitted a similar licence, especially

5 when this is not self-indulgent, but necessary? So when by the privilege granted to poets you have invoked the gods and among the gods* him whose deeds, achievements, and plans you are to proclaim, you must cast off the ropes, spread your sails, and then, if ever, launch into the deep with the full wind of your genius—for in converse with a poet, why should I not wax poetic?

6 At this moment I make it a condition that you send me the initial sections as you complete them, or rather, even before you complete them, in their rough-and-ready state while newly composed, like

7 newborn babies. Your reaction will be that fragmented parts cannot please as much as when they are assembled, nor initial attempts as much as the finished article. I know that, so they will be assessed as first drafts, regarded as detached sections, and kept in my desk to await your final polish. Allow me to have this pledge of your affection in addition to the rest, to gain acquaintance with secrets which you

8 would not wish anyone to know. In short, I shall perhaps be able to approve and praise your writings the more when they are more slowly and more carefully produced, but I shall love you the more and praise you the more, the more speedily and unwarily you send them. Farewell.

5 *To his friend Geminus* 107–8

Our friend Macrinus* has sustained a heavy blow, for he has lost his 1
wife, who even if she had lived long ago would have been what she
has been, a model wife beyond compare. He lived with her for thirty-
nine years without wrangling or animosity. What respect she demonstrated for her husband, and she deserved it herself likewise to the
highest degree! Think of the number and the depth of the virtues
which she assembled and mingled in herself, acquiring them at the
different stages of her life! True, Macrinus has the great consolation 2
of having possessed that blessing for so long, but this intensifies his
loss all the more, for the grief of missing her is increased through the
past enjoyment of pleasures. So I shall suffer anxiety on this dearest 3
friend's behalf until he can lend himself to distractions, and endure
the scar of his wound. Nothing can achieve this so much as necessity
itself, length of time, and sufficiency of grief. Farewell.

6 *To his friend Montanus*

You must now be aware from my letter that I recently noticed Pallas' 1
tomb bearing the inscription: 'For his loyalty and devotion to his
patrons, the Senate decreed to him the insignia of a praetor, together
with 15 million sesterces, but he was satisfied merely with the distinction.' Later I decided that it was worthwhile to look out the 2
senatorial decree. I found it so verbose and effusive that the supreme
arrogance of the inscription seemed modest and humble by comparison. I pass over the men of old like Africanus, Achaicus, and
Numantinus;* those of most recent date, men like Marius, Sulla, and
Pompey (I am reluctant to go on) should assemble and intermingle;
they will fail to rise to the glories of Pallas. Am I to regard those 3
who passed that decree as men of wit* or poor wretches? I would call
them men of wit, if wit were appropriate in the Senate; or wretched,
except that no man is so wretched as to have that measure foisted
upon him. So was it ambition, or lust for advancement? But who
is so lunatic as to desire advancement by way of personal and civic
shame, in a city in which exploitation of the most illustrious distinction lay in being able to be first to praise Pallas in the Senate?

I pass over the fact that praetorian insignia were offered to Pallas, 4
a slave,* for those who offered them were slaves; I pass over the fact

that they decreed that he should be not merely encouraged, but even compelled to wear a gold ring,* for it would have been an affront to 5 the majesty of the Senate for a praetorian to wear an iron one. These are minor issues to be passed over; what must be mentioned is that the Senate in Pallas' name (and the Senate House was not subsequently purified), in Pallas' name the Senate gave thanks to Caesar both because Claudius himself had attached the highest honour to mention of his name, and because he had granted the Senate the 6 opportunity of attesting their good will towards him. For what more splendid gesture could the Senate make, than to show itself suitably grateful to Pallas? Appended to the decree are these words: 'That Pallas, to whom all confess their obligation as best they can, should most deservedly obtain the reward for his unique loyalty and unique diligence.' You would think that he had extended the boundaries of empire, or brought armies back safely to the state!

7   Subjoined to those words we read: 'Since the Senate and the Roman people could have no more welcome means of showing their generosity than if they had been able to lend support to the wealth of the most abstemious and reliable guardian of the resources of the *princeps*.'* This was the prayer of the Senate at that time, this was the special source of joy of the people, this was the most welcome opportunity for their generosity, that they should enrich Pallas' resources by disbursing public funds.

8   Then what came next? That the Senate sought to decree that 15 million sesterces be awarded him from the treasury, and the further his disinclination withdrew him from base longings of that kind, the more earnestly to beg the father of the state to force him to yield 9 to the wishes of the Senate. The only thing lacking was that there should be discussion with Pallas by the authority of the Senate; that Pallas should be requested to yield to the Senate, and that Caesar as sponsor should be called on to counsel him in that most arrogant self-denial, so that he would not refuse the 15 million sesterces. He did refuse them; when such great wealth was offered him by the state, this was the only way he could have acted more arrogantly than 10 by accepting it. Yet the Senate greeted even this gesture with praises in tones of complaint with these words: 'Since the best of emperors and the father of the state, on the plea of Pallas, desired that the section of the proposal referring to the gift to him of 15 million sesterces should be rescinded, the senators bore witness that they

had willingly and deservedly taken steps to decree this sum to Pallas, together with the other distinctions, to mark his loyalty and his conscientiousness, but that they were obeying the wish of the *princeps* in this matter, since they believed that it was not right to oppose him in any issue.'

Just picture Pallas vetoing, so to say, the senatorial decree, restricting the honours conferred on him, and rejecting the 15 million sesterces as excessive, after accepting the praetorian insignia as of lesser account! Just picture Caesar deferring to the plea, or rather the command, of a freedman in the presence of the Senate (for it was a command which the freedman imposed on his patron, when he made the request in the Senate). Just imagine the Senate going so far as to bear witness that it had begun, deservedly and willingly, to decree this sum to Pallas, together with the other distinctions, and that they would have proceeded with this had they not deferred to the wishes of the emperor, for it was not right to oppose him on any issue! So what was necessary to prevent Pallas obtaining the 15 million sesterces from the treasury was his own deference and the obedience of the Senate, who especially in this matter would not have obeyed had they not thought it right in no respect to refuse their obedience.

Do you think this is the end of the story? Hold on, and hear the major part. 'In particular, since it is expedient that the benevolence of the emperor, which shows the greatest alacrity in praising and rewarding those who deserve it, should be famed everywhere, especially in those places where men charged with the administration of his affairs could be fired to imitate him, and the well-tried loyalty and integrity of Pallas could by his example incite enthusiasm to emulate such honourable conduct, the statement read out by the best of emperors before our most distinguished order on 23 January last, together with the decrees of the Senate on these matters, should be engraved in bronze, and this bronze tablet should be affixed to the mailed statue of the deified Julius.'*

So it seemed insufficient that the Senate House should witness scenes of such disgrace. The most crowded place in Rome was chosen where they were displayed to be read by contemporaries, and read too by posterity. It was decreed that all the honours of this most arrogant slave should be inscribed on bronze, both those which he had rejected and those which he sported so far as the proposers

envisaged it. The praetorian insignia of Pallas were incised and
carved on public monuments to last for ever, as if they were ancient
15 treaties or hallowed laws. So monstrous was the—I cannot find the
word for it—of the emperor, of the Senate, of Pallas himself, so that
Pallas might purpose to have his shamelessness, and Caesar his long-
suffering, and the Senate its humiliation, inscribed before the eyes of
all. They were not ashamed to offer a pretext for their base conduct,
indeed a worthy and honourable pretext, so that the rest of the world
could be challenged by the example of the rewards to Pallas to show
16 enthusiasm in emulating him. Such was the cheapness in which
honours were held, even those which Pallas did not disdain. Yet men
from honourable families were found to seek and to aspire to what
they saw was offered to a freedman, and promised to a slave.

17   How consoling it is that I had no experience of those times,* of
which I am ashamed as if I lived during them! I have no doubt that
your reaction is like mine. I know how lively and noble you are in
mind, so that though I have perhaps at some points let my anger
transgress the bounds of a letter, you may more easily believe that
my resentment is understated rather than excessive. Farewell.

7 *To his friend Tacitus*

1 It was not as master to master, nor as pupil to pupil as you state,
but as master to pupil (for you are the master and I am the opposite,
and you bid me return to school while I am still stretching out the
2 Saturnalia) that you have sent me your book.* I could hardly compose a longer hyperbaton* than that, could I, and thus prove that I
am the sort who is unfit not only to be called your master, but even
your pupil? But I will adopt the persona of the master, and exercise
over your book the rights that you have granted, all the more willingly because in the meantime I am going to send you none of my
own on which to take vengeance. Farewell.

8 *To his friend Romanus*   107

1 Have you at any time seen the source of the Clitumnus?* If not yet
(and I imagine 'not yet', for otherwise you would have described it to
me), you must visit it as I did recently. I am ashamed at having been
so slow in going there.

There is a hill which rises to a moderate height, thickly wooded 2
and shaded with ancient cypresses. Below the hill the river emerges
at its source, is forced out in several channels of varying size, and
having struggled clear of the whirlpool which it creates, it opens out
into a broad basin, its waters clear and glassy, so that you can count
the coins which have been thrown in, and the pebbles reflecting the
light. It is borne along from there, not because it goes downhill, but 3
by its own force and apparent weight, At one moment it is a rill, and
at the next the broadest of rivers, capable indeed of bearing boats.
Even when these confront it, and strain and struggle in the opposite
direction, it bears and carries them along. Its current is so strong
that the boat which hastens along with it, even over level ground,
needs no help from oars, whereas if the current is against it, one
overcomes it only by the use of oars and poles, and with the greatest
difficulty. Those who take to the water for amusing relaxation 4
enjoy the twin pleasure of hard work alternating with idleness, and
idleness with hard work, as they vary their course.

The banks are clad in thickly planted ash trees and poplars. The
crystal-clear stream allows us to count their green reflections lying
buried deep within it. The icy temperature of the water competes
with snow, and its sheen is as bright. Close by, an ancient temple 5
stands, invested with religious awe. Clitumnus himself stands there,
clad and adorned in a toga with purple border; oracular responses*
attest the presence of divine and prophetic power. Scattered around
are several tiny shrines, with gods matching their number. Each has
its separate cult and name, and indeed some have their own running
waters, for, in addition to the father-figure among them, there are
lesser streams rising from different sources, though they merge with
the river, which is crossed by a bridge.

The bridge marks the boundary between sacred and secular. 6
Above it, only sailing is allowed, whereas below it bathing is permitted. The citizens of Hispellum,* to whom the deified Augustus presented the site, maintain a civic bathing area there, and also an inn,
and there are houses lining the river-bank, enticed by the beauty of
the river.

In short, there is no aspect which will not afford you pleasure. For 7
you will also have things to study; you will read many inscriptions
written by many hands on all the pillars and on all the walls, which
hymn the waters and the god. Several of them you will praise, and

a few will make you laugh.* But such is your charitable nature that
you will not laugh at them. Farewell.

9 *To his friend Ursus*

1 It is some time since I held a book or a pen, and for some time I have
known no leisure or relaxation—in short, that sluggish but blessed
life of doing nothing and being nothing. So exacting are the many
concerns of my friends,* which allow me neither to retire from Rome
2 nor to get down to study, for no attention to books is of such importance as to cause me to abandon the obligations of friendship, which
those very books counsel us* to perform with the most scrupulous
observance. Farewell.

10 *To Fabatus, his grandfather-in-law*   c. 107

1 Your eagerness to see us providing you with great-grandchildren
will make you all the sadder to hear that your granddaughter has
suffered a miscarriage.* She had a girl's ignorance that she was pregnant, and for that reason she both failed to take the precautions
which pregnant women should take, and did things which she ought
not to have done. She has paid for her mistake with harsh realization,
2 for her life was in the greatest danger. So on the one hand you must
reluctantly accept that your old age has been deprived of the posterity
which seemed forthcoming, but on the other hand you must thank
the gods that for the time being they have denied you great-grandchildren to preserve your granddaughter; and they will provide those
children, for her fertility offers more certain hope of this, though it
has been unhappily ascertained.
3   At this time I offer you the same encouragement, advice, and
assurance that I offer myself, for your yearning for great-grandchildren is no more fervent than is mine for children. I shall, it
seems, bequeath to them as descendants from both of us, a favourable route to high offices, names more widely acknowledged, and an
ancestry firmly established. I pray that by their being born they may
transform our present sorrow into joy. Farewell.

11 *To his dear Hispulla* *c.*107

As I ponder your affection for your brother's daughter, which is ı more tender than the fondness of a mother, I am conscious that I should first report the news of what came later, so that the prior accession of joy may leave no scope for anxiety. Yet I fear that your thankfulness may revert to fear, and that your joy at hearing that she is out of danger may be affected by your horror at the crisis which has attended her.

She is now cheerful, restored to her former self and to me, as she 2 begins her recovery and assesses the danger through which she has passed by regaining her health. At one time her life was in the greatest danger (I do not wish to tempt Providence), not through any fault of her own, though her age was partly to blame. This was the cause of her miscarriage, the melancholy proof of the pregnancy of which she was unaware.

So though your yearning for your lost brother has not brought you 3 the consolation of a grandson or granddaughter of his, you must bear in mind that this is delayed rather than denied to you, because she who can be the source of our hope is safe and sound. Meanwhile give your father an explanation of the accident, for women make a readier allowance for it. Farewell.

12 *To his friend Minicianus*

This is the one day for which I plead exemption,* for Titinius Capito* ı is to give a recitation; I do not know whether a sense of obligation or enthusiasm impels me the more to hear him. He is a splendid man who is to be counted among the outstanding glories of our era. He is an enthusiast for literature and is fond of literary men, whom he nurtures and advances. Many who devote themselves to creative writing find in him a harbour, a haven, and a refuge. He is an example to all. In short, he revives and reforms the study of letters, which were now declining.* He opens his house to those who offer 2 recitations, and shows remarkable indulgence in joining audiences, not merely in his own house; at any rate, so long as he has been in Rome, he has never let me down.

It would accordingly be all the more disgraceful not to return the favour, as my reason for doing so is the more honourable. If I were 3

being harassed by lawsuits, I should believe that I was duty-bound to the man standing surety for me; surely, then, at this moment when all my business and all my concern is with literature, I have an equal obligation to the man who devotes such close attention to me. I can
4 show that obligation to him especially, if not to him alone. But even if I owed him no return and no reciprocal obligation, I should still be influenced either by the man's talent, which is most splendid, most outstanding, and in spite of his most serious demeanour, most affecting, or by the high worth of his subject.

He writes books on the deaths of famous men,* some of whom
5 were most dear to me. So it seems that I am performing a dutiful role, for though I could not attend their funeral rites, I can now be present at their funeral panegyrics, so to say, admittedly after the event but all the more sincerely. Farewell.

13 *To his friend Genialis*

1 I think it is good that you have read my slight works together with your father. It is relevant to your development to learn from a man of the greatest eloquence what you are to praise and what to censure, and at the same time to be educated in becoming accustomed to
2 speak the truth. Your eyes are on the person you are to emulate and in whose steps you are to tread. How blessed you are to have as your model that one and the same person who is both the finest man on earth and your closest relative! In short, you possess for imitation the one above all whom nature desired that you should most closely imitate. Farewell.

14 *To his friend Aristo* 105

1 As you are the greatest expert on private and public law, a part of which is concerned with senatorial procedure, I am extremely keen to have your views on whether I acted wrongly or otherwise in the Senate the other day. My aim is to seek enlightenment not on what is past—it is too late for that—but for the future, in case something
2 similar occurs. You will respond: 'Why do you enquire about something which you ought to have known?' My answer is that the slavish situation of former days casts a kind of forgetfulness and ignorance over senatorial procedures* as over other most honourable pursuits,

for how few of us have the patience to wish to learn what we shall not ₃
apply in practice? Then too it is difficult to retain what you have
learnt unless you practise it. So the resumption of freedom has
found us ill-educated and ignorant, but, fired by the sweetness of
that freedom, we are compelled to perform certain duties before we
are acquainted with them.

In days of old the custom was that, not merely by listening, but ₄
also by observing, we used to learn from our elders the procedures
which we were next to follow, and then in our turn we were to pass
them on to the younger generation. Thereafter our young men were ₅
then lent immediate experience in periods of military service, so that
they grew accustomed to command by obedience, to exercise leader-
ship by following others. Then before becoming candidates for
office, they would stand at the doors of the Senate House* to observe
state policy before sharing responsibility for it. Each individual had ₆
his father as his teacher; the greatest and the oldest men in the state
took on parental duties for those who were fatherless. Thus men
were instructed by example (the most reliable means of attaining
knowledge) about the powers of proposers, the rights of voters, the
discretion of magistrates, and the freedom of the rest. They also
learnt when they should yield and when they should hold out, the
time for silence and time limits for speaking, the distinction between
competing proposals, the way of introducing supplements to existing
motions—in short, the entire conventions of senatorial procedure.

Admittedly, when we were young men, we performed military ₇
service, but at that time military excellence was under suspicion,
sluggishness was rewarded, leaders had no authority, and common
soldiers showed no deference. Authority was nowhere in evidence,
nor obedience either, for the whole scene was lax, disorganized, and
topsy-turvy. In a word, all was better forgotten than remembered.
We then trained our gaze on the Senate, but a Senate which was ₈
fearful and speechless, for it was dangerous to express your convic-
tions, and humiliating to repress them. What was it possible to learn
at that time, or what point was there in having learnt such things,
when the Senate was summoned to be wholly idle or wholly wicked,
when it was kept in being to be now a laughing-stock and now ripe
for grief? Once we became senators, for many years we witnessed ₉
and endured the same evils in which we then took part, so that our
talents were blunted, broken, and bruised by them, affecting even

10 our later days. There has been only a brief period (for every era of greater happiness is shorter) in which it has been our pleasure to come to know our identity, and to apply that knowledge.

So I am the more justified in begging you, first to pardon any error which I may have made, and second, to remedy it by your knowledge, for it was always your speciality to be familiar with laws both public and private, ancient and modern, exceptional and everyday.

11 Moreover, I believe that even those whose regular handling of numerous cases did not allow for any ignorance, will have found the kind of question which I am putting to you not sufficiently commonplace, or even unfamiliar. Accordingly, I shall win further forgiveness if I happen to have erred, and you will be more deserving of praise if you can offer guidance on a matter which one doubts one ever learnt.

12 The trial before the Senate implicated the freedmen of the consul Afranius Dexter.* It was not clear whether his death was attributable to suicide or to the crime or the obedience of his servants. Following the investigation, one senator (who? I myself, but no matter) thought that they should be acquitted, a second that they should be relegated to an island, and a third that they should be punished with death.

13 These proposals were so different from each other that they could only be considered one by one, for what have execution and relegation in common? No more indeed than relegation and acquittal, though a vote for acquittal is somewhat closer to a vote for relegation than is one for execution, for the first two leave a man with his life, but the third deprives him of it. Meanwhile those opting for punishment by death and those voting for relegation were sitting together, seeking to postpone their disagreement by a momentary pretence of harmony.

14 I demanded that the three proposals be counted as three, and that two of them should not be united in a short-lived truce. So I insisted that those who thought that the freedmen should be executed should detach themselves from those proposing relegation, and that in the meantime they should not combine in opposing those voting for acquittal, when later they would be at odds with each other. I argued that it mattered very little whether they both disagreed with one

15 proposal, since they were not supporting the same one. A further point which seemed to me surprising was that the man who had proposed relegation for the freedmen and execution for the slaves

had been compelled to subdivide his proposal, whereas the proposer
of death for the freedmen was being counted in with the advocate of
relegation. For if it had been necessary for the subdivision of one
because he was combining two issues, I did not see how the proposals
of two such different submissions could be combined.

So let me now render an account of my understanding of the 16
situation to you as if you had been there, and though the case is
terminated, as though it were still undecided; let me now assemble at
leisure the points I then made intermittently in the face of many
loud protests. Let us imagine that three judges only had been 17
assigned to this case, and that the first of them had decided that the
freedmen should be executed, the second that they should be relegated, and the third that they should be acquitted. Will the first two
judgements combine forces and eliminate the third, or will each of
the three separately have the same validity as each of the others, so
that the first cannot be joined to the second any more than the
second to the third? So in the Senate likewise, the proposals 18
advanced as different ought to be accounted differently. But if the
one identical person submitted that the freedmen should be both
executed and relegated, they would surely not suffer both death and
relegation on the basis of a single judgement. In short, a judgement
combining such diverse punishments could surely not be considered
a single one. So when one person proposes that they be executed and 19
another that they be relegated, how can this be seen as a single
judgement advanced by two persons, when it did not appear as one
advanced by one person?

Again, does not the law* clearly teach that proposals for execution
and for relegation must be distinguished from each other, when it
prescribes a division in these words: 'You who make this judgement
proceed to this side, and you who support all other measures proceed
to the side which you approve'? Scrutinize and weigh each word.
'You who make this judgement', that is, you who believe that they
are to be relegated, 'proceed to this side', that is, to the side where
the proposer of relegation is seated. This makes it clear that those 20
who believe that they should be executed cannot remain at that side.
'You who support all other measures': note that the law was not
content to say 'other measures', but added 'all'. So there is surely
no doubt that those who opt for execution take a wholly different
view from those who support relegation. 'Proceed to the side you

approve': surely the law itself seems to summon, compel, and drive those who dissent to proceed to the opposite side? Does not the consul, too, not merely by the ritual words but also by a gesture of the hand, indicate where each is to remain or to cross over?

21 But the objection can be made that if the proposals advanced for execution and relegation were separated, the proposal for acquittal would prevail. What relevance has this to the voters? It is certainly unfitting for them to wage war by every means and on every count to prevent the outcome of a more merciful proposal. However, those voting for execution and those who advocate relegation ought to be mustered against those for acquittal, and then against each other. Just as in some public shows the lot extracts and preserves an individual to join battle with the victor, so perhaps in the Senate there are certain primary and certain secondary contests, and when two of the proposals clash, the third awaits the one which comes out on top.

22 What of the fact that if the first proposal is approved, the rest fall? What rational basis, then, can there be for not affording the proposals equal standing, when they have no such standing sub-
23 sequently? Let me repeat my point more clearly. When the proposer of relegation pronounces his opinion, unless those who favour execution cross to support a different measure, it will be vain for them subsequently to dissociate themselves from the proposer with whom they were in agreement a little before.

24 But why should I assume the mantle of the teacher, when I wish to learn whether the proposals should have been separated or voted upon one at a time? I obtained the result I demanded,* but none the less I wish to know whether I should have demanded it. How did I obtain it? The person who was proposing the exaction of the death penalty was defeated by the fairness, if not perhaps the legality, of my demand. He renounced his proposal, and went over to the proposer of relegation, doubtless because he feared that, if their motions were separated, which seemed likely on other grounds, the proposal for acquittal would gain the majority of votes. Indeed, there were far
25 more supporters of this one motion than of each of the others. Then those, too, who had been attracted by his authority were left high and dry when he crossed over, and they abandoned the motion which the sponsor had renounced, and they trooped after him whom they fol-
26 lowed as a leader as if he had become a deserter. So the three motions became two, and once the third was eliminated, the second prevailed.

For since the third could not prevail over both of the others, it chose which of them would prevail over it.* Farewell.

15 *To his friend Junior*

I have burdened you with the dispatch of so many volumes at once. 1 The reason why I have burdened you is, first, because you demanded them, and secondly, because you wrote that your vine-harvest was so thin that I knew well you would have leisure to read a book, as the saying goes. I have the same report from my own poor estate,* so I 2 too will be free, and can write something for you to read, so long as I have the wherewithal to buy paper. Otherwise I shall have to erase whatever I have written,* good or bad. Farewell.

16 *To his friend Paternus*

Illnesses and also deaths among my servants,* some of them young, 1 have affected me deeply. I have two consolations, which though in no way commensurate with the overwhelming grief, are none the less consolations. The first is my readiness to grant them their freedom (I seem not to have lost them wholly before their time, when they were free as I lost them), and the second is my permitting those who remain slaves to make a sort of will; such documents I guard as if they are legal. The slaves issue their instructions and requests 2 according to their wishes, and I fall in with them as though under orders. They allocate, bestow, and bequeath their possessions, with the proviso that they are confined to the household, for the household is for slaves a sort of republic* and citizen-state.

But though these consolations ease my mind, I am badly affected 3 and heartbroken, owing to the same human feelings which led me to grant that concession. I would not wish, however, that I were more insensitive on that account. I am well aware that others regard happenings of this kind as nothing more than financial loss, and that they regard themselves on that account as men of importance and wisdom. Whether they are important and wise I do not know; they are certainly not men, for it is part of being human to be assailed by 4 grief and to have feelings, but to struggle against them and to acknowledge consolations rather than to have no need of them.

I have perhaps dwelt on these matters longer than I ought, but 5 more briefly than I wished, for there is a sort of pleasure even in grieving, especially if you weep in the embrace of a friend who accords ready praise or pardon to your tears. Farewell.

17 *To his friend Macrinus*

1 Surely you are not enduring such harsh and stormy weather as we are? Here we have had continual storms and frequent flooding. The Tiber has left its channel* and burst its banks further downstream to
2 a considerable height. Though its impact has been reduced by the channel dug by the abundant foresight of our emperor, it is oppressing the valleys, inundating the plains, and, where there is level ground, before our eyes is an expanse of water covering it. In consequence it confronts and drives back the tributaries which it usually absorbs and carries with it down to the sea, and so it covers the fields, which it does not itself reach, with these immigrant waters.

3 The Anio,* that most sumptuous of rivers—hence the villas on its banks seem to entice and hold fast to it—has broken off and carried away most of the glades with which it is shaded. It has undermined the hillside, and in several places it is blocked by massive landslides. In its search for its lost course, it has battered buildings and forced
4 its way, extricating itself over the fallen masonry. Those on higher ground who have borne the force of the storm have witnessed in some places the fittings and weighty furniture from wealthy establishments, in others farm equipment, here, oxen and ploughs and ploughmen, there, herds of cattle at large and unsupervised, and among them tree-trunks and beams and roofs of houses, all floating
5 along higgledy-piggledy over a wide area. Even areas not reached by the rising river have not escaped the calamity. Instead of river-floods they have had incessant rain, tornadoes hurtling down from the clouds, walls levelled enclosing valuable estates, and burial structures battered and even brought crashing down. Many people have been enfeebled, crushed, and smothered by such disasters, so that mourning for the dead is accentuating the financial losses.

6 I fear that something comparable to this hazard has struck your region. I beg you to take thought for my anxiety and to let me know if nothing of the kind has occurred. But let me know also if something similar has happened. There is very little difference between enduring adversity and awaiting it, except that there is a limit to

grieving, but not to apprehension; for grief is limited by knowledge of what has happened, but apprehension by what can happen. Farewell.

18 *To his friend Rufinus*

The popular belief that wills reflect people's characters is certainly 1 untrue, seeing that Domitius Tullus* has given a much better impression in death than in life. Though he had made himself available to 2 legacy-hunters,* he has left as his heiress the daughter* whom he shared with his brother (she was his brother's daughter, and he had adopted her). He also left numerous legacies most agreeably to his grandchildren, and one also to his great-granddaughter. In short, all the bequests reflected totally his devotion to family, and were on that account all the more unexpected.

So there is varying gossip throughout the city. Some are calling 3 him insincere, ungrateful, and unappreciative, and in upbraiding him they betray themselves with their wholly demeaning expressions of guilt, for their complaints are levelled at a father, a grandfather, and a great-grandfather as if he were childless. Others, by contrast, are praising the very fact that he has cheated the shameless expectations of certain men, for their being deceived is in keeping with the manners of our day. They also make the point that he was not free to make a different will at death, for he had not left, but restored, the money to his daughter, since it was through her that he was enriched by it. What happened was that Curtilius Mancia* loathed his son-in- 4 law Domitius Lucanus, the brother of Tullus, and he had made his granddaughter his heiress only on condition that she was released from her father's control. Her father had then released her, and her uncle had adopted her. In this way, the brother shared in the inheritance by circumventing the stipulation of the will, for having released her from his control, he transferred her to the control of his brother, and thus by deceitful trickery of adoption he restored her to his own control, together with her very substantial riches.

In general, fate seemed to have endowed these brothers with the 5 opportunity of becoming rich at the expense of most unwilling donors. Why, even Domitius Afer,* who adopted them, left a will drawn up eighteen years previously, which was subsequently so displeasing to him that he ensured that their father's possessions should

6 be impounded. His harshness was remarkable, but so was their good fortune; for his harshness removed from the citizen-roll the man who had been his associate in rearing the children, and their good fortune lay in their being adopted by a father who had removed their 7 natural father from the scene. However, this inheritance* from Afer, like the rest of the riches shared with his brother, were to be bequeathed to his brother's daughter, for that brother had made Tullus his sole heir, thus preferring him to his own daughter in seeking to win his affections.

So the will was all the more praiseworthy because it was dictated by family feeling, loyalty, and a sense of decency, for by it he returned the favours owed to all his kin for the services each had 8 bestowed on him. He has likewise repaid his wife for her efforts, for she has inherited most handsome houses and a considerable amount of money. That excellent woman* had borne her lot with supreme patience. and she was all the more deserving of better treatment from her husband because of the criticism she incurred in marrying him, for she had a distinguished pedigree, and an honest character, and is now in her declining years. She had earlier been a mother, but was for long widowed, and it had seemed rather inappropriate that she should have sought marriage with a rich old man so wasted with illness that he could have been wearisome even for a wife whom he 9 had wed when he was young and healthy. In fact he was gnarled and crippled in every limb. He attended to his massive wealth only by eyeing it, and even in bed he could change his posture only with help from others; disgusting and pitiful to relate, he had even to have his teeth washed and brushed for him. He was often heard to say, when he was complaining about the indignities of his weakened state, that 10 every day he licked the fingers of his slaves. Yet he continued to live on, and wanted to live on, sustained above all by this wife, who by her perseverance had transformed the obloquy incurred at the beginning of their marriage into good repute.

11 You have here all the talk of the town, for all the talk is about Tullus. The sale of his goods is awaited, for he was so well endowed that on the very day he bought the hugest gardens, he adorned them with numerous statues of the greatest antiquity, so large was his collection of most handsome works of art, which were lying uncared for in his store-rooms.

12 In turn, if you have anything in your habitat worth a letter, do not

begrudge it; for on the one hand there is always pleasure at hearing something new, and on the other particular incidents educate us on the ordering of our lives. Farewell.

19 *To his friend Maximus*

I find joy and consolation in literature. There is no happiness that 1 literature does not intensify, and nothing so sad that literature does not relieve it. So in the anxiety caused by my wife's sickness and by the life-threatening maladies of my servants,* and indeed the deaths of some of them, I have had recourse to my studies as the sole alleviation of my distress, for they ensure that I become aware more clearly of my misfortuncs, but also that I bear them with greater equanimity.

But it is my practice, before consigning a work to the hands of the 2 public at large, to try it out first on the judgement of friends, and especially on yours. So now if ever please address your mind to the book which you will receive with this letter, for I fear that in my depression I have not addressed my own mind to it sufficiently. I was able to master my grief sufficiently to write, but not with a mind unpreoccupied and serene. It is certainly the case that as literary studies give rise to joy, so the contented mind inspires our writing. Farewell.

20 *To his friend Gallus*

Though we often embark upon a journey and cross the sea to 1 enhance our knowledge of certain things, we ignore those which lie before our eyes. This is possibly because we are disposed by nature to show no interest in things close at hand, but to investigate what lies far away. Or possibly eager interest in everything fades when opportunity readily offers, or perhaps we postpone going to observe what we can set eyes on whenever we are so inclined, on the grounds that we will often see it in the future. Whatever the reason, there are 2 numerous things in this city of ours and in the vicinity that we fail not merely to set eyes upon, but even to read about, whereas if they were a feature of Greece or Egypt or Asia or any other country abundant in and boastful of its wonders, we would have heard and read of them, and visited them.

3   At any rate, I myself quite recently heard of and witnessed something I had neither heard of nor seen before. My grandfather-in-law had requested me to cast an eye over his estate in Ameria. As I was walking round it, a lake lying below it called Vadimon* was pointed out to me, and at the same time some astonishing facts about it were
4 recounted to me. I went to take a look at it. The lake is shaped like a wheel lying on its side, enclosed in proportion all round. There are no inlets, no irregular features, all symmetrically balanced, hollowed and cut out as though by the hand of a craftsman. Its colour is somewhat paler than blue, but with a tinge of darker green. It reeks of sulphur, and has a medicinal taste; the water contains the property to heal fractures. It is modest in extent, but large enough to feel the
5 force of winds and to swell with waves. No ship sails on it because it is sacred, but there are floating islands,* all of them grassy with reeds, sedge, and such other plants as more fertile marshland bears at the lake's edge. Each island has its individual shape and size. The edges of all of them are shaven, because they often collide with the shore and with each other, and thus they chafe or are chafed. They are all of equal height, and are equally buoyant, for like a ship's keel their
6 roots lie low in the water. These are visible from every side, floating above and submerged beneath the water in equal measure. At one time, as they join and are locked together, they look like unbroken mainland; then at another they are separated by warring winds, and frequently, when abandoned by windless weather, they float separ-
7 ately. Often the smaller islands cling to the larger, like small craft to merchant ships, and often smaller and greater compete in a sort of race; in turn they are all driven to the same point of the shore, and dislodge the earth there where they take up their stations. They restore or remove the expanse of the lake on one side or the other. Only finally when they occupy the centre do they not diminish its size.
8   It is known that cattle, in their search for grazing, often set foot on the islands as though they are on the edge of the lake, and only when they are drawn from the shore do they realize that the ground is moving beneath them, as if they have been herded onto a ship, and lodged there. They are aghast at finding the lake surrounding them on all sides. Later, having disembarked where the wind has taken them, they have no more awareness of having left the islands than of having mounted them.

The lake also debouches into a river, which remains visible for a 9
short time until it descends into a cave, and maintains its course
buried deep below. Whatever object it has received before retiring
below, it preserves and produces on re-emerging.

I have recounted this to you because I imagined that it was as little 10
known to you as to me, and no less acceptable to know, for nothing
is so delightful, in your eyes as in mine, as the works of nature.
Farewell.

21 *To his friend Arrianus*   107

As in life, so in literature I regard it as the most handsome and 1
civilized thing to mingle the serious with the genial,* so that the first
does not lapse into melancholy, nor the second into wantonness.
This is the rationale which leads me to intersperse more serious 2
works with playful and sportive ones. In order to publicize these
lighter pieces, I chose the most apposite time and place, and so that
people could henceforward become accustomed to hear them at
leisure and over dinner, during the month of July when litigation is
especially at a standstill, I settled my friends on chairs placed in front
of the couches.

It so happened that in the early morning of that same day, I was 3
suddenly asked to act as an advocate, and this circumstance offered
me a pretext for introductory remarks. I begged that no one should
accuse me of being cavalier towards the composition which I was to
read out—admittedly to friends merely, and to a small number,
which is another way of saying to friends—because I had not abandoned my business in the courts. I added that this was the priority
I followed also in writing, putting needs before pleasures and serious
things before pleasant ones, and that I wrote first for my friends, and
only secondly for myself.

The work consisted of a variety of brief pieces in various metres.* 4
Such is the regular practice of those of us with insufficient confidence in our abilities, to avoid the danger of inordinate length. My
recitation extended over two days, as was demanded by the kind
reception of my audience. But whereas others pass over certain
sections, and charge such omissions to their credit, I omit nothing,
and moreover I say that I am omitting nothing. My reason for reading everything is to correct everything, whereas those who recite

5 merely selected passages cannot achieve this. You may say that their practice is more restrained and perhaps more sensitive towards others, But mine is more straightforward and affectionate, for true affection is shown by one who believes that he is held in such affection that he does not fear he is wearying people. And in any case, what is the use of friends if they assemble solely for their own pleasure? The person who prefers to listen passively to a good work rather than help to create it,* is a frivolous person, and virtually an ignoramus.

6   I have no doubt that, in accordance with your general affection for me, you are eager to read as early as possible this book while it is still immature. Yes, you will read it, but only following the revision which was the purpose of my recitation—though in fact you are already acquainted with parts of it. These sections, when they have been later corrected (or, as sometimes happens following a more protracted delay, changed for the worse), you will find apparently new and revised when you read them again. For when most passages have been amended, the sections left unaltered seem likewise to have been changed. Farewell.

22 *To his friend Geminus*

1 You doubtless know the type of person who, while being subject to every low pleasure, waxes angry at the vices of others as though envious of them, and who comes down most heavily on those whom he chiefly resembles. On the other hand there are those in no need of anyone's forbearance, whose most apposite quality is their tolerance.

2 For my own part, I regard as best and most unblemished the character who is indulgent to the faults of others as if he were guilty of them day after day, yet eschews faults as though he would forgive none of them.

3   So this should be our abiding rule at home and abroad and in every sphere of life, to show no mercy to ourselves, and to be indulgent to those who refuse to pardon all faults but their own. Let us commit to memory what Thrasea,* gentlest of men, used often to say with the attitude which contributed to his greatness: 'The man who loathes faults, loathes men.'

4   Perhaps you are asking what has moved me to write this. The other day a certain person—but I had better tell you of him face to

face, or rather not even then; for I fear that my condemnation of such persecution, sniping, and judgement which I condemn may militate against the precept which I particularly lay down. So I must make no mention of the man's identity and his character, for to reveal him offers no useful lesson, and to refrain from exposing him is the greatest mark of decency. Farewell.

23 *To his friend Marcellinus* 108–9

All my studies, preoccupations, and distractions have been driven, 1 expelled, and excluded from my mind by the most crippling grief which I feel at the death of Junius Avitus.* He had assumed the broad 2 senatorial stripe in my house, and by my vote he had been assisted to obtain offices. Moreover, his affection and respect for me were such that he engaged me to mould his character and to be in a sense his teacher, an unusual trait in our young men of today, for how few of 3 them defer to the age or authority of another and regard themselves as of lesser account? They have immediate access to wisdom, they know everything, they respect nobody, and imitate nobody; they are their own models.

Avitus was not like these, for his outstanding wisdom lay in considering others wiser than himself, and his outstanding learning lay in his eagerness to learn. He always came to seek advice on his 4 studies or on his everyday obligations, and he always went away as if better for it. Indeed, he had become better, either from the advice he received or from the fact that he had sought it at all. What deference 5 he showed to Servianus,* that most scrupulous man! When he was military tribune, and Servianus was governor, he so came to know him and so took to him that when Servianus was transferred to Pannonia from Germany, Avitus followed him, not as a fellow-soldier but as a companion on his serving staff. When he was quaestor,* what diligence and modesty he showed in making himself no less genial and accommodating than useful to his consuls (he served several)! What activity and watchfulness he displayed in canvassing for the office of aedile, from which he has been so untimely taken! This is what makes my grief especially painful. Those pointless labours, those 6 fruitless pleadings,* the position which he deserved but did not attain, pass before my eyes. My mind dwells on the broad stripe which he assumed in my house. I keep recalling those first and last supporting votes of mine, the discussions and the consultations which he held.

7   What deeply affects me is his youth, and the bereavement suffered by his relatives. He had an aged mother, a wife whom he married as a maiden a year ago, and a daughter whom he had recently seen born. So many hopes, so many joys, have become

8   disappointments and griefs in a single day. This man, of late an aedile-designate, so recently a husband and a father, has left behind an office never filled, a mother bereft of her son, a widowed wife, a dependent daughter who never knew her father. What intensifies my tearful grief is that I was away, all unaware of the looming evil. I heard of his illness simultaneously with his death, affording my fears no time to accommodate themselves to this overwhelming sadness. I am in such torment as I write this that my letter contains this news alone, for I can neither think or speak of anything other at present. Farewell.

24 *To his friend Maximus*

1   My affection for you compels me, not to instruct you (for you need no instructor), but rather to remind you to hold fast to what you know and to abide by it, or to have no knowledge of anything better.

2   Bear in mind that you have been dispatched to the province of Achaia,* which is the true and genuine Greece in which civilization, literature, and agriculture too are believed to have been first invented. Remember that you have been sent to order the condition of free states, dispatched in other words to men who are men in the highest sense, to free citizens, free in the highest sense, who have maintained the rights which nature bestowed on them by virtue of their excellence, merits, political friendships, treaty, and finally

3   religious devotion. Show respect for their founder-gods and the names of those gods; show respect for their ancient glory and old age, which in men is worthy of respect, and in cities is sacred. Show honour to their antiquity, to their mighty achievements, and also to their legends. Take nothing away from any man's dignity, his

4   independence, or even his boasting. Keep before your eyes that this is the land which conferred rights and bestowed laws on us,* not after conquering us, but in response to our appeals; that it is Athens to which you are to go, and Sparta which you are to govern; and that it

would be harsh, merciless, and even barbaric to rob cities of the last vestige and remaining title of freedom.

You observe that although in sickness slaves and free men do not 5 differ, yet physicians treat free men better and more gently. Remember what each city has once been, and do not despise it because it has ceased to be such. Show no arrogance or brutality, and do not fear 6 being despised for this. Surely no man who wields supreme power and its insignia is despised, unless he is degraded and shabby, and despises himself first? It is wrong for authority to flex its muscles by insults towards others, and wrong for respect to be won by terror. Affection is far more effective than fear for attaining your purpose, for fear disappears once you depart, whereas affection remains, and, just as fear begets hatred, so affection breeds respect.

Again and again you must remember (for I shall re-emphasize 7 this) the title which your office bears, and you must clarify in your mind the nature and importance of the task of ordering the condition of free cities; for what is more fitting for cities than due order, and what is more precious than freedom? And further, what is more 8 demeaning than if that order should be overthrown, and freedom transformed into slavery?

There is the additional challenge of a personal nature. The outstanding reputation as quaestor which you brought back from Bithynia* lies heavily upon you, as does the emperor's recommendation, and your tenure of the tribunate, the praetorship, and this very role as commissioner, bestowed on you as a reward. So you are to 9 strive all the more not to appear to have been more civilized, more efficient, and more experienced as an official in that distant province than in this one closer to Rome, nor among that subject people than among free men, nor when chosen by lot than here specially selected, nor when inexperienced and unknown than well tried and approved. For in general, as we have often heard and we often read, it is much more humiliating to lose a reputation than to fail to win it.

Do please believe, as I said at the outset, that I have written this 10 to remind rather than to instruct you, though I am instructing you as well, for I am not apprehensive that my affection has taken me too far, There is no danger that what should be of the greatest importance goes too far. Farewell.

BOOK NINE

1 *To his friend Maximus*

1 I have often advised you to publish with all speed the written versions of the speeches which you made in self-defence or against Planta* (or rather, both in self-defence and against Planta, as the subject demanded). I urge and advise it now especially, having heard that he

2 has died. Though you have recited the speeches to many, and have distributed them to be read, I should not like anyone to think that they were finally begun only after his death, whereas you completed

3 them when he was still alive and well. Your reputation for consistency must be preserved, as it will be if both friend and foe realize that you did not pluck up courage to write after your enemy's death, but that the work was already completed when his death forestalled

4 its publication. At the same time you will avoid the charge that 'it is unholy to boast over the slain'.* For what is written and recited about a man still alive can still be published after his death as though he were still alive, so long as it is published at once.

So if you have some other work on hand, abandon it for the time being, and put the final touches to this work which those of us who read it some time ago regard as already perfected. You too must now take the same view, for both the subject and consideration of the time brook no delay. Farewell.

2 *To his friend Sabinus*

1 How agreeable of you to demand not merely a horde of letters, but also very long ones! I have been more sparing with them partly because I feared you were busy with your routine tasks, and partly because I myself was considerably distracted by affairs, predominantly tedious, which both divert and reduce my powers of concentra-

2 tion. Then, too, no subject offered itself for further writing, for my situation is different from that of Marcus Cicero, whom you invite me to imitate. He had not only the most abundant talent, but also matched it with the most lavish supply of varied and important topics.

3 You realize even without my mentioning it within what narrow

boundaries I am circumscribed, unless perhaps I opt to send you a letter reeking of the school of rhetoric and of the philosopher's shade, so to speak. But I consider nothing to be less suitable when I 4 think of you under arms, and your camp, and bugles and trumpets, and the sweat and dust and heat of the sun.

So this is what I consider a reasonable excuse, though I doubt 5 whether I want you to accept it. For it is the mark of boundless affection to deny forgiveness for brief letters sent by friends, even if one knows that there is good reason for them. Farewell.

3 *To his friend Paulinus*

Different people hold different views, but I regard as wholly blessed 1 the man who enjoys the anticipation of a good and lasting repute, and lives in certainty of the survival of his name and future fame. If the reward of immortality were not in prospect, my choice would be for a life of idle and utter leisure. Indeed, I believe that all must 2 opt for either immortality or mortality. Those who choose the first must strive and struggle, while those who opt for the second must live peacefully in relaxation, without wearying their short-lived existence with transient toil, as I see many doing,* who, after chasing the wretched and thankless shadow of hard work, attain only a tawdry end for themselves.

I share these thoughts with you as I share them with myself each 3 day, so that if you demur, I shall abandon them. But you will not demur, since you are always pondering some splendid work which will bring immortality. Farewell.

4 *To his friend Macrinus*

I should be afraid you might think that the speech you will receive* 1 with this letter is too long, if it were not of the type which is seen to incorporate frequent beginnings and frequent conclusions, for each indictment is treated as a separate case. So wherever you begin and 2 then lay aside the speech, you will be able to read what immediately follows both as a fresh beginning or an attachment to what goes before, and thus you will be able to account me interminable in the whole, but very economical in each part. Farewell.

5 *To his friend Tiro*   107–8

1 You are doing splendid work (for I am taking soundings). Carry
on the good work in administering your justice to the provincials in
that most civilized way. This wins you the affection of the lesser
2 citizens, and at the same time the regard of the leading men. Many
people, in their fear that they may bestow too many favours on the
3 powerful, gain a reputation for bad manners and even ill-will. I am
well aware that you have distanced yourself far from this fault, but
I cannot refrain from making my praise sound like advice, in your
observing due discretion in preserving distinctions* between men of
different rank and status, for if they are thrown together, confused,
and intermingled, there is nothing more unequal than the resultant
equality. Farewell.

6 *To his friend Calvisius*

1 All these recent days I have spent in the most agreeable tranquillity
among my tablets and my books. 'How could you manage that in this
city?' you ask. The races were on,* and I take not the slightest interest*
in that type of performance. There is no novelty, no variation, noth-
2 ing for which a single viewing would not suffice. This makes me
wonder all the more that so many thousands should be so childishly
keen, time after time, to see horses galloping and drivers hunched
over their chariots. If the attraction for them lay in the speed of the
horses or the skill of the riders, there would be some justification for
it, but as it is they show their support and affection for the colour of
the shirt, and if in mid-course, while the race was being run, the
colours should be changed, then the enthusiasm and support of
the crowd will be transferred, and in a moment they will forsake the
drivers and the horses which they identify repeatedly from afar, and
3 whose names they repeatedly bawl. So devout is the popularity and
the authority residing in a single shirt of the cheapest kind, not merely
among the common crowd (which is cheaper than the shirt), but
among certain men of dignity. When I call these men to mind settling
down so insatiably to watch the pointless, tedious, continual pursuit,
4 I get some pleasure in not being captive to such low enjoyment, and I
feel the utmost delight in devoting my leisure to literature during the
days which others are wasting on the idlest of pursuits. Farewell.

7 *To his friend Romanus*

You write that you are engaged in building.* That's good, because it 1
means that I've found some justification, for I have a warrant for
my own building since I am in harmony with you. Moreover, our
situations are not dissimilar, because you are building near the sea,
and I near lake Comum, on the shore of which I have a number of 2
houses. Two of them in particular give me much pleasure, but also
much labour. One of them looks out on the lake, being set on rocks 3
in the manner of houses at Baiae, and the other, as at Baiae, abuts
on the lake's edge. So I often call the first Tragedy and the second
Comedy, for the one rests on tragedy's high boots, and the other on
comedy's slippers. Each has its peculiar charm, and each seems
more attractive to its owner because it is different. The first gazes 4
more closely on the lake, and the second has a more extensive vista
of it. The first takes in a single bay which winds gently round, and
the second lies between two bays on a very high ridge. The second
has a straight drive, which stretches above the shore to its distant
boundary; the first has the widest of terraces winding gently round.
The second is not lapped by the waves, whereas the first breaks
their impact. From the second you can observe the fishermen,
and from the first you can yourself fish, casting your line from
your bedroom and virtually even from your bed,* as though from a
small boat.

These are my reasons for building additions onto both houses,
in view of their numerous amenities. Yet why should I render an 5
account to you when you will be doing the same in kind? Farewell.

8 *To his friend Augurinus*

If I begin to praise you after your praise of me, I fear that I may 1
seem not so much to express my considered judgement as to
return a compliment. But in spite of such appearances, I do think
that all your writings are very fine, and especially those about me.
This is attributable to one and the same reason: for your part, 2
you write best when the subject is your friends, and I for my
part in reading your works regard those about me to be the best.
Farewell.

9 *To his friend Colonus*

1 Your grief at the death of Pompeius Quintianus, which leads you to deepen your affection for your departed friend owing to your sense of loss, wins my vehement approval. You are not like many, who love men only in life—or rather, pretend that they do, and even that pretence extends only to those who are successful, for they exclude the unsuccessful from their thoughts, just as they do the dead. But your loyalty is enduring, and your unswerving love is so great that it can be bounded only by your own death.

2 Quintianus was indeed worthy of affection since he himself demonstrated it. He showed affection to the successful, protected the unsuccessful, and felt the loss of those who died. Then too what decency showed itself in his features, and in his speech what reserve, equally balanced between seriousness and geniality! What enthusiasm and what fine judgement he had on literary matters! What devotion he showed in a life spent with his father who was utterly different, though the excellence of the son did not prevent the father from appearing to be outstanding!

3 But why do I intensify your grief? Yet your affection for the young man was such that you prefer these sentiments to my saying nothing about him, especially as they come from me, for you believe that his life can be enhanced, his memory prolonged, and these very years from which he has been torn restored to him by my praise. Farewell.

10 *To his friend Tacitus* 107–8

1 I am eager to follow your instructions, but there is such a shortage of boars that it is not possible to cope with both Minerva and

2 Diana,* who you say should be equally cultivated. So I must render service to Minerva alone, but in a relaxed way, as is appropriate in summer retirement. On my way here I strung out a few lighter pieces not worth preserving for a moment, which were composed in the sort of chatter in which conversation is carried on in a carriage. To these I appended a few more in the house here, when no other activity appealed. So no voice is found for those poems which you think are most appositely composed among groves

3 and glades. I have revised one or two short speeches, though this

category of writing has no charm or attractiveness,* and approximates more closely to the toils than to the pleasures of country life. Farewell.

11 *To his friend Geminus*

I have received that most agreeable letter of yours, which was 1 particularly welcome since you asked for something to be dedicated to you so that it can be included in a collection of my works.* A suitable topic will occur to me, either the one which you indicate or something else more suitable, since your suggestion contains some comments of a slightly offensive nature; take a look, and they will strike you.

I did not imagine that there were booksellers at Lugdunum,* 2 and I was all the more pleased to learn from your letter that my writings are on sale there. I am delighted that they are continuing to attract the favour which they have won at Rome. I begin to regard my work as quite the finished article when the opinions of people scattered over such widely different regions are as one about it. Farewell.

12 *To his friend Junior* 107–8

A certain individual rebuked his son for buying horses and dogs 1 which cost a little too much. When the young fellow had gone off, I said to his father: 'Come on now, did you never do anything deserving a rebuke from your father? I put that in the past tense, but do you not sometimes act in a way which your son would censure as harshly if he suddenly turned father, and you turned son? Aren't we all misguidedly drawn into one mistake or another? Don't different people indulge themselves in different ways?'

It was because I was prompted by this instance of excessive harsh- 2 ness that I have written these lines to you out of the affection we have for each other, in case you too at some time should be too sharp and too hard on your son. Just remember both that he is a boy and that you have been the same, and play your role as father in such a way as to recall that you are human and the father of one who is human. Farewell.

13 *To his friend Quadratus*

1   The more eagerly and attentively you read the written versions of
the speeches which I composed on the vindication of Helvidius,* the
more insistent was your demand that I pen for you the details not
covered in them, and the background information to them; in short,
the entire sequence of the affair which your youth did not allow you
to witness.

2   Following the murder of Domitian,* after some thought I reached
the conclusion that there were important and edifying grounds for
prosecuting the guilty, avenging the unhappy victims, and achieving
personal advancement. In particular, though many individuals had
committed many crimes, none seemed more outrageous than that in
the Senate House a senator should have committed violence* against
a senator, a praetorian against an ex-consul, and a judge against a man
3   on trial. Another circumstance was that I was a friend of Helvidius,
in so far as this was possible with a man who in fear of the times
was keeping his notable fame and his equally notable virtues under
cover in retirement. I also enjoyed friendship with Arria and Fannia,*
the second of whom was Helvidius' stepmother, and the first, her
mother. But it was not so much private obligations as the rights of
the community, the outrageous nature of the deed, and consider-
4   ation of the precedent which fired me. In fact, during the first days
when freedom was restored,* men on their own account in disordered
and uncontrolled uproar had indicted their enemies and brought
them down—so long as these were lesser figures. My own thinking,
both less self-seeking and more resolute, was to bring pressure upon
a most notorious culprit, based not upon the general odium of that
era, but on a specific charge involving him, at a time when the initial
outbursts had subsided, and when anger was every day abating, and
justice had been restored in its place. Although at that time I was
especially downcast owing to the recent loss of my wife,* I contacted
Anteia, widow of Helvidius, asking her to visit me, since the period
of mourning was still under way, and was confining me indoors.

5   When she arrived, I said to her: 'I have decided not to allow your
husband to go unavenged. Tell this to Arria and Fannia' (they had
now returned from exile). 'Think it over, and ask their views, whether
you all wish to be enrolled in this. I have no need of an associate,
but I am not so bent on my own glory as to begrudge you a share in

it.' Anteia conveyed the instruction, and the two ladies promptly agreed.

Conveniently enough, the Senate met two days later. I used invari- 6 ably to refer everything to Corellius,* for I knew him to be a man of the greatest foresight and wisdom of our age. But on this occasion, I remained content with my own decision, because I feared that he would veto the plan, for he was rather hesitant and circumspect. How- ever, I could not contemplate refraining from telling him on that very day that I was about to undertake the course of action which I intended to carry through without further deliberation; for experience dictates that when you have made a decision, you should not consult those men to whom you ought to defer when you have consulted them.

I entered the Senate, sought permission to speak, and for a short 7 time my words won the greatest approval. But when I began to refer to the charge, and to indicate the culprit* (though as yet not naming him), shouts arose against me from every side. One man cried: 'Let us know who the individual is to whom you are referring out of turn!' Another said: 'Who is this person being indicted before any motion has been put?' Then a third: 'We have survived, so let us 8 play safe!' I listened, serene and showing no fear; so strong was the integrity of the case which I had undertaken, and it makes such a difference in instilling confidence or fear, whether people object to your action or merely disapprove of it. It would be tedious to 9 review all the claims advanced on both sides. Finally the consul said: 'Secundus, if you wish to make a proposal, you must make it in your due turn.'* I replied: 'You had granted me the discretion which you granted to everyone up to this moment.'

I sat down. Other business was conducted. Meanwhile a certain 10 friend from the ranks of former consuls took me aside, and in care- fully ordered words rebuked and restrained me, on the grounds that I had advanced too boldly and rashly; he warned me to hold back, and then he added: 'You have brought yourself to the notice of future emperors.' 'So be it,' I replied. 'So long as they are wicked 11 ones.' He had scarcely left me when a second one harangued me in turn: 'What are you presuming to do? Where are you rushing to? To what dangers are you exposing yourself? Why do you repose such confidence in the present when you are uncertain of the future? You are gunning for a man who is already a prefect of the treasury, and will soon be consul. Moreover, think what influence and what

friendships he can call upon!' (He named a man who at that time
was in command of the most massive army* in the East, the subject
12   of some significant gossip, and one causing apprehension.) I replied:
'I have anticipated and thought through all this beforehand. I do not
shrink from paying the penalty for a most honourable deed in
punishing a most wicked man, if fate so decrees.'

13   It was now time for the verdicts. The consul-designate, Domitius
Apollinaris, Fabricius Veiento, Fabius Postuminus, Bittius Proculus,
the colleague of Publicius Certus (who was the man under investigation) and the stepfather of the wife who had died on me, all spoke,
and after them Ammius Flaccus.* Each and all defended Certus as
though I had named him, though I had not yet done so, and took up
14   the defence of the charge, though as yet it had not been tabled. There
is no need to recount their additional comments, for you have them
in the written version, since I have recorded their words verbatim.

15   Avidius Quietus and Cornutus Tertullus* spoke on the other side.
Quietus said that it was most unjust that the complaints of the
aggrieved parties should be disregarded, and therefore that Arria
and Fannia should not be deprived of their right to complain. He
16   added that it was not a person's rank that was relevant, but the case
he had to answer. Cornutus stated that the consuls had appointed
him as guardian to Helvidius' daughter at the request of her mother
and stepfather, and that at this juncture too he did not contemplate
abandoning the role dictated by his obligation. However, he was
limiting his own resentment, and was conveying the most moderate
sentiments of those excellent women. He said that they were content
to remind the senate of Publicius Certus' bloodstained flattery, and
to request that if punishment for his most blatant wickedness was
remitted, that he should at least be branded with the equivalent of
the censor's stigma.*

17   Then Satrius Rufus* took a moderate and ambivalent line. 'My
view', he said, 'is that if Publicius Certus is not acquitted, he is
wronged. His name has merely been mentioned by the friends of
Arria and Fannia, and by his own friends. This should not trouble
us, for we who take a favourable view of him will also be his judges. If
he is innocent, as I hope and would wish and believe until there is
proof to the contrary, you will be able to acquit him.'

18   These were the views advanced by those senators when called to
speak in the due order. When my turn came, I rose, and after my

initial remarks in the written version, I responded to each observation. It was astonishing how those who had previously objected loudly listened to every word with close attention, and with cries of approval. Such was the change of heart attending upon the seriousness of the business, or the success of the speech, or the integrity of the speaker. When I finished, Veiento* began to oppose my view, but no one 19 allowed it, and the opposing din and clamour reached such a pitch that he said: 'Conscript fathers, I implore you not to compel me to invoke the aid of the tribunes.' Immediately the tribune Murena responded: 'Veiento, most distinguished senator, I give you leave to speak.'

This led to further loud objections. During the ensuing delay, the 20 consul called out our names, and after the division was completed, he dismissed the Senate. Veiento was left still on his feet, trying to speak. He complained at length about what he called 'this insult', citing a line of Homer: 'Aged sire, these youthful fighters are sore distressing you.'* There was virtually no one in the Senate who did 21 not embrace and kiss me as the members vied with each other in heaping praise upon me for having reintroduced the practice, for long discontinued, of consulting the public interest at the cost of incurring personal enmities, and in short of delivering the Senate from the odium it had aroused among the other orders for being harsh on the rest and being indulgent only to senators by their turning a blind eye towards each other's guilt.

These proceedings took place in the absence of Certus, for he 22 either suspected that some such business was in hand, or the excuse was that he was ill. Caesar, however, did not cite him in any proposal sent back to the Senate. But I had gained my purpose, for the consul- 23 ship was awarded to the colleague of Certus, and his office passed to a successor.* Thus what I proposed in my closing words came to pass: 'The reward which he received from the worst of emperors he should relinquish under the best.'

Later I reassembled my speech as best I could, and made many additions. By a coincidence, though it did not appear coincidental, a 24 very few days after the speech was published, Certus became ill, and died. I have heard it said that there swam before his eyes and mind an 25 image of my coming before him with a sword. I should not presume to claim that this was true, but the apparent truth of the story serves a useful example.

26   You now have a letter—and considering what the length of a letter
should be, what you have is no shorter than the written version of
the speech you have read! But blame yourself for not having been
content with the published speech. Farewell.

14 *To his friend Tacitus*

1   You do not blow your own trumpet, and no writing of mine is more
sincere than that referring to you. Whether generations to come will
pay any attention to us I do not know, but at any rate we deserve
some notice, not for our talent (that would be an arrogant claim), but
for our application, labour, and veneration for posterity. Only let us
proceed on our established path. Though it has led few into the light
of eminence, it has none the less allowed many to emerge from the
darkness and silence of anonymity. Farewell.

15 *To his friend Falco*

1   I have taken refuge among the Etruscans* to arrange everything
according to my inclination. I cannot, however, achieve this, even
among the Etruscans, so numerous and so plaintive are the written
requests of the country-folk which trouble me from all sides. I read
these somewhat more unwillingly than my own writings—for these
2   too I read reluctantly. Why? I am revising a few minor speeches, a
tedious and disagreeable task after some time has elapsed. My
accounts are not being worked upon, as though I were not here.
3   However, from time to time I mount a horse and assume the role of
proprietor in so far as I ride round part of my estate, though only
for the exercise. Do continue your practice of informing me by letter
of events at Rome, for I live the life of a peasant here. Farewell.

16 *To his friend Mamilianus*   107–8

1   I am not surprised that you obtained supreme pleasure from that most
fruitful hunting-expedition of yours, since you write as historians do
that the number of beasts defied counting. I have neither time nor
inclination for hunting; no time, because the grape-harvest is on
2   hand, and no inclination because the harvest is so meagre.* But in
place of new wine I am bringing home new verses, and at your most

engaging request I shall send them to you as soon as they stop fermenting.* Farewell.

17 *To his friend Genitor*

I have received your letter, in which you complain that you found 1 a dinner-party tedious in spite of its most lavish provision, because wits and catamites and clowns roamed round the tables. Shouldn't 2 you try a little to stop frowning? I myself don't lay on anything of that sort, but I bear with those who do. Why do I not have them? Because I derive absolutely no unexpected or gratifying pleasure from the effeminacy of a catamite, the wantonness of a city-wit, or the stupidity of a clown. What I recount to you is not my logic, but 3 my feelings—and on that score how many people do you think there are who are alienated by the entertainments which enthral and attract you and me, when some of them regard them as idiotic, and others as supremely boring? When a reader or lyre-player or comic actor* is ushered in, how many request their sandals, or lie back and listen with as much boredom as you had to endure with those monstrosities, as you call them. So let us indulge other people's pleasures 4 so that we may obtain our own. Farewell.

18 *To his friend Sabinus*

Your letter reveals the concentration, enthusiasm, and finally powers 1 of memory with which you have read my modest works. So when you entice and invite me to agree to share with you as many of my writings as possible, you are responsible for imposing this trouble on yourself. I 2 shall comply, but by sending it piecemeal, as the saying goes. In this way I hope to avoid confusing that memory of yours, which I gratefully acknowledge, with the constant presence and abundance of material, and not to overburden and overwhelm it, and thus compel it to dispense with individual parts in the interests of the greater number, and the earlier ones in the interests of the later. Farewell.

19 *To his friend Ruso*

You indicate that you have read in a letter of mine* that Verginius 1 Rufus* commanded these lines to be inscribed on his tomb:

Rufus lies here; of old by routing Vindex,
He freed the imperial power for Rome, not for himself.

You censure this instruction of his, and you add that Frontinus* acted in a better and nobler way by forbidding any tombstone whatsoever to be erected for him. Finally, you ask me for my feelings about both men.

2 I loved them both, but I had more admiration for the one whom you censure. My admiration was so great that I considered no praise
3 could be adequate for him. I must now undertake his defence. I regard all who have achieved something important and memorable as most deserving not merely of pardon but even of praise, if they pursue the immortality which they have deserved, and if by their epitaphs too
4 they strive to prolong the glory of a name which will live on. I do not readily think of anyone other than Verginius whose fame in achieve-
5 ment was matched by his modesty in proclaiming it. I myself, as one who was held in close affection and esteem by him, attest that only once in my hearing did he go so far as to make reference to his achievements. This was when on one occasion Cluvius* in conversation with him remarked: 'Verginius, you are aware of the good faith which is owed to history, so I ask your pardon if you read in my historical writings anything which does not please you.' Verginius replied: 'Are you not aware, Cluvius, that I have acted as I did so that you historians could be free to write what you wanted?'

6 So let us now compare Frontinus, whom you mentioned, on this very issue on which you regard him as more sparing and restrained. He forbade the construction of a tombstone, but what were his words in doing so? 'Spending money on a tombstone is superfluous; my memory will survive if my life has merited it.' So do you think that it shows greater restraint to proclaim a message to be read throughout the whole world that his memory will endure, than to signal one's achievements in one place with two short lines?

7 However, my purpose was not to denigrate Frontinus but to defend Verginius, and what more appropriate defence of him can
8 there be than by comparison with the person you preferred? My judgement is that neither is worthy of blame, for each strove for fame with the like aspiration, but by different routes, the one by requesting the epitaph due to him, and the other by preferring to appear to have despised it. Farewell.

20 *To his friend Venator* 107–8

Your letter was all the more welcome to me owing to its greater 1
length, and especially since it was wholly concerned with my writings. I am not surprised that they give you pleasure, since you are as
fond of all that concerns me as you are of myself.

At this particular moment I myself am gathering in the grape- 2
harvest,* thin but more abundant than I had anticipated—if 'gathering' is the right word for plucking the odd grape, visiting the press,
testing the new wine from the vat, and stealing up on my city-servants
as they now superintend the peasants, leaving me to my secretaries
and my readers. Farewell.

21 *To his friend Sabinianus*

Your freedman, with whom you said you were angry, has approached 1
me,* and grovelling at my feet he has clung to them as if they were
yours. His tears were copious, as were his pleas and also his silences.
In short, he persuaded me that he was genuinely sorry, and I believe
that he has turned over a new leaf because he feels that he has
misbehaved. I know that you are furious with him, and I know also 2
that you are rightly so, but praise for forbearance is especially due
when the grounds for anger are more justified. You were fond of 3
him, and I hope that you will be so in the future; meanwhile it is
enough that you allow yourself to be appeased. It will be possible for
you to renew your anger, if he deserves it, and you will have greater
justification if you have been prevailed upon now. Make some allowance for his youth, for his tears, and for your own benevolence. Do
not cause him pain, to avoid paining yourself, for you pain yourself
when your mild disposition turns to anger.

I fear that I may seem to be applying pressure rather than to be 4
pleading with you, if I join my prayers to his, and I shall do this all
the more fully and frankly for having rebuked him more sharply and
severely, having threatened that I shall never plead with you again
after this. That threat was addressed to him, for it was necessary to
scare him, and not to you; indeed, I shall perhaps plead with you
again, and my plea will again be granted, provided only that it is
fitting for me to request it, and for you to grant it. Farewell.

22 *To his friend Severus*

1 The illness of Passennus Paulus* has been causing me great concern, and indeed for the greatest number of justified reasons. He is the best and most honourable of men, who shows the greatest affection for me, and besides, his writings challenge, imitate, and reproduce those of the ancients, especially those of Propertius, of whom he is a descendant, a true offspring who resembles his forebear most 2 closely in the genre in which Propertius excelled.* Take Paulus' elegies into your hands, and you will read work which is refined, tender, and attractive, written closely in the Propertian tradition. He has recently moved on to lyric poetry,* in which he reproduces Horace as competently as he does Propertius in his elegies. You would think that if kinship influences literary art, he was a relative of Horace as well. His writings show great variety and great dexterity; he writes of love like the truest of lovers, of grief like one who finds it hardest to bear, of praise as the most generous of men, and sportiveness as a man of the greatest wit. In short, his poetry as a whole is as good as each part.

3 For this friend and this talent I was as sick in mind as he was in body, but now at last I have found him restored, and myself likewise. So felicitate me, and felicitate also literature itself, which through the hazard to his life came as close to danger as his recovery will enhance its fame. Farewell.

23 *To his friend Maximus*

1 It has often happened to me in the course of pleading that members of the Centumviral court, after for long preserving the authority and serious demeanour appropriate to judges, have suddenly got to their feet and complimented me, as if overcome and compelled to do so. 2 Often, too, I have won from the Senate the glory to which I particularly aspired. Yet never have I experienced greater pleasure than from a conversation the other day with Cornelius Tacitus. He told me that seated next to him at the recent chariot-races* was a Roman knight, who after diverse conversation of a learned kind asked: 'Are you Italian or a provincial?',* and that he replied: 'In fact you know 3 me from my published work.' Thereupon the knight asked: 'Are you Tacitus or Pliny?' I cannot describe how pleasurable I find it to have

our names associated with literature, and belonging to it, so to say, rather than to our identity, and also that each of us should be known from our writings to people to whom we are otherwise unknown.

Something similar occurred a very few days ago. A man of note, 4 Fadius Rufinus,* was reclining at table next to me, and beyond him was a fellow townsman who had come to Rome that day for the first time. Rufinus pointed me out to him, and asked: 'Do you see this gentleman?', and he spoke at length about my writings. Whereupon the man said: 'Why, it's Pliny!' I shall tell the truth: I obtain a great 5 reward for my labours. Surely, if Demosthenes was justified* in his pleasure when an old Attic woman recognized him with the words 'It's Demosthenes', I ought to be glad because my name is celebrated? For myself, I am delighted, and I admit that I am delighted. I do 6 not fear being thought too boastful when I retail the judgement of others rather than my own, especially to you, for you begrudge praise to none, and you cherish that accorded to me. Farewell.

24 *To his friend Sabinianus*

It was commendable of you to restore to your home and affection the freedman who was earlier dear to you, after my letter had guided him back to you. Your gesture will be of service to you; at any rate it is gratifying to me, first because I see that you are sufficiently amenable to be able to accept guidance when angry, and secondly because you repose sufficient trust in me either to follow my authority or to be open to my pleas. So you win both my praise and my thanks, but at the same time, my advice for the future is that you show yourself ready to forgive the misdemeanours of your servants, even if there is no one to plead for them. Farewell.

25 *To his friend Mamilianus* 107–8

You complain about the crowd of camp-duties, yet as if you were 1 enjoying the height of leisure you read and admire and demand my sportive trifles, and urge me pressingly to compose others like them. I am indeed beginning to seek from this type of writing not only 2 pleasure but also repute following your assessment, for you are a most learned, serious, and candid judge.

3   At the moment the performance of my court-duties is a minor distraction, but none the less a distraction. Once I have disposed of them, I shall land something inspired by these same Muses into that most accommodating lap of yours. You must allow my little sparrows and little doves to spread their wings among your eagles,* but only if you find them pleasing; be sure to confine them to their cage or nest if they are merely gratifying to themselves. Farewell.

26 *To his friend Lupercus*

1   In commenting upon a certain orator of our era, whose style was sound and sensible, but lacking in grandeur and not highly wrought, I think my judgement was apposite: 'His only fault is that he has no
2   faults.' For an orator ought to be elevated and exalted, and from time to time glowing with heat in a transport of passion, often drawing close to a headlong fall, for usually lofty and exalted language approximates to the precipitous. The lower and more pedestrian path over level ground is safer. Sprinters fall more often than those who creep along, but no praise accrues to crawlers who do not
3   stumble, whereas runners gain some glory even if they fall. Eloquence is like certain other skills in winning approval above all from its hazards.* You observe what loud shouts are often aroused by men who practise tightrope walking* at a great height, when they seem
4   about to fall at any moment. For the mòst remarkable feats are those which are most unexpected and most hazardous, and which Greeks better express as *téméraires*. Hence the skill of a helmsman in sailing on calm waters is by no means commensurate with journeying on a stormy sea. On the first, he attracts no admiration as he enters harbour winning no praise or glory, but when the ropes are creaking, and the mast bends over, and the rudder groans, he then achieves fame, and attains a stature closest to the gods of the sea.

5   Why do I make these observations? The reason is that you seemed to have designated some passages in my writings as inflated, when I thought them lofty, as pretentious, when I thought them bold, as overblown, when I thought them fully expressed. It makes the greatest difference whether you signal blameworthy faults or striking
6   features, for everyone notices what is out of the ordinary and out of the common run, but it requires keen concentration to discriminate between the extravagant and the high-flown, between the lofty and

the monstrous. Let me cite Homer as the pre-eminent example. Who, I ask you, cannot fail to notice and assign to one or other of these the phrases 'the lofty heavens trumpeted forth' and 'his spear reclined upon a cloud', and that whole passage which begins: 'Nor did the wave of the sea bellow so loudly . . .'.* But there must be 7 scrutiny and weighing to decide whether these phrases are outrageous and meaningless on the one hand, or magnificent and divine on the other. I do not here believe that I have voiced, or can voice, utterances like these (I am not as crazy as that!), but I want to make it clear that eloquence should be given free rein, and that the impact of talent should not be confined within a very circumscribed course.

The objection may be raised that the role of orators is one thing, 8 and that of poets another. But was Marcus Tullius any less audacious? However, I disregard him, for I believe that there is no doubt in his case. But what of the great Demosthenes, the very model and standard of the orator? He does not confine and restrain himself, does he, when he utters those most celebrated words:* 'Blackguards, flatterers, and wretched creatures!', and again: 'It was not with stones or bricks that I fortified the city', and immediately following: 'Was it not to throw up Euboea as a defence for Attica on the seaward side?' Elsewhere he has: 'By the gods, men of Athens, I believe that the man is intoxicated by the greatness of his achievements.' And 9 what is bolder than that very fine and very lengthy digression which begins: 'An epidemic . . .'? Again, this passage is shorter than what goes before, but is equally audacious: 'Then, when Pytho was playing the braggart, and was pouring heaps of abuse on us . . .'. On the same lines are the words: 'When a man like this has obtained power by rapacity and villainy, then the first pretext and some minor stumble overthrows and destroys everything.' Similar is the phrase: 'Debarred by every right that obtains in the city', and again, in the same speech: 'Aristogeiton, you have betrayed your children's right to pity, or rather, you have destroyed it totally. Do not then seek anchorage in the harbours which you yourself have barricaded and filled with stakes.' Earlier he had said: 'I do not see that any one of these topics offers a firm basis for the defendant. All that lie before him are precipices, ravines, and gaping pits.' Then too we read: 'I fear that in some men's eyes you will appear to be acting as trainer to each and every citizen who seeks to be wicked.' Nor is that enough; he also writes: 'For I do not assume that your forebears built these

law courts for you so that you could plant men such as these in them.'
And again: 'If he is a huckster and importer and dealer in wickedness
. . .'. There are a thousand similar phrases, not to mention those
which Aeschines* labels 'monstrosities, not words'.

10   I am beset here with opposition, and you will say that Demosthenes
too is blameworthy on these counts. But observe how much greater
an orator is the man being criticized than the critic, and greater too
11   for these very features. In other passages his vigour shines out, but in
these his grandeur. And surely Aeschines himself did not refrain
from the usages which he censured in Demosthenes? 'For, men of
Athens, the orator and the law ought to deliver the same message,
but when the law says one thing and the orator another . . .'. Elsewhere he has: 'Then he appears totally absorbed in the decree.' And
again in another place: 'But if you sit lying in wait for him as you
12   listen, you must drive him into discussion of the illegality.' He so
greatly approved of this expression that he repeats it: 'Drive him as
on the racetrack to maintain the same course on this topic.' Again,
is this passage more circumspect and restrained? 'You reopen old
wounds, and you care more for speeches at the moment than for the
safety of the city.' He rises still higher with: 'Will you not remove
this man, this disaster shared by all Greeks? Or rather, seize him and
take vengeance on him as a pirate in political life who sails through
the state on his ship of words?'

13   I anticipate that you will delete from this letter certain expressions
like 'the rudder groans', and 'a stature closest to the gods of the sea',
with the same censure with which you delete the passages which I
cite; for I realize that in begging pardon for my previous faults,
I have fallen into those very errors which you have condemned.
But you can delete them, so long as here and now you fix a day on
which we can face to face analyse both those past and these present
instances. Then you will either make me more circumspect, or I shall
make you adventurous. Farewell.

27   *To his friend Paternus*

1   On other occasions I have often felt the great force, dignity, majesty,
and finally divine power of history, as I did the other day. Someone
had been reciting a most truthful account,* and he had held back a
2   part of it for another time. Would you believe it, but friends of a

certain individual came begging and pleading with him not to read out the rest. Such great shame do men feel at hearing the account of their actions, though they felt none at doing things which make them blush to hear. The performer granted the request, as his probity allowed, but the written word, like the events themselves, remains and will remain to be read for all time, and all the more for not being read there and then; for men are roused to discover facts reserved for the future. Farewell.

28 *To his friend Romanus*

A lengthy period elapsed before I received your letters, but three 1 have arrived simultaneously, all of them most elegant and most affectionate, the sort which ought to have come from you since I was particularly longing for them. One of them imposes on me the most agreeable task of bearing your letter to Plotina,* that most upright lady, and I shall carry out this commission. In the same letter you 2 brought to my favourable notice Popilius Artemisius,* and I have immediately complied with his request. You also inform me that your grape-harvest was meagre. This lament I share with you, though in a totally different part of the world.*

Your second letter reports that you are now dictating and writing 3 a great deal, recording your impressions of me. I am grateful, and would have been more so if you had desired me to read what you are writing and dictating. It would be fair for me to gain acquaintance with your writings as you are acquainted with mine, even if yours referred to someone other than myself. At the close of your letter, 4 you promise that when you have more definite information about my future plans,* you will take flight from your domesticity and wing your way at once to me. I am already forging fetters for you, and there is no way you can break out of them.

The third letter contained the information that the speech on 5 behalf of Clarius* had been delivered to you, and that it appeared more extensive than when I delivered it in your hearing. It is indeed more extensive, for I made many subsequent insertions. You said that you have sent a letter composed with particular care,* and you ask if I have received it. I have not, and I am keen to get it. So dispatch it at the first opportunity with the interest added, which I shall calculate at twelve per cent annually, for surely I cannot charge you less? Farewell.

29 *To his friend Rusticus*

1 On the one hand, it is better to achieve one thing with distinction than several things with modest success, but on the other hand it is better to do numerous things with modest attainment if you cannot achieve one with distinction. With this thought in mind, I am trying myself out at different types of literature, since I have insufficient 2 confidence in any one of them. So when you read one or other of my pieces, you must excuse each individually, since each is not the only one. In the other arts, excuse for failure is granted to one among many, so why should the law for creative literature, in which success is more difficult, be harsher? Yet why do I harp on pardon as though I am ungrateful? Why, if you greet my recent work as indulgently as my earlier pieces, I am to anticipate praise rather than beg for pardon—though pardon is enough for me! Farewell.

30 *To his friend Geminus*

1 You praise your friend Nonius* to me both often when we meet and now in a letter, because of his generosity to certain people. I too praise him, so long as his giving is not confined to those you mention. My aspiration for the man who would be truly generous is that he should bestow his gifts on his native land, his neighbours, his kin, and his friends. When I say 'friends', I mean impoverished ones, unlike men you know who direct their gifts chiefly at people who are 2 best able to be donors themselves. I believe that such people do not bestow their own possessions, but lay their hands on those of other people by smearing their gifts with bird-lime, and equipping them with anglers' hooks. Similarly crafty are men who take from Peter what they give to Paul, seeking a reputation for generosity by resort 3 to avarice. Our first obligation is to be content with what we have; and the second is to support and cherish those who we know are especially in need, and to encircle them, so to say, with friendliness.

  If Nonius discharges all these duties, he is wholly praiseworthy. If he discharges any one of them, he is still praiseworthy, but to a lesser 4 degree—so out of the ordinary is the man who is a model of even qualified generosity. Lust for ownership has come to dominate men so much that they seem to be possessed by their wealth rather than possess it. Farewell.

31 *To his friend Sardus*

After leaving you, I remained with you no less than when I was in 1
your company. This was because I was reading your book, to which I
have reverted repeatedly and especially (I will not lie) to your profuse
discussion about myself. How numerous and how varied were the
comments you have made, without repetition on the same theme yet
not diverging from it! Am I to offer praise as much as thanks? I can 2
do neither adequately, and even if I could, I should be afraid of
boastfully praising you for the things which won my thanks. I shall
add this one comment, that the whole work seemed the more worthy
of praise as it was the more agreeable, and the more agreeable as it
was the more worthy of praise. Farewell.

32 *To his friend Titianus*

What are you doing at present, and what do you plan to do? I am
living the most agreeable life, in other words, the most idle. For
this reason I refuse to write longer letters, but I should like to read
some, the first because I am self-indulgent, and the second because I
am unoccupied; for there is nothing so idle as men who are self-
indulgent, and nothing so inquisitive as those who are unoccupied.
Farewell.

33 *To his friend Caninius*

I have come across a subject which is factual but very close to fable, 1
worthy of that talent of yours which is very luxuriant, lofty, and
eminently characteristic of a poet. I lighted upon it over the dinner
table, when diverse marvels were being exchanged to and fro. The
author of this account is highly reliable*—though what concern
have poets with reliability?—he is, however, a source whom you
would have done well to trust even if you were going to compose a
history.

The colony of Hippo in Africa* lies very close to the sea. Adjoining 2
it is a lagoon on which boats sail and from which an estuary flows like
a river, at one time to join the sea, and at another back into the
lagoon, alternating as the tide impels the water forwards or backwards.
Folk of every age spend time there, in their keenness for fishing or 3

sailing or swimming. In particular, boys are drawn there, since leisure and love of sport entice them. They gain credit for bravery by going far out into the deepest water, and the one who has left the shore and his fellow swimmers furthest in his wake is pronounced the victor.

4   In this contest, one boy bolder than the rest made his way further out. A dolphin approached him.* At one time it would swim in front of the boy, at another behind him, and at another it would circle round him. In the end it would take him on its back, then push him off, and then take him back on again. As the boy panicked, it ferried him first out into the deep, and then turned back to the shore, restoring him to land and to his mates.

5   Rumour of this wound its way through the colony. The whole community hastened together there, gazing at the lad as if he were a prodigy, questioning him, listening to him, and spreading his story around. Next day they laid siege to the shore, their eyes glued to the sea and to any waters resembling it. The boys went swimming, among them, but more circumspectly, the boy in question. The dolphin appeared at the same time as before and made for the same boy. He fled with the others. The dolphin seemed to be enticing and urging him back, for it would leap up and dive underwater, and curl

6 itself into different shapes and then uncurl itself. This happened the next day, on the third day, and on several subsequent days, until those men who had been nurtured by the sea grew ashamed of their fears. They approached the dolphin, sported with it, addressed it, and even touched and stroked it, with its encouragement. As these trials progressed, they became increasingly bold. In particular, the boy who had had that initial experience swam close to it as it swam along, climbed on its back, and rode out into the deep and back again. He believed that the dolphin recognized him and felt affection for him, which he reciprocated. Neither of them either showed or induced fear. The boy grew more trusting and the dolphin grew

7 tamer. Other boys accompanied him on either side, offering him encouragement and advice. What was also surprising was that a second dolphin accompanied the first, but merely to observe and attend it, for it did not make or entertain similar approaches; it merely escorted the other out to sea and back to land, just as the

8 other boys escorted the dolphin's favourite. What is beyond belief, and yet is as authentic as the previous events, is that the dolphin

which was mounted and sported with the boys grew used to being dragged ashore, where it would dry itself on the sand, and when overcome by the heat would roll back into the sea.

It is known that Octavius Avitus,* the governor's legate, was 9 induced by debased superstition to pour perfumed ointment on the dolphin as it was enticed ashore, and that it fled from the unaccustomed odour into the deep and was not sighted until many days later, when it appeared listless and unhappy. But subsequently its strength was restored, and it recovered its previous playfulness and its usual offices. All the magistrates* would flock to watch it, 10 and their arrival and lodging there inflicted additional expense on this small community. Eventually the place itself began to forfeit its tranquillity and privacy, and it was decided that the focus of large gatherings should be secretly destroyed.

How compassionately and profusely you will lament and adorn 11 and elevate this event! Yet you need not invent any additions to it. It is enough that these true details should not be underplayed. Farewell.

34 *To his friend Tranquillus*

Do solve my anxiety. I am told that I read badly—verses at any rate; 1 that I read speeches quite competently, but verses all the worse by comparison. So as I am about to give a recital to intimate friends, I am contemplating trying out a freedman of mine. A further pointer to that intimacy is my choice of a man who will not read well, though I know that he will read better so long as he is not on edge, for his 2 role as reader* is as recent as mine as poet.

For myself, I do not know what I should do while he is reading. Am I to sit still and mute as though uninvolved, or as some do, attend his delivery with murmur and movement of eyes and hands? The trouble is that I think I am no better at mimic portrayal than at reading. So I shall ask you again to solve my anxiety. Write back to tell me honestly whether it is better to read very badly than either to mime or to avoid miming. Farewell.

35 *To his friend Atrius*

I have received the book which you sent, and I thank you for it. I am 1 extremely busy at the moment, however, so I have not yet read it, though in other circumstances I would be extremely eager to do so. But the respect I owe both to literary studies, and to your writings especially, is such that I consider it impious to take up the book

2 unless my mind is free to concentrate upon it. Your industry in revision of your writings meets with my emphatic approval, but there must be a limit to it, first because excessive care impairs rather than improves, and secondly because it draws us back from our more recent compositions, allowing us neither to polish off our earlier work nor to embark upon new writing. Farewell.

36 *To his friend Fuscus*

1 You ask how I spend my day in summer among the Etruscans.* I wake when I like, usually about the first hour of daylight, but often before, and occasionally later. My shutters remain closed, for the silence and the darkness divert me from distractions, leaving me free in my own company. My thoughts are not dictated by what I see, but my eyes follow the direction of my thoughts, for when the eyes do not light on other things they concentrate on the same things

2 as the mind. I turn my thoughts to the work I have on hand, choosing exact wording and improving the text. The changes I make are sometimes fewer and sometimes more numerous, depending on the difficulty or the ease with which they could be constructed or remembered. I then call in my secretary, let in the light, and dictate what I had fashioned; he leaves me, and is again called in and sent away a second time.

3   At the fourth or fifth hour of daylight (the time is not fixed or carefully measured out) I retire to the terrace or the covered colonnade, according as the weather advises, and there I ponder the remaining changes, and dictate them. I then mount my carriage, and there too I follow the same routine as when strolling or in bed, for my concentration is strengthened and the change itself refreshes it. After a short sleep and a stroll, I next read aloud a Greek or Latin speech clearly and deliberately to exercise the gullet* rather than the voice, though the voice too gains strength from this.

4 Once again I take a stroll, then oil and exercise myself, and take a bath.

If I take dinner with my wife or a few friends, a book is read* to us, and after the meal we listen to the reading of a comedy, or to a lyre-player. I then take a stroll with my servants, among whom are men of learning. In this way the evening is drawn out with intellectual conversation, and even the longest days of summer are happily rounded off.

Sometimes there are changes in this routine, for, if my lie-in or my walk has been lengthy, I do not ride in my carriage following my siesta and my reading, but on horseback, for this is speedier and so less time-consuming. Friends from the nearest towns drop in to occupy part of the day, on occasion alleviating my weariness by their timely interruptions. Sometimes I go hunting, but not without my writing-tablets,* so that even if I catch nothing I do not return empty-handed. Then too I devote some time to my tenants, though in their view not enough. Their rustic complaints* are a spur to my literary activities and to the civilized pursuits of the city. Farewell. 5 6

37 *To his friend Paulinus* 107

You are not the sort of person to demand from your friends those conventional, quasi-public duties which are contrary to their interests. Then again, my affection for you is too steady to fear that you may misinterpret my wishes if I fail to attend your inauguration as consul* on the first day of the month, especially as the necessity to lease my farms, which will obtain for several years, holds me back, since it involves my adopting new strategies. For during the previous four-year period,* in spite of large-scale lowering of rents, the arrears of debt have increased. So several tenants have lost all interest in reducing their debts, because they have no hope of being able to discharge them. They even seize and consume the produce from the land, since they now think that it is not in their interest to keep their hands off it. 1 2

So I must confront these increasing shortcomings, and devise a remedy for them. One solution is to lease the farms, not for money, but for part of the produce, and then appoint some members of my household to supervise the work and to safeguard the harvest. In general, there is no type of return fairer than that yielded by the soil, the weather, and the season. But this demands great honesty, keen eyes, and many hands. However, I must try this out, for, as with a long-standing malady, each and every remedial change must be applied. 3 4

5   So you realize that this is no self-indulgent reason preventing my attendance at the initial day of your consulship. But I shall celebrate it here with prayers, joy, and felicitations as though I were present. Farewell.

38 *To his friend Saturninus*

I do indeed praise our friend Rufus,* not because you begged me to do so, but because he is most worthy of it, for I have read his book, which is perfect on every count, and my affection for him greatly added to my appreciation of it. Mind you, I did peruse it critically, for critical assessment is not confined solely to spiteful readers. Farewell.

39 *To his friend Mustius*

1 On the advice of the soothsayers, I must rebuild the shrine of Ceres,* which stands on my estate, to improve and enlarge it, for it is certainly dilapidated and confining, and it is generally very crowded on
2 her feast-day. Indeed, on 13 September* a huge throng gathers from the entire area around. Many ceremonies are performed, and many vows are both undertaken and discharged. But there is no shelter
3 near at hand from rain or sun. So I shall be seen to act both generously and piously if I build as splendid a shrine as possible, and adjoin colonnades to the shrine—the temple for the goddess, and the porticoes for the people.
4   So I should like you to purchase four marble columns of the sort that gains your approval, and marble to beautify the floor and the walls. A statue of the goddess herself will have to be sculpted as well, since bits of the antique wooden one have fallen off because it is so
5 old. As for the colonnades, nothing strikes me at the moment which can be carried out at your end,* other than drawing a plan which conforms with the nature of the area. They cannot encircle the shrine because the site is enclosed on one side by the river and its
6 precipitous banks, and on the other by the road. Beyond the road there is a most capacious meadow where the porticoes can quite suitably be erected facing the shrine. But perhaps you will devise something better, for you are used to overcoming problems of terrain as part of your profession. Farewell.

40 *To his friend Fuscus*

You write that you are delighted with my letter* in which 1
you ascertained how I spend my leisure among the Etruscans in
summer, and you ask what changes I make from this routine when at
Laurentum* in winter. The answer is none, except that I forgo my 2
midday sleep, and utilize the hours of darkness before dawn or after
dusk, and, if a vital court-case is looming, as is frequent in winter,
there is no room for a performer of comedy or for a lyre-player after
dinner. Instead, I repeatedly revise what I have dictated, making
numerous improvements to assist my memory.

So now you know my routine in summer and in winter; to these 3
you can add spring and autumn, the seasons lying between them,
since they lose none of the daylight, and they appropriate little from
the hours of darkness. Farewell.

BOOK TEN

1 *Gaius Pliny to the emperor Trajan*   early 98

1 Most venerable emperor, your filial devotion had made you pray that
your succession to your father should come as late as possible, but
the immortal gods hastened to apply your merits to the guidance of
2 the state which you had already undertaken.* So I pray that all success worthy of your reign may accrue to you, and through you to the
human race. In both capacities, as private citizen and public figure, I
wish you, best of emperors, both strength and joy.

2 *Gaius Pliny to the emperor Trajan*   early 98

1 I cannot find words to express, my lord, the great joy you have
brought me by your having regarded me as worthy of the right of
three children.* Though you had granted this to the prayers of Julius
Servianus,* an excellent man and one especially devoted to you, I
none the less realize from your very reply that you granted him this
2 boon more gladly because he asked for it on my behalf. So I think
that I have gained the summit of my prayers, since as one of the first
acts of your most blessed principate you have found me worthy to be
the recipient of your personal generosity. I therefore long all the
more for the children I sought to have even in that most melancholy
3 reign, as you can infer from my two marriages.* But the gods had
better designs, for they have held back the process unimpaired for
your generosity. I preferred that I should become a father at this time
instead, when I was to be both safe and blessed.

3 A *Gaius Pliny to the emperor Trajan*   98

1 As soon, my lord, as the generosity of you both* advanced me to the
prefecture of the treasury of Saturn, I abandoned all my roles as
advocate (in general, I had never performed them indiscriminately)
so that I could leave myself free to devote my whole attention to the
2 duties assigned to me, For this reason, when the provincials chose
me as their spokesman against Marius Priscus,* I both begged to be

excused this duty, and obtained my request. But subsequently, when the consul-designate proposed that those of us granted exemption should be asked to put themselves at the Senate's discretion and to allow our names to be included in the ballot,* I thought it most in keeping with the harmonious nature of your era not to oppose the wish of that most august body, especially as it was such a modest one. I pray that you may consider this deference reasonable, for I am keen 3 that all deeds and words of mine should conform with your most venerable procedures.

3B *Trajan to Pliny*

In showing deference to the most reasonable demand of our most august order, you have performed the role of both good citizen and good senator. You will, I am sure, fulfil that role in accordance with the trust reposed in you.

4 *Gaius Pliny to the emperor Trajan* 98–9

Your kindness, best of emperors, which I experience in fullness, 1 encourages me to presume to beg you to be bound by it on behalf of my friends. Among them, Voconius Romanus* claims a quite outstanding place, for he has been a fellow student and a bosom friend from our earliest years. This was why I petitioned your deified father 2 also to advance Romanus to our most august order. However, this wish of mine was held back to await your favour, because Romanus' mother, having pledged in a written document sent to your father that she was conferring a gift of 4 million sesterces upon her son, had not at that time completed the legal formalities. Later, however, she completed these when I advised her, for she released some farms to 3 him, and completed the other formalities usually required to fulfil the transfer of property.

So now that the business which was delaying my hopes has been 4 completed, with some considerable confidence I give you my guarantee of the good character of my friend Romanus. His cultivation of the liberal arts, and his outstanding filial piety, which merited his mother's generosity as well as an immediate inheritance from his father and adoption by his stepfather, lend him distinction. These 5 qualities are enhanced by the prestige of his birth and by his father's wealth. I am sure that in addition to each of these my plea will be a strong recommendation to your gracious self.

6   Therefore, my lord, I ask that you grant me this happy outcome which is my dearest wish, and that you indulge what I hope are my honourable sentiments, so that through your adjudication I can take pride not only in myself but also in my friend.

5 *Gaius Pliny to the emperor Trajan* late 98

1   Last year, my lord, I was afflicted by an illness* so serious that my life was in danger. So I called in a physiotherapist,* whose concern and attentiveness I can repay with equal gratitude only by your gracious kindness.

2   I am therefore asking you to award him Roman citizenship, for he is a foreigner, having been manumitted by a foreign mistress. His name is Harpocras, and his patroness Thermuthis, wife of Theon, is long dead. I am also begging you to grant the rights of citizens to Media and Antonia Harmeris, freedwomen of a most distinguished lady, Antonia Maximilla.* I make this plea at the request of that patroness.

6 *Gaius Pliny to the emperor Trajan* 98–9

1   Thank you, my lord, for the speedy award of the rights of citizens to the freedwomen of my kinswoman, and of the Roman citizenship to Harpocras, my physiotherapist. However, when I was submitting details of his age and finances in accordance with your instruction, I was advised by those more expert than myself that I ought first to have obtained Alexandrian citizenship for him,* as he is an Egyptian,

2   and then that of Rome. But because I believed that there was no difference between Egyptians and other foreigners, I had confined myself to informing you in writing merely that he had been manumitted by a foreign woman, and that this patroness of his had died long ago. I do not chide my ignorance about this, since it has allowed me to be in your debt more often on behalf of the same man. So I beg you to award him Alexandrian citizenship as well, so that I can legally enjoy that kindness of yours. I have dispatched details of his age and financial status to the freedmen you requested, to avoid any further delay to your kind help.

7 *Trajan to Pliny*   98–9

In conformity with the practice of emperors, I have decided not to grant Alexandrian citizenship indiscriminately, but since you have already obtained Roman citizenship for your physiotherapist Harpocras, I do not propose to deny this further request. You will have to notify me of his native region so that I can send a letter on your behalf to my friend Pompeius Planta,* prefect of Egypt.

8 *Gaius Pliny to the emperor Trajan*   98 or 99

Your deified father, my lord, had in a most attractive address and by a 1 most honourable precedent encouraged all citizens to acts of generosity,* so I asked him to allow me to transfer statues of emperors, which I had received through several bequests and was preserving on distant estates in the condition in which I had received them, to the township of Tifernum,* and to add to them a statue of himself. He 2 had granted me this request in a fully detailed attestation. I at once wrote to the town officials, asking them to provide a piece of ground on which I could erect a temple at my own expense. They gave me leave to choose the site to do honour to the building. But initially my 3 poor health, and then that of your father, and subsequently supervision of the office* which you had consigned to me, held me back, so now seems the most convenient time for me to be able to embark on this present enterprise, for my month's duties* expire at the end of August, and the month that follows* includes several public holidays.

So first and foremost I beg that you allow me to adorn the project 4 which I am about to launch with the addition of your statue. Secondly, I ask that you grant me leave, so as to be able to perform this task with all speed. But my honesty does not permit me to conceal 5 from your kindness the fact that you will incidentally very greatly further the interests of my family affairs. The estates I own in that same area bring in more than 400,000 sesterces at least. I cannot postpone letting them out, because the new tenant must carry out the pruning very shortly. Moreover, an unbroken series of barren harvests is forcing me to contemplate reductions of rent* which I cannot calculate without being there.

So, my lord, I shall be indebted to your kindness for both the swift 6 execution of my piety and the arrangement of my affairs, if you grant me leave of absence for thirty days for this twofold mission. I cannot impose a narrower limit, since both the township and the estates which I mention are more than 150 miles away.

9 *Trajan to Pliny* 98 or 99

You have given me many reasons, all of them relevant to the public interest, for your application for leave of absence. But the mere expression of your wish would have been enough for me, for I have no doubt that you will return as soon as you can to your taxing duties.

You may erect my statue in the place you wish (though I allow distinctions of this kind only very sparingly), for I do not wish to appear to have limited the scope of your devotion for me.

10 *Gaius Pliny to the emperor Trajan* late 99

1 My lord, I cannot express in words the great joy which your letter brought me, from which I learnt that you have additionally granted Alexandrian citizenship to my physiotherapist Harpocras,* though following the precedent of earlier emperors you have decided not to grant this at random. I now inform you that Harpocras hails from
2 the district of Memphis, and accordingly I beg that you write on my behalf to Pompeius Planta,* prefect of Egypt, as you undertook to do. I beg you to allow me to meet you* as far as possible from Rome, my lord, so that I may greet you and more speedily savour the joy of your eagerly anticipated return.

11 *Gaius Pliny to the emperor Trajan* 99

1 My recent indisposition, my lord, has put me under an obligation to my doctor, Postumius Marinus. Through your kindness I can do him an equal favour, if in accord with your usual good nature you are
2 favourable to my request. So I am asking you to grant the citizenship to his relatives Chrysippus, son of Mithradates, and to Chrysippus' wife Stratonice, daughter of Epigonus, and also to the sons of this Chrysippus, Epigonus and Mithradates, on condition that they remain under their father's authority though preserving their rights* as patrons over their freedmen.* I am further asking that you grant

the rights of citizens to Lucius Satrius Abascantus, to Publius Caesius Phosphorus, and to Pancharia Soteris. I make this request of you in accord with the wishes of their patrons.

12 *Gaius Pliny to the emperor Trajan* 101–2

I know, my lord, that my petitions are embedded in your mindful 1 thoughts, which are most mindful of good works. But because you have shown favour in this matter as well,* I remind you and earnestly beg you to deign to honour Accius Sura* with the praetorship, since there is a vacancy there. He is in general most reticent in seeking 2 this ambition, but the distinction of his birth, his total integrity in his impoverished state, and above all, the happy augury of the times offer an incentive, for these times challenge and inspire the honourable thinking of your citizens to exploit your favour.

13 *Gaius Pliny to the emperor Trajan*

Since I know, my lord, that the esteem of so good an emperor enhances the assessment and praise of my character, I am petitioning you to deign to add to my standing, to which your kindness has advanced me, by awarding me the augurate or the status of septemvir,* since there are vacancies in both. Thus by virtue of a priesthood I can officially entreat the gods on your behalf, as I now entreat them with the piety of a private citizen.

14 *Gaius Pliny to the emperor Trajan* ?102

Best of emperors, I felicitate you both in your name and in that of the state for your outstandingly great and glorious victory,* most worthy of the days of old. I beg the immortal gods that so happy an outcome may attend all your projects, and that the fame of the Empire may be both renewed and enhanced by your abundant merits.

15 *Gaius Pliny to the emperor Trajan* August 110 (?109)

My lord, I am reporting to you that I have reached Ephesus by sea with my entire entourage, having rounded Cape Malea* after being held back by opposing winds. I am confident that you regard this as your concern. I now intend to make for my province, partly by coastal shipping and partly by carriages,* for on the one hand the oppressive heat impedes overland travel, and on the other the Etesian winds* are a bar to uninterrupted sailing.

16 *Trajan to Pliny*   August–September 110 (?109)

My most dear Secundus, you did well to report back, for I am interested to know the nature of your route to the province. It is wise of you to decide to make use of shipping for part of the journey, and carriages overland for the rest, according as local conditions advise.

17 A *Gaius Pliny to the emperor Trajan* September 110 (?109)

1 My lord, I enjoyed a most bracing voyage by sea to Ephesus, but once I began to journey by carriage from there, I was oppressed by the most intense heat and minor bouts of fever, so I called a halt at
2 Pergamum.* Then again, when I transferred to coastal vessels, I was detained by opposing winds, so I reached Bithynia rather later than I had expected, on 17 September. I cannot, however, grumble about the delay, since it was my good fortune to celebrate your birthday* in
3 the province, the best of omens. At present I am reviewing the expenditure, revenues, and debtors of the city of Prusa, and the process of handling these makes me realize that this exercise is more and more essential, for many sums of money are for various reasons being held back in private hands, and, again, some are being disbursed on wholly illegal outlays. This is my written report to you, my lord, upon arrival here.

17 B *Gaius Pliny to the emperor Trajan* September 110 (?109)

1 I entered the province, my lord, on 17 September, and found it in that sense of obedience and loyalty towards you such as you
2 deserve from the whole human race. You must ponder, my lord, whether you consider it necessary to send a quantity-surveyor* here, for it appears that not inconsiderable amounts of money could be recovered from contractors of public works if measurements were

conducted honestly. This at any rate is how I foresee it on the evidence of the Prusians, with whose accounts I am particularly exercised.

18 *Trajan to Pliny* October–November 110 (?109)

If only you could have arrived in Bithynia without distress to your 1 dear person and to your entourage, and if only your journey from Ephesus had been as pleasant as that which you experienced on your voyage there! I have gathered from your letter, fondest Secundus, 2 the date of your arrival in Bithynia. I believe that the provincials will understand that I have taken thought for their interests, for you too will ensure that it is clear to them that you were chosen to be dispatched to them in my place.

You must take particular care to examine the financial accounts 3 of the cities, for it is quite clear that they are not in order. As for a quantity-surveyor, I have scarcely enough for the works being conducted in Rome or the neighbourhood. But in every province men can be found who can be trusted, so you will not be without them so long as you are willing carefully to seek them out.

19 *Gaius Pliny to the emperor Trajan* late 110 (?109)

My lord, I am writing for the guidance of your advice. I am in doubt 1 whether I should maintain guard over prisoners by employing the public slaves of the cities, which has hitherto been the practice, or whether I should employ soldiers;* for my fear is that the use of public slaves may result in less reliable supervision, but on the other hand this duty may divert a not inconsiderable number of soldiers from military tasks. Meanwhile I have reinforced the public slaves 2 with a few soldiers, but I see that there is a danger that this practice may lead to neglect of duty by both, as each side feels sure that they can pin the guilt they share on the other.

20 *Trajan to Pliny* late 110 (?109)

There should be no need, my fondest Secundus, for more of our 1 fellow soldiers to be diverted to guard duties over the prisons. Let us continue with the practice which obtains in your province of

2 employing public slaves for guard-duties. Indeed, it lies with your discipline and careful attention to ensure that they do the job conscientiously; for, as you write, we must be especially apprehensive, if soldiers are mingled with public slaves, that they become more careless through relying on each other. We must rather abide by the practice that as few soldiers as possible should be called away from the standards.

21 *Gaius Pliny to the emperor Trajan* late 110 (?109)

1 Gavius Bassus, prefect of the Pontic shore,* has paid me a most respectful and dutiful visit, my lord, and has stayed with me for several days. So far as I could ascertain, he is an outstanding man, worthy of your kindness. I acquainted him with your order that, from the cohorts which you wished me to command, he should be satisfied with ten first-class privates,* two cavalrymen, and one cen-
2 turion. He replied that this number was insufficient for him, and that he would write to you to say this. This was the reason which deterred me from opining that the troops which he has in excess of that number should be at once recalled.

22 *Trajan to Pliny* late 110 (?109)

1 Gavius Bassus has likewise written to me to say that the number of troops I had included in my instructions to be entrusted to him was not enough for him. I have ordered that my reply to him* should be attached to this letter for your information. There is a world of difference between the needs of his situation and whether on this
2 pretext he wishes to employ them more widely. But my concern must be solely for what is useful, and as far as possible to ensure that the soldiers are not absent from the standards.

23 *Pliny to the emperor Trajan* late 110 (?109)

1 The citizens of Prusa, my lord, have public baths which are filthy and out of date, and they think it important to have a new building.*
2 In my view you can show favour to their request, for there will be money to finance it. In the first place, there are the sums which I have already begun to recover and to exact from private citizens, and

secondly, amounts which they habitually expend on olive oil they are ready to contribute towards the building of the baths. In general, both the prestige of the town and the splendour of your reign make this demand.

24 *Trajan to Pliny* late 110 (?109)

If the construction of the new baths is not going to impose a burden on the resources of the Prusians, we can grant this request, so long as no levy is imposed on them for that purpose, and that they do not have fewer resources available for necessary expenditure in the future.

25 *Gaius Pliny to the emperor Trajan* late 110 (?109)

My deputy, Servilius Pudens,* arrived at Nicomedia on 24 November, my lord, thus freeing me from the anxiety caused by the lengthy wait.

26 *Gaius Pliny to the emperor Trajan* late 110–early 111 (?109–10)

Your kindnesses bestowed on me, my lord, have united Rosianus 1 Geminus* with me in the closest bond of friendship, for I had him as quaestor in my consulship. I found him most attentive to me, and after my consulship he has shown me the same degree of respect, and he has enhanced the allegiance of his official relationship by informal gestures of service. So I am requesting your personal 2 indulgence that you should take to your heart his high status. You will also, if you repose any trust in me, grant him your favour. He himself will ensure, in the tasks which you enjoin on him, that he is deserving of greater things. What makes me less effusive in praise of him is my hope that his sincerity, honesty, and hard work are abundantly known to you, not only from the offices which he has held in the city before your eyes, but also from his military service with you in the field.

This one request, which because of my affection for you I do not 3 yet seem to have made in sufficient fullness, I make again and again, and I beg you, my lord, to assent at the earliest possible moment to my joy at the illustrious standing of my quaestor, which through him affects my own.

27 *Gaius Pliny to the emperor Trajan*   late 110 (?109)

Your freedman and procurator Maximus, my lord, maintains that in addition to the ten first-class private soldiers which you ordered me to allocate to the excellent Gemellinus,* he needs six soldiers more. I thought that for the moment those soldiers should be left in his retinue as I had found them, especially as he was journeying to Paphlagonia to obtain grain.* I had in fact at his request given him two cavalrymen in addition as bodyguards. Please let me know what procedure you wish to maintain in future.

28 *Trajan to Pliny*   late 110 (?109)

You acted rightly in equipping my freedman Maximus with troops, as he was setting out at the time to collect grain, for he was undertaking a special mission. When he returns to his former activity, the two soldiers you have assigned to him will be enough for him, together with the same number supplied by my procurator Virdius Gemellinus, whose assistant he is.

29 *Gaius Pliny to the emperor Trajan*   late 110 (?109)

1 Sempronius Caelianus,* an outstanding young man, has discovered and sent to me two slaves who were among the new recruits. I have postponed punishing them until I could consult you about the nature of the punishment, for you are the one who established the 2 military discipline we uphold. I am hesitant chiefly because, though they had already taken the oath, they had not yet been allocated among the units. Please write, my lord, to tell me what course I must follow, especially since this involves a precedent.

30 *Trajan to Pliny*   late 110

1 Sempronius Caelianus acted in accordance with my instructions by sending to you those who must be subject to a formal inquiry to decide whether they appear to have deserved the death penalty. It makes a difference whether they volunteered, or whether they 2 were conscripted, or were provided as substitutes. If they were conscripted, the scrutiny at recruitment was at fault. If they were

supplied as substitutes, the blame lies with those who supplied them. If they volunteered in full knowledge of their status, they are to be executed. It does not make much difference that they had not been allocated among the units, for the day on which they first passed muster was the time when truth of their origin was demanded of them.

31 *Gaius Pliny to the emperor Trajan*   late 110

Saving your eminence, my lord, you must condescend to confront 1 my worries, since you have given me the right to refer to you issues on which I was doubtful. In most cities, and notably at Nicomedia 2 and Nicaea, certain men who had been condemned to forced labour, or to the arena and to punishments similar to these,* are performing the duties and functions of public slaves, even to the point of drawing the yearly emolument of the public slave. On being apprised of this, I pondered long and hard about what I should do, for I thought 3 it extremely harsh after such a long interval to return them to their punitive status, when several of them were now old, and by all accounts were living frugal and moderate lives. Yet I thought it insufficiently fitting to keep condemned men engaged on public projects. On the other hand, I considered it inexpedient to feed them at public expense for doing nothing, while not to feed them was also dangerous. Of necessity therefore I have left the whole issue hanging 4 until I could consult you. Perhaps you will ask how it came about that they were released from the punishment to which they had been condemned. I too made enquiries, but discovered nothing to enable me to make a firm declaration. Though the decrees by which they had been condemned were adduced, there were no proofs which could established that they were freed. There were, however, some 5 who spoke up, entering pleas for them, that they had been released by orders of proconsuls or their deputies. What lent substance to this claim was that it was credible that no one had dared to maintain this without authority.

32 *Trajan to Pliny*   late 110 (?109)

We are to remember that you were sent to this province of yours 1 because many things appeared in need of improvement. What will

stand especially in need of correction is the fact that those condemned to punishment were not merely, as you write, freed without
authority, but are also enrolled in the status of responsible officials.*

2   Accordingly, those who have been condemned within the past ten
years and and have not been released by any appropriate authority
must be returned to continue their sentences. Any of more advanced
years, and the elderly who are found to have been condemned more
than ten years ago, are to be spread among duties not much different
from the punishment earlier prescribed. Such slaves are usually
assigned to the baths, or to clearing the sewers, or again, to laying
roads and streets.

33 *Gaius Pliny to the emperor Trajan*   late 110 (?109)

1   As I was touring round a different area of the province, a massive fire
at Nicomedia burnt down many dwellings of private citizens and two
public buildings, the Gerousia and the temple of Isis,* in spite of the
2   road lying between them. The fire spread quite extensively, in the
first place because of the violence of the wind, and secondly because
of the inactivity of the people. It is clear that they stood idly by
throughout, taking no action as they watched the disastrous event. In
general, there was no state provision of a pump or bucket or in short
any means of controlling fires. I have now given instructions, and
3   these things will be made available. But you, my lord, must consider
whether you think that an association of firemen* should be established, confined to a total of 150. I shall ensure that firemen only are
enrolled, and that they do not exploit the rights they are granted for
any other purpose. It will not be difficult to control such a small
number.

34 *Trajan to Pliny*   late 110 (?109)

1   Following the precedent of several others, you have in mind the
possibility that an association of firemen should be set up among the
citizens of Nicomedia. But we are to remember that the province,
and notably these cities, have suffered disturbances through factions
of this kind. Whatever title and for whatever reason we bestow on
2   those who join together for the same purpose, they will become
cabals, and that within a short time. So it is better to make provision

for the equipment which can be of help in controlling fires, and to advise owners of properties both to make use of this themselves, and if the situation demands it, to deploy for this purpose the bystanders who assemble there.

35 *Gaius Pliny to the emperor Trajan* early 111 (?110)

My lord, we have both organized and discharged the vows for your well-being,* by which the safety of the state is preserved. We have prayed to the gods that these vows will be for ever discharged and for ever fulfilled.

36 *Trajan to Pliny* early 111 (?110)

My fondest Secundus, I have learnt with pleasure from your letter that you and the provincials have discharged and pronounced the vows for my safety and well-being.

37 *Gaius Pliny to the emperor Trajan* early 111 (?110)

The citizens of Nicomedia, my lord, have spent 3,318,000 sesterces 1 on an aqueduct.* It was abandoned before it was completed, and also demolished; 200,000 sesterces were then contributed towards another aqueduct, but this too was abandoned. Hence there is need of a fresh contribution so that the citizens who have disastrously squandered all that money may obtain water. I have myself visited the source 2 from which the purest water should apparently be drawn. This was attempted on that first occasion. An arched structure was built so that the water would reach not merely the level and the low-lying areas of the city. Arches, though very few, are still in place, and some can be erected from the dressed stone removed from the previous structure. In my view some part of it should be fashioned from brickwork, an easier and cheaper process. But what is above all 3 necessary is that you send out a water-engineer or an architect so that there may be no repetition of the previous occurrence. The one point I emphasize is that the usefulness and beauty of the structure are to be worthy of your reign.

38 *Trajan to Pliny* early 111 (?110)

Every effort must be made to have water brought to the city of Nicomedia, and indeed I am sure that you will tackle the project with the necessary application. But for heaven's sake, it is up to you to make careful enquiry on whose fault it is that the citizens of Nicomedia have wasted so much money up to now. One fears that people were doing each other favours when they began work on the aqueducts and then abandoned them. So let me know your findings.

39 *Gaius Pliny to the emperor Trajan* January 111 (?110)

1 My lord, the theatre at Nicaea,* which is well on the way to completion but remains unfinished, has sucked in more than 3 million sesterces; this is what I am told, for the calculation of the cost of the 2 work has not been examined. But I fear that it is all in vain, for it is subsiding with huge cracks and holes, whether because the soil beneath is wet and yielding, or because the stone itself is porous and crumbling. It is at any rate worth pondering whether it should be completed or abandoned or even destroyed, for the props and bases on which it is supported below appear to me to be not as solid as the 3 expense indicated. Many additional features in the theatre—for example, halls on each side, and a colonnade above the auditorium— are promised by private individuals and are still due to be built, but they are now all postponed since the theatre which is to be finished 4 first is not forthcoming. The Nicaeans have also begun to restore a gymnasium,* which was destroyed by fire before my arrival, on a far more ambitious and extensive scale than its predecessor, and they have already contributed a considerable sum towards it. But the danger is that their money may be wasted, for the building is badly arranged and scattered; moreover, an architect (doubtless a rival of the one who made a start on the building) maintains that the walls though 22 feet thick are unable to bear the weight placed on them because they are centred on rubble within, and are not faced with brick.

5 The inhabitants of Claudiopolis* are also at work on a huge baths, but they are excavating rather than building it, for it lies on a hollow site overhung by a mountain. The cost is being borne by those councillors who owing to your kindness were additionally appointed.

They have already on their appointment disbursed the money, or
they will make their contribution when we demand it. Accordingly, 6
since I fear that in the first building the money of the community,
and in the second your generosity, which is more precious that any
money, is being wasted, I am compelled to ask you to send out an
architect not only for the theatre, but also for the baths. He would
consider whether it is more useful, in view of the outlays already
made, to complete the work somehow or other in the way it has been
begun, or to make the adjustments that appear necessary to be made,
and to transfer to other sites what needs to be moved, in case in
seeking to save the money which has been spent we spend badly the
additional sums necessary.

40 *Trajan to Pliny*   January 111 (?110)

At the present juncture you must best ponder and decide what must 1
be done about the theatre begun at Nicaea. It will be enough for me
to be told of the decision which you have reached. You must then
exact from private citizens the additional buildings, once the theatre
which prompted their promises is completed. The wretched Greeks* 2
are addicted to gymnasia, so perhaps this is why the citizens of
Nicaea are tackling one with greater zest. But they must remain
content with a building which can meet their basic needs.

As for the advice to be given to the citizens of Claudiopolis, in 3
connection with the baths which you state have been mounted on
an unsuitable site, you must decide. You can have no shortage of
architects,* for no province is without experienced and clever individuals. Do not imagine that dispatching one from Rome is quicker;
all architects usually hail from Greece to us as well.

41 *Gaius Pliny to the emperor Trajan*   January 111 (?110)

As I contemplate the greatness of both your position and your cast of 1
mind, it seems to me most appropriate that buildings should be
shown to be worthy of your personal fame no less than of your glory
and that they should be as useful as they are beautiful.

In the territory of Nicomedia there is an extensive lake.* Marble, 2
agricultural produce, logs, and timber are transported by ship across
it to the highway* at little cost and labour, but then with great toil and

greater expense on carts to the sea. The operation demands many hands, and indeed these are not lacking, for there are large resources of men in the countryside and a huge number in the city, and there is a sure expectation that they will gladly undertake a project which
3 will be advantageous to all. It remains for you to dispatch a surveyor or architect, if you are agreeable, to study carefully whether the lake lies higher than the sea. The draughtsmen in this area main-
4 tain that it is 40 cubits* above sea level. I have discovered that a canal was cut through the same region by a king,* but it is uncertain whether this was to drain the water from the fields around or to join the lake to the river, for it has been left unfinished. It is likewise uncertain whether the king's life was cut short or whether they lost
5 hope in the success of the project. You must bear with my eagerness to promote your glory, but what inspires and fires me in this is my desire that you complete what kings had merely begun.

42 *Trajan to Pliny*   January 111 (?110)

The lake you mention can inspire us to join it to the sea, but obviously a careful study must be made at least of the volume of water, and the sources from which it comes, in case when it is released into the sea the lake drains away completely. You will be able to ask Calpurnius Macer* for a surveyor, and I shall send out from here to you some expert* in operations of this kind.

43 *Gaius Pliny to the emperor Trajan*   January 111 (?110)

1 As I was reviewing, my lord, the very considerable expenditure of the state of Byzantium,* it was pointed out to me that a delegate is sent every year with a decree to greet you, and he is given 12,000
2 sesterces. So, being mindful of your policy, I considered that the delegate could be withdrawn but that the decree could be forwarded. Thus the cost would be relieved, and the duty of the state fulfilled.
3 This state has also been charged 3,000 sesterces, which under the heading of travelling-expenses were given annually to the delegate who goes to pronounce the state's greeting to the governor of Moesia.* My view was that this payment should be abolished in
4 future. I ask, my lord, that you communicate your views, and deign either to approve my plan or to correct my error.

44 *Trajan to Pliny* early 111 (?110)

My fondest Secundus, you were perfectly correct in relieving the Byzantines of the 12,000 sesterces spent on the delegate to greet me. They will perform this role even if the decree alone is sent through you. The governor of Moesia will likewise excuse them if they honour him less expensively.

45 *Gaius Pliny to the emperor Trajan* January 111 (?110)

Please write, my lord, and remove my doubts about whether you wish travel passes,* the date of which has expired, to be honoured in any way, and for how long. My fear is that through ignorance I may slip up one way or the other, and either approve what is unlawful or hinder what is essential.

46 *Trajan to Pliny* January 111 (?110)

Travel passes which are out of date ought not to be used. Hence one of the first rules I impose upon myself is to send new passes throughout all the provinces before they can possibly be needed.

47 *Gaius Pliny to the emperor Trajan* January 111 (?110)

My lord, when I sought to investigate at Apamea* the state debtors, 1 the revenue, and the expenditures, I was given the reply that the whole citizen body was eager for me to scrutinize the accounts of the colony, but that they had never been scrutinized by any of the proconsuls, for they had the privilege and long-standing custom of administering the state at their own discretion. I demanded that the 2 claims and the decrees they quoted be embraced in a memorandum which I have forwarded to you in the form in which I received it, though I realized that several items in it did not relate to the matter under investigation. So I am asking you to deign to guide me about 3 the procedure which you think I should follow, for my fear is that I may seem to have either gone beyond the role of my office, or not to have fulfilled it.

48 *Trajan to Pliny*   January 111 (?110)

1 The memorandum of the Apameans which you appended to your
letter has freed me from the need to weigh the motives on account of
which they wish it to appear that those who governed the province
refrained from investigation of their accounts, whereas they did not
2 refuse to allow you to inspect them. Their worthy attitude is therefore to be rewarded by now informing them that the investigation
you are about to make you will carry out in accordance with my wish,
and without prejudice to the privileges which they possess.

49 *Gaius Pliny to the emperor Trajan*   January 111 (?110)

1 Before I came here, my lord, the citizens of Nicomedia began to add
a new forum to the earlier one, in the corner of which is a shrine of
great antiquity dedicated to the Great Mother.* It must either be
restored or moved to another site, especially as it stands at a much
lower level than the building which is rising at this very moment.
2 When I enquired whether any charter had been laid down for the
temple, I discovered that the local form of dedication is different
from ours. So, my lord, decide whether you think that a shrine for
which no charter has been established can be moved to another site,
for otherwise this solution is the most practicable if there is no
religious impediment.

50 *Trajan to Pliny*   January 111 (?110)

Secundus my dearest friend, you can transfer the temple of the
Mother of the Gods to a more appropriate site without any religious
scruple, if the situation of the present site seems to demand this. The
fact that no charter of dedication is found should not give you pause,
since a site in a foreign city does not qualify for the dedication which
takes place under our religious law.

51 *Gaius Pliny to the emperor Trajan*   early 111 (?110)

1 My lord, I find it hard to express my great happiness at your
arranging for my mother-in-law* and myself the transfer of her rela-
2 tive Caelius Clemens* to this province. This gesture gives me a

further deep awareness of such abundant kindness. I do not even presume to offer you like gratitude in return, however able I could be to do so, so I take refuge in prayers, begging the gods that I may be thought not unworthy of the gifts you so regularly bestow on me.

52 *Gaius Pliny to the emperor Trajan*   early 111 (?110)

My lord we have celebrated with the joy you merit the day on which you have preserved the empire by shouldering it. We have begged the gods to keep you safe and well for the benefit of the human race, whose protection and security have rested on your safety. We have led our fellow soldiers too in the declaration of the oath* in the formal manner, and the provincials vied with them in swearing with the same devotion.

53 *Trajan to Pliny*   February 111 (?110)

My dearest friend Secundus, it was with pleasure that I learnt from your letter of the abundant devotion and happiness with which our fellow soldiers and the provincials followed you in celebrating the first day of my rule.

54 *Gaius Pliny to the emperor Trajan*   early–mid-111 (?110)

Public moneys, my lord, through your foresight and my handling 1 have already been and are still being levied, but I am fearful that they lie unused;* for there is no opportunity, or only a most occasional one, of purchasing estates, and none are found willing to become debtors to the state, especially at the rate of twelve per cent, the rate at which they borrow from private individuals. So, my lord, consider whether 2 you think that this rate of interest should be lowered, and suitable debtors enticed by this means, and if even so debtors are not found, whether money should be allotted among the city-councillors, specifying that they safeguard the welfare of the state. Even if they are unwilling and reluctant, this will be less burdensome if a lower rate of interest is established.

55 *Trajan to Pliny*   early–mid-III (?110)

I too visualize no remedy, my dearest Secundus, other than that the level of interest should be lowered, so that the public money can be more easily lent out. You must decide on the level, depending on the resources of those who will borrow. It is not in accord with the justice of our times to force men to borrow if they are unwilling, when perhaps the money will remain unused in their hands.

56 *Gaius Pliny to the emperor Trajan*   early or mid-III (?110)

1 I thank you profusely, my lord, for when you are preoccupied with the greatest issues of state, you deign to guide me also on matters on which I have consulted you. I am asking you to do this now as well.

2 A certain individual has approached me with the information that enemies of his who had been banished by Servilius Calvus,* a man of great renown, for three years, were still lingering in the province. They countered by maintaining that the same governor had restored them, and they read out his edict. This is why I thought it necessary

3 to refer the issue to you from the beginning. Your instructions specify that I am not to restore men who have been banished by another or by myself, but no provision is included for those who have been both banished and restored by another.

This is why, my lord, I had to consult you on the attitude which you wish me to maintain, and likewise indeed about those who have been banished for life and not restored, but are arrested in the prov-

4 ince; for this type of case too has come to me for a decision, since one who had been banished for life by the proconsul Julius Bassus* has been brought before me. I knew that the decisions of Bassus had been revoked, and that the Senate had granted the right of a fresh trial to all who had been subject to his decisions, provided that it took place within two years. I questioned the man whom Bassus had banished, and asked him whether he had approached and informed

5 the proconsul. He said that he had not. This was what made me consult you on whether he should be returned to continue his sentence, or a more severe one, and above all what penalty would in your view be prescribed against this man and any others whom we happen to encounter in the same situation. I have appended to this letter Calvus' decision and edict, and also the decision of Bassus.

57 *Trajan to Pliny*   early or mid-111 (?110)

The decision to be reached in the case of those banished for three   1
years by the proconsul Servilius Calvus, who were later restored by
Calvus' edict and have remained in the province, I will very soon
communicate to you once I have elicited from Calvus the reasons for
his action. The man who was banished for life by Julius Bassus, and   2
has had the opportunity for two years to appeal if he thinks he was
banished unjustly, and has refrained from doing so, continuing to
linger in the province, must be put in chains and sent to the prefects
of my praetorian guard, for it is not enough to send him back to
continue his sentence, since he has made a mockery of it by his
insolence.

58 *Gaius Pliny to the emperor Trajan*   early or mid-111
(?110)

As I was about to convene the court and was naming the jurymen,   1
Flavius Archippus* began to plead exemption on the grounds of
being a philosopher. Some persons claimed that he should not be   2
relieved of the duty to serve on the jury, but struck off entirely from
the roll of jurymen and restored to the punishment from which
he had escaped by breaking his bonds. The sentence of the pro-   3
consul Velius Paulus* was read out, and established that Archippus
had been convicted of forgery and condemned to the mines. He
produced nothing to demonstrate that he had been restored, but in
support of that restoration he presented a document which he had
sent to Domitian, together with letters from Domitian attesting his
distinction, and also a decree of the Prusans. He also submitted a
letter sent to him by yourself, and an edict and letter from your
father by which he gave proof of the benefits bestowed by Domitian.
Therefore, though such serious charges were levelled against this   4
person, I thought that no decision should be reached until I
consulted you on this matter which I thought worthy of your
decision. I have attached to this letter the documents read out on
both sides.

Letter of Domitian to Terentius Maximus

The philosopher Flavius Archippus has obtained from me his request that   5
I should command that an estate of value about 100,000 sesterces should

be bought for him in the vicinity of Prusa, his native city, so that the rental from it can support his family. I want this to be given to him. You must charge the entire cost to my generosity.

Letter of Domitian to Lappius Maximus*

6 My dear Maximus, please regard the philosopher Archippus, a sound man whose character is at one with his profession, as one recommended by me. Accord him full kindness in the matters which he will respectfully request of you.

Edict of the deified Nerva

7 Undoubtedly, citizens, the very happiness of this era legislates on some matters, and the proclamation of a good emperor is not to be awaited on those issues to which it is enough that he be understood; for the approval of my fellow citizens can guarantee even without prompting that I have put the general safety of all before my own peace of mind, so as to 8 bestow fresh kindnesses and to preserve those granted before me. But, to ensure that the diffidence of those who have obtained favours, or the recollection of him who bestowed them, does not cause uncertainty amid the public rejoicing, I have believed it to be as essential as pleasurable 9 to confront those doubters with my generosity. I do not wish anyone to imagine that what he obtained privately or publicly from another emperor is rescinded by me, so that at any rate he owes the favour to me instead. Those favours are to be ratified and secure, nor should anyone in gratitude require to renew his pleas if the imperial destiny has shown him a more benign face. They must allow me to have free scope for fresh favours, and they are to know that they need plead only for things which they do not possess.

Letter of Nerva to Tullius Justus*

10 Since the disposition of all things begun and completed in earlier days is to be respected, we must abide also by the letters of Domitian.

59 *Gaius Pliny to the emperor Trajan* early or mid-111 (?110)

Flavius Archippus, invoking your health and eternal majesty, asks me to dispatch to you the letter which he entrusted to me. The manner of his request made me believe that I should accede to it, on condition that I informed the woman who was his accuser. I have received a memorandum from her as well, and have attached it to

these letters, so that having heard, so to say, from both sides you may
consider what decision you think we should reach.

60 *Trajan to Pliny* early or mid-111 (?110)

Domitian could indeed have been unaware* of Archippus' situation 1
when he wrote at such length about his distinction. But it is more in
keeping with my nature to believe that his situation was aided by the
emperor's intervention, especially as the honour of having statues
raised to him was so often decreed by those who were well aware of
the judgement pronounced against him by the proconsul Paulus.
But, my fondest Secundus, these considerations do not lead to the 2
conclusion that if any new charge is laid against him, you should
consider that less notice should be paid to it. I have read the memo-
randa of his accuser Furia Prima and of Archippus himself which
you attached to your second letter.

61 *Gaius Pliny to the emperor Trajan* autumn 111 (?110)

My lord, you most prudently express the fear that if the lake were 1
joined to the river and thus to the sea, it would drain away. But here
on the spot I seem to have found a solution to confront this danger.
The lake can be linked to the river by a canal without its being 2
discharged into the river; a bank, so to say, can be left to contain it
and keep it separate. In this way we shall succeed in preventing the
lake being drained by mingling with the river, yet the outcome will
be as if it were mingled. For it will be easy to convey loads over that
very narrow strip of earth lying between, by means of the canal, and
in this way to transfer them to the river.

This will be the solution if we are driven to it, which I hope will 3
not be the case. For the lake is fairly deep, and pours out into a river
on the other side. If it is closed off on that side and diverted to where
we want it, it will discharge the same amount of water as it now bears
away without loss to the lake. Moreover, rivulets develop over that
area through which the canal is to be dug; if these are carefully
combined, they will increase the amount of water discharged by the 4
lake. Indeed, if it is decided to prolong the canal, to drive it deeper,
and thus to make it level with the sea, so that the water is discharged
not into the river but into the sea itself, the counter-pressure of the

sea will preserve and repress the water from the lake. If the nature of the site does not allow us any of these plans, it would still be possible to control the water-flow by means of sluice-gates.*

5 However, the surveyor whom you must obviously send out, my lord, as you promise, will research these and other problems much more knowledgeably, for this project is worthy of both your greatness and your interest. In the meantime I have written as you recommend to Calpurnius Macer,* that man of great distinction, asking him to send the most suitable surveyor possible.

62 *Trajan to Pliny* mid-111 (?110)

My fondest Secundus, it is clear that you have lacked neither practical wisdom nor thoroughness in regard to that lake of yours, since you have so many projected plans to ensure that there is no danger of its being drained, and so that it may be more useful to us in future. So choose the plan which the situation itself especially recommends. I believe that Calpurnius Macer will ensure that he provides you with a surveyor, and these provinces of yours are not short of such craftsmen.

63 *Gaius Pliny to the emperor Trajan* mid-111 (?110)

Your freedman Lycormas, my lord, has written to say, if any delegation from the Bosporus arrives on its way to Rome, that it should be detained until his arrival. In fact, no embassy has come as yet, at least to the city where I am now, but a courier from king Sauromates* has arrived. I have exploited this chance opportunity in the belief that I must send him with the courier who has preceded Lycormas on his journey, so that you could ascertain equally from Lycormas and from the king's letter anything which perhaps you ought to ascertain from both.

64 *Gaius Pliny to the emperor Trajan* mid-111 (?110)

King Sauromates has written to me that there are some matters which you ought to know as early as possible. For this reason I have accelerated the speed of the courier, whom I have dispatched to you with the letters, by affording him a travel pass.*

65 *Gaius Pliny to the emperor Trajan*   mid-111 (?110)

My lord, there is an important issue affecting the whole province 1
which concerns the status and rearing of those they call 'foster-
children'.* Having listened to pronouncements of emperors on 2
this subject and having found nothing specific or general referring to
the Bithynians, I thought that I must consult you on what procedure
you wish to have followed in this matter. I did not think that I could
be satisfied with precedents in an issue which demanded your
authority. There was in fact an edict read out before me which was 3
relevant to Achaia and was said to have been issued by the deified
Augustus. Also read out were letters from the deified Vespasian to
the Spartans, and from the deified Titus likewise to the Spartans and
to the Achaians; and from Domitian to the proconsuls Avidius
Nigrinus and Armenius Brocchus,* and also to the Spartans. I
have not sent these copies to you because they seemed to me
both uncorrected and in some cases of dubious authority, and also
because I believed that the true and corrected versions are in your
archives.

66 *Trajan to Pliny*   mid-111 (?110)

The issue which you raise relating to freeborn infants exposed and 1
then rescued by certain individuals, and brought up as slaves, has
often been discussed, but in the diaries of emperors preceding me
no entry has been found which was directed at all provinces. True, 2
there are letters from Domitian to Avidius Nigrinus and Armenius
Brocchus, which ought to be applicable, but Bithynia is not in the
provinces which his replies specified. Therefore my view is that
applications are not to be rejected in the case of those who claim
freedom on such grounds, and freedom should not have to be
purchased by payment for their rearing.

67 *Gaius Pliny to the emperor Trajan*   mid-111 (?110)

After the ambassador from king Sauromates* had lodged for two 1
days at Nicaea, where he had found me, I did not think, my lord, that
he need remain longer. My first reason was that it was still uncertain
when your freedman Lycormas would arrive, and my second was

2 that, as my duties demanded, I was on the point of setting out to
a different region of the province. I thought that I would bring
this to your notice, because I had only recently written to say
that Lycormas had asked me to detain any embassy which might
come from Bosporus until his arrival. No persuasive reason for doing
this any longer occurred to me, especially since the letters of
Lycormas, which as I previously mentioned to you I did not wish to
hold back, were likely to arrive from here some days before the
ambassador.

68 *Gaius Pliny to the emperor Trajan*　　　September 111 (?110)

Some persons have asked my permission, following the precedent
of previous proconsuls, to transfer the remains of their kin* to
some other site because of the damage attributable to long years
of river-flooding, or for particular reasons. I was aware that at
Rome the college of pontiffs is usually approached on matters of
this kind, so I thought that I should consult you, my lord, since you
are the chief priest, for the procedure which you would like me to
follow.

69 *Trajan to Pliny*　　　September 111 (?110)

To impose on provincials the requirement that they approach the
pontiffs if they seek to remove the remains of their relatives from one
site to another, for one or other appropriate reason, would be harsh.
So instead you are to follow the precedents set by those who governed the province earlier, and to grant or reject each application
according to its merits.

70 *Gaius Pliny to the emperor Trajan*　　　September 111 (?110)

1 My lord, in the course of examining where the baths at Prusa,* which
you kindly allowed to be built, should stand, a site recommended
itself on which stood a house which my information tells me was
once beautiful but is now an unsightly ruin. If we follow this course,
we shall achieve the beautification of a most unsightly aspect of the
city; moreover, we shall ensure that the city itself will be splendidly

improved without the destruction of any buildings, while those that are tumbledown with age will be developed for the better.

The situation concerning the house is this. Claudius Polyaenus 2 had bequeathed it to Claudius Caesar with the instruction that a shrine to him be erected in the peristyle, and the other parts of the house to be let. For some time the city obtained rent for it, but gradually thereafter, partly by looting and partly by neglect, the whole house including the peristyle fell down, so that now scarcely anything but the ground survives. If you, my lord, either present the site to the city, or order it to be sold, the city will regard it as a most generous gift since its position is so convenient.

I myself have it in mind, if you are agreeable, to locate the 3 baths on an open area, and to enclose with a recess and porticoes the place where the buildings stood, and to dedicate them to you. Thus by your kindness a handsome building will rise which is worthy of your name. I have sent you a copy of the will (though it is defective) from which you will gather that Polyaenus bequeathed many objects to enhance the beauty of the house. Like the house itself, they have vanished, but I shall search them out as best I can.

71 *Trajan to Pliny*　　　　　　　　　mid-September 111 (?110)

We can exploit that open area at Prusa with the house that has fallen down, for you say that it is unoccupied, in order to build the baths. But you did not indicate clearly enough whether the shrine to Claudius had been raised in the peristyle, for if it had been completed, even if it has fallen down, its religious aura has taken possession of the ground.

72 *Gaius Pliny to the emperor Trajan*　　　　mid-September 111 (?110)

Certain persons have asked that I adjudicate on the acknowledgement of children and the restoration of their freeborn status,* in accordance with the letter of Domitian to Minicius Rufus and the precedents set by proconsuls. So I have examined the senatorial decree relevant to the same type of case. It discusses only those provinces which have proconsuls as governors. Accordingly, I have

deferred a decision on the whole matter until you issue instructions
on the procedure which you want me to follow.

73 *Trajan to Pliny*   mid-September 111 (?110)

If you send me the senatorial decree which has raised your doubts,
I shall assess whether you should adjudicate on the acknowledgement of children and the restoration of their freeborn status.

74 *Gaius Pliny to the emperor Trajan*   mid-September 111
                                                  (?110)

1   Appuleius, my lord, is a soldier stationed at Nicomedia. He has
written to me about a man called Callidromus.* When he was being
kept in close confinement by the bakers Maximus and Dionysius, to
whom he had rented out his services, he took refuge with your
statue, and when hauled before the magistrates he revealed that some
time earlier he had been a slave to Laberius Maximus, that he was
captured by Susagus in Moesia, and was sent by Decibalus as a gift
to Pacorus, king of Parthia, but after serving him for many years he
had then fled and had reached Nicomedia.

2   When he was brought before me and he told me the same story,
I thought that he should be sent to you. This I did after a little delay
in which I searched for a jewel which he stated was inscribed with a
portrait of Pacorus, together with his embellishments, and which
had been taken from him. For I wished to send the jewel as well if it
could be found, at the same time, together with a small lump of ore
which he said he had brought from a Parthian mine. It has been
stamped with my ring, the device on which is a four-horse chariot.

75 *Gaius Pliny to the emperor Trajan*   mid-111 (?110)

1   A Julius Largus from Pontus, my lord, whom I have not yet seen, or
even heard of previously, has entrusted to me (he was doubtless
2   relying on your judgement of me), the handling and management of
an act of devotion towards you. In his will he has asked that I
acquaint myself with and take cognizance of his estate, and then,
after excluding the first 50,000 sesterces, that I allocate all the rest to
the cities of Heraclea and Tium,* in such a way that it would be my

decision whether I consider that buildings dedicated to your honour should be erected, or quinquennial games established to be called Trajanic. I thought that I should bring this to your notice so that you could ponder which I ought to choose.

76 *Trajan to Pliny*   mid-111 (?110)

Julius Largus opted for your reliability as if he knew you well. So you yourself must consider what will best guarantee his enduring memory in accordance with the situation in each of the two places, and follow through the plan you think best.

77 *Gaius Pliny to the emperor Trajan*   mid-111 (?110)

It was with the greatest prudence, my lord, that you ordered that 1 most distinguished man Calpurnius Macer* to dispatch a legionary centurion to Byzantium. Consider whether you think that the inter- 2 ests of the city of Juliopolis* should likewise be consulted by a similar plan, for though the city is tiny, it shoulders the greatest burdens, and endures injuries the heavier because of its greater weakness. Whatever assistance you provide to the people of Juliopolis will 3 also benefit the whole province, since the city lies at the extremity of Bithynia, and provides a passage for very many journeying through it.

78 *Trajan to Pliny*   mid-111 (?110)

The situation of the city of Byzantium, into which a horde of travel- 1 lers pours from every side, is such that we considered that we should consult the interests of the magistrates, following the practice of previous periods, by providing the protection of a legionary centur-ion. If we decide that the citizens of Juliopolis should be aided in the 2 same way, we shall burden ourselves with a precedent, for the weaker the cities are, the greater the number which will seek the same privil-ege. I have such confidence in your careful administration that I believe you will employ every means to ensure that they are not exposed to injuries. But if any persons act in contravention of my 3 discipline, they are to be forcibly restrained at once. If their crimes have been too excessive to be punished on the spot, should they be soldiers you must inform their commanders that you have arrested them, or if they are on their way back to Rome, you must inform me by letter.

79 *Gaius Pliny to the emperor Trajan* mid-111 (?110)

1 My lord, the Pompeian law* addressed to the Bithynians excluded from tenure of a magistracy or from membership of the senate anyone under thirty years old, The same law included the stipulation that those who held a magistracy should be members of the 2 senate. There next followed an edict of the deified Augustus which 3 allowed tenure of lesser magistracies from the age of twenty-two. So the question arises whether a person less than thirty years old who has held a magistracy can be enrolled by the censors into the senate, and, if that is possible, whether those who have not held a magistracy can also by the same interpretation be enrolled as senators from that age at which they were allowed to become magistrates. This has been the general practice up to now, and is said to be essential because it is a good deal better that sons of honourable men 4 be admitted to their senate than commoners. When I was asked by the censors-elect for my view, I considered that men under thirty who had held a magistracy could certainly be enrolled in the senate, both according to the edict of Augustus and according to the Pompeian law, for Augustus had allowed men less than thirty to hold magistracies, and the law allowed anyone who had held a magistracy 5 to be a senator. But as for those who had not held magistracies, though they were of the same age as those permitted to hold them, I was in doubt, and this is why the outcome was that I should consult you my lord, about the procedure which you wish to be followed. I have appended to my letter the chapters of the law and the edict of Augustus.

80 *Trajan to Pliny* mid-111 (?110)

I agree with your interpretation, my fondest Secundus, that the Pompeian law was amended by the edict of Augustus, to the extent that those of no less than twenty-two years could hold a magistracy, and that those who had held a magistracy could enter the senate of each city. But those of less than thirty who have not held a magistracy cannot in my view be enrolled in the senate of each region merely because they are eligible to hold a magistracy.

81 *Gaius Pliny to the emperor Trajan*   mid-111 (?110)

My lord, I was at Prusa near Olympus, and on the day I was to leave I   1 was free to deal with public issues in my private lodging. The magistrate Asclepiades informed me that a Claudius Eumolpus had appealed to me. When Cocceianus Dio* in council sought to have a holding in his charge assigned to the city, Eumolpus, acting on behalf of Flavius Archippus, said that the financial accounts of the building should be demanded from Dio before it could be consigned to the state, because Dio's administration had been improper. He   2 further added that your statue had been placed in the same building together with the bodies of Dio's wife and son, which were buried there; and he demanded that I should judge the case before the tribunal. When I said that I would do this at once, postponing my   3 departure, he asked me to allow him a longer period to prepare his case, and to adjudge the case in another city. I replied that I would hold the hearing at Nicaea.

When I had taken my seat to judge the case, the said Eumolpus   4 began to request a postponement on the grounds that he was insufficiently prepared, but Dio on the other hand began to demand that the case be heard. Many statements were made on both sides, some   5 of further relevance to the case. After deciding that a postponement should be granted, and that you should be consulted since the case raised a precedent, I instructed both parties to provide details of their allegations, for I wanted you to ascertain their submissions in their precise words. Dio said that he would comply; Eumolpus   6 replied that he would include in his submission his demands on behalf of the state, but so far as the buried bodies were concerned he was not the plaintiff, but the advocate of Flavius Archippus, whose instructions he had fulfilled. Archippus, for whom Eumolpus was acting as advocate as at Prusa, agreed to provide a submission. But neither Eumolpus nor Archippus have as yet provided me with their submissions, though I have awaited them for innumerable days. Dio has provided his, and I have attached it to this letter. I have been   7 there on the spot, and have also seen your statue in position in the library, and the place where the son and wife of Dio are said to have

8 been buried; it lies in an open area enclosed by colonnades. I am requesting you, my lord, to deign to guide me in this type of adjudication, for there is in general great anticipation concerning it, as is inevitable in a matter openly admitted and defended by precedents.

82 *Trajan to Pliny* mid-111 (?110)

1 My fondest Secundus, you could have entertained no doubt on this issue on which you thought I should be consulted, since you were fully aware of my decision not to gain respect for my name through
2 men's apprehension or terror, or through charges of treason. So the inquiry is to be abandoned, for I would not allow it even if it were supported by precedents. The financial accounts of the whole building which was managed under the administration of Cocceianus Dio must be scrutinized, since the welfare of the city demands it, and Dio does not and should not oppose it.

83 *Gaius Pliny to the emperor Trajan* mid-111 (?110)

My lord, since I was requested by the citizens of Nicaea speaking for the city, in the name of what is and ought to be most sacred to me, in other words your eternal glory and safety, to communicate to you their entreaties,* I thought it impious to refuse, so I have appended to this letter the document which I have received from them.

84 *Trajan to Pliny* mid-111 (?110)

You will have to direct your attention to the citizens of Nicaea, who maintain that their claim on the property of their fellow citizens who have died intestate was granted by the deified Augustus. So you must assemble all individuals affected by this issue, and bring in Virdius Gemellinus* and my freedman Epimachus the procurators, so that after taking into account the arguments against the proposal, you may together decide on what you regard as the best solution.

85 *Gaius Pliny to the emperor Trajan* mid-111 (?110)

My lord, I have found Maximus, your freedman and procurator, throughout the time we were together, to be honest, industrious, and conscientious.* He is as closely committed to the discipline you demand as he is utterly devoted to your interests. I gladly attend him as he goes with this testimonial to you, in the good faith which I owe to you.

86 A *Gaius Pliny to the emperor Trajan*   mid-111 (?110)

My lord, I have found Gavius Bassus, prefect of the Pontic shore, to be honourable, honest, hard-working, and most respectful to me in these traits. So I attend him as he goes with my best wishes and support, in the good faith which I owe to you.

86 B *Gaius Pliny to the emperor Trajan*   mid-111 (?110)

. . . than the things he is to hope for. He has been trained by his military service with you, and he owes to the discipline of that service the fact that he is worthy of your kindness. Both soldiers and civilians, by whom his justice and kindness have been thoroughly scrutinized, have vied in providing testimony before me both individually and collectively. I bring this to your notice in the good faith which I owe to you.

87 *Gaius Pliny to the emperor Trajan*   mid-111 (?110)

When Nymphidius Lupus was a chief centurion, my lord, he was in 1 service with me. When I was a military tribune, he was a prefect. Then I began to feel the affection of a friend towards him. That fondness later grew with the long-standing nature of our shared friendship. So it was that I broke in on his retirement, and demanded 2 that he give me the benefit of his advice in Bithynia. This he has already done and will continue to do in the most friendly spirit, laying aside for the time being thoughts of leisure and old age. For 3 these reasons I count his relatives among my own, and especially his son Nymphidius Lupus,* an honest, hard-working man, fully worthy of his outstanding father. He will measure up to your kindness, as you can ascertain from your first experience of him, since as prefect of a cohort he has won the most glowing commendation from those outstanding men Julius Ferox and Fuscus Salinator. You will enhance my joy and my gratitude, my lord, by thus honouring our son.

88 *Gaius Pliny to the emperor Trajan* September 111 (?110)

I pray, my lord, that you may celebrate both this birthday* and numerous others as days most blessed, and that you may enhance the glory of your virtue which flourishes with perennial fame. You will increase that glory in safety and strength with achievement after achievement.

89 *Trajan to Pliny* September 111 (?110)

I acknowledge your prayers, my fondest Secundus, in which you pray that I may spend numerous most blessed birthdays in the prosperity of our state.

90 *Gaius Pliny to the emperor Trajan* late 111 (?110)

1 The citizens of Sinope, my lord, are short of water.* It seems possible to draw a good and abundant flow from the sixteenth milestone. But close to this source, a little more than a mile away, the ground is treacherous and soft, so I have ordered it to be investigated at modest 2 expense to see if it can take and bear a structure. Money when collected at my instigation will not be lacking if you, my lord, kindly allow this kind of structure for the health and enjoyment of an extremely thirsty colony.

91 *Trajan to Pliny* late 111 (?110)

My fondest Secundus, continue the careful investigation which you have begun to ascertain whether the ground about which you are uneasy can bear the structure of an aqueduct. I regard it as beyond question that water should be brought to the colony of Sinope, as long as the colony can also achieve this with its own resources, for this amenity will vastly contribute to the health and pleasure of the city.

92 *Gaius Pliny to the emperor Trajan* late 111 (?110)

The free allied city of the citizens of Amisus* enjoys its own laws through the kindness of your generosity. I have attached to this letter a document delivered to me concerning welfare-clubs,* so that you, my lord, can decide what proposal you think should be permitted or forbidden and to what extent.

93 *Trajan to Pliny* late 111 (?110)

If the citizens of Amisus, whose document you had attached to your letter, are allowed to have a welfare-club by virtue of the laws of those who enjoy the benefit of a treaty, we cannot hinder their having one. This concession is granted the more readily if they use such funds not on gatherings or forbidden assemblies, but to relieve the poverty of those in greater need. In the other cities which are bound by our law projects of this kind are forbidden.

94 *Gaius Pliny to the emperor Trajan* late 111 (?110)

For a long time now, my lord, I have admitted Suetonius Tranquil- 1 lus,* that most worthy, honourable, and learned man, into my circle of friends, for I have long admired his character and his learning, and I have begun to love him all the more, the more I have now come to know him from close at hand. There are two reasons 2 which make it vital for him to possess the 'right of three children',* for he deserves the good opinion of his friends, and his marriage has been unsuccessful. So through your agency we must obtain from your benevolence what the malice of fortune has refused to grant him. I know, my lord, the magnitude of the kindness that I 3 seek, but I seek it from one whose generosity I experience in all my needs. You can infer how great is my desire for this, because I would not be asking for it when at a distance, if I merely sought it half-heartedly.

95 *Trajan to Pliny* late 111 (?110)

My fondest Secundus, you are intimately aware how sparingly I grant these favours, for even in the Senate I regularly declare that I have not exceeded the number which in the presence of that most august order I maintained would be sufficient for me. However, I have acceded to your request, and have ordered it to be inscribed in my records that I have awarded the 'right of three children' to Suetonius Tranquillus, subject to my usual conditions.

96 *Gaius Pliny to the emperor Trajan* late 111 (?110)

1 It is my regular custom, my lord, to refer to you all questions which cause me doubt, for who can better guide my hesitant steps or instruct my ignorance? I have never attended hearings concerning Christians,* so I am unaware what is usually punished or investigated,
2 and to what extent. I am more than a little in doubt whether there is to be a distinction between ages, and to what extent the young should be treated no differently from the more hardened; whether pardon should be granted to repentance; whether the person who has been a Christian in some sense should not benefit by having renounced it; whether it is the name Christian, itself untainted with crimes, or the crimes which cling to the name* which should be punished.

In the meantime, this is the procedure I have followed, in the cases
3 of those brought before me as Christians. I asked them whether they were Christians. If they admitted it, I asked them a second and a third time, threatening them with execution. Those who remained obdurate I ordered to be executed, for I was in no doubt, whatever it was which they were confessing, that their obstinacy and their inflex-
4 ible stubbornness should at any rate be punished.* Others similarly lunatic were Roman citizens, so I registered them as due to be sent back to Rome.

Later in the course of the hearings, as usually happens, the charge
5 rippled outwards, and more examples appeared. An anonymous document was published containing the names of many. Those who denied that they were or had been Christians and called upon the gods after me, and with incense and wine made obeisance to your statue, which I had ordered to be brought in together with images of the gods for this very purpose, and who moreover cursed Christ (those who are truly Christian cannot, it is said, be forced to do any of these things), I ordered to be acquitted.

6 Others who were named by an informer stated that they were Christians and then denied it. They said that in fact they had been, but had abandoned their allegiance, some three years previously, some more years earlier, and one or two as many as twenty years before. All these as well worshipped your statue and images of the gods, and
7 blasphemed Christ. They maintained, however, that all that their guilt or error involved was that they were accustomed to assemble at

dawn* on a fixed day, to sing a hymn antiphonally to Christ as God, and to bind themselves by an oath, not for the commission of some crime, but to avoid acts of theft, brigandage, and adultery, not to break their word, and not to withhold money deposited with them when asked for it. When these rites were completed, it was their custom to depart, and then to assemble again to take food, which was however common and harmless. They had ceased, they said, to do this following my edict, by which in accordance with your instructions I had outlawed the existence of secret brotherhoods. So I thought it 8 all the more necessary to ascertain the truth from two maidservants, who were called deaconesses,* even by employing torture. I found nothing other than a debased and boundless superstition.

I therefore postponed the inquiry, and hastened to consult you, 9 since this issue seemed to me to merit consultation, especially because of the number indicted, for there are many of all ages, every rank, and both sexes who are summoned and will be summoned to confront danger. The infection of this superstition has extended not merely through the cities, but also through the villages and country areas, but it seems likely that it can be halted and corrected. It is at any rate certain that temples which were almost 10 abandoned have begun to be crowded, and the solemn rites which for long had been suspended are being restored. The flesh of the victims, for which up to now only a very occasional buyer was found, is now on sale* in many places, This leads me readily to believe that if opportunity for repentance is offered, a large crowd of people can be set right.

97 *Trajan to Pliny* late 111 (?110)

You have followed the appropriate procedure, my Secundus, in 1 examining the cases of those brought before you as Christians, for no general rule can be laid down which would establish a definite routine. Christians are not to be sought out. If brought before you and 2 found guilty, they must be punished,* but in such a way that a person who denies that he is a Christian and demonstrates this by his action, that is, by worshipping our gods, may obtain pardon for repentance, even if his previous record is suspect. Documents published anonymously must play no role in any accusation, for they give the worst example, and are foreign to our age.

98 *Gaius Pliny to the emperor Trajan*   late 111 (?110)

1 The city of the Amastrians,* my lord, which is both smart and well appointed, has amongst its outstanding buildings a most beautiful and very extensive street. On its flank for its entire length runs a so-called river, but in reality it is the foulest of sewers. It is both unsightly in its most disgusting appearance and baneful in its most 2 noisome smell. For these reasons it is in the interests of health as much as appearance that it should be covered over, and this will be carried out if you allow it, for we will see to it that money is not lacking for construction-work both massive and necessary.

99 *Trajan to Pliny*   late 111 (?110)

My fondest Secundus, it is reasonable to have that water covered which flows through the city of the Amastrians, if by remaining uncovered it is a hindrance to health. I am certain that with your punctiliousness you will ensure that the money is not lacking for this work.

100 *Gaius Pliny to the emperor Trajan*   January 112 (?111)

My lord, the vows which we uttered last year we have fulfilled with eagerness and joy, and we have in turn undertaken new ones.* Our fellow soldiers and the provincials have vied in devotion. We have begged the gods to preserve you and the state flourishing and unharmed with that good will which you have earned by your notable piety, obedience, and honour towards the gods, in addition to your great and numerous virtues.

101 *Trajan to Pliny*   January 112 (?111)

I have gladly learnt from your letter, my fondest Secundus, that our fellow soldiers and the provincials in most joyful harmony followed your lead in discharging their vows to the immortal gods for my safety, and renewed them for the future.

102 *Gaius Pliny to the emperor Trajan*   early 112 (?111)

We have celebrated with due piety the day on which the guardian-ship of the human race was passed to you in most blessed succession.*
We commended to the gods, from whom you derive your rule, both our public vows and our joys.

103 *Trajan to Pliny*   early 112 (?111)

I have gladly learnt from your letter that the day of my accession to rule was celebrated with due joy and piety by our fellow soldiers and provincials, following your example.

104 *Gaius Pliny to the emperor Trajan*   early 112 (?111)

My lord, Valerius Paulinus* has passed over Paulinus* and committed to me his rights over his Latin freedmen. I ask you to confer the rights of full citizenship* on three of them in the meantime, for I fear that it may be going too far to invoke your generosity on behalf of all of them. I must exploit that generosity all the more moderately as I experience it more fully. Those for whom I entreat it* are C. Valerius Astraeus, C. Valerius Dionysius, and C. Valerius Asper.

105 *Trajan to Pliny*   early 112 (?111)

Since you most honourably wish opportunely through me to promote the interests of those whom Valerius Paulinus has committed to your good faith, I have ordered a note to be made in my registers that I have granted the rights of Roman citizens in the meantime to those for whom you have now sought it. I intend to do the same in the case of the rest for whom you request it.

106 *Gaius Pliny to the emperor Trajan*   early 112 (?111)

When I was asked, my lord, by P. Accius Aquila, a centurion in the sixth mounted cohort,* to send to you a petition through which he begs your generosity on behalf of the status of his daughter, I thought it harsh to refuse, since I was aware how much forbearance and kindness you regularly show to the pleas of soldiers.

107 *Trajan to Pliny* early 112 (?111)

I have read the petition of P. Accius Aquila, a centurion of the sixth mounted cohort, which you passed to me. In response to his pleas, I have granted Roman citizenship to his daughter. I have sent to you the petition with the response below, to deliver to him.

108 *Gaius Pliny to the emperor Trajan* early 112 (?111)

1 I am asking you, my lord, to state in reply what rights you wish the cities of Bithynia and Pontus to have in demanding the moneys owed to them from rents or sales or other sources.* I have found that several proconsuls allowed them the right of first claim, and that this had 2 the force of law. My view, however, is that through your foresight some procedure should be established and ratified, by means of which their interests can be protected for ever. For the decisions made by the proconsuls, though wisely conceded, are temporary and precarious unless your authority is brought to bear on them.

109 *Trajan to Pliny* early 112 (?111)

The rights which the cities of Bithynia or Pontus should wield in the matter of the moneys which for one reason and another are owed to the public weal must be decided in accordance with the law of each. If they have the privilege by which they are ranked before all other creditors, it must be safeguarded; or if they have no such privilege, it will not be incumbent on me to grant it and to do injustice to private individuals.

110 *Gaius Pliny to the emperor Trajan* early 112 (?111)

1 The state prosecutor of the city of the Amiseni,* my lord, was demanding before me from Julius Piso a sum of about 40,000 denarii, which the state awarded him twenty years previously with the joint approval of the council and the assembly, and he exploited your 2 instructions, which forbid gifts of this kind. Piso responded by saying that he had bestowed numerous gifts on the state, and had expended virtually all his wealth. In addition, he cited the lapse of time, and he pleaded that he should not be compelled to repay what he had long ago received in return for many contributions, for this

would be the ruin of what remained of his high standing. For these reasons I thought that I should postpone the entire case to consult your advice, my lord, on what you think should next be done.

111 *Trajan to Pliny*   early 112 (?111)

It is true that our instructions forbid donations from the public purse, but to ensure that the financial position of many is not undermined, it is not advisable that regulations made some time ago should be reconsidered and rendered invalid. Let us therefore in this issue ignore any transaction of twenty years ago, for I wish the interests of individuals, whatever their position, to be consulted no less than those of the public finances.

112 *Gaius Pliny to the emperor Trajan*   early 112 (?111)

The Pompeian law,* my lord, which is observed by the citizens of 1 Bithynia and Pontus, does not prescribe that those selected by the censors for the council should pay a sum of money. However, those whom your generosity has permitted certain cities to add to their lawful number, have contributed 1,000 or 2,000 denarii each. Sub- 2 sequently Anicius Maximus,* the proconsul, ordered those chosen by the censors as well to contribute various sums in a very few cities. So 3 it remains for you to decide whether in all cities all who will from now on be chosen as councillors should pay a certain sum to be admitted. For it is fitting that you should decide what will remain as a permanent arrangement, since undying fame is the necessary outcome of your deeds and words.

113 *Trajan to Pliny*   early 112 (?111)

I cannot prescribe a general rule that all who become councillors in every Bithynian city should or should not pay a fee for obtaining that office, so I believe that the law of each city is to be followed, for this is the safest procedure. But with greater certainty I imagine that those who become councillors by invitation will so act as to excel the others in their contributions.

114 *Gaius Pliny to the emperor Trajan*   early 112 (?111)

1 The Pompeian law,* my lord, allowed Bithynian cities to enrol as honorary citizens any persons they wished, provided that they were not natives of cities in Bithynia. The same law prescribes the reasons

2 for which censors can exclude members from their senate. Hence some censors have thought that they should consult me on whether

3 they ought to exclude a man from another city, since the law forbade an outsider to be enrolled as a citizen, but did not order him to be excluded from their senate on these grounds. Moreover, I was assured that in every city there were numerous councillors from other cities, and the result would be that many individuals and many cities would be deeply embarrassed by that part of the law which had for long become obsolete by a sort of tacit agreement. I thought it necessary to consult you for your views on what procedure to follow. I have attached the chapters of the law to this letter.

115 *Trajan to Pliny*   early 112 (?111)

You were right to have doubts, my fondest Secundus, about what your response to the censors should be when they consulted you on whether citizens from other cities in the same province ought to remain senators. For the authority of the law, and long-standing custom opposed to the law, could have pulled you two ways. I have decided on this compromise: we should make no change to previous practice and men though enrolled illegally from other cities should remain as citizens, but in future the Pompeian law should be observed. If we sought to maintain the force of that law retrospectively, there would inevitably be a great deal of confusion.

116 *Gaius Pliny to the emperor Trajan*   early 112 (?111)

1 Those who don the toga of manhood, or celebrate a wedding, or enter upon a magistracy, or dedicate a public building, usually invite the whole council and a fair number of common folk, and distribute one or two denarii to each* of them. I am asking you to write detailing your thinking on whether there should be such celebrations and to

2 what extent. My own feeling is that this right of invitation should be allowed, especially if the occasion is a formal one, but at the same

time I am afraid that those who invite a thousand and sometimes more may appear to be going too far, and succumbing to a form of bribery.

117 *Trajan to Pliny* early 112 (?111)

You are right to fear that an invitation may become a form of bribery when the numbers become unlimited and people assemble in blocs, and not as individual acquintances, to receive the usual handouts. But I chose you for your practical wisdom so that you would preside over the moulding of the behaviour of your province, and establish the norms which would be good for the enduring peacefulness of the province.

118 *Gaius Pliny to the emperor Trajan* 112 (?111)

The athletes, my lord, think that the prizes which you appointed for 1 the triumphal contests* are due to them from the day they were crowned, for they say what counts is not when they ceremonially ride into their native city, but when they have prevailed in the contest which enabled them to make their entry in triumph. But I by contrast would have strong doubts whether we ought not to consider apposite the time when they have made their ceremonial entry.

The athletes are also seeking allowances for the contest which you 2 declared 'triumphal', although their victories occurred before your declaration. They maintain it is appropriate that since they did not receive allowances for the contests which ceased to be triumphal after their victories, they should accordingly be given them for those contests which began to be triumphal later. On this issue too I am in 3 considerable uncertainty whether account should be taken of anyone retrospectively, and whether they should be paid allowances not owed to them when they gained their victories. So I am asking that you deign to direct my uncertainty, in other words, to specify how your benefactions are to be applied.

119 *Trajan to Pliny* 112 (?111)

I think that the triumphal reward first begins to be due when the competitor has made his triumphal entry into his city. Allowances for

those contests which I have specified as triumphal are not owed
retrospectively if they were not triumphal earlier. The fact that the
athletes have ceased to receive allowances for those contests which I
laid down as non-triumphal after their victories cannot be advanta-
geous for their claim, for though the status of the contests has
changed, the allowances earlier obtained are not being brought back.

120 *Gaius Pliny to the emperor Trajan*　　　112 (?111)

1 Up to this time, my lord, I have not issued travel passes* for anyone,
nor have I dispatched anyone on business other than yours. My
invariable restraint in this has been dislocated by what amounts to
2 necessity. When my wife heard of the death of her grandfather,* she
wished to hasten to be with her aunt. I thought it unfeeling to refuse
her a travel pass, for speed is of the essence in performing such a
favour of devotion, and I knew that you would approve the reason for
the journey, for it is prompted by family feeling. I have written to
you about this, because it seemed that I would be less grateful than I
should be if I hid the fact that among other kindnesses I owe this one
as well to your generosity. The trust that I repose in that generosity
caused me to act without hesitation as if I had consulted you, for if
I had consulted you, my action would have come too late.

121 *Trajan to Pliny*　　　112 (?111)

You were right, my fondest Secundus, to have confidence in my
attitude. No hesitation should have been felt on whether you should
have waited until you consulted me about whether your wife's journey should have been eased by the travel passes which I issued for
your official duties. For in the eyes of her aunt, your wife's duty was
to enhance the favour of her arrival with the speed of her coming.

BITHYNIA AND PONTUS

EXPLANATORY NOTES

BOOK ONE

1 SEPTICIUS CLARUS: the recipient of this and three other letters (I 15; VII 28; VIII 1) was a literary friend of Pliny and of Suetonius, who dedicated his *Lives of the Caesars* to him. He was to become praetorian prefect under Hadrian (see note to II 9.4).

1 *as each happened to come to hand*: this dedication letter accompanies the correspondence of Books I–II. The claim of casual collection conceals the careful choice and variety of topics.

2 ARRIANUS MATURUS: the first of seven letters addressed to this equestrian friend (see also II 11, 12; IV 8, 12; VI 2; VIII 21), with whom he discusses literary and political topics. At III 2 Pliny extravagantly praises his qualities in recommending him for advancement to Vibius Maximus, prefect of Egypt 103–7.

2 *Calvus*: the most prominent authority in Cicero's day to claim the label of Atticist. Atticism, which promoted a spare and austere style of rhetoric, was contrasted with the Asianic school, which was regarded as overelaborate and bombastic. Cicero was sometimes unjustly associated with this style.

by 'the favoured few': Pliny evokes Virgil, *Aeneid* 6.129 f, which describes those whom Jupiter enabled to rise from Hades to the heights of heaven.

3 *the subject matter*: Pliny probably refers here to his speech discussed in II 5.

6 *works which I have already issued*: for possible candidates at this early stage of Pliny's career, see I 8.1 and IX 13.1.

the booksellers: from the sparse evidence in these letters and in Martial (1. 66 and 117), it appears that booksellers paid authors a fee to acquire the copyright of their work, though other writers like Cicero and Regulus (IV 7.2) made their own arrangements for publication and distribution.

3 CANINIUS RUFUS: this friend was a landowner at Comum, Pliny's native town. Of the six other letters addressed to him (II 8; III 7; VI 21; VII 18; VIII 4; IX 33), virtually all are devoted to literary topics. Rufus plays no part in the politics of his day, but lives out his life in opulent retirement at Comum.

1 *the lake lying below*: lake Comum (Como); the 'service' it provides will be fish for the table.

2 *'one of a crowd'*: for the popular expression, see Cicero, *De finibus* 2.66, with the sense of 'no one special'.

4 POMPEIA CELERINA: the mother of Pliny's second wife, who died in 97. Celerina remarried, her second husband being Bittius Proculus (IX 13.13).

Her estates indicate her wealth, which she readily lent to Pliny when the need arose (see III 19.8).

1 *Ocriculum, Narnia, Carsulae, and Perusia!*: the first three were all towns (modern Otricoli, Narni, Consigliano) on the Flaminian Way, the great north road which Pliny took when journeying to his estates. In this instance he will have crossed from Carsulae to Perusia (modern Perugia), and then journeyed northward along the bank of the Tiber to his villa near Tifernum (modern Città di Castello).

5 VOCONIUS ROMANUS: this émigré from Nearer Spain became a fellow student of Pliny at Rome, and Pliny was subsequently active in recommending him for an army post (II 13), then the 'right of three children' (II 13.8), and finally advancement to the Senate (X 4). Other letters addressed to him (II 1; III 13; VI 33; VIII 8; IX 7, 28) are devoted largely to literary or domestic topics.

1 *Marcus Regulus, following Domitian's death?*: M. Aquilius Regulus, aristocrat and senator, became notorious under Nero for his role as informer in the condemnation of three consulars; see Tacitus, *Histories* 4.42 and section 3 of this letter. Under Domitian he made no further accusations, but he revelled in the condemnation of members of the Stoic opposition (see sections 2–3 below). The poet Martial is better disposed towards him, as the recipient of favours. After the death of Domitian in September 96, Pliny began gingerly to join in attacks on informers, as is indicated here and in IX 13.

2 *the trial of Arulenus Rusticus*: Q. Arulenus Junius Rusticus had reached the consulship in 92, but as an outspoken member of a Stoic family, he suffered impeachment for treason and execution while senators stood impotently by. See Tacitus, *Agricola* 45: 'Our hands dragged Helvidius into prison; the sight of Maurus and Rusticus shamed us; Senecio bespattered us with his innocent blood.'

'branded with Vitellius' scar': in AD 69 Rusticus as praetor was dispatched by the Senate to Vitellius' forces to plead for peace and reconciliation, but he was roughly received and wounded. The Stoic philosopher Musonius Rufus attended him (Tacitus, *Histories* 3. 80 f.). Pliny's comment here, 'You observe his eloquence', is ironical. Elsewhere (IV 7.5 f.) he is scathing about Regulus as orator.

3 *Herennius Senecio . . . Mettius Carus*: in 93 Senecio and Pliny indicted Baebius Massa for extortion in Baetica, and Massa countered by impeaching Senecio for treason. He was subsequently prosecuted by Mettius Carus for having written a life of Helvidius Priscus (the leading Stoic who was exiled under Nero in 68), and was executed.

Crassus . . . Camerinus: M. Licinius Crassus (consul 64) and the aged senator Q. Sulpicius Camerinus, both delated by Regulus, were among the many victims of Nero's final years. For others, see Tacitus, *Histories* 1.48; Suetonius, *Nero* 37.1.

5 *Arrionilla . . . at the request of Arulenus Rusticus*: the nature of the lawsuit is

unknown, but Arrionilla may have been a relative of Thrasea Paetus and his wife Arria, and therefore implicated in the Stoic opposition to the emperor. Pliny's evidence on her behalf rested on the judgement of Mettius Modestus, ex-governor of Lycia, who had been banished by Domitian as suspected of being in the Stoic opposition to the emperor.

6 *your view of his patriotism*: 'patriotism' translates *pietas*, here implying devotion to the state and its ruler.

8 *Celer . . . Justus . . . Spurinna*: Celer is little known; Justus was a prominent politician who became suffect consul in 102, and later governor of Syria. The elderly Spurinna was even more eminent; hence Pliny's deference. He was consul three times, finally in AD 100, and in Pliny's eyes was the model of how to live in old age; see III 1.

9 *the colonnade of Livia*: the two men encountered each other close to Pliny's house on the Esquiline (see III 21.5), in the colonnade built by Augustus in honour of his wife above the Clivus Suburanus.

10 *'I am waiting for Mauricus'*: banished in 93 (see III 11.3), he returned in 97 to become a close associate of Nerva and Trajan.

11 *our formal visit*: they were attending the installation of the new magistrate in January 97.

   Satrius Rufus: known only by the references here and at IX 13.17.

15 *dur à réprimer*: the Greek word used means 'hard to put down'.

16 *to take action or to remain quiet*: prudence prevailed, and Pliny refrained from attacking Regulus, but later in 97 he spoke up against Publicius Certus (see IX 13).

6 CORNELIUS TACITUS: the eminent historian is the recipient of no fewer than eleven letters, six in Books I–VI (I 20; IV 13; VI 9, 16, 20), and an interconnected series of five in Books VII–IX (VII 20, 33; VIII 7; IX 10, 14), this second group reflecting a closer degree of intimacy than the earlier letters.

1 *This acquaintance of yours has captured three boars*: Pliny is relaxing on his estate near Tifernum. The site of his villa there 'below the Apennines' (V 6.2) has been identified a few miles north of modern Città di Castello. Hunting was a favoured recreation of Pliny at Tifernum; see V 6.46; V 18.2; IX 36.6.

3 *Minerva . . . no less than Diana*: that is, the goddess of literature no less than the goddess of hunting.

7 OCTAVIUS RUFUS: probably the suffect consul in 80, and a relative of the historian Cluvius Rufus. Pliny again praises his verses in II 10, the other surviving letter addressed to him.

1 *Part of his prayer . . . part denied*: Pliny cites in Greek a passage from Homer, *Iliad* 16.250, where Zeus answers Achilles' prayer by allowing Patroclus to chase the Trojans from the Greek ships, but not to return safely from combat.

2 *the Baetici against a single individual*: Octavius Rufus has requested Pliny not to represent the citizens of Baetica (the province in southern Spain) in what was apparently an indictment of the proconsul of the province for extortion. Earlier in 93 Pliny had prosecuted Baebius Massa on behalf of the Baetici. In that indictment he cooperated with Senecio, who was later executed by order of Domitian. Hence the references here to services, toils, and dangers; see also VII 33.

4 *Gallus*: presumably an influential friend of the proconsul being indicted; for Pliny's connections with him, see II 17.

'*He nodded with his dark brows*': Pliny resumes the persona of Zeus (see section 1 of the letter) to indicate that he approves the words of encouragement to Gallus, as Zeus at *Iliad* 1.528 accedes to the wishes of Thetis with a nod.

5 *I am fired with such enthusiasm*: for Pliny's gushing praise of Octavius Rufus' merits as versifier, see also II 10.

8 POMPEIUS SATURNINUS: this friend is a busy advocate (I 16; VII 7) and politician (VII 15). This and other letters (V 21; IX 38) indicate that the chief bond between the two men is their enthusiasm for literature.

2 *the speech . . . before my fellow townsmen*: the speech announced Pliny's philanthropy towards the residents of his native town of Comum, details of which are recorded in an inscription from Comum which outlines his career and beneficence (*CIL* v. 5262), and in V 7.2. He donated a million sesterces for the foundation of a library, and a further 100,000 for its upkeep; he also provided the equivalent of half a million sesterces for the support of freeborn children of the town (see section 10 of this letter, and VII 18).

8 *the regret which accompanies impulsive generosity*: Pliny stresses that his own benefactions result from deep thought and planning.

10 *not for shows or gladiators*: for Pliny's disdain for the vulgar enthusiasms of the common herd, see also IV 22; IX 6.

towards the rearing of freeborn children: at VII 18 Pliny explains how he arranged this gift in the shape of property, the capital value of which remained intact while the interest was dispensed.

9 MINICIUS FUNDANUS: he is to become suffect consul in 107. The interests he shares with Pliny are primarily political; see IV 15, VI 6. But at V 16.8 he is referred to as 'a learned man, and a philosopher'. (The addressee in VII 12 may not be this Minicius; Pliny has at least five friends with that name.)

1 *each individual day in Rome*: Pliny at this time is a man of leisure, following his praetorship in 93 and his tenure of the prefecture of the military treasury in 94–6.

2 *an investiture of the adult toga*: a freeborn youth at this date assumed the man's toga at the age of 14–16. There was usually a sacrifice, followed by registration into a tribe, and then a banquet. The traditional date for it was the feast of the Liberalia (17 March).

2 *a betrothal or a wedding*: a girl could be legally married at 12, and a boy at 14. The betrothal was the occasion for a contract drawn up between the families. The contract was similarly witnessed at weddings, after which the bride was escorted to the bridegroom's home.

to witness his will: a will had to be signed and sealed by seven freeborn male witnesses to ensure rights of inheritance.

an assessor on the Bench: men with legal expertise were often called in by judges in the court of the Centumviri (see I 20.12; VI 2.7) or by the city prefect (VI 11) to act as assessors. Seneca (*De breuitate uitae* 7.7) grumbles at time expended on this duty.

4 *residence at Laurentum*: Pliny's estate south of Ostia, described in detail at II 17. The site, a mere 17 miles from Rome, has not been identified.

8 *Atilius*: Atilius Crescens was a school-friend of Pliny (see VI 8) given to pithy remarks (e.g. II 14.2).

10 ATTIUS CLEMENS: he is unknown except as the recipient of IV 2, another attack on Pliny's *bête noire* Regulus.

2 *Euphrates*: this Stoic philosopher was, like Dio Cocceianus (later Chrysostom), a professional orator of the Second Sophistic; his oratory is praised by Fronto and Epictetus, so that Pliny's eulogy seems justified. Having retired with other philosophers under the oppression of Domitian, he returned under Nerva to become a rival of Apollonius of Tyana as professional 'holy man'. He died by taking hemlock in 119.

in Syria: Pliny served as military tribune there early in Domitian's reign, employed by the legate to audit the finances of auxiliary cavalry and infantry units (see VII 31.2).

8 *Pompeius Julianus*: otherwise unknown. Apollonius, a vociferous critic of Euphrates, speaks scornfully of his rival's forceful entry into aristocratic houses (so Philostratus, *Vita Apollonii* 8.7.11). But Euphrates was not alone among leading figures of the Second Sophistic in enjoying life in high society.

10 *the most noble part of philosophy*: Euphrates echoes the conviction of Cicero that public service has a higher priority than private study of philosophy; see *De officiis*, especially the introductory section of Book 2.

11 FABIUS JUSTUS: see note to I 5.8. This and perhaps VII 2 are the only letters addressed to him, neither of them of any substance.

1 *If you are well . . . I am well*: Cicero uses this formula frequently in correspondence with his wife Terentia (*Ad familiares* 14, *passim*). Otherwise it is found only in formal addresses to him, as at *Ad familiares* 5. 9, 10a, 14. Well before Pliny's time (compare, for example, the letters of Seneca) the abbreviated greeting had fallen out of fashion.

12 CALESTRIUS TIRO: he and Pliny were long-standing friends, having served in the army together, and as *quaestores Augusti* under Domitian. They also became praetors at the same time, probably in AD 93 (see VII 16.1). Tiro eventually obtained the governorship of Baetica in southern Spain. Other

letters addressed to him (VI 1, 22; IX 5) are concerned predominantly with political affairs.

1 *Corellius Rufus has died*: he had been prominent in the later years of Vespasian as suffect consul (probably in 78), and later as governor of Upper Germany (*c.*82), but subsequently, whether through Domitian's antipathy or indifferent health, he disappeared from the political scene, to re-emerge under Nerva as a land-commissioner (VII 31.4).

3 *constrained by supreme reasoning*: Rufus was clearly of the Stoic persuasion. The Younger Cato argued: 'When a man's situation is more in accord with nature, he has the obligation to remain alive; when the opposite is, or apparently will be, the case, it is his obligation to depart from this life' (Cicero, *De finibus* 3.60). Seneca likewise argues that we are free to opt for suicide when circumstances demand it, and emphasizes that incurable illness is a sufficient motive (*Letters* 58.32 ff.).

4 *afflicted with gout*: Pliny is exceptional in not attributing gout to earlier debauched living. The description here of how Rufus coped with the condition mirrors the observation of Celsus (*De medicina* 4.31): 'Some have obtained lifelong relief by refraining from wine, mead, and venery.'

7–8 *his slaves retired . . . He swivelled his eyes round*: the oppressive era of Domitian had created an atmosphere of fear, in which critics of the regime feared accusations of treason by informers. Rufus takes precautions against betrayal by his own household.

8 *that brigand*: the Latin word is *latro*. When Domitian executed or exiled his opponents, he confiscated their property, according to Suetonius (*Domitian* 12.1), in order to meet the expenses of shows and additional payments to his soldiers.

what he wished: Pliny hints that Rufus would have participated in the assassination of Domitian, though in fact no senators did so (Suetonius, *Domitian* 16 f.; Dio 67.15 f.).

9–10 *Gaius Geminius . . . Julius Atticus*: both are little known.

10 *Je me suis décidé*: Rufus uses Greek to underline his rational decision in the Stoic tradition.

12 *my boon-companion Calvisius*: Calvisius Rufus, an equestrian friend from Comum, is the recipient of six letters (II 20; III 1, 19; V 7; VIII 2; IX 6), concerned chiefly with property and gossip.

13 SENECIO: Q. Sosius Senecio became a major political figure under Trajan, becoming consul twice in 99 and 107; he was even honoured with a public statue. He had literary connections, being a friend of Plutarch, who dedicated works to him. Letter IV 4 is also addressed to him.

1 *a healthy crop of poets*: contrast Juvenal's jaundiced view (*Satire* 1) about the rash of would-be poets and their recitations.

the whole month of April: there were three major festivals in April: the Ludi Megalenses, the Ludi Ceriales, and the Ludi Florales. Between them they accounted for eighteen days on which cultured individuals might attend public readings.

2 *in resting places*: that is, in the public areas around the houses where the recitations were mounted.

3 *Claudius Caesar ... on the Palatine*: presumably in the grounds of the palace of Tiberius, remains of which are still visible on the north-west corner of the Palatine. Claudius himself had his historical works recited by professional readers at such recitations (Suetonius, *Claudius* 41.2, 42.2).

Nonianus: M. Servilius Nonianus was a leading orator, politician, and historian. He was consul in 35 under Tiberius, and later, under Claudius, proconsul of Africa. As historian, he won praise from Tacitus (*Annals* 14.19) and Quintilian 10.1.102 ('famous for the power of his intellect'). The attraction for Claudius will have been his account of the reign of Tiberius.

6 *something not for recitation*: as Pliny's letters suggest, the recitations served a double purpose for the aspiring author. The reactions of his audience enabled him to amend his work for publication, and they were also a means by which he became more widely known.

14 JUNIUS MAURICUS: see note to I 5.10 above for this friend and mentor of Pliny. Letters II 18 and VI 14 are also addressed to him.

1 *your brother's daughter*: Mauricus' brother was the celebrated Arulenus Rusticus, whom Domitian had executed in 93 for his close association with Thrasea Paetus and Helvidius Priscus, intrepid Stoic critics of the regime. Thus Mauricus, recently returned from exile, was acting as guardian of his niece, who was about 14 years old at this time.

3 *Minicius Acilianus*: little is known of him beyond the information here and in II 16.

4 *Brixia ... that Italian region of ours*: lying midway between Milan and Verona, the town (modern Brescia) in Transpadane Gaul was close to Pliny's native habitat of Comum.

5 *Minicius Macrinus*: he is perhaps the Macrinus discussed in VIII 5.

Vespasian designated him as a praetorian: in 73–4 the emperor was seeking to fill out the depleted ranks of the Senate, following the purge by Nero and the casualties in the Year of the Four Emperors. See Suetonius, *Vespasian* 9.2.

6 *Patavium*: for its reputation as a town of worthy morals, see Martial, 11.15.7 f.

Publius Acilius: probably the recipient of III 14.

7 *the quaestorship, tribunate, and praetorship*: Augustus had reformed the ladder of offices. Anyone aspiring to a senatorial career had initially to hold one of the twenty minor offices allocated by the emperor. Election to one of the twenty quaestorships then became possible. Plebeian candidates had next to advance to one of the six aedileships or one of the ten tribunates, before becoming eligible for one of the eighteen praetorships,

9 *the legal requirements*: these were the property qualifications required for admission to the equestrian and senatorial orders; see I 19 below.

15 SEPTICIUS CLARUS: see note to I 1.

1 *I'll take you to court*: this jocular threat to a boon-companion is sustained throughout the letter.

2 *barley-water*: this is the probable meaning here of *halica*; see Martial 13.6, where it is the poor man's drink, contrasted with honeyed wine (*mulsum*) enjoyed by the rich.

Ready for each of us . . . other delicacies no less elegant: Pliny's main purpose in the inclusion of this letter was to demonstrate the simplicity of the vegetarian fare which he enjoyed, in contrast to the gargantuan meals pilloried by the satirists; see Horace, *Satires* 2.8; Petronius 31 ff.

performers of comedy . . . or a lyre-player: elsewhere (IX 36.4) Pliny states that a book was read over dinner, and a comedy or a lyre-player was the entertainment afterwards.

3 *oysters . . . performing-girls from Cadiz*: oysters and fish were expensive dishes, and Pliny contrasts this feast with his own plain fare. The girls from Cadiz who sang and danced provocatively (see Martial 5.78.26 ff., 3.63.5) were regarded with disapproval by Pliny.

16 ERUCIUS: this Erucius Clarus may be the youthful senator whose early career is discussed in II 9 (and who became consul for the second time in AD 146) or alternatively his father.

1 *Pompeius Saturninus*: see note to I 8.

a friend of mine: I translate *nostrum* as 'mine' rather than 'ours', because the evidence of this letter suggests that Erucius is not personally acquainted with Saturninus.

wide range of his talent: like other literary friends, he publishes speeches, history, verses, and (one suspects) cultivated letters.

5 *Catullus or Calvus*: intimate friends who wrote in the same wide range of poetical genres, especially love-poetry, but also satirical epigrams, miniature epics, and marriage-poems. Calvus was also highly respected as an orator of the Atticist school; Cicero pays him respectful tributes.

the bitterness of love!: or perhaps 'bitterness and passion', the first with reference to the satirical epigrams, the second to the love-poetry.

6 *he has moulded the girl he married*: the patronizing comment is reminiscent of the attitudes of Plutarch and Pliny himself towards their young wives (see IV 19.2–4), though in mitigation we are to remember that brides were usually as young as 14; see, for example, V 16.2.

7 *he is with me*: not physically, but in his writings.

17 CORNELIUS TITIANUS: known only from this letter and the note addressed to him in IX 32.

1 *Titinius Capito*: Pliny salutes him elsewhere (VIII 12) as patron of recitations and literary studies generally. His nostalgia for the Republic reflected

in his activities described here is witheringly dismissed by Syme (*Tacitus* (Oxford, 1958), i. 92) as 'the inner falsity of conventional beliefs and pious observances'.

1 *permission from our emperor*: Nerva (or Trajan) has granted this permission to hallow the memory of L. Junius Silanus Torquatus, unjustly executed by Nero in AD 65 in the aftermath of the conspiracy of Piso (Tacitus, *Annals* 16.7–9).

3 *portraits of men like Brutus, Cassius, and Cato*: earlier emperors had discouraged public veneration of these icons of Republicanism, and under Nero it was hazardous to give house-room to their portraits (Suetonius, *Nero* 37). Hence here 'whenever possible . . . in his home'.

18 SUETONIUS TRANQUILLUS: the celebrated biographer of the Caesars (born *c.* AD 70, probably at Hippo Regius in Africa) is here a youthful advocate at the outset of his public career. For a summary of his career as administrator and historian, see *OCD*³. He is the recipient of three other letters from Pliny (III 8; V 10; IX 34). Pliny hints that he is playing a valuable role in promoting his young friend's career.

1 *a bad fright from a dream*: Cicero's discussion of dreams in his treatise *De diuinatione* usefully focuses the arguments for and against dreams as prophetic messages (1.39–65 presents the Stoic case for taking dreams seriously, and 2.119–48 the caustic rebuttal of the Academic). Pliny reveals his own credulous attitude at VII 27.12, as well as that of a friend at V 5.5 ff.

the court case . . . an adjournment: Pliny and Suetonius are appearing jointly on one side in a civil case. Later in the letter, Pliny appears to change his mind about the possibility of an adjournment.

'for a dream comes from Zeus': so Achilles in Homer, *Iliad* 1.63, suggesting that the Greeks investigate by some prophetic means why Apollo is angry with them.

3 *to plead in the Four Courts*: Pliny was representing Junius Pastor (possibly the Pastor who is a friend of Martial; see Martial 9.22) in the Centumviral court, which divided the cases between four panels.

4 *'to fight for one's native land was the best and sole omen'*: so Homer, *Iliad* 12.243, where Hector rebukes Polydamas for suggesting that the omen of the snake should dissuade the Trojans from attacking the Greeks.

6 *your situation differs from mine*: since Suetonius is the junior partner, Pliny graciously offers to initiate his contribution until his friend is prepared to appear.

19 ROMATIUS FIRMUS: this former fellow student of Pliny's at the *grammaticus* in Comum is also the addressee of IV 29, where he has become one of the 180 judges in the Centumviral court.

2 *a town-councillor . . . worth 100,000 sesterces*: this passage provides interesting evidence of the financial requirement demanded of a municipal councillor in Italy.

the requirement for an eques: the figure of 400,000 sesterces needed for enrolment in the equestrian order goes back to the period of the Republic, at least from 76 BC (cf. Cicero, *Pro Roscio comoedo* 42; Horace, *Epistles* 1.1.58 provides evidence for what pertained from 67 BC).

20 CORNELIUS TACITUS: see note to I 6. This request for the great historian's view on the controversy between Atticism and Asianism was made when Tacitus was at the height of his oratorical powers (he became suffect consul in 97), but before the publication of his *Dialogus de oratoribus* (speculatively dated to *c.*101). The central theme of that discussion between three eminent rhetoricians is that eloquence has declined owing to the changed political circumstances of the day (the dialogue is set in AD 75). Pliny may have taken this as a lament for the standards of Cicero, and therefore support for his thesis; but Tacitus is characteristically ambivalent, and leaves the onus of choice to the reader.

1 *a certain man of learning and experience*: this may be Lupercus, the addressee of II 5 and IX 26; in the second of these, Lupercus is reported as criticizing Pliny's ebullient style.

nothing so much as brevity: Tacitus' renowned brevity in his historical works is no criterion for his views on rhetoric, especially at this early date.

4 *Lysias*: (459–*c.*380), the virtual founder of the Atticist school; 34 of his speeches survive. Cicero (*Brutus* 63) compares him with Cato: 'Both are sharp, elegant, and brief.'

the Gracchi . . . Cato: the brothers Tiberius and Gaius Gracchus, who, as plebeian tribunes in 133 and 123–2 BC respectively, with their pungent speeches weakened the dominance of the entrenched nobility; both had Greek teachers of rhetoric. Tiberius' oratory is known only at second-hand through Plutarch, but some fragments of Gaius' speeches survive. Artistic rhetoric at Rome began earlier with the Elder Cato (214–149 BC), numerous fragments of whose speeches survive.

Demosthenes . . . Hyperides: of this distinguished trio of fourth-century Attic orators (Aeschines and Hyperides were bitter foes of Demosthenes in politics and in the courts), Demosthenes is regarded as the master of the grand style, the others less so. See *OCD*[3], s.vv.

Pollio . . . and above all Cicero: in Tacitus' discussions in the *Dialogus de oratoribus*, little is made of these orators as exponents of the plain or grand styles. Cicero is acknowledged as the master, closely followed by Pollio, Caesar, and Caelius among others (*Dialogus* 25. 3).

Cicero's longest speech: this is the *Pro Cluentio*, in which Cicero claims to have employed all three styles of plain, medium, and grand (*Orator* 102 f.).

7 *I take the opposite view*: Quintilian (12.10.52) argues that written versions *should* excise much from speeches as delivered; Pliny claims that Cicero actually did so, citing the *Pro Murena* 57, where headings replace the detailed charges, and *Pro Vareno*, which has not survived.

8 *he followed the old procedure*: see his comments in *Pro Cluentio* 199; cf. *Brutus* 207.

9 *l'archétype*: here and at sections 15 and 22 below Pliny uses Greek expressions.

10 *in the speech against Verres*: at *Verr.* 2.4.5 Cicero refers to Verres' theft of two bronze statues of the Canophoroe sculpted by the celebrated Argive Polyclitus, whose name he affects to forget to accentuate ironically the monstrosity of Verres' conduct.

11 *The laws support this belief of mine*: Cf. VI 2.6.

14 *Regulus*: see note to I 5.1. Pliny misses no opportunity to criticize him.

17 *Pericles . . . Eupolis*: some 500 fragments survive from 19 plays of Eupolis, one of the leading playwrights of Old Comedy. This praise of the great Athenian statesman is from the *Demes*.

19 *a second comic poet*: this is Aristophanes; for the quotation, see *Acharnians* 531.

22 *I am not approving . . . with the utmost clarity*: of these three characters in Homer's *Iliad*, the first is the demagogue Thersites; for the epithet, see *Iliad* 2.212. The second is Odysseus; this description of his oratory is at *Iliad* 3.222. The third is Menelaus; see *Iliad* 3.214.

21 PLINIUS PATERNUS: the relatively uncommon surname makes it virtually certain that this is the addressee of IV 14, VIII 16, and IX 27. The first and third of these are on literary topics, and the second on slaves, both connections between the two friends implied in this letter. Paternus is probably from Comum, and one of Pliny's literary circle.

22 CATILIUS SEVERUS: this youthful friend of Pliny is to become a leading figure in the state as suffect consul in 110 and 120, and as governor of Armenia-Syria in between. Letter III 12 is also addressed to him. He was the great-grandfather of the emperor Marcus Aurelius.

1 *Titius Aristo*: this older friend of Pliny was one of the outstanding legal minds of the day, frequently cited in the Digest (the codification of Roman Law by Justinian), and adviser to Trajan on legal affairs. Letters V 3 and VIII 14 are addressed to him. Clearly he made a complete recovery from this illness.

2 *whenever I seek . . . information*: see the example at VIII 14.

6 *bodily adornment . . . does not attend the gymnasia or the colonnades*: Pliny contrasts his friend with the philosophers, chiefly Greek, who made themselves conspicuous with their groomed appearance (see e.g. Euphrates at I 10.6 f.) and philosophers' cloaks. The gymnasia had become more and more centres of education rather than of athletics, so that philosophers held their seminars there as well as in colonnades.

8 *to depart deliberately from life*: Pliny has already reflected on the arguments for and against suicide in the case of Corellius Rufus at I 12, where Rufus takes a Stoic attitude. Here, Aristo is more conscious of the Aristotelian attitude of opposition to it for the sake of family and community.

11 *for God to consent*: Pliny, like Seneca, frequently refers to the one deity under the influence of Stoic thought.

My house at Laurentum: cf. note to I 9.4.

23 POMPEIUS FALCO: he is another of Pliny's youthful friends later to attain political eminence. Almost certainly he is the Murena cited as tribune in 97 in IX 13. 19. He was governor of Lycia-Pamphylia and of Judaea, became suffect consul in 108, governor of Lower Moesia in 116–17 and under Hadrian governed Britain and then Asia.

1 *when you are a tribune*: for the tribunate as the intermediate office between quaestorship and praetorship in the imperial *cursus honorum*, see note to I 14.7. It had become less important, desirable only as a necessary stepping stone to the higher positions. Patricians were exempted from it.

2 *I . . . when tribune*: under Domitian, probably in AD 92; see the Introduction, p. xiv. Pliny the arch-traditionalist has an anachronistic view of the dignity of the office.

3 *to intervene with the veto*: there were isolated examples of the use or threatened use of the tribunician veto in the later first century (e.g. Tacitus, *Annals* 16.26.6, *Histories* 4.9), but not in the Centumviral court.

24 BAEBIUS HISPANUS: he is probably the addressee of VI 25, by then in a position of authority.

1 *Suetonius Tranquillus*: see I 18 and note. There, as here, Pliny underlines by his protective attitude Suetonius' dependence on him for social favours.

BOOK TWO

1 ROMANUS: for Voconius Romanus, see note to I 5.

1 *Verginius Rufus*: born AD 14 of an undistinguished family at Mediolanum, he reached the consulship in 63 under Nero, and became governor of Upper Germany in 67. There he crushed the revolt led by Vindex at Vesontio, and on Nero's death resisted the pressure of his army to claim the principate. His relations with Galba were cool, and when that emperor was murdered, he supported Otho, who rewarded him with his second (suffect) consulship in 69. When Otho committed suicide, he preferred to support Vitellius rather than to accede to further pressure from his troops to become emperor. Following the accession of Vespasian to the throne, nothing more is heard of Verginius until 97 when Nerva conferred a third consulship on him, but he died shortly after taking office. The public funeral over which the magistrates presided was an exceptional honour bestowed by the emperor Nerva, a 'close friend' (section 3).

2 *poems and historical works*: no verses have survived, but for evidence that Verginius was praised in the history of Cluvius Rufus, see IX 19.5.

6 *Cornelius Tacitus as consul*: see note to I 20. This letter provides the evidence for the date of Tacitus' suffect consulship.

8 *from the same district*: that is, Transpadane Gaul. The territories of Mediolanum and Comum bordered on each other, but Verginius' family also owned lands at Mediolanum.

8 *bequeathed to me as my guardian*: that is, in the will of Pliny's father, who may have made Verginius joint guardian with his brother, the Elder Pliny.

he always put forward my name: but apparently without success, for Pliny does not become augur until several years later (IV 8).

9 *as one of the quinquevirs*: for this body, see Pliny, *Panegyricus* 62.2. It was appointed to review the expenditure of the treasury administered by the Senate, the *aerarium Saturni*.

2 PAULINUS: Valerius Paulinus, recipient of IV 16; V 19; IX 3, 37, became suffect consul in 107. His death is reported in X 104.

1 *susceptibles*: rendering the Greek word for 'touchy'.

2 *on my estate*: it is not clear whether Pliny is at Laurentum or at Tifernum.

3 NEPOS: he is the recipient of III 16; IV 26; VI 19. His gentile name is reported at IV 26 as Maecilius. Mommsen suggested that it should be Metilius, suffect consul in 91.

1 *Isaeus' great reputation*: the celebrated rhetorician is known also from Philostratus, *Lives of the Sophists* 513.

2 *to make the choice . . . and often also the side he is to take*: this rhetorical exercise appears to be the *controuersia*, in which a speaker was asked to argue for or against a historical or fictitious course of action; for example, should Hannibal have marched on Rome after his victory at Cannae?

3 *he instructs, charms, and moves*: Pliny echoes the Ciceronian doctrine of the task of the orator as *delectare, docere, mouere*.

His enthymemata . . . his syllogisms: whereas the syllogism proper has a conclusion based on a combination of a major and a minor premiss, the *enthymema* is an incomplete syllogism, whether based on a single premiss or on incompatible premisses. See Quintilian 5.10.

8 *a man from Gades*: this is the sole evidence for the anecdote celebrating the fame of Livy. Gades is the modern Cadiz.

10 *that anecdote of Aeschines*: Pliny presses the story again into use at IV 5, in the context of self-praise. It appears earlier in Cicero, *De oratore* 3.213, where it is stated that the speech was *On the Crown*. Demosthenes' praise of the delivery of Aeschines is at *On the Crown* 313.

4 CALVINA: otherwise unknown.

2 *credited to your account*: that is, to wipe out the debt owed to Pliny by her father.

3 *my resources are quite modest*: attempts have been made to measure Pliny's finances. He drew about a million sesterces yearly from properties worth about 15 million, and at this date, as prefect of the treasury of Saturn he will have received a salary of at least 300,000 sesterces annually. These are modest sums compared with the wealth of Regulus, for example, who was about four times as rich.

5 LUPERCUS: this friend of Pliny, valued for his literary judgement, is also

the recipient of IX 26, where the topic again is oratory, and where Pliny defends himself against Lupercus' criticism of his pompous style.

1 *the speech which you have often requested*: Pliny clearly regarded this as a major speech, and at first sight it is tempting to identify it as the *Panegyric*, delivered to Trajan in AD 100. But the references to his native region (section 3), and the absence of laudatory mention of the *princeps*, disqualify this suggestion. Secondly, the speech delivered at Comum for the inauguration of the civic library (see I 8) is also ruled out, because that was an informal *sermo* and not an *actio*, a political or forensic speech, which is denoted here. The occasion of this speech cannot be known.

5 *in the manner not only of the historian, but also of the poet*: such pleasant diversions as geographical descriptions were a popular feature of Hellenistic historiography, as a means of charming the reader, and Roman rhetoricians approved the practice. So Cicero (*Orator* 66) states: 'History is narrated in ornate style, and a region is often described.' For Pliny's view of this relationship between history and oratory, see V 8.9 ff. History and poetry are closely associated in this sense; see Quintilian 10.1.31.

7 *through applying several types of utterance*: in this, as in much of his theories of oratory, Pliny echoes the views of his former teacher Quintilian (12.10.69 ff.).

12 *certain initial passages*: that is, sections of the prefaces which describe the nature of the works. For this sense of *principia*, see Cato, *De agricultura*, *Praefatio* 4; Quintilian 4.1.1 f.

6 AVITUS: the paternal advice offered by Pliny in this letter makes it extremely likely that the recipient is Junius Avitus, the protégé whose early death is lamented in VIII 23, where details of his career are also given.

2 *himself and a few of us*: this practice of separate fare for the host and select guests should be read in conjunction with Juvenal 5, where, at Virro's dinner-party, there are as here three categories of guests. In each course the privileged few are served elegant dishes. The second group, the clients or dependants of the host, get inferior food and cheap wine, and the third group, freedmen, starts a quarrel with them. In earlier days old Cato, and then Julius Caesar, voiced objections similar to Pliny's; see the Elder Pliny's *Natural History* 14.91; Suetonius, *Julius* 48.

3 *not for disgrace*: the Latin, *non ad notam*, evokes the censor's mark of disgrace on citizens condemned for moral lapses.

5 *'reduced to the ranks'*: the military metaphor indicates that the practice is unworthy of men wielding authority.

7 MACRINUS: Caecilius Macrinus is the recipient of five other letters (III 4; VII 6, 10; VIII 17; IX 4). They mostly report details of extortion trials in the Senate, thus suggesting that Macrinus is not a member of that body.

1 *Vestricius Spurinna*: Pliny's model for a vigorous life in old age; see III 1. Born *c.* AD 23, he held the consulship three times, finally in AD 100 (*Paneg.* 61.7 ff.; 64.5 f.). For his other public appointments, see note to III 1.12.

2 *established the king of the Bructeri*: the Bructeri were a tribe living round the river Lippe in north-west Germany. From AD 75 Roman operations were conducted against them under Vespasian and later under Domitian. Tacitus (*Germania* 33) describes an intertribal war in which more than 60,000 Bructeri fell. The settlement by Spurinna reported here is probably to be dated to this period, when the tribe was decisively weakened, rather than to the later period of 97–8. But see the note below.

3 *Cottius*: at III 10 Pliny reveals that he has written a memoir of his life.

lost while he was away: this mention of Spurinna's absence from Rome has prompted the suggestion that his settlement of the Bructeri took place in AD 97, but Spurinna was old for military operations, and he was busy at court at this time.

5 *encouraged to rear children*: for the reluctance of the rich to have children, see I 8.11, and for anxiety about the population shortage, see *Paneg.* 28.6.

8 CANINIUS: for Caninius Rufus, see note to I 7.

2 *these close-confining bonds*: his duties as prefect of the treasury of Saturn.

3 *a greater column*: Pliny envisages his string of duties as a column of slaves chained to each other as they proceed to work in the mines or the fields.

9 APOLLINARIS: L. Domitius Apollinaris, the recipient also of V 6, is cited at IX 13.13 as about to become suffect consul in 97. He frequently appears in Martial's poems as the poet's patron.

1 *The candidature of my friend Sextus Erucius*: for the reformed ladder of offices, see note to I 14.7. Erucius is now a candidate for the tribunate, for which applicants were recommended by the Senate to the centuriate assembly. The emperor (here Nerva) put forward names which the Senate duly approved. Erucius eventually made his way up to the suffect consulship in 117. He became city prefect and held a second consulship in 146, the year of his death. His eminence as a literary figure is attested by Aulus Gellius and Fronto.

2 *the broad stripe*: the *latus clauus* was a purple stripe on the tunic, signalling the initial promotion to the quaestorship and thus membership of the Senate. The passage here indicates that the emperor wielded influence over the award.

4 *Erucius Clarus . . . Gaius Septicius*: since Sextus was the first of his family to reach the Senate, his father is an anonymous figure. But his uncle C. Septicius Clarus was to become praetorian prefect under Hadrian. He was also a noted literary figure; the initial books of these letters, and the *Lives of the Caesars* of Suetonius, were dedicated to him.

10 OCTAVIUS: for Octavius Rufus, see note to I 7. This letter repeats his eagerness expressed at I 7.5 to obtain a copy of Octavius' verses.

3 *claims them as his own*: such plagiarism seems to have been rife in Pliny's day; see Martial's repeated complaints (1.28, 38, etc.). For the absence of copyright, see note to I 2.6.

4 *this one memorial*: throughout this section Pliny evokes the thought and language of Horace, *Odes* 3.30.

6 *a recitation . . . amenable to publication*: see note to I 13.6.

11 ARRIANUS: For the background of Arrianus Maturus, see III 2. Four other letters besides this and II 12 are addressed to him in his country retreat: IV 8 (Pliny as augur); IV 12 (Pliny's friend Marcellinus); VI 2 (death of Regulus); VIII 21 (Pliny's recitation). All provide details of life in Rome.

2 *Marius Priscus*: a senator from Spain who had become consul in the early 80s, and proconsul of Africa (roughly modern Tunisia and Algeria) in 97–8.

he pleaded guilty and asked for assessors: he was indicted for extortion by individuals from the province. After an initial hearing in the Senate, he pleaded guilty and asked for assessors to determine the level of restitution to be paid. By this ploy he hoped to avoid exile or relegation.

bidden to represent the provincials: the Senate put forward a list of names from which they were selected by lot.

3 *Catius Fronto*: suffect consul in 96, otherwise known only as a competent advocate, also defending Julius Bassus (IV 9.15) and Varenus Rufus (VI 13.3).

5 *Julius Ferox*: suffect consul in late 98 or early 99, curator of the Tiber in 101–3, and subsequently proconsul of Asia in 116. The content of VII 13 suggests that he is a regular correspondent of Pliny.

8 *summoned to attend, Vitellius Honoratus and Flavius Marcianus*: by the *lex Iulia de ui*, these men otherwise unknown were extradited in connection with these serious accusations.

beaten with clubs . . . strangled in prison: these punishments when imposed on Roman citizens were illegal. Condemnation to the mines involved loss of liberty and citizens' rights. Strangulation, the regular form of execution in Republican times (e.g. of the Catilinarian conspirators) had become less frequent by this date.

9 *Tuccius Cerealis*: the correct name is M. Tullius Cerialis, suffect consul in 90.

that Priscus be informed: following his condemnation, he was disqualified from attendance until summoned.

10 *the emperor as consul*: the trial took place in January 100, shortly after Trajan had been inaugurated as consul on 9 January. At the outset of his principate he was anxious to clamp down on maladministration in the provinces.

12 *recently . . . a consular and . . . a septemvir*: his condemnation had deprived him of these titles. The *septemuiri epulonum* formed the fourth class of priests after the pontiffs, the augurs, and the *quindecimuiri sacris faciundis*.

14 *four further water-clocks*: the prosecution was normally allotted six hours (see IV 9.9), which Pliny shared with Tacitus. The clocks normally ran for

a quarter of an hour each, but Pliny's first twelve were larger, running for twenty minutes.

15 *Caesar . . . showed me . . . great support*: the letters of Book X constantly reflect Trajan's interest in Pliny's welfare. His 'slender physique' is also referred to at IV 9.10, after another marathon performance of five hours.

Claudius Marcellinus: otherwise unknown.

17 *Salvius Liberalis*: his career is documented on an inscription (*ILS* 1011). He was advanced by Vespasian, but after his suffect consulship in *c*.84, he was prosecuted under Domitian, and presumably exiled (see III 9.33).

18 *the summings-up*: the *probationes* consisted of a review of the evidence, spoken and written, before the senators voted.

19 *Cornutus Tertullus*: this long-standing friend of Pliny shared the suffect consulship with him in September–October of this year (AD 100). Two letters (VII 21 and 31) are addressed to him.

deposited in the treasury: as the money was illegally offered, it was not to be restored. The *aerarium Saturni*, as opposed to the *fiscus*, the imperial treasury, traditionally received the fees for extortion.

debarred from Rome and Italy: the punishment was not exile, which would have meant loss of citizenship and of property, but the milder sentence of relegation. Juvenal (1.49 f.) acidly comments: 'Marius starts drinking from the eighth hour, and enjoys the wrath of the gods, while you, province, won your case and lament.'

20 *as far as Pompeius Collega expressed agreement*: the consuls-designate, recorded their votes first, followed by ex-consuls in order of seniority. Pompeius Collega, having held the consulship in 93, was well down the order. His counterproposal would have spared Priscus the penalty of relegation.

22 *by the consuls' chairs*: one wonders if Trajan made any gesture which affected this result.

23 *un procès*: the Greek word used by Pliny here (and at II 12.1: *liturgion*) is of uncertain meaning.

Hostilius Firminus: otherwise unknown.

the account-books of Marcianus: a city-councillor at Lepcis. Lepcis Magna, a coastal city east of Carthage in Tripolitania, was a Phoenician foundation which expanded rapidly in the early principate. Its considerable remains have attracted recent archaeological surveys; see *OCD*[3].

50,000 denarii . . . 10,000 sesterces: these sums were paid by the council of Lepcis to Priscus and Firminus respectively; a denarius was the equivalent of four sestertii. The figures were drawn from the account-books of Marcianus. The description of Firminus as 'perfumer', a role more appropriate to a slave, perhaps implies an effeminate relationship with Priscus.

12 ARRIANUS: see notes to I 2 and II 11. He receives this letter as a postscript to II 11.

1 *not satisfactorily*: Pliny would have much preferred the proposal advanced by Tertullus.

2 *the consuls-designate*: for Tertullus, see note to II 11.19. Acutius Nerva held the suffect consulship earlier in 100 than Tertullus; he then became governor of Lower Germany.

when lots were drawn: Firminus would have been eligible for one of the provinces governed by those of praetorian rank.

5 *nothing is so inequitable as equality itself*: Pliny's acceptance of the democratic process in spite of its limitations is an echo of Cicero's discussion of the government of states in *Republic* 1.46–50.

6 *a fast-moving and conscientious courier*: the public service (*cursus publicus*) was restricted to state business; see X 45 and note. For Pliny's couriers, see III 17.2; VIII 3.2.

13 PRISCUS: probably Javolenus Priscus, suffect consul in 83, governor of Upper Germany *c*.90, and legate of Syria for an extended period some time between 95 and 101. His career is outlined in *ILS* 1015. A less likely identification is Neratius Priscus, governor of Pannonia 102–3, but that date seems too late for this letter; note also in section 2, 'You have held this office for a long time'.

2 *a really massive army*: Syria housed three or four legions in the Flavian period.

4 *Voconius Romanus*: see note to I 5.; X 4. Inscriptional evidence indicates that he was from Saguntum in Spain, the son of Voconius Placidus. While at school in Rome with Pliny, his father died, and he was adopted by Licinius Macrinus.

his mother: for her wealth and prominence, see X 4.2.

a priest in Nearer Spain: as *flamen* there he not only conducted the ceremonies of the imperial cult, but also became president of the council of the province. The tenure of the office, attained by election, was for one year.

8 *the 'right of three children'*: this privilege, established by Augustus to encourage population growth, gave precedence in public offices to such fathers. It was increasingly extended to others as a favour by later emperors.

14 MAXIMUS: the identity of this Maximus is uncertain. Pliny's circle has several friends with this *cognomen*. The likeliest candidate is either Novius Maximus, the recipient of IV 20 and V 5, or Maesius Maximus, who received III 20 and IV 25. Both are apparently detached from life in the capital.

1 *Centumviral cases*: for the scope of the civil court, see Cicero; *De oratore* 1.173.

2 *Atilius*: for Atilius Crescens, see note to I 9.8.

as with Homer in the schools: cf. Quintilian 1.8.5: 'So the excellent custom has been established of beginning by reading Homer and Virgil, though there is need of more mature judgement to gain understanding of their merits.' The reference is to secondary education under the *grammaticus*.

3 *brought in by an advocate*: for a depiction of the good old days in the courts, see Tacitus, *Dialogus* 34.

4 *in the middle of the basilica*: the Centumviral court met in the Basilica Iulia (built by Julius Caesar) in the Forum.

5 *'Sophocleses'*... *'Tommy Tuckers'*: 'Sophocleses' literally means 'those who shout "How clever!"'. 'Tommy Tuckers' renders *Laudiceni* ('those who praise for their suppers').

6 *my announcers*: these were slaves of Pliny who announced to their master the names of persons encountered in the street, or received at home. The age at which boys received the man's toga was about 14–16 (see note to I 9.2).

9 *Larcius Licinus*: a celebrated advocate and rhetorician under Claudius and Nero (see Gellius 17.1.1). Later (*c*.73) he became governor of Hispania Tarraconensis, where the Elder Pliny was his procurator (see III 5.17).

my teacher Quintilian: Pliny again mentions at VI 6.3 that he was a pupil of the venerable rhetorician, who wrote his *Institutio Oratoria* in the reign of Domitian.

10 *Domitius Afer*: notorious as an accuser under Tiberius (Tacitus, *Annals* 4.52.1, 52.4, 66.1), Afer was celebrated as an advocate. Quintilian (5.7.7) states that as a very young man he became a pupil of his. Afer died in 59 (Tacitus, *Annals* 14.19).

he heard from close by: the court was divided into four sections to enable more speedy disposal of cases; see note to I 18.3.

14 *the beginning of gradual retirement*: at X 3A Pliny indicates that after becoming prefect of the treasury in early 98 until his consulship in 100, he practised rarely, but thereafter his presence becomes more frequent, as the letters of Book IV indicate.

15 VALERIANUS: Julius Valerianus, the recipient also of V 4 and 13, is otherwise unknown.

1 *your ancient Marsian lands*: the Marsi had by this date been virtually consigned to history, so that Pliny uses the adjective in a jovial sense. The area concerned is in central Italy, around the Fucine Lake and the capital Marrucinum.

2 *My mother's estate*: Pliny has difficulty superintending this property at Comum from Rome. His father had died while he was still a minor, and he was still only 17 when his uncle perished during the Vesuvius eruption. Hence his difficulties in maintaining the property.

16 ANNIUS: Annius Severus was Pliny's legal adviser, the recipient of III 6 and V 1, both concerned with legacies.

1 *Acilianus*: for this younger friend of Pliny, see the warm recommendation at I 14.3 ff.

2 *my own law*: equity, the application of the principle of natural justice to

correct or supplement the force of law, was not a feature of Roman law at this time. See further examples at IV 10, V 7.

3 *no opening for an informer*: by contrast with Domitian, Trajan discouraged the practice of delation. See *Panegyricus* 34, where Pliny states: 'We have seen the column of informers brought in like brigands and robbers . . . No will was safe from them . . .' See also X 97.2 (Trajan to Pliny): anonymous denunciations are 'foreign to our age'.

17 GALLUS: probably Clusinius Gallus, to whom Pliny writes at IV 17 concerning an impending civil case, and the Gallus to whom VIII 20 is addressed.

1 *my Laurentine . . . estate*: see note to I 9.4. Pliny's detailed description of the house has attracted many attempted reconstructions. Reproduced overleaf is the diagram and key from Betty Radice's Loeb edition of Pliny, vol. ii, appendix B, itself based on C. Pember's model in Oxford's Ashmolean Museum. Pliny's imprecise description allows only a tentative reconstruction.

2 *one can stay there*: 'the business of the day' would be complete by midday or shortly after, allowing Pliny to reach his villa by late afternoon.

   Laurentum . . . Ostia: Ostia as the port of Rome lay at the mouth of the Tiber. Laurentum, the site of a celebrated villa in the Antonine period, lay on the coast further south.

15 *a gentle, shady path*: with some hesitation I accept and translate the emendation *uia* for *uinea*, for the vine can hardly be 'soft and yielding even to bare feet'.

16 *almost like a public building*: Pliny is not making extravagant claims about its dimensions, but merely draws attention to it as an unusual feature in domestic architecture.

24 *the Saturnalia*: this celebration in honour of Saturn was gradually extended from a single day on 17 December to a whole week by Pliny's day. The slaves of his household enjoyed freedom to gamble and to sport without fear of punishment.

26 *there is a village*: this is *uicus Augustanus*, some five miles south of Ostia, close to Castel Fusano. It is in this general area that Pliny's villa is to be located. Extensive excavations have taken place there; see R. Meiggs, *Roman Ostia*[2] (Oxford, 1973), 69.

18 MAURICUS: for Junius Mauricus and his dead brother Arulenus Rusticus, see I 14.1–2. In that letter, Pliny writes to Mauricus, recently returned from exile, and therefore not fully au fait with possible candidates, in response to his request for advice on a husband for his niece; Mauricus now makes a further request for help in the education of his nephews.

1 *I am going back to school*: this passage indicates that the boys are old enough (perhaps at 13 or 14) to attend a school of rhetoric. By this time there were salaried professors (Vespasian appointed Quintilian as the first) but also private practitioners.

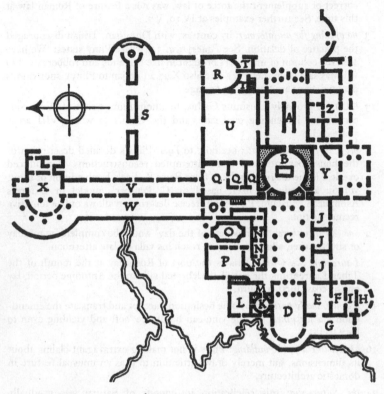

PLINY'S HOUSE AT LAURENTUM

A. Entrance hall
B. Courtyard
C. Inner hall
D. Dining room
E. Bedroom
F. Bedroom
G. Gymnasium
H. Bedroom
I. Bedroom
J. Slaves' rooms
K. Bedroom
L. Small dining room

M. Rooms and antechambers
N. Bathrooms
O. Heated swimming-bath
P. Ball court
Q. Suite with upper storey
R. Dining room, with stores above
S. Garden with vine pergola
T. Rooms behind dining room
U. Kitchen garden
V. Covered arcade
W. Terrace
X. Pliny's private suite
Y–Z. Kitchens and storerooms, not mentioned by Pliny

2 *many present of senatorial rank*: senior figures attended these performances for personal profit, or as invited friends, or (like Pliny) to assess the teachers' suitability for the education of their children or their friends' children.

3 *to report to you . . . by letter*: Pliny probably recommended Julius Genitor, as he does to Corellia Hispulla at III 3.

5 *not only resentment, but also enmity*: doubtless not only from unsuccessful candidates, but also from their patrons.

19 CERIALIS: Tuccius Cerialis. The speech which Pliny is being invited to read is probably that in which he indicted Marius Priscus as described in II 11. The ex-consul Cerialis was not only present but also made a formal proposal (II 11.9).

1 *my speech*: the speech was an indictment of extortion, which points persuasively to that described in II 11.

2 *the assemblage of judges . . . the partial audience*: in this section Pliny is generalizing about the superiority of the spoken speech, not only in the Senate but also in the Centumviral court. The references to judges (assessors) and to the audience are more appropriate to the latter.

6 *this disharmony between styles*: the controversy between the florid Asianic style and the austere Atticism has already been discussed (see e.g. I 2 and II 5). Whereas he argues in those letters for a combination of the two, in this speech he clearly deployed the more austere utterance, in view of the complexity of the legal arguments.

7 *the Greeks have something not at all dissimilar*: in his speech indicting Priscus, Pliny argued against the simple application of the law against extortion, which would have prescribed merely a financial penalty. He compares this with the Greek fourth-century practice, which led to a frequent *graphē paranomōn* (indictment for illegality). For example, after Ctesiphon proposed a decree to award a crown to Demosthenes, Aeschines brought such an indictment against him, which provoked Demosthenes to utter his famous speech *On the Crown*.

20 CALVISIUS: for Calvisius Rufus, see note to I 12.12.

1 *this princely story, or rather stories*: Pliny ends Book II with a further attack on his *bête noire* Regulus, here in his role as legacy-hunter. The satirists regard this as virtually a profession; see Horace, *Satires* 2.5; Juvenal 12.93 ff.; Petronius 116, 141, etc.

2 *Verania, wife of Piso*: L. Calpurnius Piso Frugi Licinianus, after returning from exile, was formally adopted by the emperor Galba in AD 69. This greatly enraged the Praetorian Guard, who supported Otho, and they murdered both the emperor and his adoptee. Verania secured her husband's body for burial (Tacitus, *Histories* 1.14 ff., 34 ff., 48).

Regulus approached her: for Aquilius Regulus, see note to I 5.1. The hostile relations between him and Piso were doubtless attributable to Regulus' informing under Nero, when Piso was exiled and his brother executed.

But Regulus had amended his ways thereafter, and was clearly on friendly terms with Verania.

4 *I shall consult a soothsayer*: Regulus shared the widespread belief in the efficacy of astrology and haruspicy as prophetic. See section 13 below and VI 2.2.

5 *on the survival of his own son*: the young man's death is reported in IV 2, apparently later than the publication of this letter.

7 *Velleius Blaesus*: unknown, unless he is the Blaesus whose death is signalled by Martial 8.28.

9 *the scholars' law?*: in the school of rhetoric, the topic chosen had to be illustrated by three examples.

10 *Aurelia*: mentioned as the target of a *captator* in Juvenal 5.97 f.

11 *inheritances and legacies*: the first as gifts of land, the second of other legacies.

12 *Mais pourquoi je me fâche?*: the Greek (an echo of Demosthenes, *On the Crown* 142) means: 'Why do I get exercised?'

13 *a twin set of entrails*: the size of the liver was especially significant; see e.g. Livy 27.26.14.

BOOK THREE

1 CALVISIUS RUFUS: see note to I 12.12.

1 *Spurinna*: for Vestricius Spurinna, see note to II 7.1.

4 *At the second hour*: the Romans divided the period between sunrise and sunset into twelve hours, so that an hour varied in length according to the time of the year.

7 *enhanced by the integrity of their author*: some of Spurinna's verses are risqué. Pliny justifies them by the traditional argument that they are composed by innocents at play; so also Catullus 16.5 ff.; Ovid, *Tristia* 2.754; Martial 1.4.8; and Pliny himself, IV 14, V 3.

9 *Corinthian ware*: the Elder Pliny (*Natural History* 34.2.3) states that it is made of 'bronze blended with gold and silver'.

12 *held magistracies, governed provinces*: Spurinna held the consulship three times, first under Vespasian (date uncertain), then in 98 and again in 100. He was governor of Lower Germany under Vespasian or Domitian; we have no knowledge of other governorships claimed by Pliny. Under Nerva he served on the board seeking economies in the outlays of the *aerarium Saturni*.

2 VIBIUS MAXIMUS: Pliny addresses him with both *nomen* and *cognomen* to distinguish him from other Maximi. He is probably the Vibius Maximus who became prefect of Egypt in 103.

2 *Arrianus Maturus*: see note to I 2.

Altinum: modern Altino on the Adriatic coast in Venetia. It was a thriving town; see Martial 4.25.

3 CORELLIA HISPULLA: the daughter of Corellius Rufus, whose death Pliny mourns in I 12. In IV 17 Pliny promises to represent her in court in what may be a civil case,

1 *Your father*: see I 12 and note.

3 *He has had teachers at home*: the boy has now at the age of 13–14 completed his literary studies under the *grammaticus* at home. Quintilian (1.2) discusses the rival merits of such private tuition and of attendance at school with other pupils.

5 *Julius Genitor*: see II 18, where Pliny is seeking a suitable rhetor for the nephews of Junius Mauricus. He has now made his choice, and recommends him also to Hispulla. Three later letters (III 11; VII 30; IX 17) indicate a developing relationship between Pliny and Genitor, all concerned with various aspects of the intellectual life.

7 *first upright behaviour, and then eloquence*: Pliny echoes his former teacher Quintilian in his warnings against sexual immorality and on the importance of choosing a teacher of integrity. Quintilian further recommends the appointment of a second person to accompany the pupil as a moral guide (1.2.5).

4 CAECILIUS MACRINUS: see note to II 7.

2 *a public building*: Pliny had decided to pay for the erection of a temple in the town of Tifernum; see IV 1.5; X 8.2.

leave from my prefecture of the treasury: see the Introduction (pp. xiv f.) for his tenure of this post from early 98 to his consulship in 100.

a complaint against . . . Caecilius Classicus: Pliny records the details of the trial in III 9. Classicus was proconsul of Baetica in 97–8, but his death delayed the judicial process until late 99.

3 *My colleagues*: that is, in the treasury, notably Cornutus Tertullus, who administered the civil treasury jointly with Pliny.

4 *against Baebius Massa*: for this indictment in 93 and the subsequent ramifications, see VII 33.

my formal attachment . . . as patron: this system of patronage of communities had developed from Republican days, when conquering generals undertook protection of them; see Cicero, *De officiis* 1.35, The system continued in Pliny's day, but he does not acknowledge any formal agreement with Baetica either here or at I 7.2.

6 *the considerable dangers*: Pliny uses similar language with reference to the indictment of Baebius Massa at I 7.2. He is referring to the possible displeasure of Domitian.

7 *Classicus had died*: see III 9.5: 'whether by chance or suicide'.

8 *for the third time*: following his participation in the trials of Baebius Massa and of Marius Priscus (see II 11).

5 BAEBIUS MACER: after being curator of the Appian Way, and then governor of Baetica, he became suffect consul in 103, and city prefect in 117.

1 *my uncle*: details of the career of the Elder Pliny (AD 23/24–79) and his writings will emerge from the commentary on this letter.

2 *One book on throwing the javelin from horsebook*: the work has not survived. It was probably written when Pliny was a junior cavalry officer in Germany in the late 40s AD.

the life of Pomponius Secundus: after his consulship in 44, Pomponius was governor of Upper Germany in 50–51 (Tacitus, *Annals* 12.27–8). Pliny will have gained the older man's affection during this period.

4 *Twenty books on the wars in Germany*: this substantial work covered the German campaigns from the time of Julius Caesar to the reign of Claudius. It is generally assumed that it was the source for Tacitus' account of German affairs in *Annals* 1–6. It has not survived.

Nero Drusus: this stepson of Augustus and father of Claudius campaigned in Germany 12–9 BC. He died as the result of an accident (Dio 55.1), having reached the Elbe.

5 *Three books on education*: Quintilian perused them and regarded them as fussy (11.3.143 and 148). The work has not survived.

Eight books on ambiguity: the work, which has not survived, was broader in scope than the title suggests. Pliny himself described it as *De grammatica* (*Natural History*, Preface to Book 28). It was concerned with regularity and exceptions in the forms of words (analogy and anomaly). The Younger Pliny strikes an apologetic note here, hinting that his uncle would not have devoted himself to such a work in less hazardous times.

6 *where Aufidius Bassus left off*: Bassus' history may have covered the period from the death of Julius Caesar to the later years of Claudius. Quintilian is complimentary (10.1.103). Pliny's history, which has not survived, continued to the Jewish wars in 71. The Younger Pliny's reticence about this work is striking; he may have found the account of Nero's reign uncongenial.

Thirty-seven books on natural history: this encyclopaedia of every aspect of the natural world has survived. On the author's own count it contains 20,000 facts drawn from 2,000 authors. It deservedly gained eminence in the Middle Ages, becoming a model for Isidore of Seville's *Etymologiae*.

7 *he died in his fifty-sixth year*: for the circumstances, at the eruption of Vesuvius, see VI 16.19.

duties of the greatest importance: Suetonius, in his (fragmentary) *De uiris illustribus*, states: 'With the utmost integrity he administered as procurator offices which were most splendid and in succession.' These took him to Gaul, Africa, and Spain.

friendships with emperors: *amicitia* is here technical, referring to his membership of the emperor's council, which in Vespasian's day met early in the morning. See Suetonius, *Vespasian* 2.

8 *the time of the Vulcanalia*: the feast, on 23 August, was an appropriate day on which to begin to ignite the lamps for study.

11 *he would often bathe . . . a light lunch*: he thus reversed the normal Roman pattern of exercise and bath after lunch (see Martial 4.8.1 ff.) At VI 16.4 f. he follows the same routine of bathing before lunch.

12 *we have lost ten lines and more*: the book being read was poetry, perhaps a comedy.

14 *scraped and towelled*: for the routine of oiling, strigilling, and towelling, see J. P. V. D. Balsdon, *Life and Leisure in Ancient Rome* (London, 1969), 30.

17 *a procurator in Spain . . . Larcius Licinus*: see II 14.9. The elder Pliny was in charge of the imperial finances in the province where Larcius was governor.

19 *official duties . . . services to friends?*: the combination of the two suggests that 'official duties' refers to business at Rome, when he was prefect of the treasury (between early 98 and 100) or curator of the Tiber (104–7). 'Services to friends' indicates court-appearances as advocate or as assessor.

6 ANNIUS SEVERUS: see note to II 16.

1 *a Corinthian statue*: see note to III 1.9 for Corinthian ware. Pliny probably affects ignorance of it because the satirists and others targeted pretentious owners. See Petronius 50; Martial 9.59.11; Seneca, *De breuitate uitae* 12.2.

5 *my name . . . with my titles*: Sherwin-White suggests that this points to a date after Pliny's consulship when he was busy as a leading senator and curator of the Tiber, rather than the period when he was prefect of the treasury.

7 CANINIUS RUFUS: see note to I 3.

1 *Silius Italicus*: this politician and poet (*c*.26–103) was a *nouus homo*, initially notorious as an informer under Nero, who awarded him the consulship in 68. He regained popularity under Vespasian, who appointed him proconsul of Asia (*c*.77). After retirement in Campania, he devoted himself to literature and art. His epic poem, the *Punica*, the longest surviving poem in Classical Latin, is on the Hannibalic War, with Livy as the main authority and Virgil as poetic model. Pliny's judgement in section 5 below is just.

2 *his elder son . . . has in fact attained the consulship*: so also Martial 8.66.

3 *a friend of Vitellius*: he aided him in negotiations with Vespasian; see Tacitus, *Histories* 3.65.

4 *without thought of his wealth*: the visitors were not legacy-hunting.

6 *the accession of the new emperor*: Trajan is meant. 'Accession' (*aduentu*) less probably refers to Trajan's arrival from Pannonia.

7 *un connaisseur*: the Greek *philokalos* refers to Silius' enthusiasm for collecting *objets d'art*.

8 *a number of villas*: they included Cicero's villa at Cumae (Martial 11.48; for Cicero's ownership, *Ad Atticum* 5.2.1 f.).

Virgil's tomb: Silius purchased it when it was in disrepair (Martial 11.50).

12 *father of the Piso . . . killed in Africa*: the father was consul in 27. The son, consul in 57, when proconsul of Africa in 70 was assassinated by Valerius

Festus, the legionary commander acting in the interests of Vespasian (Tacitus, *Histories* 4.48–50).

13 *tears of Xerxes*: the anecdote is recorded by Herodotus (7.45): 'None of all these thousands will be alive a hundred years from now.'

14 *in another's hands*: Pliny laments the loss of political freedom under the autocratic principate.

15 *La lutte, c'est bonne*: the Greek cited by Pliny is from Hesiod, *Works and Days* 24.

8 SUETONIUS TRANQUILLUS: see note to I 18. Pliny's condescending attitude towards his protégé is further demonstrated here.

1 *the tribunate . . . obtained from . . . Neratius Marcellus*: Marcellus was governor in Britain in 103 (and perhaps earlier). Pliny had obtained for his young friend a post as military tribune there.

4 *I am free to put Silvanus in your place*: Marcellus had obviously given Pliny *carte blanche* to enter a name in the army-list, without specifying Suetonius.

9 CORNELIUS MINICIANUS: this equestrian from Bergamum is also the recipient of IV 11 and VIII 12. His background is described in VII 22.

2 *Caecilius Classicus . . . Marius Priscus*: this letter reports the details of the trial of Classicus, governor of Baetica in 97–8, the preliminaries to which were recounted in III 4. The trial of Marius Priscus is reported in II 11; see the notes to these letters.

4 *by a single community*: as indicated here, prosecution of provincial officials could be mounted by individuals, or communities, or provincial councils. Classicus' behaviour is here shown to have been more heinous than that of Priscus.

6 *against the allies and agents of Classicus*: these were chiefly the members of the governor's staff, comprising tribunes, prefects, scribes, and the rest, as detailed in Cicero, *Pro Rabirio Postumo* 13.

7 *Lucceius Albinus*: he is reported again as cooperating with Pliny in the defence of Julius Bassus in IV 9. He may be the recipient of VI 10.

11 *the exemplary tale of Sertorius*: the anecdote is recorded in Valerius Maximus 7.3.6, and also in Plutarch, *Sertorius* 16.5–11. In his attempt to unify the revolts of the Spanish tribes against the post-Sullan regime at Rome, and to discourage isolated and ineffective attacks on the Roman forces by individual groups, Sertorius set before them an aged horse attended by a strong man, and a strong horse with an attendant who was a weakling. The two men were instructed to pull off the tails of their respective horses. The strong man sought ineffectually to wrench the tail off his horse by force; the weakling plucked out the hairs of his horse's tail one by one.

13 *a written account . . . his actual words*: these damaging documents came from Classicus' account-books and official files.

14 *their carrying out of orders was a crime*: the perennial issue of whether subordinates can justify atrocities by claiming that they were carrying out

orders is discussed by D. Daube, *The Defence of Superior Orders in Roman Law* (Oxford, 1956).

16 *Claudius Restitutus*: probably the Restitutus who is the addressee of VI 17.

17 *relegated for five years*: relegation was the lesser form of banishment, allowing retention of citizenship and property.

21 *from the judges' bench*: a panel of senators acted as judges; Pliny would have been one of them had he not been assigned as prosecutor, as described in III 4.

25 *'He will be just as innocent . . . the facts'*: Pliny employed irony in meeting these loud objections from supporters of the defendant.

28 *a technique of Homer's*: the device of *husteron proteron* which Pliny probably remembers from Cicero, *Ad Atticum* 1.16.1.

29 30 *Norbanus Licinianus . . . a prevaricator*: this letter is our sole evidence for the career of Norbanus, here accused of prevarication or collusion with the opposing counsel defending Casta, wife of Classicus.

33 *two ex-consuls*: Pomponius Rufus reappears at IV 9.3 as prosecutor of Julius Bassus. He could be either Q. Pomponius, suffect consul 95 and governor of Lower Moesia in 99, or C. Pomponius Rufus, consul 98. Libo Frugi is not otherwise known.

before a judge in support of the accusers of Salvius Liberalis: for Liberalis, see note to II 11.17. Here Norbanus appeared before a single judge, presumably appointed by Domitian. It seems curious that such evidence was admitted as relevant, unless it was argued that he was guilty of calumny and that this was relevant to the charge of collusion.

10 VESTRICIUS SPURINNA: see II 7.1 and note, and III 1. Cottia was Spurinna's wife.

1 *an account of your son*: for his death in 97, while Spurinna was conducting business abroad, see II 7.3 ff. Pliny is writing this extended obituary some three years later.

3 *for a second volume . . . in serial form*: since *uolumen* means a roll rather than a book, it is not clear whether he divided the work into two books, or merely extended the earlier one.

11 JULIUS GENITOR: see note to III 3.5.

1 *Artemidorus*: nothing is known of him other than the details in this letter.

2 *when the philosophers were banished*: in late 93 Domitian expelled the philosophers after outspoken criticisms of his autocracy.

because I was a praetor: Pliny, like Tacitus, played safe during Domitian's regime, but loses no opportunity thereafter to claim that his association with foes of the emperor made his position precarious.

3 *Senecio, Rusticus, and Helvidius*: for Senecio, see note to I 5.3; for Arulenus Rusticus, note to I 14.1. Helvidius, whose father had been executed under Vespasian for his attacks on the regime, was charged with composing a play

implicitly critical of Domitian's divorce. All three were executed in 93; see Suetonius, *Domitian* 10.3 f.; Tacitus, *Agricola* 2.

3 *Mauricus, Gratilla, Arria, and Fannia*: for Junius Mauricus, see note to I 5.10. Gratilla was the wife of Rusticus, Arria of Thrasea Paetus, and Fannia of the elder Helvidius.

5 *Gaius Musonius*: the celebrated Stoic philosopher was implicated in the conspiracy of Piso, and was banished by Nero in 65 and for a second time by Vespasian. Pliny was about thirty years his junior.

6 *firm control over his eyes and thoughts*: condemnation of idle curiosity is especially strong in Plutarch's treatise, *Moralia* 515b–23b.

12 CATILIUS SEVERUS: see note to I 22.

1 *Socratic conversation*: the phrase indicates intellectual conversation on various topics, not merely philosophy.

2 *your duties with early morning callers*: for the early morning *salutatio*, at which clients and others thronged the salons of more important citizens, see Balsdon, *Life and Leisure*, 21 ff.

Not even Cato: the Younger Cato was notorious for heavy drinking. See e.g. Plutarch, *Cato the Younger* 6: 'He drank longer than anyone else, so that he often continued over his wine till daybreak.'

Caesar's rebuke: cited from Caesar's lost work, the *Anticato*, written in two books in 45 BC in reaction against Cicero's laudatory *Cato*. See Suetonius, *Julius* 56.5; Cicero, *Ad Atticum* 12.40.1; Plutarch, *Caesar* 54.

13 VOCONIUS ROMANUS: see notes to I 5 and II 13.4.

1 *the speech*: this is the extant *Panegyricus*, which Pliny as consul delivered to the Emperor Trajan in 100; he discusses the speech further at III 18. The text is conveniently included (with translation) in the Loeb Pliny, vol. ii.

2 *the mode of expression*: lying behind Pliny's entire discussion here is the traditional fivefold division of *inuentio, dispositio, elocutio, memoria*, and *actio*. He claims that the uninitiated often excel at *inuentio* (invention of topics and argumentation) and *actio* (delivery), but that arrangement of topics and transitions (*dispositio*) and modes of expression (*elocutio*, or style) require the training such as he enjoyed under Quintilian.

4 *light . . . shadow*: Pliny has probably derived this notion from Cicero, *De oratore* 3.101.

14 ACILIUS: perhaps the P. Acilius of I 14.6, or at any rate a friend remote from Rome and its social problems.

1 *Larcius Macedo*: he cannot be positively identified. Other notorious murders by slaves are recorded at VIII 14.12, and by Tacitus, *Annals* 14.42 ff.

2 *Formiae*: on the coast of Latium, the scene of Cicero's death.

4 *as murdered individuals usually are*: when the city prefect Pedanius Secundus was murdered in 61 by a slave, his entire household of 400 was executed (Tacitus, *Annals* 14.45; for the Senate's draconian policy, cf. *Annals* 13.32.1).

6 *today's holiday*: Pliny writes at Rome, free from public duties.

in the public baths: following the example of Agrippa (20 BC), Nero, Titus, and Trajan had all erected splendid *thermae* by Pliny's day. In addition there were numerous *balnea*, less pretentious establishments which charged a mere *quadrans* for entry. See Horace, *Satires* 1.3.137; Juvenal 6.447; Balsdon, *Life and Leisure*, 26 ff.

15 SILIUS PROCULUS: otherwise unknown.

1 *Cicero*: in making this implicit comparison between Pliny and Cicero, Proculus finds a sure way to Pliny's benevolence, since Pliny likes to pose as a latter-day Cicero. For Cicero's encouragement of the young men around him, see e.g. J. P. V. D. Balsdon, 'Cicero the Man', in T. A. Dorey (ed.), *Cicero* (London, 1964), 187 ff.

2 *respect for poetry*: like so many of his contemporaries, Pliny tries his hand at verses, recorded increasingly from IV 14 onwards.

16 NEPOS: see note to II 3.

2 *Fannia*: see note to III 11.3. As the second wife of Helvidius Priscus, she was banished three times (VII 19.4), before finally returning from exile in 97 (IX 13.5). Pliny recounts her final illness in VII 19.

the famous Arria: the wife of A. Caecina Paetus became celebrated for her intrepid exhortation to her husband as she encouraged him to follow her lead in committing suicide in prison in 42.

3 *Caecina Paetus*: suffect consul in 37. The date of this illness and of his son's death is uncertain.

6 *That celebrated action*: it is recounted also by Cassius Dio (60. 15.5 f.), and by Martial (1. 13).

7 *When Scribonianus raised a rebellion*: L. Arruntius Camillus Scribonianus was governor of Dalmatia in command of two legions. His attempted *coup d'état* to restore the Republic in 42 fizzled out after five days (Suetonius, *Claudius* 13.2).

9 *the wife . . . laying information before Claudius*: Cassius Dio states that the trial took place in the Senate, in the presence of Claudius. The wife, Vibia, was relegated (Tacitus, *Annals* 12.52).

10 *her son-in-law Thrasea*: this moderate Stoic, after being consul in 56, was executed under Nero in 66. Tacitus, *Annals* 16.21 f., indignantly reviews the events leading to the execution.

17 JULIUS SERVIANUS: three times consul, and under Trajan the legate successively of Upper Germany and Pannonia, he was one of the influential figures under Trajan and Hadrian, until at the age of 90 he fell under suspicion of conspiracy, and was executed.

1 *fully stretched . . . not fully stretched*: the phrases point to his tenure as governor of Pannonia *c.*100, rather than to his campaigning subsequently with Trajan in Dacia.

few or no opportunities to write?: presumably with reference to the availability of couriers.

18 VIBIUS SEVERUS: a friend from Pliny's native region (perhaps from Mediolanum), who is the recipient also of IV 28. Both letters indicate common literary interests.

1 *My position as consul*: it appears to have been the convention that each incoming consul gave thanks for his appointment, and paid tributes to the emperor. Pliny was the third or fourth incumbent of the office in 100. For the extant *Panegyricus*, see note to III 13.1.

in a more extended . . . version: it has been hazarded that the speech as delivered was a third or a quarter the length of the written version.

5 *these literary recitals . . . are being revived*: see I 13. Note that here the revival is attributed to the change of regime after Domitian.

10 *a more luxuriant style . . . restrained and severe presentation*: Pliny reverts to the controversy of the merits between the plain style of Atticism and the baroque style of Asianism, which preoccupies him in earlier letters from I 2 onwards.

19 CALVISIUS RUFUS: see note to I 12.12.

1 *A neighbouring estate*: this is adjacent to Pliny's property near Tifernum in Etruria. This is indicated by the description of the property at V 6. Rufus, as a native of Comum, would not have needed such detail if Pliny had been referring to property there. The mention of travel-costs excludes Laurentum.

5 *woodland, which provides timber*: see V 6.8 for a similar comment about the Tifernum estate.

7 *we shall have to equip them with slaves*: the tenants will have forfeited their slaves as well as farming-equipment through their inability to pay the rent.

the economic slump: perhaps in part attributable to overproduction of wine, intensified by provincial competition. Domitian forbade new vineyards to be planted in Italy, and those in the provinces to be cut down (Suetonius, *Domitian* 7.2).

8 *money from my mother-in-law*: for Pompeia Celerina, see I 4, where her generosity towards Pliny is indicated.

20 MAESIUS MAXIMUS: aside from this letter and IV 25 (also on voting procedures), he is unknown.

1 *the lex tabellaria*: four such laws regulating voting were passed between 139 and 107 BC, the first on the proposal of A. Gabinius, plebeian tribune in 139 (see Cicero, *Laws* 3.35–7). When the secret ballot was introduced, voters were issued with a small boxwood tablet on which to record their vote. After a lapse of time, secret ballots were reintroduced by the *lex Valeria* of AD 5, but it is clear from this letter that the procedure had again lapsed, and had only recently been restored.

2 *on the day of the elections*: all magistrates (consuls, praetors, quaestors, aediles) were elected at one meeting in January.

5 *the procedure at elections*: the emperor Tiberius in AD 14 had transferred the

elections from the popular assembly to the Senate (Tacitus, *Annals* 1.15.1). Pliny's older friends will have described the procedure under Claudius.

6 *a rival's origin, age, or even character*: descendants of slaves required the lapse of three generations before becoming eligible for equestrian rank. The minimum age for a quaestor was 25. Certain mean professions, as well as public disgrace, debarred candidates from office.

9 *as in court cases*: Pliny obliquely refers to his honourable conduct as judge in extortion trials.

12 *certain streams flow*: in the more tolerant era of Trajan, greater respect towards Republican offices and procedures was shown.

21 CORNELIUS PRISCUS: After becoming suffect consul in 104 (he is called *consularis* at V 20.7) he became proconsul of Asia *c.*120–1.

1 *Martial*: the Spanish poet (*c.*40–*c.*104) was a protégé of the Younger Seneca and friend of most of the literary men at Rome, where he lived from 64 to 98, keeping on the right side of emperors. Twelve books of his *Epigrams* have survived.

2 *When he was retiring from Rome*: he retired to Spain, to his native Bilbilis, in 98, and died there.

3 *poets who had written eulogies*: Pliny thinks pre-eminently of Pindar, whose patrons included not only leading aristocrats but also the ruling houses of Cyrene, Syracuse, and Acragas.

4 *the verses for which I thanked him?*: the ten lines quoted are lines 12–21 from *Epigrams* 10.20 (19), composed at Rome in autumn 94. They are written in hendecasyllables.

5 *on the Esquiline*: Pliny's town house lay on this eminence to the east of the city.

the court of Centumviri . . . Arpinum's pages: at this early stage of his career (see above) Pliny's chief occupation was with the lawsuits in the civil court. Arpinum was the birthplace of Cicero, with whom Pliny loves to be compared.

6 *his writings will not be immortal*: for this just appraisal, compare III 7.5 on Silius Italicus.

BOOK FOUR

1 CALPURNIUS FABATUS: this equestrian landholder at Comum and else-where is the recipient of seven further letters (V 11; VI 30; VII 11, 16, 23, 32; VIII 10), chiefly concerned with family affairs and property. He was accused of being implicated in the treason charges against L. Junius Silanus in 65, but escaped by a direct appeal to the emperor (Tacitus, *Annals* 16.8.3). His death is reported in X 120.

1 *your granddaughter*: Calpurnia Fabata, Pliny's third wife, was the daughter of Fabatus' deceased son. Her virtues as wife are extolled in IV 19.

4 *a town close to our estate . . . Tifernum-on-Tiber*: Pliny inherited the estate from his uncle, the Elder Pliny, and presumably at the same time the role of patron of the town; he was 17 or 18 at his uncle's death at the eruption of Vesuvius.

5 *a shrine*: work was to start on it in 99 (III 4.2), but delays hindered its completion (X 8.3).

7 *your daughter*: Calpurnia Hispulla. Letters to her (IV 19; VIII 11) report on her niece's virtues as a wife and on her miscarriage.

2 ATTIUS CLEMENS: the recipient of I 10, otherwise unknown.

1 *Regulus has lost his son*: for Regulus, see note to I 5.1. At II 20.5 Pliny hints that Regulus is putting the boy's life at risk by swearing false oaths on his head.

2 *released him from paternal authority*: while subject to *patria potestas* the boy could not inherit (Gaius 1.132, 134).

3 *now that he has lost him*: Regulus' grief is signalled in other ways at IV 7.

5 *with his statues*: not necessarily all statues of himself; see IV 7.1 for those of his son.

3 ARRIUS ANTONINUS: suffect consul in 69 and (probably) in 97, proconsul of Asia probably in 78. He was the grandfather of Antoninus Pius. The brief notes addressed to him in IV 18 and V 15 are both concerned with his literary efforts.

3 *Homer's fabled ancient*: Nestor, the archetypal old sage, hence a flattering comparison with Antoninus. Homer (*Iliad* 1.249) writes of him: 'The speech from his tongue flowed sweeter than honey.'

4 *Callimachus or Herodas*: Callimachus flourished in the early third century BC. Of his massive poetic output six hymns and sixty epigrams survive. These cover a *mélange* of erotic, literary, and dedicatory topics. Herodas, flourishing about a generation later, wrote mimes in scazons (limping iambics). Seven of them have survived with such titles as 'The Procuress', 'The Brothel-keeper', 'The Shoemaker', and 'The Schoolmaster'.

4 SOSIUS SENECIO: see note to I 13.

1 *Varisidius Nepos*: otherwise unknown.

Gaius Calvisius: see note to I 12.12.

2 *a six-months' tribunate*: there is controversy about the exact nature of the office; the term is familiar from inscriptions. One attractive suggestion is that it covered the period of the campaigning season. The salary of 25,000 sesterces is half that of the pay of a full-blown military tribune.

5 JULIUS SPARSUS: the suffect consul of 88 and friend of Martial (12.57.3) is also the recipient of VIII 3.

1 *The story goes*: for the anecdote about Aeschines and Demosthenes (with a slightly different slant), see II 3.10 and note.

2 *a speech of mine*: probably the *Pro Basso*, detailed in IV 9.

6 JULIUS NASO: a young protégé of Pliny, who reports that he is canvassing for him to become quaestor in VI 6.

1 *Etruria . . . across the Po*: these generalities refer to Pliny's estates at Tifernum and Comum.

2 *My Laurentine estate*: see II 17.

7 CATIUS LEPIDUS: otherwise unknown.

1 *Regulus*: see note to I 5.1.

to mourn his son: cf. IV 2.

3 *'ignorance breeds daring . . . hesitation'*: the apt citation is from the funeral-speech of Pericles at Thucydides 2.40.3. Pericles claims that Athenians are superior to others in being 'most daring in action, and in reflection on deeds we are about to undertake. In others, ignorance breeds boldness, and reflection breeds hesitation.'

4 *weak lungs . . . memory*: Regulus' feeble oratory is earlier criticized at I 20.14 f.

5 *Herennius Senecio*: see note to I 5.3.

Cato's definition: see Quintilian 12.1.1: 'uir bonus dicendi peritus.'

6 *Demosthenes' words*: Pliny cites *On the Crown* 291.

8 ARRIANUS MATURUS: see note to I 2. He may have been serving in Egypt under Vibius Maximus at this time (III 2.2; IV 12.7).

1 *the augurate*: this was one of the four main colleges of priests, together with the *pontifices*, the *quindecimuiri sacris faciundis*, and the *septemuiri epulonum*. For the functions of augurs collectively and individually, see *OCD*³. In Pliny's day, appointments were in the gift of the emperor; at X 13 Pliny begs for admission to this or to the *septemuiri*.

other positions: not other priesthoods (all held for life), but other positions of prestige.

3 *Julius Frontinus*: after his first consulship in 73 or 74, he governed Britain in 74–8. After a period of obscurity under Domitian, he became curator of aqueducts in 97, and held further consulships in 98 and 100. His tenure as curator of aqueducts resulted in his treatise *De aquis*; he is probably also the author of *Strategemata*.

5 *at a much earlier age*: Cicero became consul at 43, and augur at 53; Pliny became consul at 38 or 39, and augur at about 42.

9 CORNELIUS URSUS: the recipient of three other letters (V 20; VI 5, 13) on the trial of Rufus Varenus, and of a further brief letter (VIII 9) of no consequence.

1 *Julius Bassus*: he was quaestor, then praetorian governor in Bithynia in 100–1. Of the earlier indictment under Vespasian, nothing further is known. His friendship with Domitian, leading to a strained relationship with Titus, and his relegation by Domitian, suggests involvement in court intrigues.

3 *Pomponius Rufus . . . Theophanes*: for Rufus, see note to III 9.33. Theophanes is not otherwise known.

4 *his positive qualities*: these *ornamenta*, gained in part from 'hazardous
processes', imply that the hostility of earlier emperors was regarded as a
positive merit.

5 *plotting of the informers*: the other main source for Bithynian affairs at this
date, Dio of Prusa, refers satirically to the profitable trade of informers
(43.6 f.).

other accusations: chiefly charges of cruelty and violence against individuals
(see Dio of Prusa 43.11).

6 *for he had been quaestor*: as the duties of a provincial quaestor were mainly
financial, he would have had opportunities for gain.

7 *the Saturnalia*: 17 December and subsequent days were the period for
exchange of gifts and merrymaking; see II 17.24.

9 *the law*: cf. II 11.14.

10 *my physical strength*: see similarly II 11.15.

13 *Lucceius Albinus*: see note to III 9.7.

14 *Herennius Pollio*: otherwise unknown.

15 *Homullus and Fronto*: M. Junius Homullus was suffect consul in 102, and
then governor of Cappadocia-Pontus. He defends Rufus Varenus at
V 20.6, and is mentioned as a participant in a senatorial debate at VI 19.3.
For Catius Fronto, see note to II 11.3.

16 *Baebius Macer . . . Caepio Hispo*: on Macer, see note to III 5. Caepio
Hispo (suffect consul *c*.101) became successively governor of Baetica and
of Asia.

20 *Valerius Paulinus*: see note to II 2.

21 *the consuls did not pursue the proposal*: Pliny gives the misleading impression
that Theophanes left the Senate under a cloud, and that Bassus had been
maligned. In fact, as emerges from X 56.4, all Bassus' decisions in the
province were annulled; he had got off lightly.

10 STATIUS SABINUS: almost certainly the recipient of VI 18; IX 2 and 18; a
native of Firmum and a military commander. The tone of the letters
indicates that he is not an intimate of Pliny.

1 *Sabina*: clearly a relative of Pliny's correspondent.

2 *this seems clearly mistaken*: compare II 16.2 for Pliny's praiseworthy
espousal of the principle of equity in the face of Roman law.

11 CORNELIUS MINICIANUS: see note to III 9.

1 *Valerius Licinianus*: not known outside this letter.

2 *'What sport . . . senators!'*: the lament inspired Juvenal's 'Should Fortune so
wish, you will become a consul from being a rhetor, but should she so wish,
you will become a rhetor from being a consul' (7.197 f.).

3 *'debarred from water and fire'*: the traditional formula for *deportatio*, the

stricter form of banishment. For the toga versus the Greek pallium, see Cicero, *Pro Rabirio Postumo* 25 ff.

6 *He had wanted to bury Cornelia . . . alive*: Pliny is guilty of special pleading on behalf of Cornelia throughout this letter. Other contemporary authors have little doubt about the guilt of her and of other Vestals. See especially Suetonius, *Domitian* 8.3 f.: 'The sexual depravities of the Vestals had been ignored by Domitian's father and brother, but he punished them harshly in various ways.' He states that three were allowed to commit suicide, and when Cornelia was convicted, her debauchers (plural) were beaten to death in public. Cornelia is probably the Cornelia Cossa appointed as a Vestal at a youthful age in 62 (Tacitus, *Annals* 15.22).

not to the Regia: the official residence of the chief priest (Pontifex Maximus) at the eastern end of the Forum. Pliny is hinting that the meeting held elsewhere was irregular.

He condemned Cornelia: Suetonius' account indicates that there were two hearings. At the first, when three Vestals were found guilty and committed suicide, Cornelia was acquitted; at the second, she was condemned. The date of the trials is conjectural, perhaps *c.*90.

defiled his brother's daughter: the account of Pliny is closely echoed by Suetonius, *Domitian* 22, who states that after the deaths of her father and her husband, Domitian 'loved her openly and most passionately', and later compelled her to abort her child.

7 *Priests were immediately dispatched*: the procedure is described in Plutarch, *Numa* 10, preceded by details of the privileges and the tenure of office of the Vestals. The guilty Vestal was borne on a litter through the Forum, and lowered by ladder to an underground chamber, where she was left with a modicum of food and water. Pliny's account is dramatically elaborated.

9 *'she took elaborate care . . . due decorum'*: so Euripides, *Hecuba* 569, describing the death of Polyxena, the archetypal sacrificial victim whose death was to ensure a safe crossing for the Greek ships making from Troy.

10 *Celer*: otherwise unknown. Juvenal (4.8 ff.) names Crispinus as one of Cornelia's guilty partners.

11 *he had hidden a freedwoman*: thus preventing her from giving evidence, which points to his guilt.

12 *Herennius Senecio*: see note to I 5.3. His death in 93–4 provides a *terminus ante quem* for the trial.

the 'Patroclus is dead' technique: at Homer, *Iliad* 18.20, Antilochus, son of Nestor, reports briefly the death of Patroclus to Achilles. Quintilian (10.1.49) signals it as a classic account of brevity.

13 *the mild form of exile*: not relegation, for Licinianus forfeited his goods and citizenship; perhaps indicating deportation to a more civilized region.

12 ARRIANUS MATURUS: see note to I 2.

1 *Egnatius Marcellinus*: he becomes suffect consul in 116, but at this time, as a mere quaestor, he does not get further mention in the letters.

3 *he consulted Caesar*: Trajan duly passed him on to the Senate, since this was the concern of the *aerarium Saturni* rather than the *fiscus*.

4 *Caecilius Strabo ... Baebius Macer*: these are senior senators who make their proposals at the close of the speeches. Strabo is consul-designate for 105, September to December; he is mentioned again at IV 17.1. For Macer, see note to III 5.

7 *as they journey abroad*: Arrianus is in Egypt at this time, serving on the staff of Vibius Maximus; see III 2.

13 CORNELIUS TACITUS: see note to I 6. Reference to his safe return implies that he has been on short-term duty abroad.

1 *on this Tusculan estate*: Pliny gives no indication elsewhere of owning a residence at Tusculum; this is doubtless a friend's estate.

3 *I was in my native region*: the visit was reported in IV 1.

'Are you a student?': the boy is studying at a school of rhetoric in Mediolanum. He is about 14 years old. Compare II 18.1 and note.

4 *Where could their morals be better safeguarded ... their parents' eyes?*: for the moral dangers at schools of rhetoric, see III 3.3 f.

5 *I do not as yet have any children*: his (third) marriage was recent; see IV 1.

6 *by canvassing ... teachers hired at public expense*: Pliny fears that inferior appointments may be made through influential connections. Public subsidies for such appointments had been in operation since Vespasian's time (Suetonius, *Vespasian* 18.1).

10 *the horde of students who surround you*: not that Tacitus offers formal instruction; eager students attend him as he performs in the Centumviral court.

14 PATERNUS: almost certainly Plinius Paternus, a distant relative from Comum; see note to I 21.

2 *my hendecasyllables*: this is the first mention of Pliny's verse-composition, which becomes a prominent feature throughout Books IV–IX. Pliny responds to criticism of this initial collection in V 3.

3 *In these ... more elevated style*: the range of topics parallels the collection and influence of Martial.

5 *which Catullus formulated*: see Catullus 16.5–8; in this poem in hendecasyllables, Catullus obscenely but jovially attacks his friends Aurelius and Furius for attacks on his virility.

9 *You can call them epigrams ... short poems*: traditional titles for short poems inherited by Latin versifiers from Hellenistic poets.

15 MINICIUS FUNDANUS: see note to I 9.

1 *Asinius Rufus*: this praetorian senator is mentioned in the letters only here.

3 *many regard even one child as a burden*: cf. I 8.10 ff.

Saturius Firmus: not otherwise known.

5 *you will become consul next year*: in fact, Minicius became consul in 107, a year later than Pliny had anticipated.

6 *Asinius Bassus, becomes quaestor*: of the twenty quaestors appointed annually, four were chosen as assistants to the consuls. Pliny is promoting Bassus for one of these posts.

9 *after the fashion of our ancestors*: see e.g. Cicero, *Ad familiares* 13.10.1.

16 VALERIUS PAULINUS: see note to II 2.

2 *a full seven hours . . . the length of my speech*: though Pliny speaks at great length in extortion cases in the Senate (cf. II 11.14; IV 9.9 ff.), speeches in the Centumviral court were usually confined to an hour or less (cf. VI 2.5 ff.). This exceptional case may be the speech referred to at IV 24.1, an address to all four panels of the court.

3 *some read*: that is, they read their speeches (or their verses) at a *recitatio*.

17 CLUSINIUS GALLUS: see note to II 17.

1 *Corellia*: for Corellia Hispulla, see III 3.
Gaius Caecilius: this is Caecilius Strabo, on whom see note to IV 12.4.
Corellius?: see I 12.1 ff. and notes.

3 *the distinguished office*: he is to become suffect consul in September 105, five years after Pliny.

9 *Secundus and Cornutus*: Pliny was closely associated with his older friend Cornutus Tertullus. They were colleagues as prefects of the treasury of Saturn, and later as consuls (see V 14.5).

18 ARRIUS ANTONINUS: see note to IV 3.

1 *as Lucretius puts it*: see Lucretius 1.832, where he complains of the absence of a Latin expression to render Anaxagoras' *homoeomeria* ('the likeness of parts to the whole, and to one another'). He repeats the complaint at 3.260. The view is challenged by Cicero, *De finibus* 1.10: 'I believe . . . that Latin, so far from being impoverished, is actually richer than Greek.'

19 CALPURNIA HISPULLA: see note to IV 1.7.

1 *the father she has lost*: this son of Calpurnius Fabatus, otherwise unknown, had died shortly before this third marriage of Pliny, first reported in IV 1.

5 *not my time of life or my body which she loves*: Pliny is well into his forties, while the girl is nearly thirty years younger.

7 *my mother*: Plinia, sister of the Elder Pliny. The detail in this letter, and her absence from other letters, suggests that she had died many years earlier.

20 NOVIUS MAXIMUS: see note to II 14 for possible identification with the addressee there.

1 *each of your volumes*: Novius has sent individual sections of a work for scrutiny to Pliny, who now offers a general (and generous) judgement. The work is probably the attack on Planta mentioned as still unpublished at IX 1. Pompeius Planta, governor of Egypt in 98–100, wrote an account of the civil conflicts of AD 69 which presumably included criticism of allies of Novius.

2 *your resentment*: Novius' work is obviously a bitter polemic, which lends substance to the suggestion in the previous note.

21 VELIUS CERIALIS: otherwise unknown.

1 *the Helvidian sisters!*: the daughters of the younger Helvidius Priscus, on whom see note to III 11.3. They were only recently married; their husbands are unknown.

3 *since his death*: that is, since 93, when he was executed on the orders of Domitian.

my speech and my books: the speech was the condemnation of Publicius Certus, who had prosecuted Helvidius Priscus in 93. The books were written versions of his speeches in vindication of Priscus. See IX 13.

22 SEMPRONIUS RUFUS: suffect consul in 113, and recipient of V 9.

1 *Gymnastic games . . . at Vienna*: Vienna (modern Vienne), in Narbonese Gaul, became a Roman colony under Gaius. The Greek athletic and musical contests were frowned on by Roman conservatives especially for their homosexual inclinations.

Trebonius Rufinus . . . a city-magistrate: after obtaining the status of Roman colony, Vienna boasted duumvirs elected annually, of whom Rufinus was one.

3 *Junius Mauricus*: see notes to I 5.10, II 18. Nerva had brought him back from exile in 97.

4 *Veiento*: after a chequered career under Nero, Fabricius Veiento was influential under the Flavians, becoming consul three times. Despite having been influential with Domitian, he survived and indeed prospered subsequently. Pliny's contempt for him is attributable to his association with discredited figures like Publicius Certus (see IX 13. 13 ff.).

5 *Catullus Messalinus*: he held the consulship twice with Domitian in 73 and 85. The pointed remark of Mauricus here is doubtless directed against Veiento's successful survival.

23 POMPONIUS BASSUS: after serving on the staff of the governor of Asia in 79–80, Bassus became consul in 94, governor of Cappadocia 95–100, and *curator alimentorum* in 101.

2 *the ideal old age*: compare Pliny's eulogy of Spurinna at III 1.

3 *this is what the laws prescribe*: from the time of Augustus onwards, senators were excused from attendance at the age of 70, and this was later reduced to 60 (Dio 55.31–3).

24 FABIUS VALENS: an officer with that name served with Vitellius in the civil wars of 69, but the identification is uncertain. See Tacitus, *Histories* 1.7.

1 *the four panels*: the 180 judges of the Centumviral court normally sat in four panels to expedite cases, but for major or more complex ones they sat in judgement together.

3 *friendship with the emperor*: the emperor had an advisory group, the *consilium principis*. For its activities under Nerva and Trajan, see John Crook, *Consilium Principis* (Cambridge, 1955), 53 ff.

4 *My speech-making*: translating *studia*, which here connotes speeches both

delivered and later edited for publication. Pliny makes much of the 'danger' he faced under Domitian, in his support of the Stoic opposition: he undoubtedly protests too much.

25 MAESIUS MAXIMUS: see note to III 20. This letter resumes the theme of that letter.

1 *the recent elections*: held in January 105.

the names of the campaigners: the implication being that the views of the candidates can be elicited by the identity of the sponsors.

5 *'But he who is over us . . . of that'*: from Plato, *Phaedo* 95b. Socrates there refers to God, but Pliny directs the quotation to the emperor, lamenting that the Senate takes its responsibilities so lightly that Trajan is left with more to do.

26 MAECILIUS NEPOS: see note to II 3.

2 *about to be governor of a massive province*: the province is uncertain; Pannonia and Asia have both been suggested.

27 POMPEIUS FALCO: see note to I 23.

1 *Sentius Augurinus*: Pliny's youthful admirer, who receives a note of thanks for compliments received at IX 8, became proconsul of Macedonia under Hadrian.

his short poems: Latin *poematia*, one of the terms which Pliny envisages for his epigrams at IV 14.9.

3 *if I can recall the second line*: the first two lines of this supremely forgettable epigram are omitted.

4 *seeking a love-affair . . . is loved*: referring to the fictions of love-encounters in the epigrams of Pliny and contemporary versifiers.

5 *with Spurinna and with Antoninus*: see III 1, IV 3, and notes, for these worthies. It is uncertain which of the two is his kinsman.

6 *that famous saw*: the citation is from Euripides, *Phoenix*, fr. 809 Nauck.

28 VIBIUS SEVERUS: see note to III 18.

1 *Herennius Severus*: this friend, who perhaps comes from Mediolanum, may be the Severus who is the recipient of IX 22, but is otherwise unknown.

Cornelius Nepos and Titus Catius: Nepos (*c.* 110–24 BC), biographer and friend of Catullus and Cicero, and Catius, 'an Insubrian Epicurean' (Cicero, *Ad Familiares* 15.16.1, reporting his recent death), both hailed from Mediolanum or a neighbouring township.

29 ROMATIUS FIRMUS: see note to I 19. The judges in the Centumviral court, of which he is one, were drawn from the five divisions of equestrians (*decuriae*) nominated by the emperor. Presumably each *decuria* was responsible for nominating its judges.

2 *Licinius Nepos!*: as a praetor for this year (105), this petty official has been appointed to draw up the list of judges from one of the *decuriae*. We see him busy at work again in V 4 and VI 5.

30 LICINIUS SURA: this Spaniard was a major political figure at the court of Trajan, who awarded him his second and third consulships in 102 and 107. He was also a considerable intellectual, as the epigrams of his fellow countryman Martial indicate (see e.g. 1.49; 7.47). In a further letter addressed to him (VII 27), Pliny consults him on the authenticity or otherwise of ghosts.

2 *a spring*: this is still visible today in the Villa Pliniana near Torno on the eastern side of Lake Como. The phenomenon described by Pliny here (and by his uncle, at *Natural History* 2.232) still occurs about every six hours, which is close to Pliny's 'three times each day'. Both Pliny and Seneca (*Natural Questions* 6.16 f.) argue on Stoic lines for air-pressure as the cause. The regularity is presumably attributable to the subterranean reservoir flooding when it reaches a certain level.

BOOK FIVE

1 ANNIUS SEVERUS: see note to II 16.

1 *Pomponia Galla . . . Asudius Curianus . . . Sertorius Severus*: all are otherwise unknown.

4 *'I am asking you to investigate'*: the inquiry was into the reasons for his being disinherited. This was a preliminary inquiry (*praeiudicium*) before Curianus brought his claim to court.

5 *Corellius and Frontinus*: for these distinguished men, see notes to I 12.1 and IV 8.3.

7 *the fear induced by the times*: Pliny exploits the receipt of the legacy in 104–5 to recount his leading role in the settlement a decade or so earlier, when Domitian was emperor.

8 *friendships with Gratilla and Rusticus*: for Arulenus Rusticus, executed by Domitian in 93, and his wife Gratilla, see note to I 14.1, and III 11.3.

9 *the temple of Concord*: rebuilt by Augustus in 7 BC, it lay at the north–west corner of the Forum.

10 *two years have now elapsed*: a single year was enough in Roman law to establish ownership by possession.

the same amount: Pliny offers a quarter of his legacy, like the other heirs.

2 CALPURNIUS FLACCUS: otherwise unknown.

2 *Diomedes' crafty exchange*: see Homer, *Iliad* 6.234 ff., where Diomedes craftily suggests to Glaucus that they seal their friendship with exchange of armour, Glaucus' golden for Diomedes' brazen, 'a hundred oxen's worth for nine'. Pliny suggests that he is not similarly offering in exchange even an inferior gift.

3 TITIUS ARISTO: see note to I 22.1.

2 *I also listen . . . I appreciate Sotadics*: this sardonic outburst reveals that Pliny is nettled by the criticism. His reference to listening to comedies

points to the entertainments at dinner. The mime was the most popular form of public drama in Pliny's day. Sotadics, so called after their Hellenistic originator Sotades, were obscene lampoons; see Quintilian 1.8.6.

5 *Marcus Tullius Cicero . . . Verginius Rufus*: this extensive list consists solely of senators; hence the omission of Catullus. Pliny thus justifies his own descent into light-hearted obscenities. The licentious verses of many of these worthies are attested also in other sources; Verginius Rufus is added *pietatis causa* as Pliny's former guardian (see notes to II 1.1 and II 1.8).

6 *Virgil . . . Accius and Ennius*: Pliny broadens the canvas from licentious epigrams to amatory poetry such as Virgil's *Eclogues* and dramatic episodes from the earlier playwrights. Nothing is known of the poetry of Nepos.

4 JULIUS VALERIANUS: see note to II 15.

1 *Sollers*: L. Bellicius Sollers had fought as an equestrian officer under Domitian in Germany, had reached the Senate, and attained the consulship.

Vicetia: modern Vicenza, close to Verona. The ambassadors objected to the market on a neighbouring estate because of its effect on the prosperity of their own. Such applications were rigorously controlled by the Senate, and later by the emperor, in the interests of public order.

Tuscilius Nominatus: he appears only here and in the subsequent developments at V 13.

2 *Nepos the praetor*: see IV 29.2 and note for this zealous official.

6,000 sesterces . . . 1,000 denarii: a *senatus consultum* dating to the reign of Claudius permitted a fee of 10,000 sesterces (one denarius = four sesterces) for such advocacy (by comparison, the annual pay of a legionary was 1,200 sesterces).

4 *What follows!*: see V 13 for the later development of the episode.

5 NOVIUS MAXIMUS: See note to II 14.

1 *Gaius Fannius*: his animosity towards Nero and the name Fannius may indicate kinship with Fannius Thrasea Paetus, the moderate Stoic executed under Nero (cf. III 16. 7 ff.).

5 *he dreamt*: for Pliny's preoccupation with dreams, see I 18 and especially VII 27.

6 DOMITIUS APOLLINARIS: see note to II 9.

1 *my Tuscan estate*: Pliny's residence at Tifernum-on-Tiber (modern Città di Castello) has received passing mention at IV 1, and at X 8 we learn that it was about 150 miles from Rome; hence the desirability of an extended stay. The description of the property is less precise than that of his Laurentine villa (II 17), and accordingly reconstruction is more difficult. See H. H. Tanzer, *The Villas of Pliny the Younger* (New York, 1924). The site of the villa, a few miles north of Città di Castello, has been identified.

the region is unhealthy: as Pliny indicates, Apollinaris refers to the marshes along the coast, which made malaria a hazard. The translator vividly recalls the massed croaking of frogs in the Ravenna area.

8 *varied hunting*: for Pliny's enthusiasm for the chase, see section 46 below, and I 6.

10 *when turned over nine times*: Pliny recalls the phrase of his uncle (*Natural History* 18.181), who probably owned the property previously.

16–17 *a terrace . . . hedge of box*: for the gardens, see P. Grimal, *Les Jardins romains*² (Paris, 1969) and E. MacDougall (ed.), *Ancient Roman Villa Gardens* (London, 1987).

25 *in the courtyard*: not the small yard mentioned in section 20.

27 *Beyond the disrobing-room*: the Latin *superpositum* probably means 'higher up the hill' rather than 'on top of'.

29 *a covered gallery*: not that mentioned in sections 27–8, but a second one alongside it.

32 *the riding-ground*: from here to section 40 the riding-ground (*hippodromus*) is described, a misleading name since it appears to have been used not for exercising horses but for walks (section 40) and for dining outdoors (section 37).

35 *Miniature obelisks*: it is not clear if they are of stone or of boxwood.

43 *Homer . . . Virgil*: Homer's description (*Iliad* 18.478–613) covers 136 lines and Virgil's (*Aeneid* 8.620–728) 109.

Aratus: this Hellenistic poet (born *c*.315 BC) wrote a work called *Phaenomena*, which embraces two themes, the constellations (19–732) and weather-signs (733–1154).

45 *to any in Tusculum or Tibur or Praeneste*: the allusions are pointed, since Apollinaris owned houses in these fashionable places in Latium (see Martial 10.30). Pliny had estates only at Laurentum, Tifernum, and Comum (see IV 13.1).

46 *I have never lost a single one*: neither by death nor by desertion.

7 CALVISIUS RUFUS: see note to I 12.12.

1 *Saturninus*: this former resident of Comum, not to be confused with Pompeius Saturninus (see note to I 8), is otherwise unknown. His legacy to the township of Comum was illegal, because Roman law as formulated by Gaius (2.217 ff.) specified that municipalities could not be designated as heirs.

2 *In my eyes . . . to be prefered to the law*: here, as on earlier occasions (II 16.2; IV 10.2), Pliny suggests that the law is an ass.

3 *slightly more than the one-third:* if the 400,000 sesterces to be allocated to the municipality represented a quarter of Saturninus' estate, and Pliny and Rufus as heirs inherited the other three-quarters, Pliny's share ought to have been three-eighths, not one-third; but perhaps Rufus had been named as first heir, and was to receive more than Pliny.

8 TITINIUS CAPITO: see note to I 17.1.

2 *no awareness of personal guilt*: as often (cf. III 11.3), Pliny (perhaps too vehemently) asserts that his behaviour under Domitian was above reproach.

3 *'any path . . . to flit victorious on the lips of men'*: Pliny cites Virgil, *Georgics* 3.8 f., where Virgil aspires to literary fame, evoking the epitaph of Ennius (*Varia* 18).

'*Yet oh . . .*': so Virgil, *Aeneid* 5.195. Mnestheus claims not to seek victory for his ship in the boat-race, but hopes that Neptune will intervene in his interest. Similarly, Pliny dismisses his chances of immortality, but none the less hopes for it.

5 *My uncle . . . wrote works of history*: see III 5 and notes.

8 *in my nineteenth year*: that is, in AD 80. His first important case, the defence of Junius Pastor (I 18.3), came probably a few years later.

9 *oratory and history*: Pliny retails the views of his former teacher Quintilian, who (10.1.31) states that history is akin to poetry and is written 'not for immediate effect and immediate strife', but 'as a reward for posterity'.

11 *in Thucydides' words*: see Thucydides 1.22, where the historian defines history as 'a possession for ever' rather than an *agonisma* for the present. Pliny interprets the Greek word as 'contest' or 'conflict', an appropriate sense for oratory.

12 *the research is available*: this passage is often cited as illustrating the tendency of Roman historians to reproduce the accounts of earlier writers without undertaking original research.

a recent period not yet covered?: at the date of this letter, Tacitus was probably gathering material for his *Histories*, which covered the period 69–96, and his *Annals* came later.

9 SEMPRONIUS RUFUS: see note to IV 22.

1 *the Basilica Iulia*: this building on the south side of the Forum was the regular home of the Centumviral court.

3 *the praetor Nepos*: see IV 29.2; V 4.2. His reforming policies were probably addressed to criminal cases initially, but are now affecting civil suits as well.

4 *the senatorial decree*: this is probably the decree mentioned by Tacitus at *Annals* 11.7.4, in which Claudius specified a limit of 10,000 sesterces for such legal advice.

10 SUETONIUS TRANQUILLUS: see note to I 18.

1 *your writings*: perhaps the *De uiris illustribus*, or a section of it, rather than *De uita Caesarum*, which Suetonius published later.

11 CALPURNIUS FABATUS: see note to IV 1.

1 *your son*: he had died (IV 19.1), probably recently in view of this memorial to him.

2 *our native region wins renown*: the colonnade was erected at Comum, the home of Fabatus and the native region of Pliny.

12 TERENTIUS SCAURUS: this is his sole appearance in the letters, and nothing certain is known of him from other sources.

3 *the subject matter*: Pliny suggests that Scaurus will identify the nature and occasion of the speech from the title and the content. At V 8.6 Pliny states that he is revising speeches which he has made 'in important and serious lawsuits', and this is doubtless one.

13 JULIUS VALERIANUS: see note to II 15. This letter to him is a continuation of V 4. The roles of Nepos and Nominatus are outlined there.

2 *would incur greater odium*: clearly Pliny has not reported the events fully in V 4; Nominatus, not a senator, had been given a rough time by supporters of Bellicius Sollers, the senator who had applied to conduct a market on his estate.

4 *Afranius Dexter*: having been appointed suffect consul for May–July 105, he died in dubious circumstances in June of that year; see VIII 14.12 ff.

5 *Fabius Aper . . . citing the law*: the proposal by Aper (the gentile name is uncertain; it should perhaps be Flavius) of disbarment from advocacy for a fixed period was the regular penalty for this offence. The law cited here was the *lex Iulia de senatu habendo* of 9 BC, which regulated all aspects of senatorial procedure.

6 *Nigrinus . . . an . . . important document*: C. Avidius Nigrinus rose to the suffect consulship in 110 and subsequently to the governorship of Dacia or Moesia, but was executed for treason under Hadrian. The problem of fees for advocacy had been a running sore under previous emperors; see e.g. Tacitus, *Annals* 11.6 f. (on AD 47).

8 *the public records*: the *urbis acta*, published from 59 BC (Suetonius, *Julius* 20.1), at this date included details of senatorial proceedings; see VII 33.3. For their wide circulation, see Tacitus, *Annals* 16.22.3 (on AD 66).

10 *keep labelling me a prophet*: Pliny claims that his own clean record has been a forerunner of the stricter regulations introduced.

14 PONTIUS ALLIFANUS: this Campanian friend is the recipient also of VI 28 and VII 4, the second indicating a shared interest with Pliny in literary matters.

1 *Cornutus Tertullus*: see II 11.19 and IV 17.9 and notes. He later succeeded Pliny as governor of Bithynia-Pontus, and *c.*117 became proconsul of either Asia or Africa.

curator of the Aemilian Way: this was the 176-mile highway between Ariminum and Placentia. Often conjoined with such supervision was the administration of the scheme of *alimenta*, grants to poor parents for the upkeep of their children. The emperor delegated such posts to chosen senators.

5 *as my mentor . . . as a father*: Cornutus was nearly twenty years older than Pliny.

6 *not, as earlier, encountering hazards*: see *Panegyricus* 90.5 for Pliny's claim that both Cornutus and himself were endangered under Domitian.

8 *with my grandfather-in-law*: this visit to Calpurnius Fabatus at Comum is probably later than that described at IV 1.

15 ARRIUS ANTONINUS: see note to IV 3. At IV 18 Pliny reports that he is translating Arrius' Greek epigrams, and presumably he is still labouring at them.

16 AEFULANUS MARCELLINUS: he is the recipient of VIII 23, another death-notice, but is otherwise unknown.

1 *the daughter of our friend Fundanus*: for Minicius Fundanus, see note to I 9. The girl's commemorative urn and epitaph have been found on a site near Rome (*ILS* 1030), recording her age as 12 years, 11 months, and 7 days. Either Pliny's figure is corrupt, or he was misinformed.

3 *her attendants, and her teachers*: some girls from the upper and middle classes attended the school of the *grammaticus* (hence her attendants); others were educated privately at home.

6 *the wedding day*: the minimum age for the marriage of girls was 12, and 13 or 14 was normal.

8 *a learned man, and a philosopher*: Fundanus was a friend of Plutarch, who reports (*Moralia* 420–53) that he was inclined to Platonism, though he studied under the Stoic Musonius Rufus in his youth.

10 *a consolation . . . expressed with kindness*: Pliny's humane attitude contrasts strongly with the Stoic tradition, as represented, for example, by Servius Sulpicius' letter to Cicero on the death of his daughter (*Ad Familiares* 4.6), and Seneca's similar admonition to a friend on the death of his daughter (*Letters* 99).

17 VESTRICIUS SPURINNA: see II 7.1; III 1 and notes.

1 *Calpurnius Piso*: there is a C. Calpurnius Piso who became consul in 111, but the Piso praised here seems too youthful to be identified with him. Calpurnii Pisones had held consulships as early as 148 and 133 BC; when Pliny laments the eclipse of such noble families, he thinks of these and of the Piso who conspired against Nero in AD 65.

2 *Translations to the Stars*: this work doubtless recounted the myths which described the metamorphoses of humans into stars. The Greek title (*Katasterismoi*) was earlier the title of a work by Eratosthenes (*c.*285–194 BC). Doubtless Piso drew heavily on such works as this and the mythological sections of Aratus' poem *Phaenomena*.

18 CALPURNIUS MACER: he was suffect consul in 103, and later became governor of Lower Moesia (*c.*109–12) while Pliny was in Bithynia (X 42, 61, 62, 77). He is probably the Macer who is the recipient of VI 24; if so, he hails from Comum or somewhere close.

1 *a man . . . most blessed*: presumably a pun on an eminent Felix who cannot be certainly identified.

19 VALERIUS PAULINUS: see note to II 2.

2 *Homer's phrase*: at *Odyssey* 2.47, Telemachus so describes his father Odysseus, who he believes is dead.

3 *more than a reciter of comedies need be*: normally such dependants specialized in particular forms of entertainment; see e.g. I 15.2.

7 *Forum Iulii*: in Narbonese Gaul (modern Fréjus in Provence).

20 CORNELIUS URSUS: see note to IV 9.

1 *the case of Julius Bassus*: for his trial, see IV 9.

Varenus Rufus: his tenure as proconsul of Bithynia is mentioned also by Dio Chrysostom, *Letters* 48.1. The proceedings of this indictment are continued in VI 5 and 13; VII 6 and 10.

2 *Varenus asked . . . in his defence*: the request was illegal; see section 7 below, and Quintilian 5.7.9, who states that witnesses can be subpoenaed only by the prosecution.

4 *Fonteius Magnus*: not otherwise known. Pliny's criticism may be explicable in part by his arrogating the role of a Roman advocate.

5 *Julius Candidus*: this senior figure was consul for the second time in 105.

if we believe Marcus Antonius: with Licinius Crassus, he was the outstanding orator in Cicero's boyhood, and is praised by him extravagantly in *Brutus* and *De oratore*.

6 *Homullus . . . Nigrinus'*: for the first, see note to IV 9.15.; for the second, note to V 13.6.

Acilius Rufus: the suffect consul for 107 adheres to his proposal later (VI 13.5).

7 *Cornelius Priscus*: see note to III 21.

8 *what Homer says*: at *Odyssey* 1.351 f., Telemachus rebukes his mother Penelope for requesting the minstrel to sing a song other than that depicting the pitiful return of the Achaeans from Troy.

21 POMPEIUS SATURNINUS: see note to I 8.

2–3 *Julius Valens . . . Julius Avitus*: both are otherwise unknown.

BOOK SIX

1 TIRO: for Calestrius Tiro, see note to I 12.

1 *in Picenum*: in central Italy, east of the Apennines, around Ancona.

2 ARRIANUS: for Arrianus Maturus, see note to I 2.

1 *Marcus Regulus*: see note to I 5.1. Though earlier, in several letters, Pliny has criticized him, now that he has recently died he nostalgically praises him for his traditionalism in legal conventions.

2 *paint round . . . his eyes . . . sport a white patch*: for Pliny, these idiosyncrasies are superstitions, but Martial twice mentions such patches (2.29.9 f., 8.33.22) in non-judicial contexts.

he would always consult a soothsayer: Pliny mentions this earlier, at II 20.

3 *he would ask for unlimited time*: in civil cases, the length of speeches was agreed between the two sides in discussion with the judges.

4 *without being a public menace*: Regulus' role as informer was confined to

Nero's reign, though he took pleasure in the condemnation of Stoic rebels under Domitian.

5 *two water-clocks or one*: see II 11.14 for the normal running-time of a clock as a quarter of an hour.

6 *so many hours*: cf. II 11.14; IV 9.9; but these refer to criminal cases.

3 VERUS: otherwise unknown. The tone of the letter suggests that he is a tenant of Pliny's, doubtless on the estate at Comum, where Pliny would have had a nurse in his childhood.

4 CALPURNIA: for Pliny's wife, see the Introduction, p. xx, and note to IV 1.1.

1 *my routine tasks*: chiefly his involvement in the numerous court cases described in letters later in this book.

for your convalescence in Campania: Calpurnia will have retired to her grandfather's residence (see VI 30.2).

5 URSUS: for Cornelius Ursus, see note to IV 9.

1 *I reported earlier*: see V 20 and notes

Licinius Nepos: for this praetor's previous attempts to regularize court procedures, see IV 29.2; V 4.2, 9.3, 13.1.

2 *the same power . . . of investigation*: that is, at a sitting prior to the trial proper. See V 20.1.

4 *Juventius Celsus*: he later became consul twice under Hadrian, and as an eminent jurist became head of the Proculian school of law, which laid emphasis on principle and consistency in application of the laws.

5 *that the emperor would look kindly . . . on both*: these senators assumed that the final decision on Nepos' proposal rested with the emperor. Trajan appears not to have been present.

6 FUNDANUS: for Minicius Fundanus, see note to I 9.

1 *Julius Naso*: see note to IV 6. He may be a candidate for the vigintivirate, the first step on the revised ladder of offices (see note to I 14.7), or for the quaestorship, which would admit him to the Senate.

3 *his father*: though a senator, he had not risen to prominence.

to listen to . . . Quintilian and Nicetes Sacerdos: for the various reasons why mature citizens attended the lectures in the schools of rhetoric, see note to II 18.2. For Quintilian as Pliny's teacher, see II 14.9 and note. Nicetes Sacerdos, the teacher of Greek rhetoric, is not rated highly in Tacitus, *Dialogus* 15.3.

6 *my humble writings*: presumably referring to his hendecasyllabics, initial recitations of which Naso will have attended.

7 CALPURNIA: for Calpurnia's absence, see VI 4.

8 PRISCUS: his identity is uncertain, since Pliny has many friends with that name. He may be Cornelius Priscus (see note to III 21) or Neratius Priscus (note to II 13).

1 *Atilius Crescens*: see note to I 9.8. His native town was probably Mediolanum, 30 miles away.

3 *'Personne ne fera . . . je vivrai'*: Pliny cites the Greek of Homer, *Iliad* 1.88, where Achilles reassures the augur Calchas against the anger of Agamemnon.

4 *Valerius Varus . . . Maximus*: Varus is unknown. Of the several Maximi of Pliny's acquaintance, this may be Novius (see note to II 14).

5 *no profits . . . his modest income*: Crescens has no landed property providing a financial return. He may be a teacher of rhetoric.

9 TACITUS: see note to I 6.

1 *Julius Naso*: Pliny has already reported in VI 6 that he has been canvassing on his behalf.

10 ALBINUS: probably Lucceius Albinus, for whom see III 9.7.

1 *my mother-in-law at Alsium*: for Pompeia Celerina, mother of Pliny's second wife, see I 4. Alsium (modern Palo), on the west coast about 30 miles north of Rome, was a convenient stopping-place for Pliny on his way to Centum Cellae; see VI 31.

Verginius Rufus: see note to II 1.1.

3 *nearly ten years after his death*: for his death in 97, see II 1.

11 MAXIMUS: there are nine acquaintances of Pliny recorded with this name, and no detail here identifies the recipient.

1 *the city prefect called me in as assessor*: it appears that the emperor delegated the city prefect to adjudicate on criminal cases involving the lowest classes of society. This passage suggests that advocates from aristocratic families were now taking on such cases.

Fuscus Salinator and Ummidius Quadratus: these young men of promise both rose to the consulship in 118. Salinator marries Hadrian's niece (VI 26). He is the addressee of VII 9; IX 36 and 40. Quadratus is the recipient of VI 29 and IX 13. Thus both retain their close relationship with Pliny. Subsequently they both lost favour with Hadrian, and Salinator was executed in 136.

3 *the whitest of pebbles!*: the Romans inherited from the Thracians (so Pliny, *Natural History* 7.131) the practice of marking up good days with white pebbles, and bad days with black (cf. Martial 12.34.5 ff.). Hence Pliny regards this as the equivalent of a red-letter day.

12 FABATUS: for Calpurnius Fabatus, see IV 1 and note.

2 *Bittius Priscus*: otherwise unknown. (The MSS have Bettius, and there is a strong case for emending to Vettius.)

13 URSUS: for Cornelius Ursus, see note to IV 9. This is a continuation of the preliminaries of the trial of Varenus described in VI 5.

2 *the emperor in his absence*: Trajan may have been still in Dacia in the aftermath of the second Dacian war of 105–6.

Claudius Capito: otherwise unknown.

3 *Catius Fronto*: see note to II 11.3.

5 *Acilius Rufus*: see note to V 20.6.

14 MAURICUS: for Junius Mauricus, see I 5.10, I 14, and notes.

1 *Formiae*: see note to III 14.2.

15 ROMANUS: for Voconius Romanus, see note to I 5.

1 *Paulus*: C. Passennus Paulus was a native of Asisium (modern Assisi), the birthplace of Propertius (*c.*57 BC–AD 2), whose celebrated love-poems were all composed in elegiac couplets. Paulus imitated this forebear; at IX 22 Pliny states that his poems, also in elegiacs, resemble those of Propertius closely.

2 *Javolenus Priscus*: this distinguished jurist (he was head of the Sabinian school, founded by Masurius Sabinus) held the consulship in 86, and subsequently governed successively Upper Germany, Syria, and Africa. Hence Pliny's account of his foibles may be exaggerated.

16 TACITUS: see note to I 6.

1 *a more truthful account*: at this date Tacitus was gathering material for his *Histories*, which covered the period from 69 to 96. But only four and a quarter of the 14 books have survived, covering only the years 69–70. We are thus deprived of his account of the eruption in 79.

2 *he wrote numerous works*: detailed in III 5.

3 *deeds worth chronicling or . . . accounts which deserve to be read*: echoing Sallust, *Catiline* 3.1.

4 *At Misenum . . . command of the fleet*: Misenum lies at the northern tip of the Bay of Naples. It was the headquarters of the western fleet, command of which was largely a bureaucratic post. It was held by freedmen until the reign of Vespasian, who appointed the Elder Pliny a year or two before his death.

5 *The pine tree*: the stone-pine or umbrella-pine, common in Mediterranean countries.

7 *I preferred to work at my books*: see VI 20.5 for this 17-year-old's preferring to read Livy rather than to take part in this adventure.

8 *from Rectina, wife of Tascius*: if, as seems probable, Tascius is identical with the Pomponianus at section 11, the villa was at Stabiae (modern Castel-lamare), south of Vesuvius. It would be natural for Pliny to head there, since he had set out with this purpose. Since they have to cross the middle of the bay to reach the villa, the ships must have been near Naples and Herculaneum. (Casci should perhaps be read for Tasci.)

19 *at once collapsed*: Suetonius' brief life of the Elder Pliny states: 'He was overcome by the force of dust and ashes, or he was killed by a slave of his, whom he had begged to hasten his death when he was overcome by the heat.'

21 *Meanwhile . . . at Misenum*: Pliny continues the story, at Tacitus' request, at VI 20.

17 RESTITUTUS: he may be the Claudius Restitutus who spoke on the other side from Pliny in the case of Caecilius Classicus; see III 9.16.

18 SABINUS: for Statius Sabinus, see note to IV 10.

1 *Firmum*: in the mid-Adriatic region, south of Ancona. It became a Roman colony in 264 BC to control the Piceni who had revolted five years earlier, and a *municipium* of Roman citizens in 90 BC.

19 NEPOS: see note to II 3 for Maecilius Nepos, though identification with him is not wholly certain.

1 *deposit money*: that is, on loan.

3 *Homullus*: see note to IV 9.15.

6 *the time for . . . buying in the provinces*: if the addressee is Maecilius Nepos, and he is governor of a province at this time, he was debarred from purchasing land in his own province.

20 TACITUS: see note to I 6.

1 *'though aghast . . . I shall begin'*: so Virgil, *Aeneid* 2.12 f., where Aeneas at Dido's request reluctantly agrees to recount the fall of Troy.

3 *they were frequent in Campania*: in AD 62 Pompeii had been severely damaged by an earthquake (Tacitus, *Annals* 15.22.3; Seneca, *Natural Questions* 6.1.1 ff.). For these earlier tremors in 79, see Dio 66.22.

5 *from Spain*: the Elder Pliny had served there as procurator (III 5.17).

10 *your brother . . . your uncle . . .*: addressing first Pliny's mother, and then Pliny himself.

21 CANINIUS: for Caninius Rufus, see note to I 3.

1 *Nature is not so weary*: a recurrent issue posed in Pliny's day was whether the Roman literary genius had by a natural process faded after the Augustan age. Tacitus' *Dialogus* focuses on this 'ancients versus moderns' issue; Quintilian 1.1.2 rebuts the notion that the young are deficient in intelligence. Sallust had earlier (*Catiline* 53.5) posed the question in more general terms: 'As mothers' powers become exhausted with child-bearing, so for a long time at Rome no one was great in excellence' (*uirtute magnus*).

2 *Vergilius Romanus*: not otherwise known. For 'iambic mimes' (that is, mimes written in scazons or limping iambics), see note to IV 3.4.

22 TIRO: for Calestrius Tiro, see note to I 12. He had just been designated as proconsul of Baetica in Spain. Later letters refer to his appointment, journey, and tenure (VII 16, 23, 32; IX 5).

2 *Bruttianus . . . Atticinus*: both are unknown. The advice to Tiro suggests that Bruttianus was proconsul of his province, and Atticinus a *comes* invited to accompany him.

I was an assessor: not at a senatorial hearing, but at the emperor's court, as at IV 22.

3 *foul crimes*: it appears that Atticinus was tampering with documents to accuse the proconsul of extortion, of which he himself was guilty (section 4).

5 *indicted*: the Latin word means 'requested' (the votes of the assessors).

banished to an island: this was not exile (which involved loss of citizenship and property), but the most severe form of relegation.

23 TRIARIUS: otherwise unknown.

1 *not for nothing*: fees were legally permitted (see notes to V 4.2 and V 9.4), but Pliny followed the Republican custom of waiving them.

2 *Cremutius Ruso*: as one of Pliny's bright young men, he is a correspondent of his; see IX 19.

24 MACER: probably Calpurnius Macer; see note to V 18.

3 *his wife demanded to take a look*: this facet of the anecdote casts a revealing light on the puritanical propriety of married couples in sexual matters.

5 *that most celebrated deed of Arria*: see note to III 16.2.

25 HISPANUS: probably Baebius Hispanus, the addressee of I 24. Since he is investigating a missing notable, he may have become the *praefectus uigilum* at Rome.

1 *Robustus . . . Atilius Scaurus*: neither is otherwise known. With Pliny's help, Scaurus is being summoned to Rome, presumably from Transpadane Gaul. Ocriculum, the stopping-place where he parted from Robustus, is in southern Umbria, north of Falerii, a mere day's journey from Rome.

2 *Metilius Crispus*: otherwise unknown, but probably a member of his town-council (? at Comum), since centurions who had not risen through the ranks were recommended for appointment from such *decuriones* by influential individuals to the emperor.

26 SERVIANUS: for Julius Servianus, see note to III 17.

1 *Fuscus Salinator*: see note to VI 11.1.

27 SEVERUS: Vettenius Severus was to become suffect consul for May–August 107.

1 *what proposal . . . to honour the emperor*: following the consular elections, the consuls-designate were expected to propose in the Senate some honorific award. The speeches are not those (like Pliny's *Panegyricus*) made on assuming office, but those at an earlier meeting. So when Pliny made his modest proposal, one of his fellow designates moved that Trajan be awarded a fourth consulship (see *Panegyricus* 79).

2–3 *forced to make . . . the unworthiest recipients*: Pliny contrasts his own situation under Trajan with 'the necessity of former times' (*Panegyricus* 55.2) under Nero and Domitian, when obsequious proposals were inevitable.

5 *the recent achievements*: Trajan had in 106 rounded off his conquest of Dacia.

28 PONTIUS: for Pontius Allifanus, see note to V 14.

1 *to Campania*: in VI 4 and 7, we read that Pliny's wife Calpurnia has retired to convalesce in Campania, presumably at her grandfather's villa (see VI 30.2). This brief visit to Pontius' country residence will have taken place when he was joining her.

29 QUADRATUS: for Ummidius Quadratus, see note to VI 11.1.

1 *Avidius Quietus*: this man, now dead, had been governor of Achaea, suffect consul in 93, and governor of Britain in 98.

Thrasea: see III 16.10, He was executed in 66, so that his contemporary Quietus was much older than Pliny.

5 *Pollio's*: Asinius Pollio (76 BC–AD 4) had in retirement become the most celebrated orator and writer of the Augustan age.

6 *Isocrates*: this Athenian (436–338) gained fame as orator largely through his written speeches and his role as teacher.

7 *necessity . . . partakes of reason*: for Stoics especially, the acceptance of necessity was a fundamental feature of rational thought.

8–11 *I represented the Baeticans . . . the request was granted*: Pliny reviews his most important cases, claiming that his interventions have resulted in greater equity in the conduct of extortion trials. For that of Baebius Massa in 93, see VII 33; against Caecilius Classicus in 101, III 4; against Marius Priscus in 100, II 11–12; for Julius Bassus in 102–3, IV 9; for Varenus in 106–7, V 20, VI 5.

30 FABATUS: for Calpurnius Fabatus, see note to IV 1.

5 *Rufus*: perhaps Sempronius Rufus, on whom see IV 22, V 9.

31 CORNELIANUS: since no such person is known, the name may be a corruption of Cornelius Minicianus (see note to III 9)

1 *at Centum Cellae*: modern Civitàvecchia. It lies south of Tarquinii on the Etruscan coast. Trajan held his court there because he was developing the harbour as an additional port to Ostia. The emperor employed a panel of advisers distinct from those appointed in the Senate and in the Centumviri court; see also IV 22; VI 22; VII 10.

3 *Claudius Aristion*: he is known from inscriptions to have been not only the chief magistrate of Ephesus, but also the president of the provincial council of Asia.

4 *a charge of adultery*: the *lex Iulia* passed by Augustus made extramarital sexual intercourse a serious crime, punishable by relegation, as here, This case was referred to the emperor's court because of the social status of the married couple.

7 *the will of Julius Tiro*: this indictment for forgery, punishable by Sulla's *Lex Cornelia de falsis*, was heard in the emperor's court because one of the defendants was his freedman. None of the parties mentioned is otherwise known.

9 *'That freedman is not Polyclitus, and I am not Nero'*: for Polyclitus' enormous power and influence, see Tacitus, *Annals* 14.39, a sardonic description of his costly journey to Britain to heal the rupture between the procurator Classicianus and the governor Suetonius Paulinus.

12 *Comprenez bien*: Trajan uses a Greek word.

15 *The very handsome house . . . a harbour*: the site of the villa has been identified inland from the harbour, which is also described by the fifth-century poet Rutilius Namatianus, who recounted his journey from Rome to Gaul in 417 in elegiacs. The poem (conventionally called *De reditu suo*) devotes 1.239–45 to the harbour.

17 *the name of its founder*: hence, Portus Traiani.

32 QUINTILIAN: clearly not the celebrated Quintilian, the teacher of Pliny, who if still alive would have been over 70 by this date.

 1 *Tutilius*: a rhetorician of this name is cited (and praised) with Pliny by the great Quintilian (3.1.21), and mentioned by Martial (5.56.6).

 Nonius Celer: otherwise unknown.

33 ROMANUS: for Voconius Romanus, see note to I 5.

 1 *'Put all away . . . begun'*: Pliny aptly cites Virgil, *Aeneid* 8.439, where Vulcan bids his assistants in the forge to lay aside the work in hand, to fashion the arms of Aeneas.

 2 *Attia Viriola*: 'a woman of distinguished birth', a close relative of Trajan's praetorian prefect, Attius Suburanus, consul in 101 and 104.

 the assembly of four panels: cach panel usually conducted cases separately; they combined only for important hearings.

5–6 *The outcome was divided . . . the stepmother . . . lost her case. So did Suburanus*: each panel passed judgement on one of the four claims. Pliny reports only the two on which he was successful. The precise identity of this Suburanus, and his connection with Attia Viriola, will have been clarified in the speech. These details do not emerge here.

11 *my On the Crown*: the most celebrated speech of Demosthenes, with whom Pliny modestly compares himself.

34 MAXIMUS: of the many associates of Pliny bearing this name (see note to VI 11), the identity of this Maximus cannot be established.

 Verona: the birthplace of Catullus had become a Roman colony by AD 69 (Tacitus, *Histories* 3.8).

 1 *a gladiatorial show . . . most fittingly as a funeral tribute*: such shows (*munera*) were Etruscan and religious in origin, mounted at funerals of leading men. But later they passed 'from honours to the dead to honours for the living' (Tertullian, *De spectaculis* 12), and were mounted by ambitious politicians.

 3 *African beasts*: lions and especially panthers; see Livy 39.22.2, etc.

BOOK SEVEN

 1 GEMINUS: Rosianus Geminus appears for the first time here in the letters, though he had been Pliny's consular quaestor in 100. Later he became proconsul of Achaea, suffect consul in 125, and proconsul of Africa in 142. Five further letters are addressed to him (VII 24; VIII 5, 22; IX 11, 30).

4 *once I had a high temperature*: Pliny had a serious illness in 96–7 (see X 5.1, 8.3).

2 JUSTUS: probably Fabius Justus (see notes to I 5.8 and I 11).

1 *unremitting duties*: the duties as described in this letter suggest that Justus is on military service, when winter evenings would be unoccupied.

3 PRAESENS: Bruttius Praesens has not appeared earlier in the letters. But later he emerged from the idyllic existence described here to participate as legionary legate in Trajan's Dacian campaigns, and later to hold two consulships, in 119 and 139.

4 PONTIUS: for Pontius Allifanus, see note to V 14.

1 *my hendecasyllables*: see note to IV 14.2.

3 *returning . . . on the island of Icaria*: Pliny served as a young man in Syria (I 10.2). Icaria lies in the eastern Aegean, between Samos and Delos.

Asinius Gallus: he married Vipsania Agrippina after Tiberius was forced to divorce her. In AD 30 he was imprisoned on a charge of treason, and starved himself to death (Tacitus *Annals* 6.23).

his father: Asinius Pollio, the celebrated orator and historian of the Augustan age (see note to VI 29.5).

Tiro: Cicero's confidential secretary was probably 50 years old when manumitted in 53. He is no youthful cup-bearer.

4 *the most eminent orators had practised this genre of writing*: see V 3.5 and note.

6 *When I was reading . . . fire me more?*: surprisingly, Pliny is inspired to compose in heroic hexameters rather than in hendecasyllabics. My iambic hexameters duly reflect the mediocrity of the Latin.

8 *when travelling*: like his uncle (see III 5.15), Pliny wastes no time in his carriage; see IX 10.2.

9 *the harp and . . . lyre*: the first (*cithara*) is appropriate for public performances, the second (*lyra*) for private entertainments, but it is doubtful if Pliny is making this distinction here.

5 CALPURNIA: this is the third in the series of letters sent by Pliny to his wife when she was convalescing in Campania; see VI 4, 7.

1 *like a locked-out lover*: the *exclusus amator* theme, imported from Greece and much favoured by the Augustan love-elegists (see Propertius 1.16; Tibullus 1.2, 1.5; Horace, *Odes* 3.10, *Epode* 11; Ovid, *Amores* 1.6), is treated by F. C. Copley, *Exclusus Amator* (Baltimore, 1956).

6 MACRINUS: for Caecilius Macrinus, see note to II 7.

1 *the case of Varenus*: for the earlier episodes of this case, see V 20; VI 5 and 13. The provincial council of Bithynia was obviously split between two factions. After Fonteius Magnus had departed to indict Varenus (V 20.4), Polyaenus' faction had the indictment rescinded.

2 *the excellent man Nigrinus*: see V 13.6, 20.6; the complimentary phrase indicates that opposing advocates were often on cordial terms.

6 *before the emperor held a hearing*: his role here was not to rule on the main issue of extortion, but to decide whether the indictment could or should be withdrawn on Polyaenus' request.

8 *charges of forgery and poisoning*: both were capital charges, for which Sulla had established separate *quaestiones*. Such double indictments were at this date exceptionally heard together in the Senate (Quintilian 3. 10.1).

Julius Servianus: see note to III 17. He and Attius Suburanus (section 10) were close advisers of Trajan. Suburanus had been praetorian prefect, and consul twice, in 101 and 104.

11 *grandson of the celebrated orator*: the grandson is otherwise unknown. The grandfather was regarded by Quintilian as one of the two most outstanding orators he had ever heard (10.1.118), though given to pedantry, long-winded sentences, and extravagant metaphors. Passienus Crispus, a wealthy orator of earlier days, was the stepfather of the Emperor Nero.

7 SATURNINUS: for Pompeius Saturninus, see note to I 8.

1 *Priscus*: this Priscus, the recipient of the note that follows this, cannot be certainly identified among the many Prisci known to Pliny.

8 PRISCUS: see previous note.

1 *Saturninus*: see note to I 8.

Proceed as you have begun: an unconscious(?) echo of Cicero, *In Catilinam* 1.10.

9 FUSCUS: for Fuscus Salinator, Pliny's youthful protégé, see note to VI 11.1.

2 *from Greek into Latin*: Pliny echoes the advice of his mentor Quintilian (10.5.2).

7 *Your particular interest*: for Fuscus' debut in court, see VI 11.

9 *those which are pungent and brief*: the hendecasyllables which Pliny himself has taken up. For the content (section 13), see IV 14.3.

11 *Wax wins . . . wide-ranging skills*: Pliny's verses are in elegiac couplets, which I render with alternating iambic hexameters and pentameters.

10 MACRINUS: for Caecilius Macrinus, see note to II 7.

1 *Varenus and the Bithynians*: this letter reports the outcome of the discussions reported in VII 6.

2 *the will of the province*: not on the guilt or otherwise of Varenus, but whether the indictment should stand. The absence of further mention of it suggests that the case was dropped.

11 FABATUS: for Calpurnius Fabatus, see note to IV 1.

1 *You express surprise*: Pliny and his coheirs had agreed to sell the estate as a whole at auction, after an arbitrator had divided the lands between them. Fabatus' surprise stems partly from Pliny's overriding this informal agreement, and partly from his accepting less than the market value, on which see VII 14 and note below.

3 *Corellia . . . Corellius Rufus*: Corellia is to be distinguished from Corellia Hispulla, daughter of Corellius Rufus, whose suicide in 97 is described in I 12.

4 *Minicius Justus*: since he was a prominent supporter of Vespasian in 69 (Tacitus, *Histories* 3.7), he was now at an advanced age.

her son: mention of him here indicates that he had died. Pliny has not elsewhere alluded to his games over which his friend presided. From the time of Augustus onwards praetors organized and bore the cost of games on major festivals (Dio 54.2.3 f.).

12 MINICIUS: probably Minicius Fundanus (see note to I 9), for he is a literary man (see V 16.8).

2 *to improve it . . . or to make a mess of it*: Pliny humorously alludes to Minicius' preference for Atticist rhetoric. Pliny uses a common Greek expression for the Atticists, which I have rendered in French.

3 *the passages which you will find marked*: less flowery alternatives have been offered at some points in the speech.

13 FEROX: for Julius Ferox, see note to II 11.5.

14 CORELLIA: the content of this letter is a development from that of VII 11.

1 *a twentieth part*: a levy of 5 per cent was imposed as inheritance-tax which was taken in land, not in cash, but the collectors allowed Corellia to buy this proportion of the land. It is notable that the tax is still gathered by the tax-collectors (*publicani*).

15 SATURNINUS: for Pompeius Saturninus, see note to I 8, and more immediately VII 7 and 8.

1 *my public service . . . aid to my friends*: his public service is as curator of the Tiber, a position held probably from 103/4 to 106/7. Aid to his friends is legal advice as advocate or assessor.

2 *those you prefer*: for Saturninus' literary interests, see I 16.

supervision . . . arbitration: Saturninus' legal and oratorical expertise (see VII 7.2) presumably extends to the welfare of his municipality.

3 *friendship with my Priscus*: see note to VII 7.1

16 FABATUS: see note to IV 1.

1 *Calestrius Tiro*: see note to I 12. After service as tribune with Pliny in Syria, he was chosen (again with Pliny) as *quaestor Augusti* by Domitian, became tribune in 91 (a year early because he had fathered a child during the previous year) and praetor in 93. He is now in April 107 taking up the governorship of Baetica in Spain.

3 *by way of Ticinum*: this town (modern Pavia) lay on the Via Aemilia in Cisalpine Gaul. Tiro is travelling overland to Spain. Fabatus is at Comum, a day's journey to the north.

4 *if you wish formally to free the slaves*: the presence of a magistrate was necessary to translate informal manumission into *manumissio iusta*, which included amongst other rights the power to make a will.

17 CELER: possibly the Caecilius Celer mentioned at I 5.8.

2 *people who reproached me for reciting my speeches*: this letter is of interest for its implication that recitation of speeches was much less common than that of other literary genres. See Pliny's misgivings at II 19, and his surprise at the cordial reception recorded at III 18.

4 *speeches . . . often recited . . . by some Romans*: cf. Suetonius, *Augustus* 89.3: the emperor listened patiently to readings 'not only of poetry and history, but also of speeches . . .'.

11 *Pomponius Secundus*: he was sufficiently eminent in his day under Claudius to merit a two-volume biography by Pliny's uncle (see III 5.3). But the gloss here ('the composer of tragedies') suggests that he is no longer much read.

13 *what Cicero ascribes to the pen*: cf. *De oratore* 1.150: 'The pen is the best and most outstanding creator and teacher of eloquence.'

18 CANINIUS: for Caninius Rufus, see note to I 3.

2 *to pay for the rearing of freeborn boys and girls*: at I 8.10 ff. Pliny records this purpose of his benefaction, but without mentioning the amount, or the method of disbursing it.

I was to pay 30,000 sesterces: this yearly rental amounts to 6 per cent of the 500,000, which is more generous than the 5 per cent for which he was liable.

4 *I seem to have paid rather more than the sum I donated*: though Pliny has reacquired the property, the decline in its value plus the annual rental amounts to much more than the original bequest.

19 PRISCUS: for the difficulty in identifying him, see note to VII 7.1.

1 *Fannia's*: see notes to III 11.3, 16.2.

the Vestal Virgin Junia: she was perhaps the sister of Junius Arulenus Rusticus and Junius Mauricus, on whom see I 5.2 and 10. Vestal Virgins were under the supervision of the pontiffs, one of the four main colleges of priesthoods.

3 *her husband Helvidius and her father Thrasea*: she was the second wife of the elder Helvidius Priscus, exiled by Nero in 66, and again exiled in 74–5 under Vespasian, and later executed. Her father, Thrasea Paetus, was executed in 66 (Tacitus, *Annals* 16.21 ff.).

4 *banished a third time*: the third banishment, under Domitian, lasted from 93 to 97 (see III 11.3).

5 *Senecio*: Herennius Senecio was indicted by Mettius Carus and executed in 93 (I 5.3; III 11.3).

her mother: this was the younger Arria, relegated with Fannia in spite of her alleged ignorance (see IX 13.5).

8 *Her very house . . . shaking and shattered*: Pliny refers to the death of two daughters of the younger Helvidius Priscus, stepson of Fannia (IV 21).

'She has descendants' refers to the surviving member of the family, reported in the same letter.

10 *when they were banished . . . on their return*: in 93 and 97 respectively (III 11.3; IX 13.5).

20 TACITUS: see note to I 6.

1 *I have read your book*: there has been animated discussion whether this work was the *Dialogus* or a part of the *Histories*. Stylistic arguments (possible influence of the *Dialogus* on the *Panegyricus*) put the publication of the *Dialogus* as early as 101. The *Histories* (or a part of it) is therefore more probable, especially as Pliny provides material for them at VI 16 and 20, and at VII 33.

2 *my own book*: there is no indication of its nature.

3 *identical in age and distinction*; Tacitus was about six years senior; both had held the consulship, Tacitus in 97 and Pliny in 100.

4 *'closest, but by a long distance'*: see Virgil, *Aeneid* 5.320, the foot-race in Sicily, in which Salius lies second behind Nisus.

21 CORNUTUS: for Cornutus Tertullus, see notes to II 11.19, V 14.1.

1 *dearest colleague*: he was a colleague in the strict sense as prefect of the treasury of Saturn in 98–100, and as consul in 100 (V 14.5), but it is improbable that this letter is to be dated so early; they are 'colleagues' in the more general sense in their tenure of the posts of curator of the Tiber (*curator Tiberis*) and curator of the Aemilian Way (*curator uiae Aemiliae*) respectively, positions of equal distinction.

Here: Pliny is presumably at his Laurentine villa, since the problem with his eyes will have precluded a longer journey to Tifernum or Comum.

22 FALCO: for Pompeius Falco, see note to I 23. As the governor-designate of Judaea, he has promised to offer an appointment to Pliny's friend.

2 *Cornelius Minicianus*: see note to III 9.

23 FABATUS: for Cornelius Fabatus, see note to IV 1. He has now replied to VII 16, and this letter is a response to that reply.

1 *to meet Tiro at Mediolanum*: for Tiro, see note to VII 16.1. It would have taken the old man a day's journey to meet Tiro at Milan.

24 GEMINUS: for Rosianus Geminus, see note to VII 1.

1 *Quadratilla*: she was the daughter of Ummidius Quadratus, suffect consul in 40 and later governor of Syria.

2 *her grandson*: this is Pliny's protégé Ummidius Quadratus; see note to VI 11.1.

4 *indulged them more extravagantly than was fitting*: at *Panegyricus* 46.4, Pliny calls pantomime-dancing a 'perverted art', unworthy of the age.

6 *sacerdotal games*: so called because they were held predominantly at sacred festivals.

8 *Gaius Cassius . . . the Cassian school*: Cassius Longinus, suffect consul in 30

and governor of Syria 49–51, was exiled by Nero but returned to Rome in 69. As a redoubtable jurist, he established the 'Cassian' or 'Sabinian' school of jurisprudence, headed at this time by Javolenus Priscus (see VI 15. 2–3). The other main school was the 'Proculian', represented by Titius Aristo (see note to I 22.1).

25 RUFUS: probably Caninius Rufus, a frequent addressee (see note to I 3), but perhaps Octavius Rufus (see note to I 7).

2 *Terentius Junior*: this recent acquaintance receives letters at VIII 15 and IX 12.

Narbonensis: this province of southern Gaul had its capital at Narbo (Narbonne). Founded in 118 BC, it was administered by the Senate.

26 MAXIMUS: See note to VI 11.

1 *a certain friend*: probably Rosianus Geminus; see note to VII 1.

27 SURA: for Licinius Sura, sce notc to IV 30.

1 *whether you believe ghosts exist*: both Epicureans (see e.g. Lucretius 4.45 ff.) and Stoics (as in Cicero, *De diuinatione*, 1) had theories to justify the existence of *simulacra* and epiphanies. But Cicero, Pliny's mentor, as an Academic poured scorn on them (see *De diuinatione* 2.119 ff.). Hence Pliny's divided mind.

2 *what I am told happened to Curtius Rufus*: having risen from obscurity to the praetorship with the backing of Tiberius, Rufus became suffect consul in 43, legate in Upper Germany in 47–8, and thereafter proconsul of Africa, where he died in 53. This anecdote of the apparition is recorded also by Tacitus, *Annals* 11.21, who sets the scene in a colonnade in Hadrumetum. Rufus is almost certainly the author of ten books of a *History of Alexander*, of which Books 3–10 survive.

5 *At Athens*: suspiciously, the *Philopseudes* of Lucian contains a similar story of a haunted house in Corinth, visited by a Pythagorean philosopher called Arignotus.

7 *Athenodorus*: probably the Stoic philosopher from Tarsus and friend of Cicero; if so, the story is old hat.

14 *if Domitian . . . had lived longer*: Pliny as elsewhere unconvincingly claims to have narrowly escaped indictment under Domitian. Mettius Carus was a notorious informer of that era (see note to I 5.3).

28 SEPTICIUS: for Septicius Clarus, see note to I 1.

29 MONTANUS: this unidentified correspondent is the recipient of a longer letter on the same subject as this, at VIII 6.

2 *Pallas*: he was Claudius' favourite freedman, whom the emperor appointed as his secretary of finance, but who fell out of favour under Nero and was executed (Suetonius, *Claudius* 28; Tacitus, *Annals* 13.14; 14.65). His wealth (Dio 62.14.3 claims that he had 40 million sesterces at his death) and arrogance made him deservedly notorious.

the Senate decreed: this award in 52 is recorded by Tacitus, *Annals* 12.53.2; see also at VIII 6.13 below.

30 GENITOR: for Julius Genitor, see note to III 3.5.

3 *complaints . . . suitable tenants*: the identical laments appear at IV 37. 1 ff.; Pliny is probably at Tifernum.

5 *comparing my speech . . . with Demosthenes' oration*: for the speech against Publicius Certus vindicating the younger Helvidius Priscus, see IV 21.3. Demosthenes' speech against Meidias arose out of the conflict with Eubulus, the dominant statesman at Athens, in their differing policies towards Philip of Macedon. Meidias, a close ally of Eubulus, had slapped Demosthenes' face at the Dionysia of 348. But the case was settled out of court; the speech (ed. D. M. MacDowell, Oxford, 1990) was never delivered.

31 CORNUTUS: for Cornutus Tertullus, see note to II 11.19.

1 *Claudius Pollio*: this minor personage does not appear elsewhere in the letters.

2 *When we served in the army together*: for Pliny's service as military tribune in Syria, see I 10.2; III 11.5; VIII 14.7.

3 *advanced to most distinguished offices*: he became governor of the Graian Alps, and later controller of the inheritance-tax office.

4 *our friend Corellius*: see note to I 12.1 for this friend of Pliny and Cornutus (see IV 17.9 and note).

purchase and allocation of lands: Nerva established a commission with a fund of 60 million sesterces to allocate lands to very poor citizens (Dio 68.2.1).

5 *attestations at death . . . Annius Bassus*: the attestations took the form of bequests. Annius Bassus was a supporter of Vespasian, who rewarded him with the consulship, probably in 71. See Tacitus, *Histories* 3.50.

32 FABATUS: for Cornelius Fabatus, see notes at IV 1 and VII 23.

1 *my friend Tiro*: cf. VII 16.1, VII 23.

to grant freedom: see VII 16.4 and note.

2 *as Xenophon remarks*: in his *Memorabilia* 2.1.3, Xenophon makes Prodicus recount to Hercules the altercation between Virtue and Vice. Virtue tells Vice that, though she is one of the immortals, she is an outcast from the company of the deities, and she never hears praise of herself, the sweetest of all sounds.

33 TACITUS: See note to I 6.

1 *your histories*: Tacitus had been gathering material for the 12 (or 14) books of the *Histories*, of which only the first four and a half have survived. The work covered the years 69–96, so that this trial of 93 fell within its scope, See III 4.4, VI 29.8.

3 *the public records*: for the *urbis acta*, see note to V 13.8.

4 *not to allow the dispersal*: following condemnation on the charge of extortion, Massa was sentenced to relegation, and his possessions were seized until the claims of plaintiffs were met. Massa was himself attempting to have some of his property released.

5 *your relationship with the province*: see note to I 7.2.

7 *that Senecio be indicted*: though Senecio was indicted and executed later in 93, it was not on this charge. See note to I 5.3.

9 *the deified Nerva*: before becoming emperor he was one of Domitian's trusted lieutenants.

10 *you will make it better known*: it seems doubtful if Tacitus accorded Pliny's intervention more than a passing mention.

BOOK EIGHT

1 SEPTICIUS: for Septicius Clarus, see note to I 1.

1 *the journey*: to his villa at Tifernum, from where he visits the Clitumnus and lake Vadimon (VIII 8 and 20).

2 *Encolpius*: not mentioned elsewhere. For Pliny's concern for the welfare of his servants, cf. V 19.

3 *To whom will my ears be pinned*: as Pliny's *lector*, Encolpius reads out both serious works and (especially over dinner) works for relaxation.

2 CALVISIUS: for Calvisius Rufus, see note to I 12.12.

1 *I had sold my vine-crop*: that at Tifernum, the visit to which is described in VIII 1.

3 *'none should leave without a prize'*: so Virgil, *Aeneid* 5.305, where Aeneas at the Sicilian funeral-games offers prizes to all who participate in the foot-race.

8 *'wicked and honourable men are equally respected'*: Homer, *Iliad* 9.319, where Achilles angrily explains to Odysseus his reason for refusing to go into battle.

3 SPARSUS: for Julius Sparsus, see note to IV 5.

1 *a certain very learned person*: at VII 20.2, Pliny awaits the comments of Tacitus on his recent work; perhaps the reference is to him.

2 *but perhaps I flatter myself!*: reading *etsi tamen* for *et quia tamen* in the Oxford text.

4 CANINIUS: for Caninius Rufus, see note to I 3.

1 *to write on the Dacian war*: Rufus proposes to glorify Trajan's campaigns in an epic poem in Greek. Details of the two wars are known to us only from Dio (68.6–14) and from the scenes on the spiral frieze of Trajan's column. In the first war (AD 101–2), King Decebalus was compelled to accept peace and to become a Roman vassal. In the second war (105–6), claiming that the king had broken the treaty, Trajan stormed the capital Sarmizegeth-usa, and the king committed suicide. The two triumphs of Trajan mentioned in section 2 below were held in 102/3 and 106/7.

2 *new rivers . . . over rivers*: Decebalus diverted the Sargetia (Dio 68.14.4); the Romans constructed a stone bridge over the Danube, visible on Trajan's column (cf. Dio 68.13).

2 *a king, refusing to despair*: Decebalus had intrepidly united the Dacians against Roman forces since the days of Domitian, who by the peace of 89 recognized him as king.

3 *a talent like yours*: at IX 33.1 Pliny again offers homage to Rufus' poetic talent.

4 *if Homer is allowed ... his verse*: for linguistic variations in Homer, see G. S. Kirk, *The Songs of Homer* (Cambridge, 1962), esp. 142 ff.

5 *among the gods*: such deification of living emperors was a poetic convention, beginning with Virgil (*Georgics* 1.24 ff.) and Horace (*Odes* 3.5.2), and continuing with Lucan (1.33ff.) and Statius (*Siluae* 1, in praise of Domitian).

5 GEMINUS: for Rosianus Geminus, see note to VII 1.

1 *Macrinus*: almost certainly Caecilius Macrinus (see note to II 7), for as the recipient of several letters, he is clearly a close friend.

6 MONTANUS: see VII 29 and note. This letter is a continuation of the same topic, lambasting the honours paid to Claudius' freedman, who was the emperor's financial secretary.

2 *Africanus, Achaicus, and Numantinus*: these were three great heroes of the Republic. Scipio Africanus was the victor over Hannibal, Mummius Achaicus sacked Corinth in 146, and Scipio Aemilianus, destroyed Carthage in 146 and stormed Numantia in Spain in 133.

3 *as men of wit*: Pliny ironically half-suggests that the honours paid to Pallas were ironical.

4 *a slave*: Pallas was in fact a freedman, as Pliny knows well.

   to wear a gold ring: this privilege was restricted to those of equestrian or higher status.

7 *guardian of the resources of the princeps*: Pallas was head of the imperial treasury, which was directly controlled by the emperor.

13 *affixed to the mailed statue of the deified Julius*: this statue, elsewhere unattested, presumably stood in front of the temple of the deified Julius, This temple in the Forum, together with the adjoining temple of Castor, housed the offices and the vault of the imperial treasury,

17 *no experience of those times*: both meetings of the Senate took place in January 52, a decade before Pliny's birth.

7 TACITUS: see note to I 6.

1 *your book*: probably the second instalment of the *Histories*, following that mentioned in VII 20; see the note there.

2 *hyperbaton*: the figure which Pliny's mentor Quintilian defines as 'transposition of a word to some distance for ornamental effect' (8.6.65). Here it refers to the delayed appearance of 'that you have sent me', following the lengthy parenthesis.

8 ROMANUS: for Voconius Romanus, see note to I 5.

1 *the Clitumnus?*: this stream in Umbria, which flows into the Tinia, a tributary of the Tiber, was famed in ancient lore because cattle drinking from it were thought to turn white. See Virgil, *Georgics* 1.146; Propertius 2.19.25; Statius, *Siluae* 1.4.128 f., etc.

5 *Clitumnus himself . . . oracular responses*: the statue of the god, clad in the toga of a priest or magistrate, stood in the temple together with a chest containing the wooden tablets, which when shaken together offered a message to the enquirer. See Cicero, *De Diuinatione* 2.86 for a similar scene at Praeneste.

6 *Hispellum*: modern Spello.

7 *a few will make you laugh*: illiterate graffiti rather than votive tablets.

9 URSUS: for Cornelius Ursus, see note to IV 9.

1 *the many concerns of my friends*: chiefly referring to his roles as advocate and as judge in the Centumviral court.

2 *the obligations of friendship, which those very books counsel us*: Pliny thinks especially of Cicero's *De amicitia* and *De officiis* 3.43.

10 FABATUS: for Calpurnius Fabatus, see note to IV 1.

1 *a miscarriage*: one wonders if pregnancy had been the reason for Calpurnia's indisposition reported in VI 4 and 7; VII 5. The unhappy event is again the subject of the letter that follows.

11 HISPULLA: for Calpurnia Hispulla, see note to IV 1.7.

12 MINICIANUS: for Cornelius Minicianus, see note to III 9.

1 *I plead exemption*: that is, from his business duties.

Titinius Capito: see note to I 17.1.

letters, which were now declining: Pliny believes that the Domitianic era witnessed such a decline, from which signs of recovery are evident; see I 10, 13, 16.

4 *books on the deaths of famous men*: earlier (see I 17.3) Capito had written verse-biographies of Republican heroes; here he is depicted as the author of panegyrics of those who had died during the persecutions under Domitian.

13 GENIALIS: he is one of the circle of young men who look to Pliny for oratorical guidance and advancement. Neither he nor his father is otherwise known.

14 ARISTO: for the eminent lawyer Titius Aristo, see note to I 22.1.

2 *ignorance over senatorial procedures*: Pliny repeatedly draws attention to this, for example at VI 5.1–2. The attribution of the ignorance to Domitian's tyranny is in keeping with Pliny's lament for the loss of the good old days.

5 *they would stand at the doors of the Senate House*: this venerable Republican practice (Valerius Maximus 2.1.9) was revived by the emperor Augustus (Suetonius, *Augustus* 38.2).

12 *the consul Afranius Dexter*: the Fasti (calendar of consuls) date his death to 24 June 105. Traditionally, when a master was killed in his own home, the slaves of the household were executed if they had failed to go to his aid. Freedmen were exempted, but this exemption was withdrawn by a decree of AD 57 (Tacitus, *Annals* 13.32.1). When in 61 the city prefect Pedanius was murdered, and all 400 slaves of his household were executed, a proposal to banish the freedmen was vetoed by the emperor Nero (Tacitus, *Annals* 14.45.2). Thus the proposals for execution and for relegation were both in order, but Pliny's support for acquittal probably had the tacit agreement of Trajan, if the participation of freedmen in the murder was in considerable doubt.

19 *the law*: this is the *lex Iulia de senatu habendo* of 9 BC.

24 *the result I demanded*: namely, to have the proposals separated.

26 *which of them would prevail over it*: the proposer of execution chose to support the motion for relegation. Pliny does not indicate here whether his motion for acquittal prevailed.

15 JUNIOR: for his career and retirement, see VII 25.2 ff. and note.

2 *my own poor estate*: since there were meagre grape-harvests at both estates, Pliny probably refers to his lands at Tifernum, and Terentius Junior's at Perugia (see *ILS* 6120).

I shall have to erase whatever I have written: this mock-affectation of poverty indicates that Pliny will have to revert to his wax tablets, as at I 6.

16 PATERNUS: for Plinius Paternus, see note to I 21.

1 *deaths among my servants*: perhaps including Encolpius; see VIII 1.2. Pliny again laments these deaths at VIII 19.1.

2 *the household . . . a sort of republic*: for this commonplace, see also Seneca, *Letters* 47.14.

17 MACRINUS: for Caecilius Macrinus, see note to II 7.

1 *its channel*: Flooding was a perennial problem at Rome; hence Augustus' appointment of *curatores riparum et aluei Tiberis* (see Suetonius, *Augustus* 17). Both Claudius and Trajan had canals dug to carry off flood water.

3 *the Anio*: the river rises in Sabine territory, and joins with the Tiber just north of Rome. The damage reported by Pliny is in the area around Tibur.

18 RUFINUS: this is the sole letter addressed to him. He may be L. Fadius Rufinus, suffect consul in 113, a fellow guest of Pliny's at IX 23.4.

1 *Domitius Tullus*: he and his younger brother Lucanus (see section 4), already prominent under Vespasian, had both attained the consulship under Domitian.

2 *made himself available to legacy-hunters*: for this ghoulish practice of attending the dying for financial profit, see note to II 20.1. Tullus' vociferous critics in section 3 below are the disappointed ones criticized by Pliny for their 'shameless expectations'.

his heiress the daughter: she is Domitia Lucilla, grandmother of the future emperor Marcus Aurelius.

4 *Curtilius Mancia*: this father-in-law of Lucanus was consul in 55, and governor of Upper Germany thereafter (Tacitus, *Annals* 13.56).

5 *Domitius Afer*: see note to II 14.10. He died in 59, and therefore adopted the boys in 41–2. His prosecution of their father, which led to his banishment, is not elsewhere attested.

7 *this inheritance*: that is, After's bequests to his adopted sons.

8 *that excellent woman*: otherwise unknown.

19 MAXIMUS: not certainly identifiable; see note to II 14.

1 *my wife's sickness . . . the life-threatening maladies of my servants*: see VIII 10.1, 16.1 and notes.

20 GALLUS: cf. note to II 17.

3 *Ameria . . . Vadimon*: modern Amelia and Laghetto di Bassano in south Umbria, some 42 miles from Rome. Vadimon was celebrated as the site of a battle against the Etruscans and their Gallic allies in 283–282 BC (Polybius 2.20; Livy 9.39).

5 *floating islands*: they are mentioned earlier by the Elder Pliny (*Natural History* 2.209), a passage surprisingly unknown to his nephew, and by Seneca, *Natural Questions* 3.25.8.

21 ARRIANUS: for Arrianus Maturus, see note to I 2.

1 *to mingle the serious with the genial*: in this letter Pliny resumes the apologia for his verse-compositions earlier voiced in IV 14, V 3, VII 9.

4 *in various metres*: perhaps indicating a development in his efforts at versification, from the hendecasyllabics earlier mentioned.

5 *rather than help to create it*: by offering positive criticisms at the close of the recitation.

22 GEMINUS: for Rosianus Geminus, see note to VII 1.

3 *Thrasea*: for Thrasea Paetus, see note to III 16.10.

23 MARCELLINUS: Aefulanus Marcellinus is known only as the recipient of this letter and of V 16, another death-notice.

1 *Junius Avitus*: as this letter indicates, the young man was at the beginning of a senatorial career, as reception of the broad stripe (section 2) indicates. After serving as military tribune, he had attained the quaestorship and then the aedileship.

5 *Servianus*: this notable, Ursus Servianus, after holding the consulship, was legate of Upper Germany in 98, and was in Pannonia (? with Trajan) in 99.

quaestor: four of the twenty quaestors were chosen as assistants to consuls. Avitus will have served both the ordinary and the suffect consuls during his year of office.

6 *those fruitless pleadings*: that is, his attempts to gain support when canvassing for office.

24 MAXIMUS: the hortatory tone to a younger friend suggests that this is the Maximus addressed in VI 34 and VII 26; nothing is known of him beyond the details found in these three letters.

2 *the province of Achaia*: having been established as a separate province by Augustus in 27 BC, it was declared free by Nero in 66, but re-established as a province by Vespasian. Pliny's advice to his young friend to show respect to the country to which he has been sent as imperial commissioner appears to be based on Cicero's letter to his brother on his appointment as proconsul of Asia (*Ad Quintum fratrem* 1.1).

4 *bestowed laws on us*: Pliny echoes the tradition that in 454 BC an embassy was sent from Rome to Athens to obtain a copy of the laws of Solon, and to investigate the customs and rights of other states (Livy 3.31.8), as a result of which the decemvirs established the Twelve Tables.

8 *the outstanding reputation . . . from Bithynia*: at *Panegyricus* 70.1, Pliny refers to a quaestor who on Trajan's initiative 'settled the finances of an important city'. This official has been plausibly identified with our Maximus.

BOOK NINE

1 MAXIMUS: the identity of this older Maximus is uncertain. For the likelier candidates, see note to II 14.

1 *against Planta*: this is probably Pompeius Planta, governor of Egypt 98–100. He is known to have composed a history of the civil conflicts of 69, and it is feasible that the dispute with Maximus centred on differing loyalties in their accounts of that period.

4 *'it is unholy to boast over the slain'*: Homer, *Odyssey* 22.412, where Odysseus bids his old nurse Eurycleia not to exult over the bodies of the suitors.

2 SABINUS: probably Statius Sabinus; see note to IV 10. Letter IX 18 below is also addressed to him. From section 4 we infer that he is on active service in a hot climate such as that of Syria.

3 PAULINUS: for Valerius Paulinus, see note to II 2.

2 *as I see many doing*: the implied contrast is between those who seek immortality through public service or through literature, and those who opt for a strenuous commercial career.

4 MACRINUS: for Caecilius Macrinus, see note to II 7.

1 *the speech which you will receive*: Pliny regularly sends Macrinus details of criminal cases, and the description of the speech here fits closely with the aftermath of the indictment of Caecilius Classicus by the Baeticans (see III 9.12 ff.).

5 TIRO: for Caelestrius Tiro, see notes to I 12, VII 16.1. He has now been appointed proconsul of Baetica. The proprietorial tone of the letter reminds us that Pliny is patron of the province (III 4.5 f.).

3 *preserving distinctions*: Pliny characteristically warns Tiro to give to

dignitaries of the province their proper due. There may also be a hint that he should keep an appropriate distance from the lesser orders.

6 CALVISIUS: for Calvisius Rufus, see note to I 12.12.

1 *The races were on*: from the era of Augustus, 17 of the 77 days of public games were devoted to chariot-racing in the Circus Maximus or the Circus Flaminius. The four factions were the Greens, Blues, Reds, and Whites. These were briefly augmented under Domitian by the Purples and the Golds. Racing between four-horse chariots was the norm, but lesser and greater teams were more occasionally on view. For further detail of the races, see Balsdon, *Life and Leisure*, 248, 314–24.

not the slightest interest: Pliny's *snobbisme* reflects Cicero's disdain for public games as at *Ad Familiares* 1.1.2; cf. Seneca, *Letters*, 7.4.

7 ROMANUS: for Voconius Romanus, see note to I 5.

1 *you are engaged in building*: Pliny offers no indication of where Voconius is building, unless the references to Baiae offer a clue. Baiae was the popular watering place for Roman city-dwellers on the Bay of Naples. It was famous for its hot springs.

4 *casting your line ... even from your bed*: Martial, 10.30.17 ff., similarly mentions fishing from bedroom and bed at Formiae on the coast of Latium.

8 AUGURINUS: for Sentius Augurinus, see note to IV 27.1.

9 COLONUS: neither this addressee nor the Pompeius Quintianus mentioned in section 1 are otherwise known.

10 TACITUS: see note to I 6.

1 *to cope with both Minerva and Diana*: these references to the goddesses of the arts (including literature) and of hunting are anticipated in an earlier letter to Tacitus (I 6.3). Pliny is writing from his estate at Tifernum, where the availability of good hunting is noted earlier, at V 18.2.

3 *no charm or attractiveness*: for revision of speeches on holiday envisaged as a chore, compare IX 15.2.

11 GEMINUS: for Rosianus Geminus, see note to VII 1.

1 *in a collection of my works*: this is the more probable meaning of the Latin than 'of your works', since Geminus requests a letter or speech of Pliny of which he has seen an earlier draft. Such a contribution would fit oddly into a collection of Geminus' works.

2 *booksellers at Lugdunum*: Geminus has recently returned from a visit to Lugdunum (Lyons). Founded in 43 BC, the city had become the capital of the three Gauls, and an important commercial centre. It is hardly surprising that Pliny was ignorant of the book trade there, since this is the first attested reference to any bookseller outside Rome.

12 JUNIOR: for Terentius Junior, see VII 25.2 f. and note. During the visit described in that letter, Pliny will have met Junior's son, and perhaps noted the strict supervision of his father.

13 QUADRATUS: for Ummidius Quadratus, see note to VI 11.1.

1 *the vindication of Helvidius*: Helvidius Priscus, together with Herennius Senecio and Arulenus Rusticus, was indicted for treason in 93 and executed (see note to III 11.3).

2 *Following the murder of Domitian*: the emperor was murdered by his entourage on 18 September 96; Pliny delivered and published his speech in the following year.

committed violence: the precise circumstances are unknown. Certus may have 'committed violence' against Helvidius by proposing his condemnation and having him hauled off to prison.

3 *Arria and Fannia*: the Younger Arria, wife of Thrasea Paetus, and Fannia, wife of the elder Helvidius Priscus, had both suffered exile following the condemnation of the Younger Helvidius in 98; see III 11.3.

4 *when freedom was restored*: that is, with the accession of Nerva.

the recent loss of my wife: his second wife, daughter of Pompeia Celerina, the addressee of I 4. Pliny followed the custom of not appearing in public during the period of mourning (nine days).

6 *Corellius*: see I 12.1 ff. and notes.

7 *the culprit*: Publicius Certus, as prefect of the treasury of Saturn, and anticipating the consulship, could expect the support of many senators.

9 *in your due turn*: Pliny had been given leave to speak informally (section 7), but following objections, the consul indicated that he must await his due turn before making a formal proposal.

11 *he named a man . . . in command of the most massive army*: such a man with the backing of a powerful force might have designs on the principate. Perhaps the reference is to the legate of Syria, Javolenus Priscus.

13 *Domitius Apollinaris . . . Ammius Flaccus*: these supporters of Certus had all prospered under Domitian. Apollinaris was consul-designate for 97 (and therefore first speaker). Veiento had been awarded a third consulship under Domitian. Postuminus was suffect consul in 96. Bittius Proculus, now married to Pompeia Celerina (see note to section 4) was a prefect of the treasury, soon to become consul in 98. Flaccus is cited separately as a figure of lesser account.

15 *Avidius Quietus and Cornutus Tertullus*: see VI 29.1, IV 17.9, V 14.5 and notes.

16 *the equivalent of the censor's stigma*: no censors were appointed after 22 BC. Their role as guardians of morals was taken over by the emperors or their nominees. The aggrieved women were demanding the expulsion of Certus from the Senate.

17 *Satrius Rufus*: see note to I 5.11.

19 *Veiento*: a *bête noire* of Pliny (see IV 22.4 and note). Tacitus, *Annals* 14, 50, recounts earlier misdemeanours of his under Nero.

20 *'Aged sire . . . distressing you'*: Homer, *Iliad* 8.102, where Diomedes

addresses the aged Nestor, and takes him into his chariot to protect him from Trojan attacks.

23 *the consulship . . . to the colleague of Certus, and his office . . . to a successor*: Bittius Proculus, his fellow prefect at the treasury, became consul in 98 in place of Certus. Proculus and Certus were replaced at the treasury in 98 by Pliny and Tertullus.

14 TACITUS: see note to I 6. This short note is probably a reply to Tacitus' acknowledgement of VII 20; it resumes the theme in that letter of the future fame of the two friends.

15 FALCO: for Pompeius Falco, see note to I 23. He had recently returned from governing Judaea to be awarded the consulship.

1 *among the Etruscans*: he is on holiday at his estate at Tifernum.

16 MAMILIANUS: this is his first appearance. At IX 25 he is in command of an army as consular legate, and accordingly he can be reasonably identified as Pomponius Mamilianus, suffect consul in 100, the year of Pliny's consulship.

1 *the harvest is so meagre*: this disappointing harvest at Tifernum is further mentioned at IX 20, IX 28.2.

2 *as soon as they stop fermenting*: Pliny's two activities on his estate at Tifernum are likewise connected by jocose metaphor at VIII 21.6.

17 GENITOR: for Julius Genitor, see note to III 3.5.

3 *a reader or lyre-player or comic actor*: Pliny thus carefully distinguishes between his own entertainments and the more vulgar amusements at the house of Genitor's host. For entertainments at dinner parties in general, see Balsdon, *Life and Leisure*, 44 ff.

18 SABINUS: for Statius Sabinus, see note to IV 10. At IX 2 he is on service in an eastern province, and Pliny promises to send him some of his works to relieve the tedium.

19 RUSO: for Cremutius Ruso, see note to VI 23.2.

1 *in a letter of mine*: the letter with the verse epitaph has survived (VI 10).

Verginius Rufus: his death in 97, together with a fulsome tribute, is recorded in II 1. See the notes to that letter.

Frontinus: for the career of Julius Frontinus, see note to IV 8.3.

5 *Cluvius*: Cluvius Rufus was an important source for Tacitus for the reign of Nero (*Annals* 13.20.2; 14.2.1) and for the Year of the Four Emperors (*Histories* 4.43.1). It is probable that he criticized Verginius' role in the massacre of the army of Vindex in 69.

20 VENATOR: otherwise unknown.

2 *gathering in the grape-harvest*: at Tifernum.

21 SABINIANUS: the recipient of this letter, and of IX 24, is otherwise unknown.

1 *Your freedman . . . has approached me*: St Paul offers a striking parallel in his

letter to Philemon, where he pleads on behalf of Philemon's slave Ones-
imus, with whom Paul had struck up an acquaintance while in prison.

22 SEVERUS: there are five Severi among Pliny's correspondents, of whom the
likeliest recipient here is either Vibius Severus, who received IV 28, or
Herennius Severus, mentioned in that letter.

  1 *Passennus Paulus*: see VI 15.1 and note.

  the genre in which Propertius excelled: of the four books of elegies composed
  by this poet of the Augustan age, the first two are devoted largely to love-
  poetry, centring on his mistress Cynthia. Books 3 and 4 contain themes
  ranging more widely, including the aetiological poems of Book 4, which
  bolster the poet's claim to be the Roman Callimachus.

  2 *moved on to lyric poetry*: his model, Horace, was an older contemporary of
  Propertius. He wrote his four books of *Odes* after 30 BC, covering a wide
  range of topics in a variety of metres.

23 MAXIMUS: for the possible identity of this elder Maximus, see note
  to II 14.

  2 *at the recent chariot-races*: Tacitus clearly does not share the *snobbisme* of
  Pliny towards the races (cf. IX 6), at which knights and senators were given
  reserved seats (see Balsdon, *Life and Leisure*, 260).

  '*Are you Italian or a provincial?*': Tacitus does not answer the question
  directly, which makes Syme (himself a provincial) suspect that Tacitus was
  not a blue-blooded Italian, but from Narbonese Gaul.

  4 *Fadius Rufinus*: perhaps L. Fadius Rufinus, suffect consul in 113.

  5 *if Demosthenes was justified*: Pliny recounts the story from Cicero, *Tusculans*
  5.103, with its mild criticism ('petty-minded') of the Greek orator.

24 SABINIANUS: see note to IX 21.

25 MAMILIANUS: for Pomponius Mamilianus, see note to IX 16.

  3 *among your eagles*: that is, among the legionary standards.

26 LUPERCUS: see II 5 and note. This letter embodies Pliny's reaction to the
  criticism by his friend of the speech mentioned in that letter, or a later one.
  In general, Pliny claims to take the middle ground between the plain style
  of the Atticists and the exuberance of the Asianists, but here he inclines
  towards the more florid style.

  3 *winning approval ... from its hazards*: the resemblance to the view of
  'Longinus', *On the Sublime*, has been noted here, and the suggestion made
  that the common source of both is Pliny's former teacher of Greek rhetoric
  Nicetes Sacerdos (see VI 6.3).

  tightrope walking: Horace, *Epistles* 2.1.210 f., comparing the tightrope
  walker to the poet, may be Pliny's inspiration here.

  6 '*The lofty heavens trumpeted forth ... bellow so loudly*': the three Homeric
  passages here are all from the *Iliad* (21.388; 5.356; 14.394). The first is
  cited also by 'Longinus' more extensively as an example of grandeur (9.6).

The third extract is followed by other similes from nature, all describing the dread war cries of Trojans and Achaeans.

8 *those most celebrated words*: the thirteen examples of vivid expressions which follow do not come over with the same force in English. The passages in order are from *On the Crown* 206, 299, 301; *Philippics* 1.49; *On the False Legation* 259; *On the Crown* 136; *Olynthiacs* 2.9; *Against Aristogeiton* 1.28, 84, 76, 7, 48, 46; *Against Timarchus* 176.

9 *Aeschines*: this Athenian orator and political foe of Demosthenes criticized his style in the speech *Against Ctesiphon*. The phrase 'monstrosities, not words' is from *Against Ctesiphon* 167, and the fourth of the six passages which follow is from *Against Timarchus* 176. The others are all from *Against Ctesiphon* (16, 101, 206, 208, 253).

27 PATERNUS: for Plinius Paternus, see note to I 21.

1 *Someone . . . reciting a most truthful account*: the letter clearly indicates that the work is a contemporary history, and the attractive suggestion has been made that the work being read was the *Histories* of Tacitus.

28 ROMANUS: for Voconius Romanus, see note to I 5.

1 *Plotina*: the wife of Trajan; Pliny has easy access to the emperor's residence.

2 *Popilius Artemisius*: presumably a freedman in Romanus' household.

a totally different part of the world: Romanus hails from Saguntum in Spain; the phrase here suggests that he is in residence there.

4 *my future plans*: perhaps referring to his imminent appointment as governor of Bithynia.

5 *on behalf of Clarius*: the speech is otherwise unknown. The name may be a corruption of Ciartius.

composed with particular care: so the three letters received are brief and businesslike. This further letter has been lost, and Pliny assumes that Romanus has kept a copy. For Romanus' literary abilities, see II 13.7.

29 RUSTICUS: he cannot be identified with certainty. It is bold to assume that he is Fabius Rusticus, the celebrated historian of the reign of Nero used as source by Tacitus (*Annals* 13.20.2; 14.2.2; 15.61.3).

30 GEMINUS: for Rosianus Geminus, see note to VII 1.

1 *Nonius*: his identity is uncertain. Pliny's acerbic tone suggests that Nonius' generosity is confined to gifts to well-to-do friends. Pliny's ideal philanthropy, expressed here, reflects his own practice.

31 SARDUS: not otherwise known. It has been speculated that he is the historian in IX 27, and that the compliments to Pliny refer to events after the death of Domitian in 97, but this theory cannot be substantiated.

32 TITIANUS: for Cornelius Titianus, see note to I 17.

33 CANINIUS: for Caninius Rufus, see note to I 3.

1 *the author . . . is highly reliable*: Pliny may well refer to his uncle, who

recounts this anecdote at *Natural History* 9.26 as one of several dolphin stories. The two accounts are strikingly similar, except that in section 9 here it is the proconsul's legate who pours the ointment on the dolphin, whereas in the Elder Pliny it is the proconsul himself.

2 *Hippo in Africa*: Hippo Diarrhytus (modern Bizerta) near Utica, as the Elder Pliny makes clear, not Hippo Regius in Numidia.

4 *A dolphin approached him*: stories documenting the friendly play of dolphins and their helpfulness to men are numerous in the ancient world, beginning with Herodotus' account (1.23 f.) of the rescue of Arion. A modern counterpart of dolphins' affection for children recounted by the Elder Pliny is recorded by T. F. Higham, 'Nature Note: Dolphin Riders', in *GR* 7 (1960), 82 ff., describing (with photographs) the behaviour of dolphins off the coast of New Zealand.

9 *Octavius Avitus*: otherwise unknown. The proconsul cited by the Elder Pliny, Tampius Flavianus, earlier governed Pannonia (see Tacitus, *Histories* 2.86, etc.).

10 *all the magistrates*: they descended on Hippo from Carthage, the capital of the province.

34 TRANQUILLUS: for the historian Suetonius Tranquillus, see note to I 18.

1 *his role as reader*: Pliny's excellent readers Zosimus and Encolpius (V 19.3, VIII 1) were reported as ill, and may have died (VIII 19). He may now be training a successor.

35 ATRIUS: the reading is uncertain. The addressee may be Attius Clemens, the recipient of I 10 and IV 2, but the admonitory tone of this letter does not suggest a close acquaintance. Emendation of the Latin to 'Satrio' has been suggested (cf. IX 13.17).

36 FUSCUS: for Fuscus Salinator, see note to VI 11.1.

1 *among the Etruscans*: at his villa near Tifernum, described in V 6.

3 *to exercise the gullet*: so Celsus, writing in the reign of Tiberius, states: 'If anyone has stomach-trouble, he should read loudly' (*De medicina* 1.8).

4 *a book is read*: in more elaborate company the entertainment might be more ambitious; cf. III 1.9.

6 *not without my writing-tablets*: cf. I 6.

Their rustic complaints: so too at VII 30.3, IX 15.1. For a general account of the daily routine of the literary bourgeoisie when on holiday, see Balsdon, *Life and Leisure*, ch. 6.

37 PAULINUS: for Valerius Paulinus, see note to II 2.

1 *your inauguration as consul*: Paulinus held the suffect consulship from September to December 107.

2 *the previous four-year period*: though the *lustrum* is normally a period of five years, the word is also used of a four-year term. Pliny appears to refer here to the years 103–7.

38 SATURNINUS: for Pompeius Saturninus, see note to I 8.

   Rufus: probably Caninius Rufus (see note to I 3), but possibly Octavius Rufus (note to I 7).

39 MUSTIUS: this is the sole letter addressed to the architect (see section 6).

1 *the shrine of Ceres*: this is a temple distinct from that built by Pliny for the inhabitants of Tifernum (IV 1). Ceres, as the goddess of growth, is an appropriate deity to be honoured in Pliny's rustic estate close by.

2 *on 13 September*: not the feast of the Cerialia, which coincided with the growing season in April, but a local feast to celebrate the harvest.

5 *at your end*: whether Mustius is practising his profession in Rome is uncertain, but Pliny's details of the site suggest that he is not familiar with it. Presumably a visit would be necessary before he could plan the layout.

40 FUSCUS: for Pedanius Fuscus Salinator, see note to VI 11.1.

1 *delighted with my letter*: see IX 36.

   at Laurentum: for Pliny's Laurentine villa, see II 17.

BOOK TEN

1.1 *the guidance . . . you had already undertaken*: This was following his adoption by Nerva in October 97. His accession to the throne followed the death of that emperor in January 98. See *Panegyricus* 8–10.

2.1 *the right of three children*: see note to II 13.8.

   Julius Servianus: see III 17 and note.

2 *my two marriages*: the death of his second wife in 97 is mentioned in IX 13.4. Marriage to his third wife Calpurnia followed after 100 (see IV 1).

3A.1 *the generosity of you both*: Nerva and his designated successor Trajan nominated Pliny for the prefecture in January 98.

2 *the provincials . . . against Marius Priscus*: see II 11.

   our names to be included in the ballot: a senator was assigned by lot as advocate for a province unless a request for an individual had been made.

4.1 *Voconius Romanus*: see note to I 5. There is no evidence that Pliny's request was granted.

5.1 *an illness*: this can be dated to early 97; see X 8.3.

   a physiotherapist: this physician superintended convalescence rather than treated illnesses. In Petronius (28), the three *iatroliptae* are no more than masseurs.

   Antonia Maximilla: this remote kinswoman of Pliny (see X 6.1) is otherwise unknown.

6.1 *I ought first to have obtained Alexandrian citizenship for him*: this passage indicates that Egyptians not belonging to the Greek cities were not eligible for Roman citizenship, presumably because of their ignorance of municipal institutions; see Tacitus, *Histories* I.11.

7 *my friend Pompeius Planta*: for Planta, see notes to IV 20.1 and IX 1.1. His status as prefect was equivalent to that of an equestrian governor. The expression 'my friend' does not necessarily indicate a close relationship with Trajan, but is conventional in addresses to equestrians in such posts.

8.1 *encouraged . . . to acts of generosity*: Pliny refers to Nerva's encouragement of gifts of land and *alimenta* to needy families. See VII 31.4; for Pliny's participation in the scheme, VII 18.4 f.

to the township of Tifernum: see III 4.2 and IV 1.5 for earlier mention of the temple which Pliny promised to the township.

3 *the office*: the prefecture of the treasury of Saturn, awarded to him jointly by Nerva and Trajan.

my month's duties: Pliny and his fellow prefect Cornutus Tertullus exercised supervision in alternate months.

the month that follows: Pliny would normally be required to be on hand when his colleague was in charge, but the *ludi Romani* alone occupied most of the period 4–19 September, and there were minor festivals on other days of the month.

5 *barren harvests . . . reductions of rent*: see IX 37 for these problems exercising Pliny over several successive years.

10.1 *Alexandrian citizenship to . . . Harpocras*: see X 6. His provenance, Memphis, was the centre of the administrative district of Middle and Upper Egypt.

2 *Pompeius Planta*: see note to X 7.

to meet you: Trajan was returning from inspecting the troops in Pannonia. Pliny proposes to meet him in northern Italy.

11.2 *though preserving their rights*: the Latin is ambiguous, and may refer to the rights of the parents Chrysippus and Stratonice rather than to those of their sons.

as patrons over their freedmen: when slaves were manumitted, they owed obligations to their former owners, who could in addition claim part of the freedman's estate on his death.

12.1 *in this matter as well*: that is, in granting favours on behalf of friends and dependants.

Accius Sura: this senator is otherwise unknown. The vacancy in the ranks of the praetorship must have occurred because one of the men designated has died or withdrawn.

13 *the augurate or the status of septemvir*: the augurs and the *septemuiri epularum* were two of the four main priestly colleges, together with the *pontifices* and the *quindecimuiri sacris faciundis*. The augurate, which

Trajan granted to Pliny's request (see IV 8), was particularly congenial to him since Cicero had held it.

14 *your glorious victory*: referring to either Trajan's victory in the first Dacian war of 102 or to that of the second Dacian war of 106. See note to VIII 4.1.

The remaining letters in Book X were written after Pliny took up his appointment as governor of Bithynia-Pontus. The date of arrival was autumn in either 109 or 110. A map of Bithynia-Pontus appears on p. 287.

15 *Cape Malea*: at the south-eastern tip of the Peloponnese. Pliny took this route rather than that through the Corinthian gulf because of favourable winds.

partly by carriages: these had been provided by local cities since the time of Augustus, who established them for speedier intelligence of provincial affairs (Suetonius, *Augustus* 49.3).

Etesian winds: these 'yearly' winds, according to the Elder Pliny, blow from the north for forty days from 26 July (*Natural History* 3.123 f.)

17A.1 *a halt at Pergamum*: this was after a taxing 80-mile journey from Ephesus northward along the coast. Pliny then prudently took the longer sea-journey through the Propontis to Apamea, and thence overland to Prusa.

2 *Your birthday*: 18 September. The birthdays of emperors, beginning with Augustus, were celebrated with public games.

17B.2 *a quantity-surveyor*: Trajan intimates in the next letter that he cannot dispatch one. Those he employs were fully occupied with building-works. Though his Baths were completed in 109, his Forum was to be dedicated in 113, with his basilica and markets adjoining it. A new aqueduct was being constructed for Rome, and new harbours were being built at Ostia and at Centum Cellae (see VI 31.15–17).

19.1 *public slaves . . . or . . . soldiers*: public slaves were owned by the cities, and were paid a small salary for performing such duties as this. This province, like others long peaceful, had no standing army, but Pliny had a few cohorts of auxiliary troops assigned to him as governor (see X 21.1; X 106).

21.1 *Gavius Bassus, prefect of the Pontic shore*: inscriptional evidence from Ephesus reveals that this was Bassus' crowning appointment. His command was independent of Pliny, and probably covered the entire southern shore of the Black Sea.

first-class privates: soldiers below the rank of centurion who were selected for special missions.

22.1 *my reply to him*: the tone of Trajan's letter suggests that Bassus' request was rejected.

23.1 *to have a new building*: at first sight this looks like an issue which Pliny need hardly have referred to Rome, but the emperor seems to have insisted that applications for new buildings should be referred to him;

cf. X 70, 90, 98. Trajan's concern was that profligate spending should not divert funds from essential works.

25 *Servilius Pudens*: otherwise unknown. Previous governors of the province had been proconsuls, and their deputies were appointed by the Senate; Pliny, as *legatus Augusti pro praetore*, has his deputy chosen by the emperor.

26.1 *Rosianus Geminus*: see note to VII 1 for this regular correspondent. Pliny does not specify a particular role for his friend, for fear of twisting the emperor's arm, but perhaps he hopes for the governorship of a province for him.

27 *Maximus ... Gemellinus*: Maximus was the assistant to Virdius Gemellinus, the equestrian procurator independent of Pliny in the province. His main role was to raise taxes, but, as here, was given other commissions.

to Paphlagonia to obtain grain: Paphlagonia lay between Bithynia and Pontus, extending southward to the border of Galatia. The corn was collected to feed army units on the Euphrates and the lower Danube.

29.1 *Sempronius Caelianus*: his role, independent of Pliny, was as recruiting officer of auxiliary troops. Slaves were not permitted to enlist. Trajan's reply in the next letter is characteristically incisive and clear.

31.2 *punishments similar to these*: such sentences included working in the mines, fighting as gladiators or being exposed to wild beasts at the games, and building roads. These harsh and hazardous occupations contrasted with the roles of public slaves, on which see X 19.

32.1 *the status of responsible officials*: Trajan probably refers to public slaves working as clerks in conducting the business of the province.

33.1 *the Gerousia and the temple of Isis*: the Gerousia was an association of elderly citizens established in many Greek cities, providing a social service for the bourgeoisie rather than for poor citizens. By this date the worship of the Egyptian goddess Isis was widespread among the cities of the empire. See, for example, Apuleius, *Metamorphoses*, especially Book 11.

3 *an association of firemen*: whereas in cities in the West the ever-present hazard of fires was met with permanent units of *vigiles* (Rome had a force of 7,000 by the early third century AD), no such organization was permitted in eastern cities because of the civic disturbances which such societies caused. The rigorous suppression of Christianity reported in X 96–7 was largely motivated by this fear.

35 *vows for your well-being*: at every new year throughout the Empire, public vows were offered for the safety of the emperor on 3 January. This ceremonial was distinct from the commemoration of Trajan's accession on 28 January (see X 1), and from the greetings to him on his birthday on 18 September (see X 17A).

37.1 *an aqueduct*: though this means of providing water for cities had long been commonplace in the West, in the East aqueducts were an innovation, and lack of experience in building them accounts for the failures described here. On the need to obtain the approval of the emperor for such building-projects, see note to X 23. Note that Trajan ignores the request for expert help from Rome, as he refuses it at X 18.

39.1 *Nicaea*: the city (modern Iznik, later celebrated for the Ecumenical Council of 325 which formulated the Nicene Creed) competed with its neighbour Nicomedia in the claim to be the most important in Bithynia.

4 *gymnasium*: in Greek cities this was a complex of exercise rooms, training ground, and lecture-halls.

5 *Claudiopolis*: this city in the south-east, earlier Bithynium, was renamed in honour of the emperor Claudius.

40.2 *The wretched Greeks*: Trajan's patronizing *Graeculi* ('Wretched Greeks') echoes Juvenal 3.78.

3 *You can have no shortage of architects*: Trajan again rebuts Pliny's request.

41.2 *an extensive lake*: lake Sophon (modern Sapanca Gölü) lies 18 miles east of Nicomedia. It drains by way of a stream (the Melas) into the river Sangarius which flows north into the Black Sea. Another river flows westward into the Propontis (now the Sea of Marmora), and Pliny's plan was to cut a canal between the lake and this river, and thus to reverse the flow and to allow access by water from the lake into the Propontis. The scheme becomes clearer with the further discussion at X 61.

the highway: the road from Ancyra to Nicomedia.

3 *40 cubits*: about 60 feet. Today the lake lies more than 120 feet above sea level.

4 *by a king*: either Nicomedes IV, the last of the Bithynian kings who ceded the kingdom to Rome in 74 BC, or one of his predecessors.

42 *Calpurnius Macer*: see note to V 18.

I shall send . . . some expert: Trajan appears to soften his earlier refusal to send technical help, but cf. X 62.

43.1 *the state of Byzantium*: though the city lay in the province of Thrace, under the Flavians it became the responsibility of the governor of Bithynia.

3 *to the governor of Moesia*: Moesia lay between the Danube and Thrace to the south. In AD 74 it was divided into Superior (west) and Inferior (east). Byzantium had strong trade links with Inferior; hence this cultivation of cordial relations.

45 *travel passes*: Augustus had established an efficient transport system for imperial officials (Suetonius, *Augustus* 49.3). Local cities provided

carriages and lodgings. The passes issued from Rome were probably valid for a year, though these letters are the only evidence for the expiry-dates cited here.

47.1 *to investigate at Apamea*: this town in the south-west of the province had become a Roman colony under Julius Caesar or Mark Antony. It was exempt from direct taxation, and had financial autonomy.

49.1 *a shrine . . . dedicated to the Great Mother*: the Magna Mater, Cybele, had been admitted to the Roman pantheon following the formal reception of her statue from Phrygia in 205/204 BC (see Livy 29.11.4 ff.). Pliny wonders if Roman sacral law applies in Bithynia. Trajan assures him that it does not.

51.1 *my mother-in-law*: Pompeia Celerina, mother of Pliny's former wife.

Caelius Clemens: otherwise unknown. He was probably appointed as commander of an auxiliary unit.

52 *declaration of the oath*: for this formal acknowledgement of the emperor's accession on 28 January, see note to X 35.

54.1 *I am fearful that they lie unused*: Pliny's talent in scrutinizing city-accounts has produced a handsome surplus. But the usual avenues of investment were blocked; few estates were available for purchase, and interest at 1 per cent per month was too high to attract borrowers. Hence the need for a reduction in the interest rate.

56.2 *Servilius Calvus*: nothing further is known of this former governor, and no further communication from Trajan on Calvus' handling of the case, beyond the holding reply of X 57, survives.

4 *Julius Bassus*: for the condemnation of this former proconsul, see IV 9, VI 29.10.

58.1 *Flavius Archippus*: Vespasian had granted exemption from jury service to physicians and teachers; Archippus presumably claimed exemption under this latter heading.

3 *Velius Paulus*: this proconsul in the early years of Domitian's reign had passed sentence on Archippus for forgery, perhaps of a will, but Domitian clearly regarded the charge as frivolous (see section 5).

5–6 *Terentius Maximus . . . Lappius Maximus*: Terentius was an equestrian procurator rather than proconsul, as the letter of Domitian indicates. Lappius was proconsul before 86, the year of his first consulship.

10 *Tullius Justus*: he was probably proconsul in 96–7 or 97–8.

60.1 *Domitian could . . . have been unaware*: Trajan implies that Domitian was hoodwinked by the eminence of Archippus; the statues raised to him, mentioned below, will have played their part. Pliny is urged to concentrate on the factual evidence of any new charges.

61.4 *sluice-gates*: such gates were set in stone, and were raised and lowered like a portcullis. X 61 and 62 resume the topic broached earlier, in X 41–2, reflecting the keen interest which Pliny shared with his uncle in natural philosophy and technology.

5 *Calpurnius Macer*: see X 42. Trajan tacitly withdraws his offer of an expert from Rome.

63 *Sauromates*: he was king of Cimmerian Bosporus (east of the Black Sea), 92/3–124, and an enthusiastic dependent ally of Rome.

64 *a travel pass*: see note to X 45.

65.1 *foster-children*: exposure of unwanted offspring was so common in the Graeco-Roman world that commentators show surprise at encountering abhorrence of the practice in other societies; see e.g. Tacitus, *Histories* 5.5, *Germania* 19.5. For characteristic evidence of the practice, see Petronius 116; Apuleius, *Metamorphoses* 10.23. Such exposed children were often rescued as a means of obtaining slaves.

3 *Avidius Nigrinus and Armenius Brocchus*: these otherwise unknown persons were proconsuls of provinces other than Bithynia.

67.1 *Sauromates*: see note to X 63.

68 *to transfer the remains of their kin*: Pliny's punctilious attitude towards matters religious elicits a brusque response from Trajan.

70.1 *the baths at Prusa*: see X 23–4 for earlier discussion of this project. Presumably the temple to Claudius was never erected, so that the religious issue did not arise. Trajan inherited the house as heir to the possessions of a previous emperor.

72 *restoration of their freeborn status*: the issue is more general here than that raised by Pliny in X 65, which is restricted to children exposed and rescued.

74.1 *Callidromus*: this fugitive slave posing as a free man, who when exploited by his employers claimed the emperor's protection, had been the slave of Laberius Maximus, governor of Lower Moesia. He alleged that he was taken prisoner by the Dacian general Susagus during the first Dacian war, and sent by the Dacian king Decibalus as a gift to king Pacorus of Parthia about 104. Doubt has been cast on his story by modern scholars, but the bizarre detail has the ring of truth.

75.2 *Heraclea and Tium*: both cities were in Pontus.

77.1 *Calpurnius Macer*: he was governor of Lower Moesia at this date. This was the province nearest to Byzantium with legionary forces. The dispatch of a centurion and detachment was to offer military support to local magistrates in suppression of disturbances caused by the heavy influx of travellers.

2 *Juliopolis*: the town lay on the south-eastern border of the province. Travellers from Galatia would enter Bithynia there.

79.1 *the Pompeian law*: after the final defeat of Mithradates, Pompey in 66 BC established the province of Bithynia-Pontus, and imposed a system of administration based on the practice at Rome, in which thirty was the minimum age for tenure of the lowest magistracy, the quaestorship, and for consequential membership of the senate. Augustus lowered the age-qualification at Rome to 25, and in Bithynia to 22. Pliny's suggestion that those under 30 who were magistrates could become senators (that is, city-councillors) is accepted by Trajan.

81.1 *Cocceianus Dio*: also known as Dio Chrysostom, this celebrated orator, many of whose speeches have survived, was charged with misappropriation of public funds, and with treason for having buried his wife and son in a building containing the emperor's statue. The accuser was Flavius Archippus, a noted philosopher (see X 58–9). The accusations seemingly arose out of enmity between these two leading citizens. In his reply, Trajan angrily rejects the charge of treason, but insists that Pliny should investigate the financial accusation.

83 *their entreaties*: the city-council claimed for the city of Nicaea the property of those who died intestate, invoking a concession by the emperor Augustus. This apparently impinged on the rights of heirs, but doubtless the council was claiming the property only of those who died without any.

84 *Virdius Gemellinus*: Pliny's equestrian procurator; see X 27–8.

85 *I have found . . . conscientious*: this letter, and the two that follow, are conventional testimonials in support of administrators in the province. They would be filed at Rome, and consulted when promotion to other posts was being considered. The name of the official in 86B has fallen out of the text.

87.3 *his son Nymphidius Lupus*: this testimonial for a man not serving in Bithynia, the son of a veteran chief centurion who had served with Pliny in Syria and now in Bithynia, is supported by references to the son's commanding officers. For these two ex-consuls, see II 11.5 and VI 26.1.

88 *this birthday*: this is the regular yearly acknowledgement of Trajan's birthday on 18 September; see X 17A.2.

90.1 *Sinope . . . short of water*: the town lay on the coast of Pontus. Letter X 23 indicates that all building projects be referred to the emperor for approval; see also X 98.

92 *Amisus*: the remotest coastal city in Pontus was awarded its status as a free city by Julius Caesar, a privilege confirmed by Augustus.

welfare-clubs: this Greek institution enabled members to subscribe to provide communal meals. Trajan approves this traditional privilege, but forbids it elsewhere, for fear it leads to factional disorder.

94.1 *Suetonius Tranquillus*: for Pliny's patronizing friendship with him, see note to I 18.

2 *the 'right of three children'*: see note to II 13.8.

96.1 *hearings concerning Christians*: this celebrated letter, together with X 97, provides detailed evidence from a non-Christian source of the growth and practice of Christianity in the Greek-speaking provinces of the

East as early as 90 (see section 6). Tacitus (*Annals* 15.44; cf. Suetonius, *Nero* 16.2) describes how Nero made Christians the scapegoats at Rome for the great fire of 64, and executed some of them. Probably from then onward they were proscribed as a subversive group (see section 7). But Pliny's ignorance of indictments at Rome on this count indicates that such trials were infrequent.

2 *the crimes which cling to the name*: 'homicide or sacrilege or incest or treason' (so Tertullian, *Apology* 2). These were accusations traditionally levelled against subversive sects from the time of the Bacchanalia (186 BC: Livy 39.8–18) onwards.

3 *their obstinacy . . . should . . . be punished*: contumacia, wilful disobedience to a judicial command, was in Roman eyes a crime; see X 57.2. But Roman citizens had the right to appeal to the emperor against decisions of provincial governors, who tended to dispatch them to Rome for formal trial.

7 *accustomed to assemble at dawn*: the weekly gathering was on the day after the Jewish sabbath. The description of the liturgy suggests a much simpler ritual than that recounted by Justin Martyr fifty years later. This included scripture-readings, a sermon and the eucharist (*First Apology* 67). The reference to assembling again to take food probably refers to the *agape* (see 1 Corinthians 11: 17 ff.).

8 *deaconesses*: cf. Romans 16: 1.

10 *flesh of the victims . . . now on sale*: in Roman sacrifices, the more inedible portions were burnt, and the rest was sold.

97.2 *they must be punished*: this clearly answers Pliny's initial query. It was the name 'Christian' itself which was to be punished.

98.1 *the city of the Amastrians*: a leading city of Pontus, Amastris later became capital of the Pontic shore.

100 *the vows . . . new ones*: for the customary vows taken by troops and provincials on 3 January, see X 35–6.

102 *We have celebrated . . . most blessed succession*: the celebration of the day of the emperor's accession, probably 28 January.

104 *Valerius Paulinus*: see note to II 2.

has passed over Paulinus: probably Valerius' son, the joint heir with Pliny. He was 'passed over' only so far as the Latin freedmen were concerned. Pliny was probably named by Paulinus because he had greater influence.

full citizenship: Latin freedmen at death surrendered their property to their patron, who could also nominate an outsider as his successor. Full citizenship gave a freedman total control over disposal of his property.

Those for whom I entreat it: on being manumitted, freedmen acquired the forename and gentile name of their former master.

106 *the sixth mounted cohort*: this unit of 600 auxiliary troops consisted of

four-fifths infantry and one-fifth cavalry. The centurions were mostly Roman citizens. Aquila's daughter was born of a Bithynian mother, a non-citizen. Marriage to non-Romans was forbidden to soldiers at this date. Trajan's reply indicates the nature of the centurion's request.

108.1 *rents or sales or other sources*: in addition to the lease or sale of land and provision of services, collection of taxes could be included under this heading.

110.1 *the city of the Amiseni*: see X 92–3. As a free city, it had self-governing laws, and the prosecutor was attempting to nullify these with Trajan's regulation, but the emperor defends the status quo.

112.1 *the Pompeian law*: see note to X 79.1.

2 *Anicius Maximus*: 'subsequently' indicates that he had become pro-consul after Trajan became emperor; the precise year is unknown.

114.1 *the Pompeian law*: see note to X 79.1. The purpose in excluding natives of other cities was to ensure that some areas were not deprived of prominent citizens by their flocking to the larger towns.

116.1 *one or two denarii to each*: the councillors will have received the larger sum. Pliny was doubtless correct to suspect that such handouts were a species of bribery to gain support for political or economic measures. There is a note of impatience in Trajan's reply; he must have found Pliny's continual requests for guidance trying.

118.1 *the prizes ... contests*: the competitors (who included musicians and actors as well as athletes) were demanding concessions for having come first in the respective competitions. Trajan appears to have laid down the amount of prize money which was to be conferred by the city to which each contestant belonged.

120.1 *travel passes*: see X 45–6.

2 *her grandfather*: for Fabatus, see IV 19 and note.

INDEX I: ASPECTS OF SOCIAL LIFE

INDEX II: PLINY'S CORRESPONDENTS

INDEX III: GENERAL

The Oxford World's Classics Website

www.worldsclassics.co.uk

- Browse the full range of Oxford World's Classics online
- Sign up for our monthly e-alert to receive information on new titles
- Read extracts from the Introductions
- Listen to our editors and translators talk about the world's greatest literature with our Oxford World's Classics audio guides
- Join the conversation, follow us on Twitter at OWC_Oxford
- Teachers and lecturers can order inspection copies quickly and simply via our website

www.worldsclassics.co.uk

American Literature

British and Irish Literature

Children's Literature

Classics and Ancient Literature

Colonial Literature

Eastern Literature

European Literature

Gothic Literature

History

Medieval Literature

Oxford English Drama

Poetry

Philosophy

Politics

Religion

The Oxford Shakespeare

A complete list of Oxford World's Classics, including Authors in Context, Oxford English Drama, and the Oxford Shakespeare, is available in the UK from the Marketing Services Department, Oxford University Press, Great Clarendon Street, Oxford OX2 6DP, or visit the website at www.oup.com/uk/worldsclassics.

In the USA, visit www.oup.com/us/owc for a complete title list.

Oxford World's Classics are available from all good bookshops. In case of difficulty, customers in the UK should contact Oxford University Press Bookshop, 116 High Street, Oxford OX1 4BR.

A SELECTION OF   **OXFORD WORLD'S CLASSICS**

Bhagavad Gita

The Bible Authorized King James Version
With Apocrypha

Dhammapada

Dharmasūtras

The Koran

The Pañcatantra

The Sauptikaparvan (from the
Mahabharata)

The Tale of Sinuhe and Other Ancient
Egyptian Poems

The Qur'an

Upaniṣads

ANSELM OF CANTERBURY   The Major Works

THOMAS AQUINAS   Selected Philosophical Writings

AUGUSTINE   The Confessions
On Christian Teaching

BEDE   The Ecclesiastical History

HEMACANDRA   The Lives of the Jain Elders

KĀLIDĀSA   The Recognition of Śakuntalā

MANJHAN   Madhumalati

ŚĀNTIDEVA   The Bodhicaryàvatàra